LOTUS
A Formula One
Team History

Bruce Grant-Braham

The Crowood Press

First published in 1994 by
The Crowood Press Ltd
Ramsbury, Marlborough
Wiltshire SN8 2HR

British Library Cataloguing-in-Publication Data
A catalogue record for this book is available from the British Library.

ISBN 1 85223 803 8

Dedication

To Chubby, Dan and Anika

Picture Credits
A particular thank you to the Ford Motor Company for many of the illustrations.
All other photographs were supplied by LAT Photographic, *Autosport*, and the author.

Throughout this book, 'he', 'him' and 'his' have been used as neutral pronouns and as such refer to both males and females.

Acknowledgements
I should like to thank Cathy Ager, Mario Andretti, Ann Bradshaw, Peter Collins, CSS Promotions, Johnny Dumfries, Ford Motor Company, Andrew Ferguson, LAT Photographic, John Miles, Satoru Nakajima, Steven Tee, John Watson.

Typeset by Dorwyn Ltd, Rowlands Castle, Hants
Printed and bound in Great Britain by BPC Hazell Books Ltd
A member of The British Printing Company Ltd

Contents

Introduction

The first F1 race I ever witnessed was the 1970 British Grand Prix at Brands Hatch. I had arrived at some unearthly hour of the morning and had found a vantage point pressed against the palings on the outside of Druids hairpin. I was already blooded as a marshal for the British Automobile Racing Club so I thought that I would be used to the speed of Grand Prix cars, but my introduction to F1 took my breath away. From my position I could see the cars scream along the pit straight and could hardly believe that they were able to slow in time to plunge down Paddock Hill before surging up again towards me. Down the box they went, then slid through the corner and away, only for their roar to reverberate through the trees a few moments later as invisibly they lunged behind me towards Pilgrims Drop. I was hooked. There was the young Ickx in his Ferrari, Amon and Stewart in new Marches, Jack Brabham − a near neighbour when we had lived in Surbiton − and my hero Graham Hill in his Brooke Bond Oxo/Rob Walker Lotus 49.

The Gold Leaf Team Lotuses caught both my patriotic and technical attention as I have always been fascinated by innovation, and the state of the art Lotus 72 looked a winner. I willed Jochen Rindt's car on all day and couldn't believe it when he snatched the win from Brabham at the eleventh hour. I loudly cheered both the Austrian and Chapman on their celebratory lap and then suffered with them when the announcement came that they had been disqualified. It was with great relief that this nineteen-year-old learned later from the BBC that the winner had been reinstated to crown my unforgettable introduction to Grand Prix motor racing.

From that day I have always observed the performance of Team Lotus in its many guises. A Grand Prix grid would be strangely naked without a Lotus and even when the Team sank into the doldrums and was nearer the back of the grid than the front it was unthinkable for there not to have been a Lotus present. Lotus is a corner-stone of the Grand Prix establishment and it was desperately sad when, a few years back, it seemed they might disappear altogether.

When the opportunity came to record the history of Team Lotus I decided that my contribution would be a race-by-race record of all the Team's 475 Grand Prix races to date. I have also set out to try to establish facts such as the single most successful individual Lotus chassis and driver. This book should therefore be regarded solely as reference material of Lotus's on-track F1 racing, and I hope that within its pages you may track down the facts you require, while at the same time rekindling some patriotic and technical memories.

Bruce Grant-Braham
1994

CHAPTER 1

The Power Brokers

COLIN CHAPMAN

Colin Chapman was unambiguously the single individual who created one of the most successful of modern Grand Prix racing Teams. To many, Team Lotus has, since 1958, flown the patriotic banner in a sport and industry in which Britain has led the world; and whilst the Team has undergone numerous changes over the years, not least since the untimely death of its founder, it is difficult to imagine to the present day a Grand Prix grid without a Lotus presence. Lotus, along with Ferrari, is a name synonymous with Grand Prix racing, and whilst McLaren and Williams will one day gain such recognition they still have some way to go.

Colin Chapman was born in Richmond-upon-Thames on 19 May 1928. In his early years there was little indication of the fame he was to achieve on the world's motor racing circuits; the first clue came in October 1945 when he commenced his studies at London University. There, an early passion for things mechanical was harnessed: he read engineering at University College.

His family lived in North London in the suburb of East Finchley. Perhaps they subconsciously perceived yet another clue to their son's successful future when, as nervous parents, they witnessed an obsession with speed and pushing things to the limit. During some practical 'research' the young Chapman crashed his 350cc Panther motorcycle, and for Christmas 1945 his safety-conscious father, Stan, replaced it with a Morris 8 Tourer of 1937 vintage. So by this time Chapman possessed not only a developing passion for engineering but a fascination with speed. All he needed to complete his curriculum vitae, by becoming a Grand Prix Team Owner, was an inside knowledge of, and aptitude towards, business.

Entirely coincidentally, whilst at university Chapman, in conjunction with family friend Colin Dare, set up a used car business which they ran between 1946 and 1947; this eventually failed because of the effects of petrol rationing – a circumstance well beyond their control. The only car to survive from the arrangement was an Austin 7 saloon of approximately 1930 vintage, which Chapman stripped and converted into a trials

The Dream Team. When Colin Chapman (left) created his Grand Prix Team and invited Jim Clark to drive, a perfect pairing was created. The partnership was unbeatable and it is all the more tragic that two such talents should have such a cruelly short time in which to prove themselves.

By 1967 the irresistible combination of Jim Clark, Colin Chapman's Lotus 49 chassis and the Ford Cosworth DFV engine started to dominate Grand Prix racing. Here Clark gracefully slides to victory at Silverstone.

car. Interestingly, this machine later evolved into the Lotus Mk 1. Secretarial work was undertaken by one Hazel Williams who would become Mrs Colin Chapman in 1954.

When university examinations came closer Chapman concentrated on his qualifications and gained a BSc thanks to some intensive last minute work and his knack of being able to assimilate a lot of information quickly. Not only had he both studied and run his business, but he had also joined the University Air Squadron, notching up 35 hours of solo flying, and this was to lead him briefly to join the RAF full time. Whilst there he built a number of Mk 2 Lotuses as a hobby. The thought of being a pilot indefinitely did not appeal and he retired from the RAF in 1949. Eventually, of course, he would use his flying expertise to transport himself to races in his own aircraft.

Chapman now took a job with the British Aluminium Company, whilst using his savings to work on things mechanical in his garage in Alexandra Park Road, North London. For relaxation he campaigned his Lotus Mk 2 in the 1950 trials season and for 1951 the Lotus Mk 3 was built, which was specifically designed for circuit racing in the 750 Formula. Once released onto the circuits in his own car Chapman soon became a dominant driver. Building on his racing success Lotus Engineering was formed in January 1952 in premises owned by Stan Chapman in Tottenham Lane, Hornsey. A series of Lotus cars were produced with helpers such as Mike and Frank Costin, Michael Allen and Peter Ross 'Mac' Mackintosh becoming involved. By 1954 Lotus had split into two, with Lotus Engineering building production cars and components and Team Lotus designing and running racing cars.

In the mid-fifties the name Lotus became synonymous with small sports cars, such as the Lotus 7, which were excellent performers on the track; indeed Chapman was quite satisfied with Lotus's performance in sports cars, Formula Two and in producing the road-going Lotus Elite. It was only the combination of the enthusiasm of his drivers and the obvious potential of the Climax FPF engine that convinced him that he ought to relent; even so, it was almost reluctantly that he went into Grand Prix racing in 1958. Having initially dipped his toe into Formula One, though, he soon became totally immersed and his success was to become legendary.

A Genius?

Colin Chapman was subsequently to be regarded by people such as Walter Hayes of Ford as a genius. Lotus World Champion Mario Andretti, though, partly disagreed preferring instead to emphasize that 'He could pull the best ideas from everyone. There is a misconception that he was the sole genius but he in fact extracted ideas from all around making what were to be the final decisions. He had an absolute craving for ideas.' This impression is critically confirmed by John Miles: 'Colin saw engineering opportunities faster than anyone I have met, but sometimes failed to develop new ideas to their best potential – he moved too fast on occasions.'

Andretti continues by saying that

Colin was the stimulating force behind every big effort at Lotus, having the ability to get the best out of everyone when he was on form himself. When he was

Chapman brought obvious commercial sponsorship into F1 by replacing British racing green with Gold Leaf's cigarette colours. Here Fittipaldi wins the 1970 US GP in his Lotus 72, ensuring that Jochen Rindt became World Champion.

The youthful Nigel Mansell regarded Colin Chapman as a father figure. The relationship certainly worked and it is now obvious that without the support of the Lotus boss, Britain would have been later deprived of a most popular World Champion.

distracted, as at one point he was by his boat-building business, the Team suffered tremendously. After Long Beach in 1976 Chapman was somewhat down, and at breakfast I said to him that if he gave 100 per cent, and let the boats go to someone else, I would give 100 per cent. He promised to do just this and Hazel [Chapman] told me that his attitude was completely transformed as a result. When he was right on Team Lotus was right on and if one looks back at the span of Lotus there are peaks and troughs which correspond with Colin's moods.

Others rated Chapman as a difficult man who, whilst he inspired loyalty, could also be both rude and brusque. Indeed many outsiders thought that Chapman had taken leave of his senses when he decided to give Nigel Mansell a testing contract in 1980. In considering Mansell Chapman had positively decided to back a British driver whom he perceived to be not only promotable but who also was in need of a break. Lotus, in

Chapman and Peter Wright devised the Lotus 78 for the 1977 season, harnessing the concept of ground effect. The 'reverse wing research project' helped Andretti to win at Monza and influenced all future F1 designs.

turn, was a Team that Mansell identified with, and Chapman meant a lot to him: he was inspired by the Lotus boss. He recognized that Chapman's positive attitude meant that he knew where he was going and admired that fact that he always had an open mind where innovation was concerned. In his two years with Lotus Mansell treated Chapman not only as an employer but also as a father-like figure. The two could quite happily discuss problems together, although they had arguments too, and they had a mutual respect; even when they had rows no grudges lingered and unlike others, such as Innes Ireland and Elio de Angelis, Mansell was always happy that he was being treated fairly.

Chapman was certainly resilient and admired by many for being able to recover from the traumas of the deaths of Lotus World Champions Jim Clark and Jochen Rindt, both of which ironically plucked Lotus from great pinnacles of success and plunged the Team into the abyss of despair. On both occasions somehow

The 1979 season was utterly dominated by the Lotus 79s of Andretti and Peterson. The Swede was the faster on many occasions, but as seen here at Hockenheim he loyally stayed behind his team leader as orders demanded.

Warr had first joined Lotus in 1958 after he had finished his National Service prematurely as the result of a leg injury. He immediately hit it off with Chapman during a casual visit to Lotus's premises at Hornsey and he quickly took up the offer of a sales position. He continued to race himself, even winning the 1963 Japanese Grand Prix at the wheel of a Lotus 23B.

During his first period with the Team he stayed until 1966, when he declined to move with Lotus to Norfolk, preferring instead to remain in London. Three years later Andrew Ferguson was about to vacate the position of Team manager and alerted Warr, who jumped at the opportunity. Warr arrived for the tail end of the 1969 season and was in control for Rindt's ultimately successful but posthumous World Championship season of 1970. He stayed with Lotus until the end of the 1976 season when he moved to Reading and Walter Wolf Racing. That team's progress gradually reduced and when a merger occurred with the Fittipaldi Team, Warr was persuaded to return again to Lotus. On Chapman's death in November 1982 Warr inherited the reins to face the particularly difficult task of coping without the company's charismatic founder. He remained in Norfolk until midway through the 1989 season. Throughout his time with Team Lotus, Warr was renowned as being both a meticulous administrator and extremely accomplished in the handling and cultivating of sponsors.

Chapman persuaded himself to continue, but inwardly they must have taken their short-term mental and long-term physical toll. In fact, the double blow of Clark and then Spence being killed within days of each other in 1968 hit Chapman particularly badly: he kept himself to himself at home for some time, and insiders felt that after this tragic episode his former carefree attitude towards racing never reappeared.

Andretti concludes his appreciation of Chapman by reminding us that, 'unusually for a team owner he would ask me, as a driver, what I wanted in a car's design and if I said something like a lot of downforce and no drag, he wouldn't say that that was impossible, he would give it a try. He knew that somewhere there would be a way and as a result he was a supreme innovator.'

PETER WARR

Peter Warr had the unenviable task of stepping into Chapman's shoes immediately after his death and trying to keep the Lotus name afloat in Formula One.

Peter Warr inherited the unenviable task of keeping Team Lotus afloat after Colin Chapman's death.

Australian Peter Collins brought Team Lotus back from the dead and started a struggle to regain its former glory. At times it was neither an easy nor a comfortable task . . .

PETER COLLINS

At a time when so much of Britain's emerging culture is directly influenced by things Australian it is perhaps fully fitting that the modern-day saviour of Lotus hails originally from Sydney.

At the tender age of twelve, Peter Collins had watched the 1961 Monaco Grand Prix on film and, having seen Moss win in a Lotus and Clark on the front row, he was completely hooked. It would take, though, until 1964 for him to spectate at his first race, which was a Tasman series event at Warwick Farm. Collins instantly became a Jim Clark fan and an avid reader of anything to do with motoring. In a curiously similar way to Chapman, he too developed a fascination with things mechanical and became a team helper for Chris Amon's Tasman Ferrari for two races.

His first 'proper job' was in a shipping company, and

even though he was successful he moved on to Air New Zealand knowing that this would enable him to travel to Europe to see more races. Geoff Sykes at Warwick Farm was a great help to the young Collins, who became a freelance journalist; and when Peter Windsor (most recently with Williams) left the position of press officer at Warwick Farm, Collins replaced him.

As a journalist he attended many races in Europe, but he stopped at Long Beach in 1975 when Warwick Brown invited him to help with a fledgling F5000 team. This only lasted a short time and he then had brief flirtations with other teams before he decided to get married.

Just as life seemed to be on the verge of being settled, a telegram arrived from Peter Windsor drawing his attention to the Team Manager's job at Lotus, which was on offer. On the day of his wedding, Collins pursued Colin Chapman, but he was to be out of luck; he then decided to leave Australia, with all his worldly goods, and to work for Ron Tauranac. A year later the Lotus job became vacant again and, after a fraught interview with Chapman, he was offered the job in December 1978.

He stayed with Lotus for three years, at a time when the Team was undergoing the problems of cars such as the Lotus 80, only to fall out with Chapman and to move to ATS. After just a few months personalities conflicted again and he moved to Williams, where he stayed until half-way through 1985. Collins had secretly harboured the desire to set up his own team and he targeted Toleman – which was promptly taken over by Benetton. Collins joined Rory Byrne there instead and made the team into a front runner, helped considerably by the use of Ford engines.

When Lotus seemed on the brink of oblivion in 1990, Collins returned to become literally its saviour. He says that both he and his partner Peter Wright 'took an enormous risk'.

> Everything that we've earned in our working careers is tied up in making Team Lotus successful again. There are a lot of teams that have more money than Lotus and don't do as good a job. We've both believed ever since we returned to Lotus that it's not necessarily the quantity of resources that you have, it's the way you utilize them. You also have to be prepared to take a good, calculated risk. If you sit there saying "we can't do that, it's too expensive," then you never will. But if you try to find a way, quite often you can.

CHAPTER 2

Lotus Takes to the Grand Prix Circuits

In 1956 Colin Chapman built his first single-seater racing car, the 12, which had been destined for what was then Formula Two. The car sported the 1,475cc twin-cam FPF Coventry Climax engine and, unbeknown at the time, would in the following years become the basis for the famous entry of Lotus into the world of Formula One.

The Lotus 12 took Team Lotus into Grand Prix racing for the first time at Monaco in 1968. Cliff Allison spun his way to a sixth-placed finish to prove wrong all those who had thought that what was really a F2 car would be too fragile.

═══ 1958 ═══

Lotus 12

It comes as quite a surprise to many to find that Colin Chapman never really intended to go GP racing; he was personally much more interested in producing road cars such as the Elite, and competing with both sports cars and F2 machines. Accepting the boss's philosophy, it is therefore of no surprise to find that Lotus's first GP car, the Lotus 12, started life firmly in F2 and only gradually evolved into a full F1 challenger as the necessary engines were developed by Coventry Climax. To put the record straight, to actually compete in the World Championship was not a deliberate step in any preconceived master plan; it just seemed the logical way for Lotus to go at that particular time.

The Lotus 12 had evolved in the autumn of 1956 as a stylish space-frame front-engined single-seater with a novel double-wishbone front and De Dion rear suspension. The Climax FPF 1,475cc F2 engine was installed and the car was soon to be seen racing in F2 in a limited number of events during 1957. The following season, 1958, was to be very much an educational one as Lotus learned all about F1; they followed the trend set by Brabham, who had raced his F2 car at Monaco in 1957 with an enlarged engine. Both Rob Walker and John Cooper would go down the same road in 1958. Before Lotus really knew it, they were GP racing with the Lotus 12 at Monaco in the same year.

Typically chassis and suspension fragility were to be the major problems throughout the season. Of Team Lotus's two chosen drivers, Cliff Allison was to be the most successful during 1958 as he achieved much more

in the way of results than Graham Hill, who scored no World Championship points at all in his first season of F1. All that year Lotus were at a disadvantage against the 2.5-litre Ferraris, Vanwalls and BRMs.

The first competitive F1 race for Lotus was in fact to be in the International Trophy at Silverstone. There Graham Hill was eighth in his 1.96-litre Lotus Climax (353), finishing one lap behind the winner. A fortnight later Team Lotus would become a GP Team for real with Hill similarly starting what would be an eminent GP career.

The Monaco GP of 1958 was to be the first World Championship event entered by Lotus, albeit with undersized 2-litre engines in what were still really F2 cars. The opportunity was there to make use of the 2.2-litre

Colin Chapman (centre) holds his first ever press conference, in the Monte Carlo pits.

Climax F1 engine, which was in fact physically present in Monaco, but it was decided instead to err on the side of caution. The two pristine lightweight Lotus 12s made an impressive sight in Monaco as they were made ready for the Team's first GP, complete with their enlarged fuel tanks. Knowledgeable paddock inhabitants expressed their worries, though, that the apparently fragile cars would not be durable enough to compete around the demanding Monegasque circuit. It was to be brake problems that were in fact to dog Hill throughout practice, which culminated in his hitting the straw bales at the Station Hairpin, giving the mechanics some hard overnight work. Both the cars disappointingly qualified well down the grid – Hill tied with Bonnier's Maserati for last place! – but at least they were in their first GP, which was restricted to a mere sixteen starters overall.

The start of the event was chaotic, but Allison drove through to sixth place despite a big spin and two stops to top up the water of his over-heating machine – the point should be made, though, that sixth place was in fact last place! Hill had retired from that very same sixth place after seventy laps when his car's revs increased and he spun round exiting Portier. At first he thought his gears had jumped out but then he noticed he had lost a wheel as a result of a drive-shaft having failed. He promptly jumped out of the car and collapsed, as he hadn't realized that he was suffering from heat exhaustion! That night, even though in reality the cars had been outclassed, Chapman, Allison and Hill celebrated Lotus's first GP in the famous Monte Carlo Casino where Hill won the princely amount of £120 – no small sum in 1958.

From Monaco it was off to Holland, where the

Dutch GP had last been run in 1955. This year Moss would dominate with his Vanwall; where Lotus was concerned, Cliff Allison made use of the new 2.207-litre Climax engine in his Lotus 12 for the first time at the Zandvoort circuit. This larger-capacity engine was to provide him with his best results of the season. In

Following a high-speed crash in practice, Hill (16) was to end up physically pushing his car during the Dutch GP at Zandvoort. The team omitted to top up his Lotus 12 with water and he would retire with over-heating.

practice the two cars had the wrong gear ratios but even so they were soon well under the existing track record. Hill was lucky to escape from a 100mph (160kph) trip into a twenty-foot deep ditch at one point in practice; then in the race he physically pushed his 12 into the pits on lap 22 as a result of a broken ignition. Having returned to the race, over-heating was later to claim him after the Team should have replenished his car's water during that initial pit stop. Allison excelled himself, coming home in sixth place, and was to go on to use the larger engine to good effect too at Spa, where he very nearly won Team Lotus its first GP. If that had actually happened, after only three events, it would have been sensational.

Allison was one of those drivers who adored the high speeds achievable at Spa, whilst Hill was initially scared stiff of the velocities he was experiencing for the very first time. The Belgian GP itself saw the leading three cars of Tony Brooks (Vanwall), Mike Hawthorn (Ferrari) and Stuart Lewis-Evans (Vanwall) all run into trouble towards the end. At the La Source hairpin, at the immediate summit of the short plunge down to the finish, Brooks's Ferrari started to stutter the last few yards to the line with a seized gearbox; then, Hawthorn's engine blew up and he slowed dramatically at the same spot seconds before Lewis-Evans appeared with damaged suspension – a wishbone had broken! As a result, Allison very nearly scored Lotus's maiden victory with the first serviceable car to finish but had eventually to settle for fourth place. If only the race had lasted another lap or if the final drop from the La Source hairpin had instead been an uphill climb . . . The only problem Allison had encountered during the race had been with his car's exhaust, which had at one point started to work itself free. Virtually forgotten in the excitement of the finish was the fact that Hill had retired as a result of a con-rod failure in his engine on lap 12.

Lotus 16

Chapman's next GP car was the Lotus 16, with its front-positioned Coventry Climax engine, and it turned out to be a less than memorable representative of the marque, often proving unreliable. In truth, it was a modification of the 1957 Lotus 12 F2 design; outwardly it seemed very similar to the GP Vanwall and, as a result, was in fact affectionately known as the 'Mini Vanwall'. The aerodynamic body was widely attributed to the design talents of Frank Costin, when in fact it had been body-builders Williams & Pritchard who had given the 'Mini Vanwall' its distinctive treatment. It possessed a tubular space-frame with a coil-spring front suspension and double wishbones, as well

as the typical 'strut' rear suspension that was now almost a trademark of Colin Chapman. Keith Duckworth's gearbox had an extremely short working life measured in minutes rather than hours, and disagreements with Chapman over a new replacement drove him to leave and set up Cosworth Engineering, together with an equally dissatisfied Frank Costin, although the latter still stayed at Lotus for some time following a generous offer from Chapman.

Thanks to problems with engine installation – it was originally intended that the 16 should have its engine canted over on to its side at 60 degrees, which was later altered to 30 degrees – the new car did not debut until the French GP when modifications were finally completed.

At the French GP at Rheims Mike Hawthorn (Ferrari) won his first World Championship F1 event for five years and Juan Manuel Fangio bowed out of racing. Both entries from Team Lotus unfortunately retired before lap 12 thanks to their engines giving out in the heat of the Champagne countryside. At one point, at well over 150mph (240kph), the crowd were amazed to see Hill take Gueux corner virtually standing up in the cockpit. The reason for this unusual behaviour was that his gearbox was spewing out boiling oil on to his legs, so hot had the ambient temperatures become!

At the outset everything looked promising at the British GP at Silverstone, especially as Allison had trusty service from his 'old' Lotus 12, which took him to fifth place on the grid ahead of both the newer 16s – a performance that greatly impressed all those who witnessed it. Both Hill and new F1 Lotus recruit Alan Stacey pitted when their cars over-heated and the drivers too were also suffering again from hot gearboxes.

Unfortunately all three of the Lotus entries were to retire – Hill's gearbox gave out as he battled with the BRM of Harry Schell – suffering from either lack of oil pressure or over-heating. Allison retired when his engine's bearings went, so all the Lotus entries were out before one-third of their home GP had been run.

By the time of the German GP, Chapman had decided that the upright engine mounting was the way to go and previous experiments were scrapped. Whilst Graham Hill raced in the F2 division at the Nurburgring, only Allison had a true Lotus F1 car, although both machines were now equipped with larger radiators. Allison had spent much of the previous week learning the circuit at the wheel of his road car.

Hill managed to damage Allison's borrowed 2-litre car in practice, when the engine had seized and sent him off into the bushes, but luckily the car turned out to be repairable. Its usual driver, despite a superb practice time, couldn't complete sufficient qualifying laps – six were required – and was therefore forced to start from the back of the grid. An amazing first lap saw Allison in fourth place, and he was to pass both the Ferraris of Collins and Hawthorn – the former would receive fatal injuries later in the race in a tragic accident – and the Vanwall of Brooks. Revelling in second place (Moss had retired), Allison's hastily repaired radiator header tank split. This forced him to pull into the pits, thereby dropping the bitterly disappointed driver, who knew he could have won, to last place by the time further

repairs had been successfully carried out. Enzo Ferrari, though, had noticed Allison's drive and later offered him a place at Ferrari largely on the strength of it. Hill, meanwhile, had started at the back of the grid only for an oil pipe to split, the contents of which poured on to the exhaust and caused his retirement at Adenau Bridge in a cloud of smoke, through which he had been trying to guess which way the track went!

In the break before Portugal, the 16/363 had its engine modified to sit 17 degrees from vertical as well as being equipped with bigger radiators and a rerouted

---

TEAM LOTUS RESULTS 1958

Drivers:
Cliff Allison: British; Graham Hill: British; Alan Stacey: British
Car:
Lotus 12 Engine: Coventry Climax 1.9-litre, 2.207-litre★
Lotus 16   Coventry Climax 1.9-litre

CAR	CHASSIS	DRIVER	PRACTICE	SESSION	GRID	RACE	LAPS	%	REASON	CHAMPIONSHIP POSITION	POINTS
MONACO GP, Monte Carlo – 18th May – 100 L, 195.42 miles (314.50km) (1)											
12	357	Allison	1m 44.6s	2	13th	6th	90	90.0	–	–	–
12	353	Hill	1m 45.0s	1	15th	R	70	70.0	Engine	–	–
DUTCH GP, Zandvoort – 26th May – 75 L, 195.40 miles (314.47km) (2)											
12	357	Allison	1m 39.4s	2	11th	6th	73	97.3	–	–	–
12	353	Hill	1m 39.8s	2	13th	R	42	56.0	Gasket	–	–
BELGIAN GP, Spa – 15th June – 24 L, 210.27 miles (338.40km) (3)											
12	357★	Allison	4m 07.7s	2	12th	4th	24	100.0	–	15th=	3
12	353	Hill	4m 17.8s	2	14th	R	12	50.0	Engine	–	–
FRENCH GP, Reims – 7th July – 50 L, 257.93 miles (415.10km) (4)											
12	357★	Allison	2m 49.7s	–	20th	R	7	14.0	Engine	16th=	3
16	363	Hill	2m 40.9s	–	19th	R	12	24.0	Engine	–	–
BRITISH GP, Silverstone – 20th July – 75 L, 219.52 miles (353.29km) (5)											
12	357★	Allison	1m 40.4s	–	5th	R	22	29.4	Bearings	17th	3
16	362s	Hill	1m 43.0s	–	14th	R	18	24.0	Engine	–	–
16	363	Stacey	1m 58.8s	–	20th	R	20	26.6	Engine	–	–
GERMAN GP, Nurburgring – 3rd August – 15 L, 212.60 miles (342.15km) (6)											
16	362	Allison	9m 44.3s	–	24th	10th (5th F1)	13	80.0	–	17th	=3
PORTUGUESE GP, Oporto – 24th August – 50 L, 230.12 miles (370.35km) (7)											
16	363★	Hill	2m 46.22s	–	12th	R	26	52.0	Accident	–	–
16	362	Allison	Accident	–	DNS	–	–	–	–	17th=	3
ITALIAN GP, Monza – 7th September – 70 L, 250.10 miles (402.50km) (8)											
12	(F2) 357★★	Allison	1m 47.8s	–	16th	6th NC	62	88.6	–	18th=	3
16	363★	Hill	1m 46.0s	–	12th	5th NC	62	88.6	–	–	–
MOROCCAN GP, Casablanca – 19th October – 53 L, 250.88 miles (403.75km) (9)											
12	357★	Allison	2m 33.7s	–	16th	10th	49	92.4	–	18th=	3
16	363	Hill	2m 27.1s	–	12th	16th (11th F1)	55	87.3	–	–	–

Key:
DNS = Did Not Start
NC   = Not Classified
★   = made use of Coventry Climax 2.207-litre engine
★★   = used both 2.207 and 1.5-litre engines
R   = Retired
L   = Laps

Literally shoehorned into the cockpit of his Lotus 16 in Oporto, Hill (20) was to crash, thanks largely to his cramped conditions. The Lotus 16 was more sophisticated than the Lotus 12 but never achieved the results that its sleek design promised.

exhaust. A previously cramped Hill was given more room too with an enlarged screen.

Oporto's urban track claimed Allison's Lotus 16 in practice when he got crossed up on the road circuit's tramlines and shunted heavily into the bales – luckily without personal damage – after just missing a brick wall and a lamppost. The severely damaged suspension and engine mountings were not repairable in time for the GP, so once released from his contract by Chapman, Allison went off to race for Mimo Dei's Scuderia Centro Sud in what was a heavy Maserati 250F in comparison to his more usual mount.

Hill crashed his Lotus 16 in the race – his hand had jammed against his thigh in the tight cockpit – following a dice with Roy Salvadori's Cooper when understeer forced him into and on to the bales in front of the pits. The Team's stock of Lotus 16s had been decimated in Portugal, and Chapman responded to Hill's complaint by crudely moving the dashboard on his 16 to give him more room.

Allison was back in the faithful Lotus 12 in the heat of Monza only for his 2-litre engine to fail and a 1.5-litre to have to be installed instead. Hill qualified ahead of Allison but when going well in the race – dicing with Gregory and Trintignant – he had to pull in as the insulation of a plug lead had broken down sufficiently to cause a misfire. Added to this problem were brake failure, several stops to have the radiator topped up with water and a minor fire ! He rejoined to eventually come home sixth – coasting across the line now out of fuel – with Allison just behind in seventh having stopped at one point to try to establish why he was becoming covered in oil. The Lotus positions became fifth and sixth when fourth-placed Gregory was subsequently disqualified.

The final event of the 1958 season was in Casablanca for the Moroccan GP. Allison crashed in practice and Hill, who had qualified well, was held back by a number of stops for water which dropped him to last. Allison drove steadily into tenth place whilst the main

WORLD CHAMPIONSHIP POINTS 1958

Position	Driver	Points
1	Hawthorn	42
2	Moss	41
3	Brooks	24
4	Salvadori	15
5=	Schell	14
	Collins	14
7=	Trintignant	12
	Musso	12
9	Lewis-Evans	11
10=	Hill (P)	9
	Von Trips	9
	Behra	9
13	Bryan	8
14	Fangio	7
15	Amick	6
16=	Boyd	4
	Bettenhausen	4
18=	**Cliff Allison**	**3**
	Brabham	3
	Bonnier	3

CONSTRUCTORS' CUP 1958

Position	Constructor	Points
1	Vanwall	48
2	Ferrari	40
3	Cooper-Climax	31
4	BRM	18
5	Maserati	6
6	**Lotus-Climax**	**3**

interest of the race was Hawthorn's successful repulse of a late challenge from Moss in an unsuccessful attempt to try to take the Drivers' Championship.

1959

An enlarged Coventry Climax engine appeared on the circuits in 1959, boasting 2,495cc and giving out a splendid 240bhp. Lotus made use of the new engine in the modified Lotus 16 chassis but the year was to be yet another mediocre affair. The Team Lotus cars finished in only three of the eight World Championship races. Allison had been lured away to Ferrari the previous December so the works Lotus F1 drivers for 1959 were intended to be Graham Hill and American Pete Lovely. The year, though, was to be punctuated by mechanical and preparation deficiencies.

Initially only a singleton 2.5-litre Climax engine was available to the Team, so Hill was their only driver at the non-championship Goodwood Richmond Trophy, where he retired 16/363 with failing brakes, and in the Aintree 200, where he came eleventh (fifth in the F1 class), having endured a myriad of problems. At Silverstone's International Trophy, Hill retired when a brake pipe burst; for this race he was joined by American Pete Lovely, who was not classified thanks to oil troubles.

A pair of revised Lotus 16s were entered for the Team's tenth GP at Monaco, but they only just reached the meeting owing to the breakdown of their transporter at Valence. On close examination it was apparent that both the suspension and the space-frame had been substantially altered since the previous GP season. Weber carburettors were utilized for the first time, and because they were not yet set correctly, what was left of qualifying was a nightmare: Hill finished right down in fourteenth place, while his unfortunate American team-mate – who had his carburettors fall off – was just not fast enough and did not have sufficient time to get on to the grid. As a result Lovely decided that F1 racing was not for him and he returned to Seattle to concentrate on his businesses.

The Lotus F2 car of Bruce Halford crashed into the spinning Porsche of Von Trips and Allison's Ferrari early in the Monaco race almost bending 362/2 in half. Hill suffered an oil fire after 22 laps – the smoke from which he originally thought was coming from another car – and retired at Beau Rivage, having extinguished the now sizable fire himself with an extinguisher bodily wrenched off a marshal. Colin Chapman was left in the position of trying to find a replacement for Lovely, but he had to look no further than a name already well known to him, Innes Ireland.

Lotus made a deliberate effort to prepare properly for Zandvoort by getting in an extra day's practice, during which Ireland hammered his Ford Zephyr endlessly around the track. The Team's two drivers qualified well as a result and Hill was timed as the fastest competitor around the back of the circuit.

In the Dutch GP Hill was embroiled in an early fourth place battle with Behra's Ferrari and Moss's Cooper only for smoke to start appearing from under his Lotus. Nervous after the previous fire at Monaco, he stopped and awaited a conflagration which never came! In evacuating the car he had also ripped open his

At Zandvoort, Behra's Ferrari holds off Hill's Lotus 16 (14), which is sliding wide during a battle with Moss's Cooper. Further back, Ireland is making his Grand Prix début for Lotus. Hill was sidelined by smoke and Ireland was to finish fourth.

overalls and, without realizing it, was showing a lot more of himself to the amused crowd than ideally he would have intended! He started off again, but by now was well out of the hunt in twelfth place, although he did manage seventh at the flag. By contrast, Ireland's first race for Lotus brought a very encouraging result in the form of fourth place. He had worked through the field, nearly spinning out on some oil at one point, and could have got higher had a front tyre not come off. Colin Chapman was visibly elated by this encouraging result.

In June Lotus moved to the much-needed extra space provided by new premises at Delamare Road in Cheshunt, Hertfordshire. Controversially, the staff had been asked to work under new conditions and Len Terry, then a Lotus draughtsman, paid the price for organizing a protest, although he would return in 1962.

For the French GP improved Weber carburettors were used but the cars were still off the pace. In the incredibly hot race, Hill's radiator was holed by a stone early on and Ireland's retirement was caused by the failure of his right front wheel bearing.

At Aintree for the British GP, Ireland pulled out of practice as a result of the after-effects of a F2 accident at Rouen, so Stacey took his car over. Unusually a strike had prevented Ferrari from appearing, and Hill went particularly well in the GP, having already starred in

TEAM LOTUS RESULTS 1959

Drivers:
Graham Hill: British; Pete Lovely: United States; Innes Ireland: British; (Bruce Halford: British); Alan Stacey (British)
Car:
Lotus 16 Engine: Coventry Climax 2.5-litre

CAR	CHASSIS	DRIVER	PRACTICE	SESSION	GRID	RACE	LAPS	%	REASON	CHAMPIONSHIP POSITION	POINTS
MONACO GP, Monte Carlo – 10th May – 100 L, 195.42 miles (314.55km) (10)											
16/1	368	Hill	1m 43.9s	–	14th	R	22	22.0	Fire	–	–
16/2	364	Lovely	1m 47.9s	–	DNQ	–	–	–	–	–	–
16F2	363(2)	Halford	1m 44.8s	–	16th	R	2	2.0	Accident	–	–
DUTCH GP, Zandvoort – 31st May – 75 L, 195.40 miles (314.47km) (11)											
16/2	364	Ireland	1m 38.3s	–	9th	4th	74	98.6	–	9th=	3
16/1	368	Hill	1m 36.7s	2	5th	7th	73	97.3	–	–	–
FRENCH GP, Reims – 5th July – 50 L, 257.93 miles (415.10km) (12)											
16/2	364	Hill	2m 23.7s	–	14th	R	8	16.0	Radiator	–	–
16/5	365	Ireland	2m 24.2s	–	15th	R	14	28.0	Wheel	11th	3
BRITISH GP, Aintree – 18th July – 75 L, 225.00 miles (362.10km) (13)											
16/2	364	Stacey	2m 02.8s★	–	12th	8th	71	94.6	–	–	–
16/5	365	Hill	2m 00.0s	–	9th	9th	70	93.3	–	–	–
16(F2)	363	Piper	2m 06.0s	–	22nd	R	20	26.6	Over-heating	–	–
GERMAN GP, Avus – 2nd August – 60 L, 309.44 miles (498.00km) (14)											
16/5	365	Hill	2m 10.8s	–	10th	R	11	18.3	Gears	–	–
16/2	364	Ireland	2m 14.6s	–	13th	R	8	13.3	Gears	13th=	3
PORTUGUESE GP, Lisbon – 23rd August – 62 L, 209.58 miles (337.28km) (15)											
16/2	364	Ireland	2m 18.47s	2	16th	R	4	6.4	Gears	14th	3
16/5	365	Hill	2m 15.55s	2	15th	R	6	9.7	Accident	–	–
ITALIAN GP, Monza – 13th September – 72 L, 257.25 miles (414.00km) (16)											
16/1	368	Hill	1m 42.9s	–	10th	R	2	2.7	Engine	–	–
16/2	364	Ireland	1m 43.5s	–	14th	R	15	20.8	Brakes	14th	3
US GP, Sebring – 12th December – 42 L, 218.41 miles (351.50km) (17)											
16/5	365	Ireland	3m 08.25s	–	9th	5th	39	92.8	–	12th=	5
16/2	364	Stacey	3m 13.8s	–	12th	R	2	4.8	Clutch	–	–

Key:
DNQ = Did Not Qualify
★ = Practice time set by Ireland who was subsequently taken ill and did not race
R = Retired
L = Laps

the supporting sports car race; but he then spun at Tatts Corner through a crowd of officials, only to indulge in a fraught fight with Salvadori's Aston Martin. Sadly his clutch let him down so he slowed to an eventual ninth place.

The organizers of the German GP at Avus were reluctant to allow Lotus to enter, so poor had the Team's results been up to that point. The high-speed banked circuit in West Berlin was hardly ideal hunting ground for the Lotus entries for Hill and Ireland, which were eventually accepted. The track wrought havoc with the chassis of the cars and both 16s retired early from the first heat and took no further part in the proceedings.

The long trek to Lisbon for the Portuguese GP took its toll on the transporter, which broke down again and qualification time, which included coping with brake and gear troubles, was therefore minimal. Hill's fuel tank had ruptured, which would cause major problems for him in the race. As Ireland approached his car on the grid he spotted a fatigued tube, to which the front suspension was attached! Urgent welding was undertaken to ready the car for the long afternoon's race during what was hardly a confidence-inspiring moment for the driver. Ireland in fact retired early on with gear problems, whilst Hill spun on his own leaking fuel and disappeared over a bank on lap 6 only to be collected by the Ferrari of Phil Hill on the other side. Both cars were retired as a result of the ensuing collision damage and the Lotus driver was briefly knocked unconscious.

Criticisms of the apparent lack of preparation of cars at Lotus were already being widely voiced, and it was thought that Chapman must be concentrating too much of his time on the development of the road-going Elite.

Hill's 16/364 had been so badly damaged in Portugal that parts of it were rebuilt into the 16/368 in time for Monza; all this was to be to little effect because Hill was only to race for two laps before his clutch gave out. On the way to the grid he noticed his steering wheel was loose, and though this was repaired in time, he was so infuriated by yet another mechanical retirement in the GP itself that he walked out on Lotus to join BRM in mid-December. His rushed departure from the Team subsequently provoked a breach-of-contract claim from Chapman, which was settled out of court.

Ireland's brakes had given out on lap 15 of the Italian GP for a mechanically disastrous event. Hill, though, had two more non-championship races with Lotus prior to his departure to pastures new. The first, the International Gold Cup at Oulton Park yielded him a fifth place, but in the Silver City Trophy at Snetterton he retired the same car again with a drive-shaft failure –

just as he felt poised to win against Ron Flockhart's BRM – whilst Ireland similarly left the race early when an anti-roll bar broke.

Concurrent with these events, the Cheshunt premises of Lotus were officially opened on 14 October by Godfrey Lagden, MP.

In Sebring for the final GP of the year Ireland was promoted to no. 1 driver and Stacey completed the line-up. Stacey was out of the race early when his clutch failed but Ireland kept a steady fifth place, having fought with the Ferraris of both Brooks and Allison.

The 1959 GP season could hardly be described as a rip-roaring success for Lotus but the results were hardly surprising so much was Chapman trying to undertake simultaneously. In June the whole racing and road-car manufacturing business had moved to Cheshunt, and so wide in variety were the tasks being taken on, it was a minor miracle that the GP effort survived at all.

Indeed for the first time in its history, and not the last, Team Lotus, the GP sister of Lotus Cars, could so easily have closed down, so low were everyone's spirits. It was widely discussed in the press that thanks to their lack of reliability, Lotus would not be able to obtain entries for future World Championship meetings thereby forcing their withdrawal; Chapman, however, was not someone to capitulate and his tenacity would be richly rewarded in 1960.

WORLD CHAMPIONSHIP RESULTS 1959

Position	Driver	Points
1	Brabham	31
2	Brooks	27
3	Moss	25.5
4	Hill (P)	20
5	Trintignant	19
6	McLaren	16.5
7	Gurney	13
8=	Bonnier	10
	Gregory	10
10	Ward	8
11	Rathmann	6
12=	**Ireland**	**5**
	Schell	5
	Thomson	5

CONSTRUCTORS' CUP 1959

Position	Constructor	Points
1	Cooper-Climax	40
2	Ferrari	32
3	BRM	18
4	**Lotus-Climax**	**5**

CHAPTER 3

The Scottish Era

=== 1960 ===

Lotus 18

1959 had been dominated by rear-engined cars, particularly Jack Brabham's Cooper, and Chapman decided to introduce the lightweight rear-engined Lotus 18 for 1960. It was the first such Lotus and even though it wasn't as aerodynamic as its predecessor, its very low frontal area, which made drivers recline slightly, was an entirely new approach to the reduction of wind resistance. A check on straight-line speed during the Dutch GP was to confirm that the Lotus 18 was the fastest car, and from that moment onwards the importance of an aerodynamic shape would universally influence racing-car design. Additionally, fuel could be carried nearer the centre of gravity, and the complete redesign of the adjustable suspension was another Chapman concept. The chassis could now be tuned via the anti-roll bars and the tyres cambered to remain in better contact with the road.

Chapman had wanted a simple concept after the problems encountered the previous season, and so adaptable was the Lotus 18 design that over 120 Formula Junior versions were to be constructed in the first year of production. Indeed, so simple was the design that Moss, the most successful F1 driver of the 18, referred to it as 'a biscuit-box on wheels'. Outward appearances, though, belied the fact that it had a much stiffer chassis than the opposition cars and, crucially, it kept its front tyres well and truly on the road when turning into high speed corners. Furthermore, this sophisticated handling was introduced in the first season in which Team Lotus made use of full capacity 2,495cc FPA Coventry Climax engines.

Graham Hill had by now moved to BRM, and had been replaced by Innes Ireland, who took over as no. 1 driver to début the Lotus 18 in Argentina. The car had only just been finished in time to allow for brief testing before it had to be crated and delivered to the airport! The other cars had already left by ship.

Innes Ireland

When Team Lotus eventually arrived in Buenos Aires

– the journey had been somewhat hair-raising – Ireland was briefly gaoled for a traffic offence. As if that wasn't enough, the new car was stranded in customs; so Chapman and the mechanics seized it along with a local official, who was then persuaded to complete the paperwork once they had all returned to the circuit! The two 16s only just arrived from their delayed ship in time for the end of the final practice session.

Only Moss's Cooper was faster in practice in Argentina as Ireland overcame enormous vibrations caused by a dented wheel. From Team Lotus's first Grand Prix front row position Ireland led the race away, only to spin shortly afterwards when a gear jumped out; even so, the very promising début for the new Lotus ended with sixth place, with the car having briefly led the race before a kerb-hopping moment deranged the suspension and dropped it back. The Mk 3 'queerbox' was the only problem, but luckily it held together to the flag. The Team were very happy about the promise shown by their new car and a curious Moss was to cast a close eye over Chapman's new creation in the paddock.

Transmission failure forced both Ireland and Stacey out of Cordoba's non-championship Buenos Aires City GP before Team Lotus returned home to compete in Goodwood's Richmond Trophy. There Ireland won, suitably impressing Moss who now insisted that he too should drive a Lotus 18. A deal was swiftly done whereby Rob Walker would soon become a major private entrant contributor to Lotus's GP history.

Ireland won the Silverstone International Trophy and his early season victories attracted the attention of the media, who now regarded him as a threat to Moss, who had up until then been Britain's undisputed best driver. What was ignored, though, was that the Lotus 18 was a far superior car to Moss's existing Cooper.

Rob Walker's Lotus 18 (376) was delivered a mere week before the Monaco GP and a brief test at Goodwood encouraged Moss. He was four seconds under the lap record in Monte Carlo, and this statistic guaranteed that the pole-sitting Lotus would be raced. Overwhelmed at the start, Moss caught and passed Brabham to chase after the BRM of Bonnier, who was now in the lead in the treacherously wet conditions. Moss took the lead on lap 17 but Brabham was then to get back

. . . Standing proudly on the steps of the Royal Box as the national anthem is played, Moss is admired by Prince Rainier and the stunningly beautiful Princess Grace of Monaco.

The honour of winning Lotus's first Grand Prix was to fall to Moss at Monaco in 1960. The chunky Lotus 18 of the private Rob Walker team pulled out an immense lead and Moss is seen here overtaking Bonnier's fifth placed BRM . . .

past, only to spin out on lap 41 at St Devote. Despite a 14-second lead, lap 60 saw Bonnier back at the front, as a plug lead detached itself on Moss's car. This necessitated a quick pitstop, with the driver fearing this might enforce retirement. Once back in the race his pit crew misinformed him, saying that there were fewer laps to go than there really were, and Moss speeded up to catch the BRM on lap 68 and take Lotus's first Grand Prix victory. Later it was found that the winning car's engine mountings were broken and the Climax power plant was in fact perched on a cooling pipe! Team Lotus's own cars did not perform so well, as Stacey struck one of Monaco's many kerbs and Surtees had terminal gear-selection troubles. Ireland, who was stranded out on the track after a misfire – a magneto earth had fouled the chassis – pushed his beast back into the pits where he was treated for exhaustion.

Jim Clark

After the race Lotus travelled directly to Holland. On the actual day of the Dutch GP, Surtees had a clashing motorcycle commitment so Chapman's impressive new signing, Jim Clark, replaced him. Team Lotus had calculatingly been present at a Goodwood test day, knowing full well that Clark would be there running the Aston Martin GP car. It was suggested to Clark that he might try the Lotus 18 Junior car; the Scot was duly impressed and well and truly caught in the Lotus web. When Aston Martin withdrew from F1, Clark, who was already making a name for himself with Lotus in Junior events, was set for his F1 début at the Dutch GP.

Lotus F1 cars were evenly distributed throughout the Zandvoort grid from pole position, snatched by Moss, through to eleventh place. In the race Moss took things relatively easy – being conscious of his undeserved car-breaking reputation – but was sidelined from his lead fight with Brabham, who had thrown up a 26lb (12kg) piece of rubble, puncturing his tyre and damaging a wheel; at 140mph (225kph) Moss spun, coming perilously close to a tree as he did so! A chaotic pitstop followed at the hands of Alf Francis and the Walker Team – as they had to swiftly borrow wheel and tyre replacements from the works outfit – before a tigering Moss set a new lap record on his way to fourth from twelfth position! Impressive débutant Clark had been holding fourth place, before his retirement through gearbox failure; this performance secured his place with Team Lotus.

Spa was to go down as a grim day in motor racing history. The Lotus drivers, particularly Ireland, were becoming more than concerned at the number of mechanical breakages. In Belgium, Moss had ironically expressed his concern about the consequences of an accident on the ultra-fast circuit, and unfortunately proved his point by crashing his 18 heavily in practice at the bumpy Burnenville corner at a speed in excess of 135mph (217kph). He fractured both his legs as he was thrown out on to the track, and the other drivers could not believe that the accident had been caused by anything other than a mechanical failure; the left-rear wheel had obviously come off before the impact. When the wreck was closely examined it was found that a rear hub had failed and similar faults were found on the works cars. Chapman immediately ordered new parts to be flown out in time for the race.

Shortly afterwards Mike Taylor crashed into the Rivage wood when his prototype 18 suffered steering failure to add to the catalogue of Lotus problems, which had also included a steering failure for Alan Stacey. Chapman had actually driven Ireland's 18 out to Burnenville where Moss had suffered his accident to have a close look at the wreckage, the works cars being 'grounded' in the pits until his return. Lotus were later to settle a claim for negligence brought by Taylor.

The race proved to be even worse. Clark's in-built dislike of the track after his début there two years previously was rekindled. Having stalled on the grid, the Scot was greeted by the scene of marshals clearing up the accident in which Chris Bristow had been killed when his Cooper had got away from him and then Alan Stacey, at the time running in sixth place from the back row of the grid, went missing. This was Stacey's first visit to the Belgian track and he had made it known that he would take the race easily but he was still to suffer a freak accident that had proved fatal. He had been struck in the face by a pheasant before his car cart-wheeled off the track. By now Ireland, a close friend of Stacey's, had retired and he only found out the seriousness of the accident when he visited the returning ambulance in the paddock. Clark finished fifth.

Following a troubled 24-hour Le Mans sports-car race, Ireland was deeply shocked by the injuries suffered by his co-driver Jonathan Sieff. Coming as it did so soon after the traumas of Spa, the Scot was forced to gather his thoughts, and although he did not give up racing he was inwardly troubled for some time. Clark, meanwhile, had come home third at Le Mans.

At Reims all of Lotus's drivers were Scottish, much to the amusement of Chapman, with Flockhart having joined the line-up with the newest canted-engine 18/374. Having qualified well, the Lotus cars avoided the mêlée of the start only for Ireland to pit at two-thirds of the distance with wheel troubles – spending an agonizing 6 minutes in the pits as the correct nut was retrieved from the transporter – whilst Clark and Flockhart fought each other fiercely. Team Lotus were to finish fifth, sixth and seventh in the order of Clark, Flockhart and Ireland.

Clark took over the newest car for Silverstone, where practice times were in fact slower than they had been for the International Trophy back in May. At the start of the British GP, the eventual winner Brabham took the lead only to come quickly under pressure from Ireland, who in turn was eventually overtaken by an on-form Graham Hill. Clark's third place was sacrificed to a collapsed wheel whilst Surtees held on to third to then be promoted to second at the finish as Hill spun wildly.

The Brands Hatch Silver City Trophy was to be the next F1 race and Surtees was again the highest Lotus finisher in sixth place.

Thankfully Stirling Moss had by now recovered sufficiently to take part in the Portuguese GP in which Jack Brabham was to secure the World Championship as a result of his win. The major difference now between the Rob Walker 18/376 and the works cars was that it had been rebuilt after Spa with a Colotti gearbox, which was a great improvement on the old 'queerbox'. In practice on the Oporto circuit both Surtees (crown-wheel and pinion) and Ireland (gears) had mechanical gremlins, whilst Clark crashed, after which his car needed some rather unsubtle straightening. Jim Endruweit and Chapman used wire from a fence to help weld and repair the damage!

Consequently the car's handling would never be quite right again and Clark was instructed to take things easy. This advice he promptly ignored to record his best finish of the year with a superb third. Surtees, having led the race, crashed when his foot slipped off the break pedal, thanks to leaking petrol. Ireland suffered fuel system bothers too and finished seventh, whilst Moss's Walker car was disqualified for being push-started against the traffic after he had spun (because of a locking brake) on lap 51.

Team Lotus was to join Cooper, BRM and Rob Walker in boycotting the Italian GP at Monza because of the perceived danger of running on the steep banking, and the next race was therefore the Lombank Trophy at Snetterton, which was won by Ireland. The Oulton Park Gold Cup was won by Moss, as all three Team Lotus entries retired.

In preparation for the United States GP, Moss comfortably won the Watkins Glen Formula Libre GP. The extra practice at Watkins Glen obviously helped Moss, who took both his and Lotus's second GP win of the year at Riverside, having started from pole position. He overcame oil-pressure troubles in the final

TEAM LOTUS AND PRIVATE LOTUS RESULTS 1960

Drivers:
Innes Ireland: British; Rodriguez: Argentinian; Alan Stacey: British; John Surtees: British; Jim Clark: British; Ron Flockhart: British
Car:
Lotus 18 Engine: Coventry Climax FPF

CAR	CHASSIS	DRIVER	PRACTICE	SESSION	GRID	RACE	LAPS	%	REASON	CHAMPIONSHIP POSITION	POINTS
ARGENTINE GP, Buenos Aires – 7th February – 80 L, 194.46 miles (312.96km) (18)											
18	369	Ireland	1m 38.5s	–	3rd	6th	79	98.75	–	6th	1
16/5	365	Larreta	1m 45.0s	–	15th	9th	77	96.2	–	–	–
16/2	364	Stacey	1m 43.6s	–	14th	R	25	31.25	Engine	–	–
MONACO GP, Monte Carlo – 29th May – 100 L, 195.42 miles (314.50km) (19)											
18	371	Ireland	1m 38.2s	–	7th	9th	56	56.0	–	9th	1
18	370	Stacey	1m 38.9s	–	13th	R	24	24.0	Suspension	–	–
18	373	Surtees	1m 39.0s	–	15th	R	18	18.0	Gears	–	–
18 W	376	Moss	1m 36.3s	–	1st P	1st W	100	100.0	–	2nd	8
DUTCH GP, Zandvoort – 6th June – 75 L, 195.40 miles (314.47km) (20)											
18	371	Ireland	1m 33.9s	–	3rd	2nd	75	100.0	–	5th	7
18	370	Stacey	1m 35.4s	–	8th	R	58	77.3	Drive	–	–
18	373	Clark	1m 36.3s	–	11th	R	43	57.3	Gears	–	–
18 W	376	Moss	1m 33.2s	–	1st P	4th	75	100.0	–	2nd	11
Fastest Lap & Record: 1m 33.8s – 99.994mph (160.925km/h)											
BELGIAN GP, Spa – 19th June – 36 L, 315.41 miles (507.60km) (21)											
18	373	Clark	3m 57.5s	–	9th	5th	34	94.4	–	16th=	2
18	371	Ireland	3m 55.4s	–	7th	R	14	38.8	Accident	5th	7
Fastest Lap: 3m 51.9s – 136.010km/h (218.887km/h) – Shared											
18	370	Stacey	4m 17.6s	–	16th	R	25	69.4	Accident	–	–
18 W	376	Moss	–	–	DNS	–	–	–	Accident	3rd	11
18 T&C	369	Taylor M	–	–	DNS	–	–	–	Accident	–	–
FRENCH GP, Reims – 3rd July – 50 L, 257.93 miles (415.10km) (22)											
18	373	Clark	2m 20.3s	–	12th	5th	49	98.0	–	10th=	4
18	374	Flockhart	2m 19.5s	–	8th	6th	49	98.0	–	21st	1
18	371	Ireland	2m 18.5s	–	4th	7th	43	86.0	–	6th=	7
16 RB	368	Piper D	–	–	DNS	–	–	–	–	–	–
BRITISH GP, Silverstone – 16th July – 77 L, 225.38 miles (362.71km) (23)											
18	373	Surtees	1m 38.6s	–	11th	2nd	77	100.0	–	8th=	6
18	371	Ireland	1m 36.2s	–	5th	3rd	77	100.0	–	3rd=	11
18	374	Clark	1m 37.0s	–	8th	16th	70	90.9	–	13th=	4
16 RB	368	Piper D	2m 05.6s	–	23rd	12th	72	93.5	–	–	–
PORTUGUESE GP, Oporto – 14th August – 55 L, 253.14 miles (407.38km) (24)											
18	374	Clark	2m 28.36s	–	8th	3rd	55	100.0	–	6th=	8
18	371	Ireland	2m 27.52s	–	7th	6th	48	87.2	–	3rd=	12
18	373	Surtees	2m 25.56s	–	1st P	R	37	67.2	Radiator	11th=	6
Fastest Lap: 2m 27.53 – 112.309mph (180.744km/h) on lap 33											
18 W	376	Moss	2m 26.19s	–	4th	DSQ	51	92.7	Driving	4th	11
US GP, Riverside – 20th November – 75 L, 245.60 miles (395.25km) (25)											
18	372	Ireland	1m 57.0s	–	7th	2nd	75	100.0	–	4th	18
18	371	Clark	1m 55.6s	–	5th	16th	61	81.3	–	8th=	8
18	373	Surtees	1m 56.6s	–	6th	R	4	5.3	Accident	12th=	6
18 W	376	Moss	1m 54.4s	–	1st P	1st W	75	100.0	–	3rd	19
18 H	–	Hall J	1m 58.2s	–	12th	7th	73	97.3	–	–	–

Key:
DNS = Did Not Start
DSQ = Disqualified
R = Retired
L = Laps
P = Pole
W = Win

Private Lotus Entries:
H = Jim Hall
RB = Robert Bodle
T&C = Taylor & Crawley
W = R.R.C. Walker

Innes Ireland took a superb second place in the United States Grand Prix at Riverside behind Moss's winning Lotus. Clark and Surtees, who were both Lotus mounted, had already crashed out.

WORLD CHAMPIONSHIP RESULTS 1960

Position	Driver	Points
1	Brabham	43
2	McLaren	34
3	**Moss**	**19**
4	**Ireland**	**18**
5	Hill (P)	16
6=	Von Trips	10
6=	Gendebien	10
8=	Ginther	8
8=	**Clark**	**8**
8=	Rathmann	8
11	Brooks	7
12=	Allison	6
12=	**Surtees**	**6**
12=	Ward	6
15=	Bonnier	4
15=	Hill (G)	4
15=	Mairesse	4
15=	Goldsmith	4
19=	Mediteguy	3
19=	Taylor	3
19=	Cabianca	3
19=	Branson	3
23	Thomson	2
24=	Bianchi	1
24=	Hermann	1
24=	Johnson	1
24=	**Flockhart**	**1**

CONSTRUCTORS' CUP 1960

Position	Constructor	Points
1	Cooper-Climax FPF	48
2	**Lotus-Climax FPF**	**34**

fifth of the race, but after Brabham's Cooper had caught fire he was untroubled. Both Clark and Surtees collided on lap 4 of the race – during the latter's spin thereby ruining their results, but Ireland came home a superb second to Moss. Jim Hall's private Lotus entry would have come home fifth had his transmission not failed on the final lap!

Over the winter Clark resisted attempts from Porsche and Ferrari to get him to transfer for the 1961 F1 season, since he found that he had a particularly good rapport with Colin Chapman. Stanley Chapman, meanwhile, was to leave his position as team manager following the winter Tasman series.

1961

Despite the protestations of the British F1 teams, the FIA introduced the new 1.5-litre Formula One from the 1 January 1961. It seemed at the time more than a coincidence that, now that British teams were established at the head of the field with their 2.5-litre engines, the goal-posts were to be moved. In truth the new regulations had been announced as far back as the end of 1958 in an effort to reduce speeds but there was still much distrust of the motives. Ferrari had all the time been researching their own highly effective 1.5-litre (190bhp) engine and as a result were to take the

1961 World Championship, thanks to the driving skills of American Phil Hill.

The weight of cars was also to be reduced from 500kg (1,100lb) to 450kg (992lb), roll-over hoops were to become mandatory and commercial fuel was to be used. Cars also had to be capable of self-starting.

Andrew Ferguson was now appointed team manager and Cedric Selzer and David Lazenby specifically looked after Clark's car as Lotus embarked on a series of non-championship races starting with the Snetterton Lombank Trophy, in which Clark was sixth. Ireland was fifth, immediately behind Moss (18/912), in the Goodwood Richmond Trophy. On the same day Lotus were contesting the Pau GP, which Clark won impressively. The Brussels GP saw Ireland take sixth.

Following Moss's win in the Vienna GP Team Lotus's next appearance was at the Aintree 200 where the highest placed works driver was Clark, in ninth. In the Syracuse GP Clark was sixth. The final 1961 non-championship event before Monaco was Silverstone's International Trophy, in which Ireland was a lowly twelfth.

Lotus 21

Chapman had recognized the benefit of reclining the driver in the Lotus 18, so it was no surprise that the same philosophy was utilized in the new Lotus 21. Again of space-frame construction, the car was a slippery slim design with coil-spring front suspension with shock absorbers and transverse-link rear suspension. The transmission was through a ZF gearbox and revised half-shafts, whilst the fuel load was carried in pannier tanks rather than above the drivers' legs. Although a Climax V8 engine was the intended power plant the Coventry Climax FPF, 2,495cc engine that was eventually used developed in the region of 152bhp – 38bhp less than those of Ferrari!

The UDT (United Dominions Trust)-Laystall team joined Rob Walker in running private 18s and the latter's driver, Moss, was to be a revelation throughout the year, thanks to the handling of his now out-of-date machine. Walker would have purchased a 21 but Lotus's oil-company sponsors made sure this was not possible.

Ireland, who now had his own aeroplane as personal transport, had to travel to Monaco by scheduled flight as his machine did not possess the necessary range. He was to undertake some further aviating in the Principality itself. After Clark had shunted his '21 at St Devote in early practice, Ireland put his similar car into second gear by mistake – he should have selected fourth on the new ZF box – inside the tunnel with the result that the back end locked up so that the Lotus crashed out of control, bouncing at top speed from wall to wall. All this happened at about 110mph (177kph), and thanks to a lack of seat belts, the driver was thrown out. An unrepentant Ireland suffered bad leg injuries but he was back driving again within five weeks. Clark put his 21 on to the front row of the grid in third place, but this was all to no avail when, after two laps of the race, the ignition failed and he had to pit to have the offending lead replaced.

Moss won Monaco again in Rob Walker's private 'old' Lotus 18 – which had its chassis welded up on the grid – fending off the Ferraris in a supreme effort, which many would say was his finest race. At the flag he was a mere 1.2 seconds ahead, having made the opposition work throughout as his obsolescent car proved impossible for Ginther to pass. By now Moss, like Walker, wanted a more up-to-date Lotus 21 but Esso, a major Lotus backer, had decreed that Walker's BP-backed team should not be permitted to purchase the

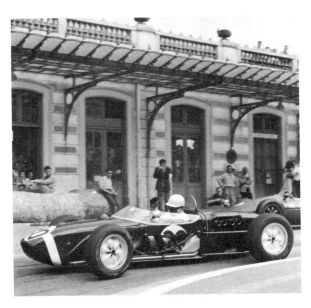

Stirling Moss won at Monaco in Rob Walker's 'old' Lotus 18 in what was widely regarded as his best-ever race. The winning margin was a mere 1.2 seconds; behind the scenes he wanted a newer Lotus 21, only for a sponsorship conflict to prevent this.

newer car. The result was that for the Belgian GP, the Walker team would field a much modified 18 (18/21), which, thanks to trusty mechanic Alf Francis, would soon closely resemble a 21.

On Whit-Monday Team Lotus was at Zandvoort for the Dutch GP with Taylor deputizing for Ireland, who was still hospitalized. In practice the Ferraris were dominant on the power circuit and in the race Clark hounded those of Ginther and Von Trips mercilessly to take third eventually. Von Trips had won despite his Ferrari being far less aerodynamic than the Lotus. Meanwhile Taylor, who finished thirteenth, had been favourably received, which was why he would eventually become a full-time member of the Lotus Grand Prix team.

Moss won the non-championship Brands Hatch Silver City Trophy, closely followed home by Clark.

The Ferraris were just too powerful again at Spa, taking the first four places on the grid, and their Phil Hill eventually won the Belgian GP. Cliff Allison was seriously injured in his UDT-Laystall Lotus 18 in a horrifying early practice crash at Burnenville, which was to end his F1 career prematurely. It was a down day for Clark too, who for once didn't have the heart to race flat out, having twice stopped to have his gearbox attended to early in the race before coming in a subdued twelfth. Ireland had an enormous engine blow-up after only ten laps, which was an inappropriate way to celebrate his welcome return to the team. Moss, in the modified 18 with new rear suspension and a 21 style body, was still outclassed in a straight line.

From Spa it was on to the ultra-fast Reims circuit, where the Ferraris were once again expected to dominate the French Grand Prix.

On a circuit where the Ferraris should have been able to make the most of their power advantage, Moss used Von Trips's version to tow him to the fourth fastest practice time. The leading Ferraris were all sidelined in the race, in which Clark and Ireland were part of a tremendous slipstreaming fight at the head of the field, which included the private Ferrari of Baghetti and the Porsche of Gurney. Running in such close proximity stones were thrown up and eventually Clark's goggles were damaged (and his face injured), and he lost his slipstreaming tow. Baghetti, having at one point pushed Ireland on to the verge at Muizon, went on to win and score his best ever result in F1, whilst Clark fought back to third. Moss retired with a wheel balance problem, followed by a suspension-damaging collision with Phil Hill. Mairesse, whose Equipe Nationale Belge entry didn't materialize, negotiated his way into the third Team Lotus car but retired at half distance.

A week later Clark was fifth in Silverstone's wet InterContinental British Empire Trophy. At a similarly wet Aintree, Ireland and Clark recorded the same qualifying time, thereby allowing them to share the grid's third row. When the British GP got under way, Ireland spun and aggravated a hand injury, which contributed to his loss of motivation. The race was held in torrential rain allowing Moss, who held second place early on, to respond brilliantly to the conditions. He spun twice at Melling Crossing, but Ferrari again took the honours after Moss eventually retired with brake troubles. Clark too pulled out from fifth place with oil system failure on lap 63.

A superb victory by Ireland at Solitude humiliated the works Porsches in their own backyard. Celebrations of Team Lotus's first win with the 21 were hectic that night, and a somewhat embellished story in the papers that Ireland had been firing a pistol into the air from the roof of his hotel ended in his being summarily banned by the organizers from the forthcoming German GP!

The ADAC Germany eventually relented and allowed Ireland to race, but after only a few minutes of the event his Lotus caught fire at Schwalbenschwanz and burned out at his feet after he had managed to abandon ship with his overalls ablaze. In practice the Ferraris had trouble with the contours of the track, as did Clark, who crashed off the circuit when a steering joint gave out. Moss out-dragged the opposition (Bon-

nier, Brabham and Phil Hill) on the first lap and was the leading Lotus driver, again coping admirably with the damp conditions. He fought off the threat of Von Trips to win by 20.4 seconds, having ignored Dunlop's advice to use dry R5 tyres (he used D12 wets instead).

In the Brands Hatch InterContinental Guards Trophy, Clark came second. It was then necessary to travel to Sweden for the Karlskoga Kanonloppet, which was won for UDT-Laystall by Moss. The return trip included the Danish GP which was again won by Moss, who made it a hat trick by winning the Modena GP too.

Ireland's intended car for Monza's thirty-second Italian GP had been destroyed in the Nurburgring fire, and as Moss had a chance of taking the Championship for Lotus he was chivalrously offered the newer Team Lotus 21 as a replacement. In effect the drivers swapped steeds with the Rob Walker driver now having use of a new Climax FPF V8; in the event, both were to retire with mechanical failure. Moss had a hub bearing fail – because of the pressures of the steep banking – after a spirited race against Gurney.

The race itself became infamous shortly after the start. The five powerful Ferraris were an obvious threat and the only way that Clark could make up for his power disadvantage was to slipstream. On lap 2 he tailed Von Trips through the Vedano corner and, on the approach to the Parabolica, he tried to overtake at about 170mph (275kph), under-braking. It would appear that Von Trips didn't see the Lotus and they touched and both spun. Whilst Clark came safely to a halt he witnessed the full aftermath: the Ferrari speared up the bank and into the crowd, killing both its driver and fourteen spectators. It was a black day for motor sport and an appalling shock for the Scot. Italian law laid the blame at the feet of the driver and Clark had to be shielded by Chapman, who quickly had him flown home. Clark's Lotus 21 was seized by the aggravated Carabineri and was not to be returned for several years; only after much litigation were Team Lotus and its driver absolved from all blame. The death of 'Taffy' Von Trips handed the title to Ferrari team-mate Phil Hill. Sadly, this was not to be the last time that the outcome of the Championship would be decided at Monza in tragic circumstances for Lotus.

The non-championship Austrian GP provided Ireland with a well-deserved win before the Oulton Park Gold Cup, where all three Team Lotus entries retired.

As the Championship had already been secured by Ferrari, they decided not to make the trip to North America, and Lotus were keen to capitalize on their absence. The new circuit of Watkins Glen was the location for the US GP. Practice saw Ireland disappear into the trackside bushes when his Lotus's steering failed. The car was repaired, and after transmission troubles, took Ireland to not only his first, but also Team Lotus's first ever GP win. Moss had led – by a margin of nearly a minute – for some time following the demise of Brabham, only for his engine to give out; Ireland nipped past to then fight off Salvadori on what was to be a memorable day for Chapman, above all. A dispirited Clark – still suffering the after-effects of Monza – was seventh, thanks to his clutch.

It had taken Team Lotus only thirty-three events to win its first World Championship GP and an ecstatic Chapman, despite a small fracas with a policeman, was absolutely delighted.

Lotus had turned the corner, being by now the most successful Climax FPF team of 1961; both they and Ireland were full of optimism for 1962, but this would soon be dissipated. Visiting the Earls Court Motor Show, Esso's Geoff Murdoch told Ireland that everything was not well within the Team. Ireland in turn sought out Chapman who reluctantly revealed the shock decision that his services would no longer be required. It later turned out that the new drivers would be Jim Clark and Trevor Taylor. A further blow was wielded when Ireland found that he was not even required for the December trip to South Africa. Clark

A characteristically irreverent gesture from Innes Ireland marks the first Grand Prix win for Team Lotus. The Watkins Glen result was achieved after Ireland had crashed in practice and also overcome transmission troubles. Chapman was delighted.

TEAM LOTUS AND PRIVATE LOTUS ENTRY RESULTS 1961

Drivers:
Jim Clark: British; Innes Ireland: British; Trevor Taylor: British; Willy Mairesse: Belgian
Car:
Lotus 21 Engine: Coventry Climax FPF

CAR	CHASSIS	DRIVER	PRACTICE	SESSION	GRID	RACE	LAPS	%	REASON	CHAMPIONSHIP POSITION	POINTS
MONACO GP, Monte Carlo – 14th May – 100 L, 195.42 miles (314.50km) (26)											
21	930	Clark	1m 39.6s	1	3rd	10th	89	89.0	–	–	–
21	931	Ireland	1m 40.5s	2	DNS	–	–	–	Accident	–	–
18 W	912	Moss	1m 39.1s	3	1st P	1st W	100	100.0	–	1st	9
Fastest Lap: 1m 36.3s – 73.054mph (117.570km/h) lap 85 with Ginther											
18 SC	914	May M	1m 42.0s	–	13th	R	42	42.0	Gears	–	–
18 UDT	916	Allison	1m 42.3s	–	14th	8th	93	93.0	–	–	–
18 UDT	915	Taylor H	1m 42.6s	–	DNQ	–	–	–	–	–	–
DUTCH GP, Zandvoort – 22nd May – 75 L, 195.40 miles (314.47km) (27)											
21	930	Clark	1m 36.9s	3	10th	3rd	75	100.0	–	5th	4
Fastest Lap: 1m 35.5s – 98.214mph (158.060km/h) on lap 7											
21	371	Taylor	1m 39.5s	3	14th	13th	73	97.3	–	–	–
18 W	912	Moss	1m 36.2s	2	4th	4th	75	100.0	–	1st=	12
18 C	905	Burgess I	–	–	DNS	–	–	–	Accident	–	–
BELGIAN GP, Spa – 18th June – 30 L, 262.84 miles (423.00km) (28)											
21	932	Clark	4m 17.7s	2	16th	12th	24	80.0	–	5th	4
21	933	Ireland	4m 20.0s	2	18th	R	10	33.3	Engine	–	–
18/21 W	912	Moss	4m 08.2s	2	8th	8th	30	30.0	–	3rd=	12
18 B	909★	Mairesse	4m 20.6s	–	19th	R	8	26.6	Engine	–	–
18 B	373★★	Bianchi	4m 27.3s	–	21st	R	10	33.3	Oil pipe	–	–
18 UDT	915	Allison/ Taylor H	–	–	DNS	–	–	–	Accident	–	–
18 M	909	Marsh T	4m 23.2s	–	DNS	–	–	–	–	–	–
18 SC	373	Seidel	4m 27.4s	–	DNS	–	–	–	–	–	–
18 C	918	Burgess	4m 34.6s	–	DNS	–	–	–	–	–	–

FRENCH GP, Reims – 2nd July – 52 L, 268.25 miles (431.70km) (29)

21	932	Clark	2m 29.0s	3	5th	3rd	52	100.0	–	7th	8
21	933	Ireland	2m 29.8s	3	10th	4th	52	100.0	–	8th=	3
21	930	Mairesse	2m 35.8s	3	20th	R	26	50.0	Fuel	–	–
18/21 W	912	Moss	2m 27.6s	1	4th	R	31	59.6	Brakes	3rd=	12
18 UDT	915	Bianchi	2m 33.4s	–	19th	R	21	40.3	Clutch	–	–
18/21 UDT	916	Taylor H	2m 40.3s	–	25th	10th	49	94.2	–	–	–
18 SC	914	May M	2m 37.9s	–	22nd	11th	48	92.3	–	–	–
18 C	905	Burgess	2m 37.9s	–	24th	14th	42	80.7	–	–	–
18 SC	373	Seidel	–	–	DNS	–	–	–	T-Car	–	–
18/21 UDT	915	Bordeu	–	–	DNS	–	–	–	–	–	–

BRITISH GP, Aintree – 15th July – 75 L, 225.00 miles (362.10km) (30)

21	933	Ireland	1m 59.2s	2	7th	10th	72	96.0	–	9th=	3
21	932	Clark	1m 59.2s	2	8th	R	63	84.0	Gauge	7th	8
18/21 W	912	Moss	1m 59.0s	2	5th	R	45	60.0	Brakes	4th	12
18/21 UDT	916	Taylor H	2m 01.8s	–	17th	R	5	6.6	Accident	–	–
18/21 UDT	917	Bianchi	2m 18.8s	30th	R	45	60.0	–	–	–	
18 SC	373	Seidel	2m 04.2s	–	22nd	17th	58	77.3	–	–	–
18 BB	903	Maggs	2m 06.4s	–	24th	13th	69	92.0	–	–	–
18 C	905	Burgess	2m 06.6s	–	25th	14th	69	92.0	–	–	–
18 A	919	Ashmore	2m 08.2s	–	26th	R	7	9.3	Misfire	–	–
18 M	909	Marsh	2m 09.6s	–	27th	R	13	17.3	Misfire	–	–
18 P	904	Parnell T	2m 16.8s	–	29th	R	12	16.0	Clutch	–	–

GERMAN GP, Nurburgring – 6th August – 15 L, 212.60 miles (342.15km) (31)

21	930	Clark	9m 08.1s	2	8th	4th	15	100.0	–	5th	11
21	933	Ireland	9m 22.9s	1	16th	R	2	13.3	Fire	11th=	3
18/21 W	912	Moss	9m 01.7s	3	3rd	1st W	15	100.0	–	3rd	21
18 M	909	Marsh	9m 37.7s	–	20th	25th	13	86.6	–	–	–
18 BB	903	Maggs	9m 45.5s	–	22nd	11th	14	93.3	–	–	–
18 SC	373	Seidel	9m 59.9s	–	23rd	R	3	20.0	Steering	–	–
18 C	914	May	10m 37.5s	–	DNS	–	–	–	Accident	–	–
18 A	919	Ashmore	10m 06.0s	–	25th	16th	13	86.6	–	–	–

ITALIAN GP, Monza – 10th September – 43 L, 267.19 miles (430.00km) (32)

21	934	Clark	2m 49.2s	2	7th	R	2	4.6	Accident	6th	11
18/21	912	Ireland	2m 50.3s	2	9th	R	5	11.6	Chassis	11th=	3
21 W	933	Moss	2m 51.8s	1	11th	R	37	86.0	Wheel	3rd	21
18/21 UDT	917	Gregory	2m 55.2s	–	17th	R	12	27.9	Suspension	–	–
18/21 UDT	918	Taylor H	3m 00.6s	–	23rd	12th	39	90.6	–	–	–
18 A	919	Ashmore	3m 03.0s	–	25th	R	1	2.3	Accident	–	–
18 P	904	Parnell T	3m 05.7s	–	27th	11th	40	93.0	–	–	–
18 SC	373	Seidel	3m 05.7s	–	28th	R	2	4.6	Engine	–	–
L-M S	902	Starrabba	3m 07.9s	–	30th	R	20	46.5	Engine	–	–

US GP, Watkins Glen – 8th October – 100 L, 230.00 miles (370.10km) (33)

21	933	Ireland	1m 18.8s	2	8th	1st W	100	100.0	–	6th	12
21	930	Clark	1m 18.3s	3	5th	7th	96	96.0	–	7th=	11
18/21 W	912	Moss	1m 18.2s	3	3rd	R	59	59.0	Engine	3rd=	21

Fastest Lap: 1m 18.2s – 105.880mph (170.39km/h) on lap 28

18/21 UDT	917	Gregory	1m 19.1s	–	11th	R	24	24.0	Gearbox	–	–
18/21 UDT	918***	Gendebien	1m 20.5s	–	15th	11th	92	92.0	–	–	–
18/21 W	372	Ryan	1m 20.0s	–	13th	9th	95	95.0	–	–	–
18/21 H	371	Hall J	1m 21.8s	–	18th	R	76	76.0	Leak	–	–
18 FH	907	Ruby	1m 21.8s	–	19th	R	76	76.0	Magneto	–	–

Key:
DNQ = Did Not Qualify
DNS = Did Not Start
* = car borrowed from T. Marsh
** = car borrowed from Scuderia Colonia
*** = car co-driven by Masten Gregory after gearbox failure on own Lotus
L-M = Lotus-Maserati
R = Retired
L = Laps
P = Pole
W = Win

Private Lotus Entries:
A = G. Ashmore
B = Equipe Nationale Belge
BB = Mrs L. Brydon-Brown
C = Camoradi International
M = T. Marsh
SC = Scuderia Colonia
UDT = UDT-Laystall Racing Team
W = R.R.C. Walker Racing Team
P = R.H.H. Parnell
S = Gaetano Starrabba
W = Jack Wheeler Autosport
H = Jim Hall Racing
F.H. = J. Frank Harrison

had been a close friend of Ireland's but the latter was now disillusioned and mystified as he had remained loyal throughout a period of Lotus F1 machinery fragility. Ireland blamed the two existing drivers for his own downfall, feeling that he had been disposed of in a most insensitive way; he went over to the UDT/BRP team for 1962, turning down the obvious choice of BRM. A feud, though, would continue to exist between him and Clark.

Out in South Africa Clark was to win the first three races in 21/937. These were the Rand GP at Kyalami, the Natal GP at Westmead and the South African GP at East London.

WORLD CHAMPIONSHIP RESULTS 1961

Position	Driver	Points
1	Phil Hill	34
2	Wolfgang Von Trips	33
3=	**Stirling Moss**	**21**
	Dan Gurney	21
5	Richie Ginther	16
6	**Innes Ireland**	**12**
7	**Jim Clark**	**11**

CONSTRUCTORS' CUP 1961

Position	Constructor	Points
1	Ferrari	40
2	**Lotus-Climax FPF**	**32**

═══ 1962 ═══

The final South African race, the Cape GP at Killarney, gave Taylor a welcome win.

Lotus 24

In 1962 Ferrari slipped from their dominant position, leaving both BRM and Lotus to fight over which was going to be top dog. In so doing Lotus ran the new V8 Coventry-Climax engine which now developed 190bhp at 8,500rpm. Clark was unlucky not to become World Champion in 1962, having at the last hurdle to give best to Graham Hill and BRM. Mechanical unreliability and a rare error were to cost Clark and Lotus dearly, but that should not take anything away from the Scot's performances whilst still a comparative newcomer to Grand Prix racing.

The Lotus 24 made its race début in Belgium at the Brussels GP with Clark taking pole position, but retiring with valve troubles. The new car was likened to a modified Lotus 21 – which it outwardly resembled – with the addition of improved steering and suspension. In reality the 24 was a space-frame insurance policy in case the forthcoming monocoque 25 was unsuccessful, and it contained many more new parts than most people perceived. The design was to be largely raced by the customer teams in the shape of UDT-Laystall and Rob Walker.

In the four further non-championship races that followed Brussels Clark won two, at Snetterton and Aintree, and came second in the Silverstone

Trevor Taylor hurls his Lotus 24 around Zandvoort in 1962 on his way to a fine second place behind Hill's BRM. Most attention, though, surrounded the appearance of the works Lotus 25, which had taken most of the paddock by surprise.

International Trophy. In the Pau GP he was eleventh, but on the same day back at Goodwood, Moss suffered an unexplained, but near fatal accident – he received a badly fractured skull – which effectively finished his GP career and from which he was lucky to recover fully.

To all those unaware that the Lotus 25 was nearing completion, the 24 certainly looked to be a promising chassis that as far as they were concerned would carry on throughout 1962.

Lotus 25

The car that started the monocoque revolution in racing car design had originally been designed on the back of a serviette by Colin Chapman during a lunchtime business meeting. The driver was even more reclined than previously (Clark would refer to himself as the first 'horizontal driver' and to the car as the 'bed on wheels'!) lowering considerably the centre of gravity – fuel was no longer carried over the driver's legs – whilst the very light design also provided both a stiffer chassis and a smaller frontal area than the 24.

Its success was largely down to the fact that the rigid chassis allowed the springs to make most use of the available Dunlop tyres; both the amount of contact with the track and wear rate were considerably improved. It should be remembered, too, that Clark's skill, although he was in his Formula One infancy, would have flattered any car.

There being no opposition in sight, Clark's 'bed on wheels' – the Lotus 25 – is seen powering into Eau Rouge amidst the packed Ardennes hillsides of Spa. This classic shot typifies the monocoque car's superiority during a dominant season.

Only on the slipstreaming power circuits did the 25 seem to be at any disadvantage to the opposition, and the work of Chapman, Dick Scammel, Mike Costin and Ted Woodley was therefore to be richly rewarded. By the time of the Dutch GP the V8 Coventry Climax engine had overcome its teething troubles.

The appearance of the monocoque Lotus 25 caused a great stir amongst onlookers at the Dutch Grand Prix. The design that had been kept so secret surprised the paddock residents, and especially those teams running private Lotus entries, who had thought that in the 24 they had purchased the most up-to-date Lotus for the 1962 season! The 25 was explained away by Chapman as a research car for the 1963 season but very few believed him.

The perfect début would have seen Clark taking pole position but this was not to be, as both gearbox and engine carburation problems saw him relegated to third on the Zandvoort grid behind Surtees (Lola) and Hill (BRM). He had, in fact, driven both the 24 and the 25 in practice before settling on the latter for its race début. Between practice and the race Chapman flew one engine back to Coventry in his Comanche to be rebuilt, and the now reliable unit was quickly fitted by the nocturnal mechanics.

In the race Clark cut into first place by the time he arrived at Tarzan, the first corner. He pulled away for a couple of laps – taking a 5-second advantage – seeming set to dominate the race, but perhaps his start was just too much for the car, as gear selection became difficult and his clutch started to slip; the lead was handed back to Hill's BRM V8 at Tarzan. Clark pulled into the pits – where the pedal mounting was repaired – eventually losing ten laps.

Taylor – whose car was being looked after by Cedric Selzer – impressed early in practice with second-best time, whilst he learned how to cope with the increased horsepower of F1, and he came home a fine second in the race – 27 seconds behind Hill. Taylor had hit the back of Ginther's BRM on the way but unlike the former had managed to continue, albeit without the front bodywork, for his best result of the season. Ireland, meanwhile, had somersaulted out of the race on lap 61. Hill's first win for BRM set the agenda for the rest of the year, as his duel with Clark would prove to be the focus of the season's action.

Clark took pole at Monaco by 0.3 seconds from Hill only to be clouted by the Ferrari of Mairesse, who tried to win the race at the first damp corner, starting off a chain of minor accidents at the Gasometer hairpin. As a result, Clark was pushed back to sixth place only to be troubled by his clutch yet again, while Taylor lost his body section. An inspired race ensued from the Scot as he chased Hill – coping, too, with a misfiring engine –

reducing the lap record as he went. Hill was luckier with the backmarkers he was overtaking and Clark dropped back at half distance only to be forced to park eventually when his gearbox and engine finally gave out on lap 56. Hill, too, subsequently retired with engine failure – letting Bruce McLaren through to win – whilst Taylor emerged from the race covered from head to foot in oil.

In the non-championship Mallory Park International 2,000 Guineas Clark retired, while at Crystal Palace's London Trophy Taylor retired too.

During practice for the Belgian GP at Spa the Team were concerned about gearbox temperatures – the cars were consequently run without their gearbox cowls – and Taylor distinguished himself by initially taking fastest practice time, on a circuit with which he was largely unfamiliar, and by even leading the race for five laps. Disaster, though, struck on lap 26 at Blanchimont when his 24 jumped out of gear at 120mph (193kph) and the hesitating Lotus was rammed by the Ferrari of Mairesse. The Lotus scythed down a telegraph pole and the Ferrari exploded into flame, with the very lucky drivers merely incurring bruising. The psychological effects of this accident, though, were to stay with Taylor for some time, which was hardly surprising as R5 was virtually cut in half . . .

Clark still disliked Spa greatly, but ironically it was here that he was to achieve his first Grand Prix success. In early practice he was bedevilled by camshaft problems, and after he had also over-revved an engine, thanks to a missed gear change, he eagerly awaited a fresh power unit for the race that was being shipped overland from England. Thanks to these problems he was only twelfth fastest in his limited practice. He succeeded in being fourth across the line at the end of the first lap of the race, however, and on his second lap he

was 5 seconds faster than he had previously managed! A five-way battle ensued involving team-mate Taylor as well as Hill, Mairesse and McLaren. Initially Clark hung back, but by mid-race, having mastered the track in the 25, he had made his move and swooped into the lead. He had suppressed his personal animosity towards Spa and the celebrations went on well into the night at the Stavelot hotel.

A double retirement occurred in the non-championship Rheims GP before the Team moved on to Rouen, which was another circuit not for the faint of heart, and it was here that two works 25s were at last fielded. A seized steering mechanism gave Clark a nasty moment in practice on his way to pole position. In the French GP he made a bad start and was worried both about a bad choice of first gear – his 25 was very slow out of the tight Nouveau Monde hairpin – as well as the car's steering. It did eventually cause his retirement when a front suspension ball joint came apart after a battle with Hill's BRM.

The fearsome downhill swoops of Rouen were also tackled by Taylor despite a jamming throttle. He had tried to repair this himself having stopped out on the circuit and had returned to the pits operating the throttle by hand! He was to finish eighth after a fight with Salvadori's Lola only to crash very heavily as he crossed the line, thanks to a mêlée of gendarmes and slowing cars. Both his 25 and the Rob Walker 24 of Trintignant were written off, but luckily both drivers as well as the crowd of spectators were unhurt. At non-championship Solitude Taylor was to come third, whilst Clark shunted his car in the unexpected rain.

The British GP meeting at Aintree was dominated by Clark in front of his home fans. An eleventh-hour pole position (by over half a second), race win and fastest lap were all to fall to the flying Scot with Hill's

Surtees's Lola gives vain chase as Clark's Lotus 25 is already starting to dominate Aintree's British Grand Prix on the opening lap. Despite a late gearbox worry, Clark won in front of his adoring home crowd, which included a young Nigel Mansell!

BRM – a hundredweight heavier than the Lotus 25 – unable to respond. Surtees's Lola had tried to offer a challenge to Clark in the early laps but when he lost fourth gear the Lotus disappeared into the distance. Taylor pitted with carburettor problems on lap 7 but still came home eighth, having shadowed and been 'towed' by Clark towards the end of the race as the winner worried that his gearbox was about to give out on the last two laps before the flag. The seven-year-old Nigel Mansell was spectating that day determined that he was going to be a racing driver for Lotus!

After Aintree, Hill and BRM went to the Nurburgring with a single point advantage over Clark and Lotus. Both Team Lotus drivers had engine trouble in practice in Germany when first Taylor's expired when being started up, and the replacement lacked oil pressure, denying him any more lappery. Taylor's original engine was subsequently cannibalized in order to help Jack Brabham début his new grand prix car. Uncharacteristically Clark had additionally managed to over-rev his Coventry Climax when R2 jumped out of gear. The UDT-Laystall Team didn't run as a result of a dispute with the organizers over start money. Taylor nearly joined them until Chapman intervened to explain that his driver had in fact covered the correct number of practice laps!

The wet German GP was the exact opposite of Aintree, being far from boring at the head of the field despite the conditions. Unfortunately Lotus were not part of the exciting equation until half distance, as on the grid Clark had forgotten to activate his Bendix fuel pump, being distracted trying to clear the lenses of his goggles. He, in fact, started last but overtook sixteen cars on the first 14-mile lap, and in a momentous drive came home fourth. With five laps to go his fuel system had denied him the chance to attack the leading trio of Hill, Surtees and Gurney. On the eleventh lap he had got himself into a 200-yard skid – so hard was he trying to catch the leaders – and despite assertions at the time his lap times certainly didn't indicate that this affected his fighting charge in the slightest.

Taylor, meanwhile, had had his engine suddenly come on song midway around the first lap, and the unexpected surge of power had caught him out: he had plunged down an embankment and off the track, but without suffering personal harm. Hill's BRM won, establishing a larger lead in the Championship.

Taylor was to take in the Roskildering Danish GP, coming home sixth on aggregate, before returning for the Oulton Park Gold Cup where Clark won and Taylor retired. Lotus travelled to Monza with Clark well positioned to take the World Championship but the event was to be shambolic for Team Lotus. The Monza road circuit rather than the banking was utilized for the

Italian GP, during which gearboxes were to be Team Lotus's Achilles' heel as a succession of failures occurred, which were later attributed to the lubricant. Clark still managed to take pole – despite damaged tappets – and snatch the lead at the start, but Hill was soon past in the BRM. Clark's transmission started to fail yet again, necessitating a pitstop on lap 3 before his electrics eventually forced his retirement after another ten laps. Another malfunctioning gearbox forced Taylor out too. The transmissions were to be extensively rebuilt before the trip to North America, but Hill had seized the initiative in the World Championship with his win.

Transmission troubles had disappeared as far as Clark was concerned by the time the Team arrived at Watkins Glen. He was easily on pole and led the race until he had problems overtaking backmarkers. Hill then got past for a short period (seven laps), but Clark retook the Englishman before setting a new circuit record and taking the chequered flag first. Taylor meanwhile came home twelfth, suffering more problems with his gear mechanism.

After Watkins Glen, Team Lotus took both Clark and a 25 chassis to Indianapolis so that Chapman could conceive a future Indy car and the Scot could pass his 'Rookie' test. There next followed a trio of non-championship races the first of which, the Mexican GP, saw Clark initially disqualified but eventually winning, having shared R2 with Taylor. The second race was the Rand GP at Kyalami where again Clark dominated, before it was Taylor's turn to win the Natal GP.

Clark journeyed to East London only nine points behind Hill, but he needed to win the race to take the World Championship – any other placing would give the Englishman the title.

A somewhat depleted entry – compared with that experienced in Europe – although it did at least include the two World Championship protagonists, Clark and Hill, made the trek to East London for the final decisive South African round of the 1962 World Championship, which would be run in front of 90,000 spectators alongside the Indian Ocean. BRM had successfully spread a rumour that their car was much lighter than it actually was and both Chapman and Lotus were completely taken in.

Clark looked well on his way to Championship victory when he took pole and then dominated the race for sixty-two laps, having made an excellent start establishing what appeared to be a safe cushion on Hill. Taylor, on the other hand, had pulled off at The Sweep when his transmission had failed him. Hill pressed hard but decided to go easy while Clark kept running at full speed, which moved Chapman to signal his driver to go cautiously. This may well have been too late, as on lap 61 smoke started coming from the back of R5 and on the next lap Clark came into the pits. Frantic activity eventually revealed that it had been a missing bolt from the crank-case – apparently there had not been a locking washer – that at the final hurdle had lost Lotus the Championship.

At the end of the 1962 season the CSI decided to continue the 1.5-litre Formula One for another two years, thus allowing the teams to continue their development work – something that caused great relief amongst the British constructors, including Lotus, who

were to be a prime beneficiary. At Lotus Len Terry had returned in September, having been involved in the Gilbey F1 project amongst others, to replace Mike Costin who had moved on to Cosworth. In October, Coventry Climax too put a spanner in the works by announcing their withdrawal from racing on financial grounds. Chapman responded by going out and persuading the major sponsors, who included tyre and fuel companies, to pay more for their engines so that Climax could cover their bills. Shortly afterwards Coventry Climax was taken over by Jaguar cars.

TEAM LOTUS AND PRIVATE LOTUS ENTRY RESULTS 1962

Drivers:
Jim Clark: British; Trevor Taylor: British
Car:
Lotus 24 Engine: Coventry Climax V8
Lotus 25   Coventry Climax V8

CAR	CHASSIS	DRIVER	PRACTICE	SESSION	GRID	RACE	LAPS	%	REASON	CHAMPIONSHIP POSITION	POINTS
DUTCH GP, Zandvoort – 20th May – 80 L, 208.43 miles (355.44km) (34)											
24	948	Taylor	1m 35.4s	1	10th	2nd	80	100.0	–	2nd	6
25	R1	Clark	1m 33.2s	3	3rd	9th	70	87.5	–	–	–
24		Spare									
24 B	947	Brabham	1m 33.9s	–	4th	R	4	–	Accident	–	–
24 UDT	942	Ireland	1m 34.1s	–	6th	R	62	–	Accident	–	–
18/21 UDT	917★	Gregory	1m 38.0s	–	16th	R	55	–	Gears	–	–
MONACO GP, Monte Carlo – 3rd June – 100 L, 195.42 miles (314.50km) (35)											
25	R1	Clark	1m 35.4s	3	1st P	R	56	56.0	Clutch	–	–
Fastest Lap and Record: 1m 35.5s, 73.666mph (118.554km/h) on lap 42											
24	948	Taylor	1m 40.0s	1	14th	R	25	25.0	Leak	4th	5
24	950	(Spare)									
24 B	947	Brabham	1m 36.5s	–	6th	R	77	–	Suspension	–	–
24 W	940	Trintignant	1m 36.8s	–	7th	R	1	–	Accident	–	–
21 F	938	Siffert	1m 38.9s	–	DNQ	–	–	–	–	–	–
24 UDT	944★★	Gregory	1m 39.2s	–	DNQ	–	–	–	–	–	–
18/21 V	912	Vaccarella	2m 01.8s	–	DNQ	–	–	–	–	–	–
BELGIAN GP, Spa – 17th June – 32 L, 280.36 miles (451.20km) (36)											
25	R1	Clark	4m 04.9s	2	12th	1st W	32	100.0	–	3rd=	9
Fastest Lap: 3m 55.6s – 133.873mph (215.449km/h) on lap 15											
24	948	Taylor	3m 59.3s	1	3rd	R	26	81.25	Accident	5th	6
24 UDT	943	Ireland	3m 59.8s	–	5th	R	9	–	Suspension	–	–
24 UDT	944★★	Gregory	4m 01.0s	–	8th	R	13	–	Withdrawn	–	–
24 B	947	Brabham	4m 08.2s	–	25th	6th	30	9.37	–	–	–
24 W	940	Trintignant	4m 09.2s	–	16th	8th	30	9.37	–	–	–
18/21 NB	918★	Bianchi	4m 18.0s	–	18th	9th	29	90.6	–	–	–
21 F	938★	Siffert	4m 11.6s	–	17th	10th	29	90.6	–	–	–
18 C	373★	Campbell-Jones	4m 26.9s	–	19th	11th	16	50.0	–	–	–
24 S	950★★	Gurney	6m 42.2s	–	DNS	–	–	–	–	–	–
FRENCH GP, Rouen – 8th July – 54 L, 219.51 miles (353.27km) (37)											
25	R1	Taylor	2m 19.1s	1	12th	8th	48	88.8	–	8th	6
25	R2	Clark	2m 14.8s	2	1st P	R	34	62.9	Accident	4th=	9
24	949	(Spare)									
24 B	947	Brabham	2m 16.1s	–	4th	R	10	–	Suspension	–	–
24 UDT	944★★	Gregory	2m 17.3s	–	7th	R	14	–	Ignition	–	–
24 UDT	942	Ireland	2m 17.5s	–	8th	R	1	–	Wheel	–	–
24 UDT	943	(Spare)									
24 W	940	Trintignant	2m 20.8s	–	13th	7th	50	90.5	–	–	–
24 F	950★★	Siffert	2m 23.4s	–	15th	R	5	–	Clutch	–	–
21 F	938	(Spare)									

BRITISH GP, Aintree – 21st July – 75 L, 225.00 miles (362.10km) (38)

25	R2	Clark	1m 53.6s	4	1st P	1st W	75	100.0	–	2nd	18

Fastest Lap: 1m 55.0s – 93.91mph (151.14km/h) on lap 36

24	949	Taylor	1m 56.0s	3	10th	8th	74	98.6	–	8th	6
24 UDT	943	Ireland	1m 54.4s	–	3rd	16th	61	81.3	–	–	–
24 UDT	942	Gregory	1m 57.2s	–	14th	7th	74	98.6	–	–	–
24 B	947	Brabham	1m 55.4s	–	9th	5th	74	98.6	–	–	–
18/21 D	P1★	Shelly	2m 02.4s	–	18th	R	6	8.0	Overheating	–	–
24 E	905★	Chamberlain	2m 03.4s	–	20th	15th	64	85.3	–	–	–
24	946★★	Seidel	2m 11.6s	–	21st	R	11	–	Brakes	–	–

GERMAN GP, Nurburgring – 5th August – 15 L, 212.60 miles (342.15km) (39)

25	R2	Clark	8m 51.2s	2	3rd	4th	15	100.0	–	2nd	21
24	949	Taylor	10m 09.6s	3	26th	R	1	6.6	Accident	8th	6
24 W	940	Trintignant	9m 19.0s	–	11th	R	4	26.6	Gearbox	–	–
21 F	938★	Siffert	9m 39.3s	–	17th	12th	15	100.0	–	–	–
24 F	950★★	Schiller	9m 51.5s	–	20th	R	4	26.2	Oil	–	–
18/21 D	P1★	Shelly	10m 18.6s	–	DNQ	–	–	–	–	–	–
24 S	946★★	Seidel	10m 38.2s	–	DNQ	–	–	–	–	–	–
18 CH	905★	Chamberlain	11m 12.9s	–	DNQ	–	–	–	–	–	–
18	373	Seiffert	(T-car)								

ITALIAN GP, Monza – 16th September – 86 L, 307.27 miles (494.50km) (40)

25	R3	Clark	1m 40.35s	2	1st P	R	13	15.1	Gearbox	3rd	21
25	R2	Taylor	1m 44.2s	2	16th	R	26	30.2	Gearbox	9th	6
24	—	(Spare)									
24 UDT	942	Ireland	1m 41.8s	–	5th	R	46	–	Suspension	–	–
24 UDT	944★★	Gregory	1m 41.9s	–	6th	12th	77	89.5	–	–	–
24 UDT	–	(Spare)									
24 V	941	Vaccarella	1m 43.4s	–	14th	9th	84	97.6	–	–	–
24 W	940	Trintignant	1m 44.4s	–	19th	R	18	–	Engine	–	–
24 S	946★★	Shelly	1m 15.6s	–	DNQ	–	–	–	–	–	–
18 A	919★	Ashmore	1m 52.9s	–	DNQ	–	–	–	–	–	–
24 F	950	Siffert	1m 52.9s	–	DNQ	–	–	–	–	–	–
18 E	905	Chamberlain	1m 59.7s	–	DNQ	–	–	–	–	–	–
18 P	913	Prinoth	1m 57.7s	–	DNQ	–	–	–	–	–	–

US GP, Watkins Glen – 7th October – 100 L, 230.00 miles (370.10km) (41)

25	R3	Clark	1m 15.8s	1	1st P	1st W	100	100.0	–	2nd	30
25	R2	Taylor	1m 18.0s	1	8th	12th	85	85.0	–	9th	6
24 UDT	944★★	Gregory	1m 17.9s	–	7th	6th	99	99.0	–	–	–
24 UDT	942	Ireland	1m 24.0s	–	15th	8th	96	96.0	–	–	–
24 Z	943	Penske	1m 21.3s	–	12th	9th	96	96.0	–	–	–
24 M	940	Schroeder	1m 24.0s	–	16th	10th	93	93.0	–	–	–
24 W	941	Trintignant	1m 25.8s	–	17th	R	32	–	Brakes	–	–
21 H	936★	Hall	1m 24.7s	–	DNS	–	–	–	–	–	–

S AFRICAN GP, East London – 29th December – 82 L, 199.72 miles (321.41km) (42)

25	R5	Clark	1m 29.3s	3	1st P	R	62	75.6	Oil	2nd	30

Fastest Lap: 1m 31.0s – 96.350mph (155.060km/h) on lap 3

25	R2	Taylor	1m 32.7s	2	9th	R	12	14.6	Gears	10th	6
24 UDT	942	Ireland	1m 31.1s	–	4th	5th	81	98.7	–	–	–
21 L	939★	Lederle	1m 33.6s	–	10th	6th	78	95.1	–	–	–
21 PI	937★	Pieterse	1m 36.8s	–	13th	10th	71	86.5	–	–	–

Key:

★	= Climax 4 engine		Private Lotus Entries:	M	= John W. Mecom Jr
★★	= BRM V8 engine	A	= G. Ashmore	NB	= Equipe Nationale Belge
DNQ	= Did Not Qualify	B	= Brabham Racing Organization	P	= E. Prinoth
DNS	= Did Not Start	C	= J. Campbell-Jones	PI	= E. Pieterse
R	= Retired	CH	= J. Chamberlain	S	= Wolfgang Seidel/Autosport Team Wolfgang Seidel
L	= Laps	D	= J. Dalton	UDT	= UDT-Laystall Racing Team
P	= Pole	E	= Ecurie Excelsior	V	= Scuderia SSS Republica di Venezia
W	= Win	F	= Ecurie Filipinetti	W	= R.R.C. Walker Racing Team
		H	= J. Hall	Z	= Dupont Zerex Anti-Freeze
		L	= N. Lederle		

WORLD CHAMPIONSHIP RESULTS 1962

Position	Driver	Points
1	Graham Hill	42
2	**Jim Clark**	**30**
3	Bruce McLaren	27
4	John Surtees	19
5	Dan Gurney	15
6	Phil Hill	14
7	Tony Maggs	13
8	Richie Ginther	10
9	Jack Brabham	9
10	**Trevor Taylor**	**6**

CONSTRUCTORS' CUP 1962

Position	Constructor	Points
1	BRM	42
2	**Lotus-Climax**	**36**

1963

For 1963 Coventry Climax developed their Mk 2 engine with Lucas fuel injection, rather than the previous Weber carburettors; it now produced 196bhp at 9,500rpm; Lotus boasted two of these power plants. Having narrowly missed the Championship the previous year, everyone expected 1963 to be a walk-over for Clark and they were to be right: he was to win seven out of ten World Championship events. The advantage was that Lotus already had their monocoque car, while the others wasted much time in trying to catch up; at least one competitor made use of a 'borrowed' detailed drawing that had disappeared! Cedric Selzer was to be Clark's mechanic during what was to be an outstandingly successful season.

The season started with six non-championship races in which Clark scored three wins, one second place and one third. Throughout these races Clark had been troubled by the 'new' R6 tyres on offer from Dunlop, much preferring the 'old' R5s with which he won the International Trophy at Silverstone.

In practice for the opening Monaco GP of the World Championship season, Clark lapped the Weber-equipped spare car almost as quickly as his fuel injection race version on his way to pole position, whilst Taylor was in all sorts of throttle troubles. Lotus loaned R3 to Jack Brabham for the race, but in common with the other two cars he was to suffer from gearbox troubles. Unfortunately, bad luck was to strike Clark for the third year in succession in Monte Carlo. At the start he was beaten away by both Hill and Ginther and it took until lap 5 for him to get back into second place

– now 1.6 seconds behind the leader. He then sparred with Hill's BRM before finally passing on lap 18 and establishing a comfortable cushion. It had been apparent that his was the quicker of the two cars on the twistier parts of the track but that he was at a disadvantage on the straights. Sadly Clark's gearbox jammed solid on lap 78 at the Hairpin, thereby ending his race against a lamppost. Taylor had been in and out of the pits with similar transmission problems but he did at least manage to finish, albeit in sixth place. It later transpired that Clark's gearbox problem had arisen because he had managed to select two gears simultaneously!

In practice at Spa, Clark – his car fitted with a new windscreen – was dogged by gearbox troubles again, which left him in a lowly eighth place. The car, which was still on its Monaco settings, persisted in jumping out of gear and oversteering simultaneously. Lotus's appalling practice continued when Taylor had a huge 130mph (210kph) accident at Stavelot when the car's suspension collapsed (a bolt had pulled out), and he savaged a wall and a hut destroying the car in the process. As a result he was only to run for five laps of the Grand Prix, being in pain from his practice injuries, which included a detached thigh muscle. In reality he had been very lucky to start the race at all. Clark made such a good flying start that he was leading by the time he reached the first corner, and he simply drew away from the opposition once Hill had been plagued by gearbox troubles on the slippery track. Unaffected by the thunder and rain at the end of the race he won easily for the second year in succession. Such was his supremacy that he finished almost 5 minutes ahead of the Cooper of Bruce McLaren, which was the only car on the same lap!

Despite his ZF gearbox jumping out Clark conscientiously worked down to an unbeatable pole time by the end of Zandvoort practice, and from this very position he proceeded to drive into the distance again in the Dutch GP. He literally lapped everyone as he became the first driver to negotiate the circuit at an average speed in excess of 100mph (160kph). The only minor snag for Clark was an altercation with the police over his pass – a problem that was soon diplomatically smoothed over. Taylor suffered from a misfire and finished well down the field in tenth place.

The third Team Lotus car (of Peter Arundell) was forbidden to start the French GP at Reims because FIA regulations stated that a driver could only enter one race on one day. He was widely regarded as the star of Formula Junior and therefore the organizers wished him to remain in that category's supporting race. If that wasn't trouble enough, Taylor's car got stuck in the mud of the paddock for much of the second practice

At Zandvoort Clark lapped the entire field on his way to another fine win with the Lotus 25. He was also the first driver to record a 100mph (160kph) lap of the Dutch seaside track. The soon-to-be-lapped field is seen here meekly trailing on the opening lap.

although he did eventually qualify seventh. Clark meanwhile had easily won the hundred bottles of champagne reward for pole position and was again to dictate the race. Clark had perceived that his Lotus 25 performed better in the corners than on the straight and he therefore made a hasty getaway – using the same set of Dunlops for the fourth successive Grand Prix and thereby showing the strengths of Chapman's suspension geometry – to leave the following drivers to slipstream each other. His tactics worked to perfection and he was then left alone to win the race from the front aided by the light drizzle. Taylor briefly held second place but then succumbed on lap 31 to the combination of a flat battery, a suspect rear axle and a Colotti gearbox failure, which stranded him at Thillois.

At Silverstone, the track to which the British GP returned, Team Lotus's cars appeared with a flattering yellow stripe on the British racing green background. The new colour scheme came about as a result of the styling used at Indianapolis which had brightened up the Lotus entries against the jazzier American designs. Taylor was again afflicted by a combination of factors including his gearbox and fuel pump. Having learned from the Reims experience R4 now possessed a manual fuel mixture control, but still suffered from a broken oil line in practice. Clark, who easily took pole, was unfortunately beaten away at the start and in the first few laps had to claw back past Brabham and Gurney before taking the lead once again and disappearing. Fuel consumption worries, thanks to a

constricted fuel bag, meant that he drove most of the way in top gear, which was luckily easy at Silverstone, and he looked well on his way to the World Championship.

A trip to the non-championship Solitude GP yielded second place for Arundell before Clark secured another pole at the Nurburgring with Surtees's Ferrari being the nearest rival. Both Team Lotus cars had gearbox problems and the Colotti versions were replaced with ZF variants. In the sunny race Clark came home second, he had led early on, then his engine went off song on to only seven cylinders, letting Ginther and Surtees past at Adenau Bridge. The next part of the car to fail was his gear linkage – he had to hold the lever in place – and he defied the predictions of many onlookers by actually finishing in the runner-up spot to Surtees: this was quite something when his adversities were taken into consideration. Taylor, too, suffered a misfire as well as odd handling, and finished in eighth place.

In the lull before the Italian Grand Prix Team Lotus competed in three further non-championship events, during which Brabham was the main opposition. Clark won on aggregate at Karlskoga and Taylor was lucky to survive the consequences of a barging match at Enna with Bandini's ex-works BRM. In the ensuing accident R2 was written off in a fiery somersault in front of the pits and its driver was ejected at over 100mph (160kpm) – miraculously to suffer only minor injuries. Clark took pole at Zeltweg with his car now boasting a new Climax V8 engine, but it was to suffer oil system failure, causing his retirement.

In the absence of Taylor (recuperating) and Arundell (clashing Formula Junior race) Mike Spence was invited into the team for the forthcoming Italian GP. Clark knew that he was threatened for the Championship by not only Surtees but also by Hill and Gurney.

World Champion

The Italian GP could settle the World Championship in Clark's favour but everything was still clouded by the ramifications of the Von Trips accident of 1961. His Climax did not have enough power to get him on to pole, originally thought to be because of a flat battery, and he had to settle for third on the grid behind Surtees and Hill. Surtees did everything he could to throw Clark off in the Grand Prix including driving on to the dirt at the Curva Grande at over 150mph (240kph), but did not succeed. The race provided the spectators with a frantic slipstreaming dice between Clark (who now possessed a new engine), Hill and Gurney, during which the lead changed no less than twenty-seven times! Both of Clark's opponents were to suffer mechanical problems allowing Clark to take the World Championship as well as the Constructors' Cup for Team Lotus. Clark's elation was rudely terminated the moment he returned to the pits when he was asked by the police to go straight away for questioning regarding the Von Trips accident two years previously. In a scenario curiously reminiscent of what would later happen to Mario Andretti at Monza, the new World Champion was denied the immediate opportunity to celebrate.

The following weekend Lotus celebrated at a Brands Hatch club meeting where the patriotic crowd applauded Clark as he undertook some exceedingly impressive sub-lap record runs in the Lotus 25. The new World Champion went straight on from there to win the Oulton Park Gold Cup – setting the first 100mph (160kph) lap of the Cheshire track.

Team Lotus were then off to America, via an Indy race at Trenton, to Watkins Glen for the United States GP, where the usual drivers were joined by Pedro Rodriguez for the last two races. Before the race Taylor was informed by Chapman that he wouldn't be required for the following season.

Hewland gearbox troubles as well as a fire in Taylor's car punctuated Watkins Glen practice, but for Clark the pressure was off, even though his engine was definitely down on power. He suffered battery failure (which he had flattened whilst trying to compensate for a faulty fuel pump) at the start of the United States GP; luckily the organizers were making use of a dummy grid, which still wasn't standard practice at the time.

He did well to get back to third – snatching the lap record on the way – at the race's conclusion, having started a lap and a half behind everyone else and coped with a fluctuating fuel pump. Both Taylor, who had used too many revs on his engine, and an impressively oversteering Rodriguez retired, although the latter had climbed as high as sixth.

The Mexican race was for the first time granted full World Championship status and appropriately the newly crowned World Champion won. Rodriguez on home ground had appalling engine troubles in practice requiring several changes, and Clark suffered in the gearbox department once again. Taylor had his gearbox strip a number of gears. Whilst Clark sailed serenely on his way from pole, his two team-mates both retired when firstly Taylor ran his bearings and then Rodriguez, who was captivating his home crowd, had the rear right suspension collapse, pushing his front left wheel high into the air: spectators were marvelling at his spirited wheel-waving driving, and the truth was only revealed during a stop that had been intended for an engine examination! Rodriguez had in fact collided with Siffert on the opening lap but had still driven with a noticeable verve.

On their way to the last Grand Prix of the year at East London Team Lotus stopped off for Kyalami's Rand GP. Both drivers suffered fuel pump failures and as a result Taylor was a lowly tenth in the new R7 (which had appeared on Lotus's stand at the London Motor Show) and Clark sixteenth on aggregate.

TEAM LOTUS AND PRIVATE LOTUS ENTRY RESULTS 1963

Drivers:
Jim Clark: British; Trevor Taylor: British; Peter Arundell: British; Mike Spence: British; Pedro Rodriguez: Mexican
Car:
Lotus 25 Engine: Coventry Climax V8

CAR	CHASSIS	DRIVER	PRACTICE	SESSION	GRID	RACE	LAPS	%	REASON	CHAMPIONSHIP POSITION	POINTS
MONACO GP, Monte Carlo – 26th May – 100 L, 195.42 miles (314.50km) (43)											
25	R5	Taylor	1m 37.2s	2	9th	6th	98	98.0	–	6th	1
25	R4	Clark	1m 34.3s	2	1st P	8th NR	88	88.0	Gears	–	–
25	R2	(Spare)									
24 BRP	944★	Ireland	1m 35.5s	–	5th	R	41	41.0	Accident	–	–
24 BRP	945★★	Hall	1m 41.0s	–	13th	R	21	21.0	Gears	–	–
24 F	950	Siffert	1m 39.4s	–	12th	R	4	4.0	Engine	–	–
25 B	R3	Brabham	1m 44.7s	–	15th	9th	87	87.0	–	–	–
24 BC	949	Collomb	1m 43.3s	–	DNS	–	–	–	Withdrawn	–	–
BELGIAN GP, Spa – 9th June – 32 L, 280.36 miles (451.20km) (44)											
25	R4	Clark	3m 57.1s	2	8th	1st W	32	100.0	–	2nd=	9
Fastest Lap: 3m 58.1s – 132.468mph (213.187km/h) on lap 16											
25	R3	Taylor	3m 58.1s	2	11th	R	5	15.6	Illness	9th=	1
25	R5	(Spare)									
24 BRP	945★★	Hall	4m 00.1s	–	12th	R	17	53.1s	Accident	–	–
24 BRP	944★★	(T-car)									
24 S	950★★	Siffert	4m 02.3s	–	14th	R	17	53.1s	Accident	–	–

DUTCH GP, Zandvoort – 23rd June – 80 L, 208.43 miles (335.44km) (45)

25	R4	Clark	1m 31.6s	3	1st P	1st W	80	100.0	–	1st	18
25	R2	Taylor	1m 35.2s	3	10th	10th	66	82.5	–	10th=	1
24 S	950★★	Siffert	1m 39.0s	–	17th	7th	77	96.25	–	–	–
24 BRP	944★★	Hall	1m 39.0s	–	18th	8th	77	96.25	–	–	–
24 P	942	(T-car)									

FRENCH GP, Rheims – 30th June – 53 L, 273.41 miles (440.01km) (46)

25	R4	Clark	2m 20.2s	3	1st P	1st W	53	100.0	–	1st	27
Fastest Lap: 2m 21.6s – 131.147mph (211.061km/h) on lap 12											
25	R2	Taylor	2m 23.7s	3	7th	13th NR	41	77.35	Axle	11th=	1
25	R3	Arundell	2m 28.5s	1	DNS★	–	–	–	–	–	–
24 S	950★★	Siffert	2m 25.2s	–	10th	6th	52	98.1	–	–	–
24 F	P1	Hill P	2m 27.7s	–	13th	14th	34	64.1	–	–	–
24 P	942	Trintignant	2m 28.3s	–	14th	8th	50	94.3	–	–	–
24 P	–★★	Gregory	2m 33.2s	–	17th	R	31	58.4	Gears	–	–
24 BRP	945★★	Hall	2m 30.9s	–	16th	11th	45	84.9	–	–	–

BRITISH GP, Silverstone – 20th July – 82 L, 240.01 miles (386.26km) (47)

25	R4	Clark	1m 34.4s	2	1st P	1st W	82	100.0	–	1st	36
25	R2	Taylor	1m 36.8s	2	10th	R	24	29.2	Disq	12th=	1
24 BRP	945★★	Hall	1m 37.0s	–	13th	6th	80	97.5	–	–	–
24 BRP	944★★	(T-car)									
24 S	950★★	Siffert	1m 38.4s	–	15th	R	67	81.7	Gears	–	–
24 P	942	Hailwood	1m 39.8s	–	17th	8th	78	95.1	–	–	–
24 P	P1★★	Gregory	1m 44.2s	–	22nd	11th	75	91.4	–	–	–

GERMAN GP, Nurburgring – 4th August – 15 L, 212.60 miles (342.15km) (48)

25	R4	Clark	8m 45.8s	3	1st P	2nd	15	100.0	–	1st	42
25	R3	Taylor	9m 33.8s	1	18th	8th	14	93.3	–	14th=	1
24 S	950★★	Siffert	9m 11.1s	–	9th	9th NR	10	66.6	–	–	–
24 BRP	944★★	Ireland	9m 14.6s	–	11th	R	1	6.6	Accident	–	–
24 BRP	945★★	Hall	9m 22.7s	–	16th	5th	14	93.3	–	–	–
24 C	949	Collomb	10m 01.0s	–	21st	10th	10	66.6	–	–	–
18/21 AP	917	Pilette	10m 20.0s	–	DNQ	–	–	–	–	–	–
18 TP	915	Parnell	11m 07.2s	–	DNQ	–	–	–	–	–	–
B-B K	914	Kuhnke	11m 23.5s	–	DNQ	–	–	–	–	–	–

ITALIAN GP, Monza – 8th September – 86 L, 307.27 miles (494.50km) (49)

25	R4	Clark	1m 39.0s	2	3rd	1st W	86	100.0	–	1st	51
25	R3	Spence	1m 40.9s	2	9th	13th NR	73	84.4	Oil	–	–
25	R6	(Spare)									
24 P	P1★★	Gregory	1m 42.1s	–	12th	R	27	31.3	Engine	–	–
24 S	950★★	Siffert	1m 43.3s	–	15th	R	41	47.6	Oil	–	–
24 BRP	945★★	Hall	1m 43.8s	–	16th	8th	84	97.6	–	–	–
18/21 AP	917	Pilette	1m 53.7s	–	DNQ	–	–	–	–	–	–

US GP, Watkins Glen – 6th October – 110 L, 253.00 miles (407.11km) (50)

25	R4	Clark	1m 13.5s	1	2nd	3rd	109	99.0	–	1st	51★★★
Fastest Lap: 1m 14.5s – 111.141mph (178.863km/h) on l 50, 59 and 61											
25	R6	Taylor	1m 15.6s	–	7th	R	25	22.7	Ignition	15th=	1
25	R3	Rodriguez	1m 16.5s	2	13th	R	37	33.6	Engine	–	–
24 S	950★★	Siffert	1m 16.5s	–	14th	R	57	51.8	Gears	–	–
24 BRP	944★★	Hall	1m 17.7s	–	16th	10th NR	76	69.0	–	–	–
24 P	P1★★	Ward	1m 19.2s	–	17th	R	45	40.9	Gears	–	–
24 P	940★★	Sharp	1m 20.0s	–	18th	R	7	6.3	Tappet	–	–

MEXICAN GP, Mexico – 27th October – 65 L, 201.94 miles (325.00km) (51)

25	R4	Clark	1m 58.8s	1	1st P	1st W	65	100.00	–	1st	54★★★
Fastest Lap: 1m 58.1s – 94.705mph (152.413km/h)											
25	R6	Taylor	2m 04.9s	1	12th	R	19	29.2	Engine	15th=	1
25	R3	Rodriguez	2m 15.3s	1	20th	R	26	40.0	Suspension	–	–
24 S	950★★	Siffert	2m 03.3s	–	9th	9th	59	90.7	–	–	–
24 BRP	944★★	Hall	2m 06.1s	–	15th	8th	61	93.8	–	–	–
24 P	940★★	Sharp	2m 07.7s	–	16th	7th	61	93.8	–	–	–
24 P	P1★★	Amon	2m 14.7s	–	19th	R	9	13.8	Engine	–	–

S AFRICAN GP, East London – 28th December – 85 L, 207.02 miles (333.17km) (52)

25	R4	Clark	1m 28.9s	2	1st P	1st W	85	100.0	—	1st	54★★★
25	R7	Taylor	1m 30.4s	3	8th	8th	81	95.2	–	15th=	1
21 L	937	Pieterse	1m 34.5s	–	12th	R	4	4.7	Engine	–	–
22 TL	22-J-17★★★★	Niemann	1m 35.6s	–	15th	14th	66	77.6	–	–	–
24 SAS	946★★	Driver	1m 36.9s	–	DNS	–	–	–	–	–	–

Key:
B-B = Lotus 'BKL-Borgward'
DNQ = Did Not Qualify
Disq = Disqualified
DNS = Did Not Start
NR = Not Running
★ = Not allowed by FIA to start two races on the same day
★★ = BRM V8 engine
★★★ = Best six results
★★★★ = Ford engine
R = Retired
L = Laps
P = Pole
W = Win

Private Lotus Entries:
B = Brabham Racing Organization
BC = Bernard Collomb
BRP = British Racing Partnership
C = Bernard Collomb
F = Ecurie Filipinetti
K = Kurt Kuhnke
L = Lawson Organization
S = Joseph Siffert
SAS = Selby Auto Spares
TL = Ted Lanfear
AP = Andre Pilette
P = Reg Parnell Racing Team
TP = Tim Parnell

The final Grand Prix of the year resulted in another victory for Jim Clark in his Championship season. This was Clark's seventh win of 1963 and beat Ascari's record set in 1953. Clark took pole and Taylor put in his season's best practice performance to occupy eighth place on the grid. They had both, though, suffered from a number of gearbox difficulties. The team leader duly won and Taylor finished eighth, despite his gear linkage coming apart, in his last race for Lotus.

WORLD CHAMPIONSHIP RESULTS 1963

Position	Driver	Points
1	**Jim Clark**	**54**
2=	Graham Hill	29
	Richie Ginther	29
4	John Surtees	22
5	Dan Gurney	19
6	Bruce McLaren	17
7	Jack Brabham	14★
8	Tony Maggs	9
9=	Innes Ireland	6★
	Lorenzo Bandini	6
	Jo Bonnier	6
12	**Jim Hall**	**3**
	Gerhard Mitter	3
	C.G. de Beaufort	2
15	**Trevor Taylor**	**1**
	Jo Siffert	**1**
	Ludovico Scarfiotti	1

★ Scored some points with Lotus chassis

CONSTRUCTORS' CUP 1963

Position	Constructor	Points
1	**Lotus-Climax**	**54**
2	BRM	36
3	Brabham-Climax	28
4	Ferrari	26
5	Cooper-Climax	25
6	BRP-BRM	6
7	Porsche	5
8	**Lotus-BRM**	**4**

1964

The Lotus 25 design was modified at the start of the 1964 season to cope with the wider 13in tyres on offer from Dunlop, which in themselves required a redesign of the suspension, to reduce roll-steer, as well as new brake discs. It was later reconverted back to 15in tyre specification.

The season started in earnest at Snetterton's Daily Mirror Trophy, in which both Lotus entries retired. Things improved for Goodwood's News of the World Trophy, in which Clark and Arundell scored a one-two. The wet Syracuse GP yielded Arundell third place.

Lotus 33

Clark was looking forward to racing the Lotus 33 design, which was a straightforward development of the 25 – the two being very difficult to tell apart in fact – and was constructed with a revised monocoque to accommodate Dunlop's new 13in wheels as well as a modified suspension. All the works 25s were to be brought up to 33 specification. Administratively, during the 1964 season, Team Lotus boasted only three mechanics, who were headed by Jim Endruweit; to put things into perspective, they were paid the princely sum of £17 10s a week! They were also entitled to a share of 10 per cent of any prize money won.

The 33 first appeared at the Aintree 200 in mid-April but teething troubles kept it back on the second row of the grid. Having dropped further back at the start, Clark fought through the field to dice with Brabham, but in trying to lap Pilette he was put on to the grass, with the end result that the new car's nose was wiped off against a trackside building. Clark was furious, especially as he seemed to be unable, with the new 33, to press home any advantage against Brabham. Whilst Arundell came home third in R6 the Lotus 33 would not reappear until the Belgian GP in June.

At Silverstone's International Trophy Arundell was third again, albeit three laps behind the leader, whilst Clark retired with engine failure at Becketts, having already lost four places when he had missed a gear. The following race was to be the first World Championship Grand Prix of 1964 at Monaco.

In Monte Carlo Clark's 25 was as near as one could actually get to a 33 without actually being one, boasting as it did modifications such as the 13in wheels as well as the newer car's rear suspension. Having commuted between Indianapolis and Southern France and then started from pole Clark's ill luck at Monaco continued, as yet again he drove well, despite brushing the straw bales at the chicane on the opening lap, only to finally swipe a marker, which knocked his suspension mountings awry. The scrutineers spotted some trailing suspension pieces and the resultant 18-second pitstop dropped him back; however, he fought through to fourth by the end, having got as high as second before his oil pressure started to drop. Arundell was a good third even though he too had similar oil pressure threats.

Ireland, meanwhile, had destroyed his 24 when in practice he braked at the top of the hill approaching the chicane, and the car's wheels locked up and wouldn't release. Having hit the wall the car flew through the air, shedding many bits and pieces as it went, before completely destroying itself. Ireland was lucky to escape from this huge accident.

Most onlookers at the Dutch GP felt that Clark's Lotus should have been credited with pole rather than Gurney's Brabham and that the timekeepers had been confused. There had been quite a fight for pole with Hill's BRM too, but it was Clark who was really intent on winning the race. He had told Chapman that he only wanted the gap to whoever was behind him shown to him from the pits, should he take the lead. In this situation he would extend the lead to 45 seconds and then hold station. The hypothetical scenario discussed before the race actually occurred with Clark achieving the allotted gap by lap 55. He was, though, suffering pain from his goggles which, having given him a severe headache, caused him to lose concentration on occasions, but he still managed to hold on to win at the finish. In the Lotus pit a spectating Steve Petrassic of Firestone was very impressed by what he saw, and the events at Zandvoort helped precipitate that company's future involvement in Grand Prix racing.

The three mechanics had their work cut out coping with three cars at Spa, especially as the 33's performance on the old 15in wheels – put on in anticipation of better handling in the event of rain – left a lot to be desired, and it was not to be raced. So much effort had been put into trying to get the car right that when the Team gave up at the end of practice it looked as if there would be no opportunity for Clark to set a good lap. In a classic piece of Chapman gamesmanship Gerard Crombac was dispatched to distract the start-line official whose job it was to signal the end of the session by standing on his flag. Clark shot past whilst this was happening to record the sixth fastest time in the 25!

Arundell briefly led at the start of the Belgian GP – both cars now being on 15in wheels – but had to stop to top up with water, as did the third-placed Clark on lap 28 (for 34 seconds). He retained his position although he was now more than 2 minutes behind the leader, Gurney. A general problem peculiar to the Ardennes circuit was fuel pick-up, and both the leading drivers, Gurney (Brabham) and Hill (BRM), ran out handing Clark a very lucky win, which was achieved, too, with assistance from a broken battery on Bruce McLaren's Cooper. Literally in the last few yards as McLaren coasted towards the line, Clark shot past the confused official with the chequered flag to win by a mere 3 seconds! Shortly afterwards he too was to run out of fuel, ending up stranded out on the circuit at Stavelot alongside Gurney.

The thronging crowd couldn't believe the tension leading up to the thoroughly unexpected finish but if the truth were known it had really been Gurney's race. The Lotuses had suffered from over-heating on the long straights, which it was perceived would be a problem at future fast circuits, so deeper radiators were fitted in advance of Rouen.

At the conclusion of the amazing race at Spa, Hill was only one point behind Clark. At Rouen, for the Golden Jubilee of the French GP, Clark took pole and looked set to improve on his points position, but in the race he lost a piston whilst in the lead – a stone having found its way into the engine's innards – and Gurney was victorious. He had already coped with his gear lever coming away in his hand! On the grid the mechanics had spotted an ominous oil leak on Clark's engine but their temporary repairs – replacing a valve cover gasket – just couldn't compensate for what had happened.

Arundell had an energetic fight with both Hill and Brabham and eventually came in fourth. Sadly, a week later, he would be seriously injured in the F2 race at Reims, so Mike Spence was to replace him for the first-ever British GP at Brands Hatch.

Clark established the first-ever Grand Prix pole position at Brands Hatch with Hill (BRM) and Gurney (Brabham) alongside. Following the Rouen problems, stone guards were fitted over the air intakes of the Lotus cars. Gurney was disposed of by the time Clark got to Druids on the first lap, and then Hill

Having taken the first-ever pole position for a Grand Prix at Brands Hatch, Clark pleased his mechanics further by driving his Lotus 33 to victory by a mere 2.8 seconds! Note the stone guard fitted over the intakes following the problems at Rouen.

commenced a nail-biting fight which would last throughout the race. As the gap between the two opened and closed it was Clark who held on to win by only 2.8 seconds to give the Scot his third successive British GP victory, although it had undoubtedly been his hardest. After the exciting British GP long-serving mechanic Cedric Selzer left Team Lotus; nearly thirty years later he would be involved in restoring Lotus 25 R5!

Clark used the Lotus 33 to win the non-championship and very wet Solitude GP from pole, whilst both Spence and Mitter retired thanks to accidents. It was by now quite clear that the days of the Lotus 25 were numbered as the opposition had caught up with the advantage originally enjoyed by what had been the bench-mark design.

A second Lotus 33 was made available to Clark at the Nurburgring but it was to be Surtees's Ferrari that took pole ahead of his second grid position. Gerhard Mitter drove the spare Team Lotus 25, but had to have a plug change early, coming home ninth just behind Spence. Surtees it was who won the German GP when Clark, who had led the first lap, retired because of a dropped valve, which had caused his Climax engine to fail. As a result of his second place in Germany, Hill went into a two-point lead in the championship.

In the non-championship Mediterranean GP at

Pergusa Clark came second and Spence was two laps behind the leaders in fifth place.

Zeltweg was a very bumpy venue for Austria's first World Championship Grand Prix and Bandini's Ferrari held up best to the battering that all the F1 cars received. The steering was to fail on both Team Lotus cars in practice, and Clark and Spence simultaneously retired when their modified Mercedes-Benz 220S drive-shafts let go in the Grand Prix; ironically the standard rubber couplings had been replaced as it was felt they wouldn't stand up to the rough nature of the circuit. The Championship seemed to be slipping away from Clark; Chapman was not present, being in America where Parnelli Jones was winning for Lotus at Milwaukee.

Thanks to a very poor engine the 33 proved too slow for Clark at Monza, so for the race he reverted to a Lotus 25, which turned out to be similarly afflicted. Surtees therefore promptly won when Clark suffered yet another engine failure, in the form of a broken piston, as the Ferraris proved uncatchable. Spence came sixth to score his first ever World Championship point.

Clark was dominant in the United States in his favourite R6 (he had recorded an identical practice time in R9), being comfortably fastest in qualifying. Spence made an amazing getaway to be up to second place early in the Grand Prix, but a slow-starting Clark was to take a commanding lead on lap 13, only for the faulty fuel injection to need a quick pitstop just when it seemed the Championship was in the bag. After another six laps the same trouble recurred, and following yet another stop Clark took over Spence's R9 in an attempt to go for Constructors' points. This ploy failed in the wake of Clark's retirement on lap 102. New Team driver Walt Hansgen, meanwhile, picked up fifth place and a useful two points in his home Grand Prix. With his win Hill took the Championship lead from Surtees, and Clark's only chance was to win at the last Mexican race.

For the now all-important Mexican GP R9 was equipped with a flat-crank Climax power unit and this combination took Clark to pole position with apparent ease. He took an early lead – which he kept for sixty-three of the sixty-five laps – but suffered an oil leak from a fractured pipe with eight laps to go. His opportunity for keeping his Championship honours evaporated along with his lubricant literally on the last lap and almost within sight of the flag on a day when Surtees was to inherit the laurels for Ferrari. Clark had been within two miles of keeping his World Championship . . .

The Lotus Team despaired in the pits as they had been certain that their man would be World

TEAM LOTUS AND PRIVATE LOTUS ENTRY RESULTS 1964

Drivers:
Jim Clark: British; Peter Arundell: British; Mike Spence: British; Gerhard Mitter: German; Walt Hansgen: USA; Moises Solana: Mexican
Car:
Lotus 25 Engine: Coventry Climax V8
Lotus 33   Coventry Climax V8

CAR	CHASSIS	DRIVER	PRACTICE	SESSION	GRID	RACE	LAPS	%	REASON	CHAMPIONSHIP POSITION	POINTS
MONACO GP, Monte Carlo – 10th May – 100 L, 195.42 miles (314.50km) (53)											
25	R4	Arundell	1m 25.5s	2	6th	3rd	97	97.0	–	3rd	4
25	R6	Clark	1m 34.0s	2	1st P	4th NR	96	96.0	Engine	4th	3
25 P	R7★★	Hailwood	1m 38.5s	–	15th	6th	96	96.0	–	–	–
24 S	950★★	Siffert	1m 38.7s	–	16th	8th	78	78.0	–	–	–
24 BRP	944★★	Ireland	1m 38.2s	–	DNS	–	–	–	Accident	–	–
24 R	P1★★	Revson	1m 39.9s	–	DNQ	–	–	–	–	–	–
24 C	949	Collomb	1m 41.4s	–	DNQ	–	–	–	–	–	–
24 P	R3★★	Amon	1m 39.1s	–	DNQ	–	–	–	–	–	–
DUTCH GP, Zandvoort – 24th May – 80 L, 208.43 miles (335.44km) (54)											
25	R6	Clark	1m 31.3s	2	2nd	1st W	80	100.0	–	1st=	12
Fastest Lap and Record: 1m 32.8s – 101.07mph (162.65km/h) on lap 6											
25	R4	Arundell	1m 33.5s	2	6th	3rd	79	98.75	–	3rd	8
25 P	R3★★	Amon	1m 35.9s	–	13th	5th	79	98.75	–	–	–
25 P	R7★★	Hailwood	1m 36.1s	–	14th	12th NR	57	71.25	Crown	–	–
BELGIAN GP, Spa – 14th June – 32 L, 280.36 miles (451.20km) (55)											
25	R6	Clark	3m 56.2s	2	6th	1st W	32	100.0	–	1st	21
25	R4	Arundell	3m 52.8s	2	4th	9th	28	87.5	–	4th	8
33	R8	(Spare)									
24 R	P1★★	Revson	3m 59.9s	–	10th	DSQ	28	87.5	–	–	–
25 P	R3★★	Amon	4m 00.1s	–	11th	R	4	12.5	Engine	–	–
FRENCH GP, Rouen – 28th June – 57 L, 231.70 miles (372.89km) (56)											
25	R4	Arundell	2m 11.6s	1	4th	4th	57	100.0	–	3rd=	11
25	R6	Clark	2m 09.6s	1	1st P	R	32	56.1	Piston	1st	21
33	R8	(Spare)									
25 P	R3★★	Amon	2m 16.4s	–	14th	10th	53	92.9	–	–	–
25 P	R7★★	Hailwood	2m 16.2s	–	13th	8th	56	98.2	–	–	–
BRITISH GP, Brands Hatch – 11th July – 80 L, 212.00 miles (341.20km) (57)											
Fastest Lap and Record: 1m 38.8s – 96.56mph (155.398km/h) on lap 73											
25	R6	Clark	1m 38.1s	2	1st P	1st W	80	100.0	–	1st	30
25	R4	Spence	1m 41.4s	2	13th	9th	77	96.25	–	–	–
33	R8	(Spare)									
25 P	R7	Hailwood	1m 41.4s	–	12th	R	17	21.25	Engine	–	–
25 P	R3★★	Amon	1m 41.2s	–	11th	R	9	11.25	Clutch	–	–
24 R	P1★★	Revson	1m 43.4s	–	22nd	R	43	53.75	Ignition	–	–
24 BRP	945★★	Taylor	1m 42.8s*	–	18th	R	23	28.75	Fatigue	–	–
GERMAN GP, Nurburgring – 2nd August – 15 L, 212.60 miles (342.15km) (58)											
33	R8	Spence	9m 09.9s	2	17th	8th	14	93.3	–	–	–
25	R6	Mitter	9m 14.1s	4	19th	9th	14	93.3	–	–	–
33	R9	Clark	8m 38.8s	4	2nd	R	7	46.6	Engine	2nd	30
25 P	R3★★	Amon	8m 54.0s	–	9th	11th	12	80.0	–	–	–
25 P	R7★★	Hailwood	9m 01.9s	–	13th	R	1	6.6	Engine	–	–
24 R	P1★★	Revson	9m 13.0s	–	18th	R	10	66.6	Engine	–	–
AUSTRIAN GP, Zeltweg – 23rd August – 105 L, 208.78 miles (336.00km) (59)											
33	R9	Clark	1m 10.21s	2	3rd	R	41	39.0	D/shaft	2nd	30
33	R8	Spence	1m 11.00s	2	8th	R	42	40.0	D/shaft	–	–
25	R6	(Spare)									
25 P	R4	Amon	1m 12.28s	–	17th	R	8	7.6	Engine	–	–
25 P	R3★★	Hailwood	1m 12.40s	–	18th	8th	95	90.4	–	–	–
ITALIAN GP, Monza – 6th September – 78 L, 278.68 miles (448.50km) (60)											
33	R8	Spence	1m 40.3s	1	8th	6th	77	98.7	–	17th=	1
25	R6	Clark	1m 39.1s	2	4th	R	28	35.8	Piston	2nd	30
33	R9	(Spare)									
25 P	R4★★	Hailwood	1m 41.6s	–	17th	R	5	6.4	Tappet	–	–
24	P1★★	Revson	1m 42.0s	–	18th	13th	72	92.3	–	–	–

US GP, Watkins Glen – 4th October – 110 L, 253.00 miles (407.11km) (61)

33	R8	Hansgen	1m 15.9s	2	17th	5th	107	97.2	–	15th=	2
33	R9	Spence (Clark)	1m 13.33s	2	6th	7th NR	102	92.7	Fuel (Clark)	3rd	30

Fastest Lap and Record: (Clark) 1m 12.7 – 113.89mph (183.3km/h) – lap 81

25	R6	Clark (Spence)	1m 12.65s	–	1st P	R	54	49.0	Fuel (Spence)	18th	–
25 P	R7**	Hailwood	1m 15.65s	–	16th	8th NR	101	91.8	Oil	–	–
25 P	R4**	Amon	1m 14.43s	–	11th	R	47	42.7	Starter	–	–

MEXICAN GP, Mexico – 25th October – 65 L, 201.94 miles (325.00km) (62)

25	R6	Spence	1m 59.21s	2	5th	4th	65	100.0	–	12th=	4
33	R9	Clark	1m 57.24s	2	1st P	5th NR	64	98.4	Engine	3rd	32

Fastest Lap: 1m 58.37s – 94.489mph (152.066km/h)

33	R8	Solana	2m 01.43s	2	14th	10th	63	96.9	–	–	–
25 P	R4**	Amon	2m 01.17s	–	12th	R	46	70.7	Gears	–	–
25 P	R7**	Hailwood	2m 04.11s	–	17th	R	12	18.4	Temp	–	–

Key:
DNQ	=	Did Not Qualify
DNS	=	Did Not Start
DSQ	=	Disqualified
NR	=	Not Running
★	=	time set in BRP-BRM
**	=	BRM V8 Engine
R	=	Retired
L	=	Laps
P	=	Pole
W	=	Win

Lotus Private Entries:
P	=	Parnell Racing Team
R	=	Peter Revson Racing
S	=	Siffert Racing Team
BRP	=	British Racing Partnership
C	=	B. Collomb

WORLD CHAMPIONSHIP RESULTS 1964

Position	Driver	Points
1	John Surtees	40
2	Graham Hill	39
3	**Jim Clark**	**32**
4=	Richie Ginther	23
	Lorenzo Bandini	23
6	Dan Gurney	19
7	Bruce McLaren	13
8=	**Peter Arundell**	**11**
	Jack Brabham	11
10	Jo Siffert	7
11	Bob Anderson	5
12=	**Mike Spence**	**4**
	Innes Ireland	4
	Tony Maggs	4
15	Jo Bonnier	3
16=	**Walt Hansgen**	**2**
	Chris Amon	2
	Maurice Trintignant	2

CONSTRUCTORS' CUP 1964

Position	Constructor	Points
1	Ferrari	45
2	BRM	42
3	**Lotus-Climax**	**37**
4	Brabham-Climax	30
5	Cooper-Climax	16
6	Brabham-BRM	7
7	BRP-BRM	5
8	**Lotus-BRM**	**3**

Champion, such had been his dominance throughout the race.

With Clark suffering a slipped disc as the result of a snowball fight (!) the Rand GP at Kyalami saw Spence come sixteenth overall when the two heats were aggregated, whilst Jackie Stewart won heat two, but could only salvage seventeenth overall in R10.

1965

For the last year of the 1.5-litre Formula One, Lotus continued to use Climax engines even though Chapman had seriously courted Honda to such an extent that a Japanese V12 mock-up had actually been delivered to the factory. This ploy is now widely accepted as having been nothing more than Chapman gamesmanship to encourage Climax to continue their engine supply, which they did.

From the word go in the first round of the 1965 World Championship, the South African GP, Clark served notice that he was going to be the driver to beat that season. He promptly outshone everyone in qualifying at East London with his short-stroke 33 and seized a commanding lead on his way to the first corner. He was closely followed by Spence, who had made an electrifying start from the inside of the second row. Spence spun twice during the race (laps 44 and 59), which dropped him back to fourth at the end. The spotlight was squarely on Clark, who won with ease,

The first round of the 1965 World Championship was held at East London in South Africa, and both Lotus and Clark served notice of their intentions by taking not only pole position, but also another commanding win.

even though he was shown the chequered flag a lap early, on the day when fellow Scot Jackie Stewart joined the F1 circus for the first time.

Clark went off to Australasia to win the Tasman series but returned to F1 for the Race of Champions at Brands Hatch, which was to be decided on the aggregate of two heats. Spence it was who won after Clark had crashed heavily on Bottom Straight.

Clark righted the situation by winning the non-championship Syracuse GP; this time it was the turn of Spence to have an accident — hitting a wall — during a fight with Bandini's Ferrari. In Goodwood's Sunday Mirror Trophy Clark was the winner of the last ever F1 event at the popular Sussex circuit. Spence had not started thanks to his car's fuel injection, which had failed him on the warm-up lap.

Clark was busy practising for Indianapolis at the time of the International Trophy at Silverstone, and in his absence Spence came third, followed home by Pedro Rodriguez. Because of the importance of Indianapolis to Lotus the team withdrew from Monaco; their prioritization paid off because Clark was to win the American Classic at his third attempt, pleasing Chapman greatly and injecting no less than $150,000 into Lotus's finances. It was whilst at Indianapolis that Clark formed a friendship with Mario Andretti, an up-and-coming rookie USAC driver, who asked the Scot to put a good word in for him with Chapman. This was

the embryonic start of a liaison that would spawn another successful Lotus World Championship.

Whilst there were no works entries at Monaco there were still a number of Lotus privateers. Paul Hawkins was still tenth although he retired in spectacular fashion with a plunge from the chicane into the harbour. Richard Attwood crashed and Mike Hailwood retired when his gearbox failed. Peter Revson in Team Lotus's Ron Harris-run F3 Lotus 35 entry did at least win the prestigious supporting event.

A Scottish one-two was the result at Spa where Clark took his fourth dominant win at the track, with the BRM of Stewart, which came in second, being his only unlapped opponent! At the start the BRMs of both Stewart and Hill had planned to block Clark, who was sandwiched between them on the front row, but the wily Scot was not going to fall for that and made the most use of the new 32-valve Climax engine on the straights in the very wet conditions to pull out a 44.8 second advantage at the end.

Spence, meanwhile, was seventh and wishing that he hadn't chosen the inappropriate Dunlop R7 tyres. As quoted in *Autocourse* Spence confided in Clark that he could not cease to marvel at his wet-weather driving — 'I was sliding all over the place when you lapped me, but you went past as if your side of the road was dry' — but Clark himself summed it all up with characteristic modesty by saying 'it was so wet that I had to keep lifting off, even on the straight. I suppose I won because I lifted off less than the others.'

For the first time the French GP was held on the switchback Charade circuit in the Auvergne, which caused suspension failures in practice for both Team Lotus drivers. Clark had also had his 32-valve engine blow up on him, but this didn't stop him from taking the first ever F1 pole at the circuit; he proceeded to drive away from everyone in the race itself to take fastest lap too — and all this was in his 'old' car! Spence had had a hairy spin at on lap 14 but he still came home seventh with a very unhealthy sounding engine — fuel pump trouble having been the cause of his original problem. Chapman's concern that his second driver was about to run out of fuel was luckily misplaced.

From the start of Silverstone practice Clark dominated, and it was eventually no surprise that he took pole for the British GP once R11 had been delivered with a new 32-valve power plant. Though Ginther cheekily took the lead at the start, this lasted barely half a lap, and Clark was soon in front tailed by Hill's BRM in a curiously similar rerun of what had happened at the British GP the previous year. Clark built up a substantial lead — more than 30 seconds — only for his engine to start cutting out, which prompted Hill to try to claw back the deficit. There was also concern towards the end of the race as Hill closed in relentlessly because not only was the oil level of Clark's car reducing dramatically – it was actually dry at the end – but also because of lack of brakes. Luckily Clark somehow managed to keep ahead – by only 3 seconds – and Lotus achieved their wish of winning their fourth successive British GP, just!

A week later in Holland, Clark was to the fore again although he was making use of the older car as the consumption of oil by R11 was unusually high in practice. It took until lap 6 of the Grand Prix for Clark to get past firstly Ginther and then Hill to take the lead before dictating the race from the front, although by a smaller margin than normal as neither driver was to lose sight of the leader during the first half of the race. Spence survived a huge spin before recording an eighth place finish. Chapman had been taken into custody after assaulting an over-zealous policeman who had not seen the Lotus supremo's official armband affixed to his belt when the start line and dummy grid were being cleared. He had been arrested after the race, following an entertaining police-versus-Lotus mechanics struggle, only to spend a couple of nights locked up. In Chapman's absence the prize-giving was postponed, only for a large band of Lotus supporters to serenade him from outside the window of his police station cell. A well-publicized court appearance luckily allowed honour to be restored in Chapman's favour.

Second World Championship

The forthcoming trip to the Nurburgring looked as if it would be the decider as far as the World Championship was concerned, such was the competitiveness of the Clark/Lotus combination. The only way this outcome might be postponed would be if the 33 proved too fragile for the bumps of the intimidating circuit. The Nurburgring was a circuit that Clark loved almost as much as Monaco. In practice he was impressively 16.3 seconds inside the previous record lap – using raised suspension – and in the Grand Prix itself he lowered the lap record with apparent ease several times. Amazingly the first lap record was set on lap 1 when the cars had started from a stationary grid!

Spence, meanwhile, retired when a drive-shaft failed and Mitter, who was racing the third Lotus on his home circuit, had a water hose grind away on the track surface, so frequently was R6 grounding. Clark went on to take his sixth successive win in a row, setting a new lap record as he went and successfully capturing his second World Championship in three years: this was energetically celebrated not only publicly by the huge crowd but also privately that night at the hotel overlooking the track. An additional cause for celebra-

tion was that Lotus-Climax had secured their second Constructors' Championship too. Even then, however, Chapman knew that this domination was threatened because for 1966 the F1 engine capacity was to be doubled to three litres, and Lotus didn't at that time have a replacement engine for those from Coventry Climax, who were still intent on pulling out of racing.

The newly crowned World Champion drove next at the Mediterranean GP at Pergusa where he was second behind Siffert – his car having caught fire in the pits in practice. Spence suffered a huge accident after being struck by a stone and was lucky to get away relatively unscathed, ending up trapped underneath his car.

Whilst it was Clark who sacrilegiously took pole away from Surtees's Ferrari at Monza, the race was to see a slipstreaming battle with Stewart and Hill in their respective BRMs. Clark led the sunny Grand Prix initially, only for both Hill and Stewart to get past when they came to the line, although places were swapping all around each lap. To the delight of the partisan crowd, Surtees's slow-starting Ferrari was up to second place by lap 11 only for his gearbox to give out – the cue for much of the crowd to depart. Clark then had electric fuel pump failure – causing him to stop at Lesmo on lap 64 and kick the errant piece of Lucas equipment – which left the door open to Stewart to take his first ever GP win. A spectating Juan Manuel Fangio was to candidly reveal that he felt that Clark was 'the best racing driver in the world'.

Monza marked the end of the European F1 season and next it was off to the Americas where Mexican Moises Solana rejoined Team Lotus as the third driver. Clark had a troubled practice at Watkins Glen where his engine failed – some timing gear teeth had sheared – and he spun wildly across the grass allowing Hill to take pole position. Curiously Hill and BRM were much more in control in the States – Hill had always gone well anyway at Watkins Glen – and Clark and Lotus looked strangely uncompetitive in comparison. Hill led, was passed by Clark, and then led again only for Clark to retire when his engine let go. Spence suffered a similar fate and it was left to Solana to record the best works position in twelfth.

The surprise of practice in Mexico was that Solana was initially fourth fastest – eventually dropping to ninth – in front of his home fans in the rarefied atmosphere of Mexico City. Clark took pole, blowing engines on the way, after an uncharacteristically problematic qualifying. His poor engine meant Clark was swamped at the start, and it was eventually to seize totally on a day when Ginther was to win for Honda. Spence had a superb day at the front of the field chasing the Honda hard, but had to settle for third place.

In the event, despite a poor showing in the final two

TEAM LOTUS AND PRIVATE LOTUS ENTRY RESULTS 1965

Drivers:
Jim Clark: British; Mike Spence: British; Gerhard Mitter: German; Giacomo Russo: Italian; Moises Solana: Mexican
Car:
Lotus 25 Engine: Coventry Climax V8
Lotus 33 Coventry Climax V8

CAR	CHASSIS	DRIVER	PRACTICE	SESSION	GRID	RACE	LAPS	%	REASON	CHAMPIONSHIP POSITION	POINTS
S AFRICAN GP, East London – 1st January – 85 L, 207.02 miles (333.17km) (63)											
33	R10	Clark	1m 27.2s	2	1st P	1st W	85	100.0	–	1st	9
Fastest Lap: 1m 27.6s – 100.097mph (161.091km/h) on lap 80											
33	R9	Spence	1m 28.3s	2	4th	4th	85	100.0	–	4th	3
25 P	R4	Maggs	1m 31.3s	–	13th	11th	77	90.5	–	–	–
21 LE	952	Lederle	1m 35.2s	–	DNQ	–	–	–	–	–	–
22 LA	22-J*	Niemann	1m 36.2s	–	DNQ	–	–	–	–	–	–
21 PI	937	Pieterse	1m 37.9s	–	DNQ	–	–	–	–	–	–
BELGIAN GP, Spa – 13th June – 32 L, 280.36 miles (451.20km) (64)											
33	R11***	Clark	3m 47.5s	2	2nd	1st W	32	100.0	–	1st	18
Fastest Lap: 4m 12.9s – 124.716mph (200.711km/h) on lap 23											
33	R9	Spence	3m 52.6s	2	12th	7th	31	96.0	–	7th=	3
25 P	R7**	Ireland	3m 57.4s	–	16th	13th	27	84.3	–	–	–
25 P	R4**	Attwood	3m 53.2s	–	13th	14th NR	26	81.2	Accident	–	–
FRENCH GP, Clermont-Ferrand – 27th June – 40 L, 200.20 miles (322.20km) (65)											
25	R6	Clark	3m 18.3s	2	1st P	1st W	40	100.0	–	1st	27
Fastest Lap and Record: 3m 18.9s – 90.590mph (145.791km/h) on lap 34											
33	R9	Spence	3m 32.4s	1	10th	7th	39	97.5	–	7th=	3
33	R11***	(Spare)									
25 P	R3**	Amon	3m 23.0s	–	8th	R	21	52.5	Fuel	–	–
25 P	R7**	Ireland	3m 50.5s	–	17th	R	19	47.5	Gears	–	–
BRITISH GP, Silverstone – 10th July – 80 L, 234.16 miles (376.84km) (66)											
33	R11***	Clark	1m 30.8s	3	1st P	1st W	80	100.0	–	1st	36
33	R9	Spence	1m 31.7s	3	6th	4th	80	100.0	–	6th	6
33	R6	(Spare)									
25 P	R3**	Attwood	1m 33.8s	–	16th	13th	63	78.7	–	–	–
25 P	R7**	Ireland	1m 33.6s	–	15th	R	42	52.5	Engine	–	–
24 G	943	Gubby	1m 45.1s	–	DNQ	–	–	–	–	–	–
DUTCH GP, Zandvoort – 18th July – 80 L, 208.43 miles (335.44km) (67)											
33	R9	Clark	1m 31.0s	1	2nd	1st W	80	100.0	–	1st	45
Fastest Lap: 1m 30.6s – 103.525mph (166.608km/h) on lap 5											
25	R6	Spence	1m 32.2s	2	8th	8th	79	98.7	–	6th=	6
33	R11***	(Spare)									
25 P	R7**	Ireland	1m 33.4s	–	13th	10th	78	97.5	–	–	–
25 P	R3**	Attwood	1m 34.6s	–	17th	12th	77	96.2	–	–	–
GERMAN GP, Nurburgring – 1st August – 15 L, 212.60 miles (342.15km) (68)											
33	R11***	Clark	8m 22.7s	2	1st P	1st W	15	100.0	–	1st	54
Fastest Lap and Record: 8m 24.1s – 101.219mph (162.896km/h) on lap 10											
33	R9	Spence	8m 33.4s	3	6th	R	9	60.0	D/shaft	8th	6
25	R6	Mitter	8m 40.4s	3	12th	R	9	60.0	Hose	–	–
25 P	R3	Attwood	8m 57.7s	–	16th	R	9	60.0	Hose	–	–
25 P	R8	Amon	8m 50.5s	–	15th	R	4	26.6	Ignition	–	–
33 DW	R8	Hawkins	9m 16.8s	–	19th	R	4	26.2	Oil leak	–	–
ITALIAN GP, Monza – 12th September – 76 L, 271.54 miles (437.00km) (69)											
33	R11***	Clark	1m 35.9s	2	1st P	10th NR	63	82.8	Fuel pump	1st	54
Fastest Lap and Record: 1m 36.4s – 133.427mph (214.730km/h) on lap 46											
33	R6	Spence	1m 37.8s	2	8th	11th NR	62	81.5	Alternator	8th	6
25	R6	Russo	1m 41.73s	2	20th	R	38	50.0	Gearbox	–	–
25 P	R3	Attwood	1m 38.85s	–	13th	6th	75	98.6	–	–	–
25 P	R13**	Ireland	1m 39.8s	–	18th	9th	74	97.3	–	–	–
US GP, Watkins Glen – 3rd October – 110 L, 253.00 miles (407.11km) (70)											
25	R6	Solana	1m 13.7s	2	17th	12th	95	86.3	–	–	–
33	R9	Spence	1m 11.5s	2	4th	R	10	9.0	Piston	9th	6
33	R11	Clark	1m 11.35s	2	2nd	R	12	10.9	Piston	1st	54
25 P	R3**	Attwood	1m 13.7s	–	16th	10th	101	91.8	–	–	–
25 P	R13**	Ireland	1m 15.0s	–	18th	R	10	9.0	Illness	–	–

MEXICAN GP, Mexico – 24th October – 65 L, 201.94 miles (325.00km) (71)

33	R9	Spence	1m 57.22s	1	6th	3rd	65	100.0	–	8th=	10
33	R11	Clark	1m 56.17s	2	1st P	R	9	13.8	Engine	1st	54
25	R6	Solana	1m 57.55s	2	9th	R	56	86.1	Ignition	–	–
25 P	R3**	Attwood	2m 00.61s	–	16th	6th	64	98.4	–	–	–
25 P	R13**	Bondurant	2m 00.80s	–	17th	R	30	46.1	Suspension	–	–
25 P	R13**	Ireland	2m 02.36s	–	DNS	–	–	–	Driver replaced		

Key:
DNQ = Did Not Qualify
DNS = Did Not Start
NR = Not Running
★ = Ford engine
★★ = BRM V8 engine
★★★ = Climax V8 32-valve engine
R = Retired
L = Laps
P = Pole
W = Win

Private Lotus Entries:
DW = DW Racing Enterprises
G = Brian Gubby
P = Parnell Racing Team
PI = Pieterse
LE = N. Lederle
LA = E. Lanfear

races, Clark was firmly the World Champion and he had undoubtedly been the star driver of the now de-funct 1.5-litre F1 racing. With a second World Championship to his name assertions were made that this might be the sensible time for him to retire – a proposition he chose to ignore . . .

WORLD CHAMPIONSHIP RESULTS 1965

Position	Driver	Points
1	**Jim Clark**	**54**
2	Graham Hill	40
3	Jackie Stewart	33
4	Dan Gurney	25
5	John Surtees	17
6	Lorenzo Bandini	13
7	Richi Ginther	11
8=	**Mike Spence**	**10**
	Bruce McLaren	10
10	Jack Brabham	9
11=	Denny Hulme	5
	Jo Siffert	5
13	Jochen Rindt	4
14=	**Richard Attwood**	**2**
	Pedro Rodriguez	2
	Ronnie Bucknum	2

CONSTRUCTORS' CUP 1965

Position	Constructor	Points
1	**Lotus-Climax**	**54**
2	BRM	45
3	Brabham-Climax	27
4	Ferrari	26
5	Cooper-Climax	14
6	Honda	11
7	Brabham-BRM	5
8	**Lotus-BRM**	**2**

1966

Lotus 33T

Climax had withdrawn from racing at the end of 1965 leaving Chapman to court BRM for a replacement engine as a stop-gap, whilst Cosworth were in the background designing and researching what would be the Ford DFV. The BRM deal agreed, Tony Rudd's H16 ran into vibration problems, delaying its debut, so Climax stepped in with a stretched Mk 9 2-litre version of their familiar engine. As events would dictate, Clark was to make use of Climax power for much of the season in what would be described as the Lotus 33T, even though it was underpowered, and what results were achieved were largely down to his mastery.

The first race of 1966, and Spence's last for Team Lotus, was the non-championship South African GP at East London. This turned out to be a fine result for Spence, who promptly won, with Arundell returning to Lotus and taking third place two laps behind.

Firestone tyres were to become an integral part of the 1966 Lotus package, replacing the offerings of Dunlop, and they were to be race tested in the Tasman series. Team Lotus suffered from a lack of suitable 3-litre cars for the usual spate of non-championship European races that traditionally preceded the World Championship season, so the first baptism of fire would literally be around the confines of Monaco.

For the first 3-Litre World Championship race Team Lotus were equipped with a 2-litre 33, which surprisingly was well suited to the sinewy Monte Carlo circuit. Whilst the Climax engine – stretched from 1.5 litres and producing only 245bhp – lost out on power to those of the opposition, Clark still managed to usurp all the other drivers to take a notably smooth pole position, complete with a new gearbox although he was unimpressed with the Firestone tyres. On the circuit, where the Climax engine looked as if it would go well, it was initially denied the opportunity when Clark's gearbox stuck in first gear and he was swamped on the opening lap. Despite fighting back strongly to second place, and dramatically reducing the gap to the leader Stewart, Clark's rear suspension failed him at the Gasworks Hairpin, and with a folded-back rear wheel he graunched to a halt on lap 61. Ironically the first ever 3-litre World Championship Grand Prix was to be won by the 2-litre BRM of Stewart!

Lotus 43

The new BRM-engined Lotus 43 was the first Grand Prix Lotus to be designed by Maurice Phillipe and it was raced throughout 1966. The year was soon to become a very long one indeed for the mechanics with the unreliable 3-litre BRM H16 power plants constantly needing attention or changing; much mental time was thus spent eagerly anticipating the arrival of Ford power in 1967. An integral part of the Lotus was the requirement for its BRM engine to be a stressed member carrying as it did the rear suspension. Very early on it was found that the engine was very over-weight (the 43 with this power plant was 410lb (185kg) heavier than the Cooper-Maserati for example) and this was to be a considerable problem all season. On the tyre front Firestone's products were to create a number of their own evolutionary problems, which contributed to what was to be a very disappointing season.

The much-heralded 43 eventually appeared at Spa for Arundell to drive, complete with the first BRM H16 engine. The self-same BRM concept had already proved troublesome in Indy racing form and it was evident that much more testing and development was going to be required to transform it into an effective F1 performer.

Arundell failed to qualify in the immaculate new 43, only putting in a total of three laps before the engine expired at top speed thanks to fuel starvation. Clark, too, suffered a practice cylinder-head failure – taking time off to fly back to Coventry with Chapman to collect a replacement – and was destined to start from a lowly tenth place, which didn't bode at all well for his attempt on a fifth Spa win. Before the race, the car's suspension had collapsed under him and hasty beefing up was necessary immediately prior to the start. Clark's Climax engine faltered at the start of the Belgian GP and once fired up, the Scot chased so hard after the field that after a few seconds the engine cried enough and he was out. He hadn't been helped by a last minute

confusion amongst his mechanics, which had caused his concentration to lapse temporarily. Elsewhere the race, which had started dry but turned treacherously wet, was characterized by a high number of accidents.

If Spa was disappointing for Clark, then Reims would be a disaster, although the outcome could have been much worse. In a practice accident, curiously reminiscent of that which had befallen Stacey at Spa back in 1960, Clark was struck in the face by a bird whilst he was flat out on the main Soissons Straight. Covered in feathers he somehow managed to wrestle the car to a stop and luckily the outcome was much less serious than the previous accident, although he was to be rendered a non-starter. Chapman had him flown back to England for treatment to his swollen and damaged eye.

Mexican Pedro Rodriguez took over R11 and got as high as fourth in the race before his engine seized as a result of a broken oil pipe. Arundell was lucky to début the Lotus 43, having twice not even got onto the circuit in practice before mechanical gremlins – particularly the shearing distributor drive – had sidelined his car. He only circulated for four laps in the race before the transmission failed him, which was hardly the most inspiring of racing débuts for a new car!

A BRM engine was fitted to Arundell's 33 for the British GP when a new 2-litre Coventry Climax engine expired, but he was to have to stop a number of times and then retire in the race with transmission troubles. Brabham won easily at Brands Hatch with Clark back in fourth having had a close fight with Hill's BRM and Hulme's Brabham. He was then forced, by a sudden lack of retardation, to stop for a couple of minutes to top up the brake fluid reservoir and whilst he went on to score his first points of the season, the World Championship was still continuing to slip away.

The day after the British GP the foundation stone of the new Lotus factory at Hethel, just outside Norwich, was laid, leading the way to the opening of the new factory in the autumn after the relocation from Cheshunt.

A superb start by Clark at Zandvoort allowed him to lead into Tarzan, the first corner on the Dutch track, where Brabham overtook only for Hulme to get past as well three laps later. On the twenty-fourth lap, whilst lapping some backmarkers, an on-form Clark spotted an opening and retook both Hulme and Brabham to lead once again only for his crankshaft damper to break, reducing his available rpm to 8,000. Taking supreme advantage of the slippery conditions, Clark held off Brabham until his car's water system sprung a leak, unfortunately requiring a pitstop. As water was quickly added Clark avoided the steam and tore back into the race two laps down on the leader, and after a tigering demonstration he was rewarded with third overall. The way in which Clark had coped without the extra litre of engine capacity possessed by the leaders had astounded everyone on what was, after all, a power circuit.

By the time of the German GP at the Nurburgring any hope of Clark winning the championship had disappeared completely. Whilst encouragingly Clark took pole position – in a car now lacking a crankshaft damper – Surtees led the race early on in his Cooper-Maserati; Clark fell back, not liking the conditions in his Firestone-shod Lotus. He had intended to race on Dunlops but had changed his mind literally at the last moment. Eventually he was caught out on lap 12 – having dropped to seventh place from his original fourth – and plunged off the circuit and down a slope, luckily without injury.

Clark at last got his BRM H16 engine at Monza and was much happier once he had the same-sized 3-litre engine as his opposition. His particular BRM power plant for once proved surprisingly reliable in a car that did not handle too well in corners. His gear linkage, too, stranded him out on the circuit in second practice. At the race start Clark was left on grid as his fuel system gave troubles, and he was forced to fight back to fifth only for a puncture-induced rear-wheel vibration to necessitate a pitstop. Both the works BRMs had retired after only a couple of laps and Clark eventually had his own gearbox fail two laps short of the flag on a day when the Italians were well pleased with a Ferrari one-two result for Scarfiotti and Parkes. Both Arundell and 'Geki' – in Clark's regular R14 – finished some way down the field.

Oulton Park's non-championship Gold Cup was the next Team Lotus F1 race and there Clark was third in after his intended car had lost its H16 engine and he commandeered Arundell's. Hill had had two rods exit the block on his H16 engine, which would greatly affect Lotus at the United States GP.

Having originally intended to make use of the more reliable 2-litre Lotus in the United States Clark took second place in practice with the 3-litre H16 engine, which did eventually give out on him, so that he had to borrow a spare from BRM (Hill's rebuilt Oulton Park engine) and hurriedly insert it overnight. The GP itself was to prove to be the only trouble-free race for Clark in 1966 and also the only race that the BRM had finished to date!

Bandini's Ferrari led away initially before Brabham took over, but both were to drop out – the latter when his timing belt went – thereby letting the admittedly lucky Clark – complete with virgin brake pads and an

The BRM-engined Lotus 43 looked the part, but it would take until the United States Grand Prix at Watkins Glen for it to be reliable enough to win. Here Clark takes the ostentatious flag to give the BRM H16 engine its one and only victory, and that a lucky one.

engine that had sounded far from perfect on the warm-up lap – through to win that was to be the only Grand Prix victory ever for the BRM H16 engine. Clark had driven a careful race, being quite distant from the leaders most of the time, but had effectively achieved what was at the time considered to be the impossible. As a bonus, there being no start money on offer, Clark's result brought a considerable amount of the large fund of prize money to Team Lotus.

Both Rodriguez and Arundell suffered accidents during the race, although the latter did manage an eventual sixth place.

In practice in the altitude of Mexico City, Clark had his Watkins Glen-winning BRM H16 engine explode on him, covering him in scalding water and oil; however, this was not before he had managed to take second place on the grid behind Surtees's Cooper-Maserati. What promised to be a good race was curtailed for Clark as he suffered from a poor replacement engine before gear linkage problems caused his retirement after only nine laps. On the day when Surtees's Cooper-Maserati won, popular local hero Rodriguez retired after an energetic but excellent drive to third place – he had been fourth fastest in the first practice session – because his final drive failed. At one point, after having already spun, Rodriguez had got all crossed up directly in front of Clark; luckily, contact was avoided. Arundell, meanwhile, managed to take an eventual seventh place.

What may now be regarded as an interim season had

TEAM LOTUS AND PRIVATE LOTUS ENTRY RESULTS 1966

Drivers:
Jim Clark: British; Peter Arundell: British; Pedro Rodriguez: Mexican; Giacomo Russo: Italian
Car:
Lotus 33T Engine: Coventry Climax V8 2-litre
Lotus 43   BRM H-16 3-litre

CAR	CHASSIS	DRIVER	PRACTICE	SESSION	GRID	RACE	LAPS	%	REASON	CHAMPIONSHIP POSITION	POINTS
MONACO GP, Monte Carlo – 22nd May – 100 L, 195.42 miles (314.50km) (72)											
33 T	R11	Clark	1m 29.9s	3	1st P	R	61	61.0	Suspension	–	–
25 P	R13★★	Spence	1m 33.5s	–	12th	R	35	35.0	Suspension	–	–
25 P	R6	Hill P	1m 42.2s	–	DNS	–	–	–	T-Car	–	–
25 B	R3★	Bonnier	1m 35.0s	–	14th	NC	73	73.0	–	–	–
BELGIAN GP, Spa – 12th June – 28 L, 245.32 miles (394.80km) (73)											
33 T	R11	Clark	3m 45.8s	1	10th	R	1	3.5	Engine	–	–
43	1	Arundell	5m 01.2s	1	DNS	–	–	–	–	–	–
25 P	R13	Spence	3m 45.2s	–	7th	R	1	3.5	Accident	–	–
FRENCH GP, Rheims – 3rd July – 48 L, 247.61 miles (398.49km) (74)											
43	1	Arundell	2m 19.6s	3	16th	R	4	8.3	Gears	–	–
33 T	R11	Rodriguez	2m 16.5s	3	13th	R	41	85.4	Oil pipe	–	–
		Clark★★★	2m 15.6s	2	DNS	–	–	–	Practice Accident	–	–
25 P	R13★★	Spence	2m 14.2s	–	10th	R	9	20.0	Clutch	–	–
BRITISH GP, Brands Hatch – 16th July – 80 L, 212.00 miles (341.20km) (75)											
33 T	R14	Clark	1m 36.1s	3	5th	4th	79	98.7	–	9th=	3
33 T	R11★★	Arundell	1m 54.3s	3	20th	R	32	40.0	Gears	–	–
25 P	R13★★	Spence	1m 37.3s	–	9th	R	15	18.7	Oil leak	–	–
DUTCH GP, Zandvoort – 24th July – 90 L, 234.49 miles (377.37km) (76)											
33 T	R14	Clark	1m 28.7s	2	3rd	3rd	88	97.7	–	8th	7
33 T	R11★★	Arundell	1m 32.0s	3	15th	R	28	31.1	Ignition	–	–
25 P	R13★★	Spence	1m 31.4s	–	12th	5th	87	96.6	–	–	–
GERMAN GP, Nurburgring – 7th August – 15 L, 212.60 miles (342.15km) (77)											
33 T	R11★★	Arundell	8m 52.7s	3	17th	12th (8th F1)	14	93.3	–	–	–
33 T	R14	Clark	8m 16.5s	3	1st P	R	12	80.0	Accident	8th	7
25 P	R13★★	Spence	8m 38.6s	–	13th	R	13	86.6	Alternator	–	–
ITALIAN GP, Monza – 4th September – 68 L, 242.96 miles (391.00km) (78)											
33 T	R11★★	Arundell	1m 34.1s	2	13th	8th NR	63	92.6	Engine	–	–
33 T	R14	Russo	1m 39.3s	2	20th	9th	63	92.6	–	–	–
43	1	Clark	1m 31.8s	2	3rd	R	59	86.7	Gearbox	10th	7
25 P	R13★★	Spence	1m 35.0s	–	14th	5th	67	98.5	–	–	–
25 P	R3★★	Baghetti	(T-Car)	–	–	–	–	–	–	–	–
US GP, Watkins Glen – 2nd October – 108 L, 248.40 miles (399.71km) (79)											
43	1	Clark	1m 08.53s	2	2nd	1st W	108	100.0	–	5th	16
33 T	R14	Arundell	1m 10.43s	2	19th	6th	101	93.5	–	17th=	1
33 T	R11	Rodriguez	1m 10.40s	2	10th	R	14	12.9	Temp	–	–
25 P	R3★★	Spence	1m 10.73	–	12th	R	75	69.4	Ignition	–	–
MEXICAN GP, Mexico – 23rd October – 65 L, 201.94 miles (325.00km) (80)											
33 T	R11	Arundell	2m 00.79s	2	17th	7th	61	93.8	–	17th=	1
43	1	Clark	1m 53.50s	2	2nd	R	9	13.8	Gears	6th	16
33 T	R14	Rodriguez	1m 54.78s	1	8th	R	49	75.3	Final drive	–	–
25 P	R3★★	Spence	1m 55.98	–	DNS	–	–	–	–	–	–

Key:
★   = Climax 2, 7 engine
★★   = BRM V8 engine
★★★   = Clark struck by bird in practice and car taken over by Rodriguez
DNS = Did Not Start
NC   = Not Classified
R   = Retired
L   = Laps
P   = Pole
W   = Win

Private Lotus Entries:
B   = Jo Bonnier Racing Team
P   = Parnell Racing Team/Reg Parnell Racing

therefore concluded on a somewhat low note compared to 1965, but all at Team Lotus were looking forward with renewed optimism to the début of their new car and engine package.

Ford, meanwhile, were keen to protect their investment and to have not only a back-up for Clark but also two world-class drivers in 'their' F1 team. As as consequence, in November Ford offered Graham Hill who had been with BRM for seven years – a large sum to come over to Lotus for 1967, which he duly accepted, thereby giving Chapman a very strong driver line-up at the expense, though, of Arundell. Hill had patched up the rivalry that had previously existed between himself and Clark, and was now pleased to be working as joint no. 1 driver on his return to Lotus.

WORLD CHAMPIONSHIP RESULTS 1966

Position	Driver	Points
1	Brabham	42
2	John Surtees	28
3	Jochen Rindt	22
4	Denny Hulme	18
5	Graham Hill	17
6	**Jim Clark**	**16**
	Jackie Stewart	14
8=	Mike Parkes	12
	Lorenzo Bandini	12
10	Ludovico Scarfiotti	9
11	Richie Ginther	5
12=	**Mike Spence**	**4**
	Dan Gurney	4
14=	Bob Bondurant	3
	Jo Siffert	3
	Bruce McLaren	3
17=	**Peter Arundell**	**1**
	John Taylor	1
	Bob Anderson	1
	Jo Bonnier	1

CONSTRUCTORS' CUP 1966

Position	Constructor	Points
1	Brabham-Repco	42
2	Ferrari	31
3	Cooper-Maserati	30
4	BRM	22
5	**Lotus-BRM**	**13**
6	**Lotus-Climax**	**8**

1967

Concern had been expressed the previous season that the overhaul costs of the BRM engines were becoming prohibitively expensive and exceeding even the start money on offer. More than ever, the Ford-powered

Lotus 49 was eagerly anticipated but, as the design took longer to evolve than anticipated, for the first Grand Prix of 1967 in South Africa Clark and Hill fielded a pair of Lotus 43s still fitted with their BRM H16 engines.

Practice in South Africa was bedevilled by mechanical problems, and Hill only managed thirteen laps over the entire three days because of a sticking throttle and leaking fuel tanks amongst a myriad of other troubles. A very hot dawn on the day at Kyalami indicated to the drivers that their tyres were going to have to be preserved by careful driving. This was something that Hill could not be accused of as he bent a front wishbone – thereby making the car droop on one side at the front and rub an oil pipe on the track – after mounting a kerb; eventually he spun at Crowthorne on oil he himself had dropped from that ruptured oil line. This was hardly an auspicious return to Lotus for the Londoner. An over-heating car dropped Clark well back after a pitstop to remove the nose and eventually he retired when the fuel pump failed. Rodriguez won the race for Cooper.

Having given the Race of Champions a miss, Hill came fourth at Silverstone's International Trophy, hoping that this would be his last non-Ford powered F1 drive. Neither the promised DFV nor the Lotus 49 were ready for Monaco, however, so a pair of Lotus 33Ts were utilized once again. Clark was not competing in any domestic English races at this time as he was in the middle of moving abroad.

In Monte Carlo both drivers reverted to alternative 2-litre engines to the H16. Hill broke his Hewland gearbox and without the appropriate spares had to borrow from Bob Anderson's private car, which caused reliability worries for Lotus on a circuit where the box is really pounded. At the track he liked so much, Clark went down the escape road at the chicane early in the event – avoiding an apparent accident, which in fact was just cement dust being thrown up – and fell right to the back of the pack. He then proceeded to push through the field, breaking the lap record on the way, to fourth place behind McLaren, which sadly he lost when his suspension failed at Tabac and he struck the wall hard, retiring on the spot. Whilst Brabham won, Hill came second with his suspension barely attached on one side. He had also coped with a recalcitrant clutch and a broken chassis en route. He was, though, deeply shocked by the fiery accident that had befallen Bandini's Ferrari at the chicane and which would later claim the popular Italian driver's life.

Lotus 49

The Lotus 49 was directly descended from the 43, with

a similar, yet lighter and slimmer, 18swg aluminium sheet monocoque, which allowed the Ford Cosworth DFV to be bolted directly on to the rear bulkhead; there was therefore no chassis behind the engine, which was now a fully stressed part of the car. The deliberately simple design was so that development attention could be devoted to the DFV engine, which would become the most successful power plant ever in Grand Prix racing. Chapman and designer Maurice Phillipe stamped their influence on to the light, yet frail, five-speed ZF (fixed internal ratios) gearbox as well as the semi-inboard brakes.

There being little spare money for testing, Team Lotus did most of their development in official practice sessions. The situation was aggravated because initially Lotus were loaned only two DFVs, so between races they had to return to Cosworth for checks and repairs. The prototype 49 was secretly run by Hill at Snetterton, where he was impressed by both and chassis and particularly the engine, although the clutch failed during a practice start. He was less happy with the car's brakes. As June drew closer the second car arrived and for their public début at Zandvoort the striking lines of the 49s drew much attention, especially as they represented Ford's entry into the world of Grand Prix racing.

Despite electrical troubles at Zandvoort, Hill was fastest, successfully taking pole position (4.2 seconds faster than the existing lap record), having fought off a challenge from Gurney's Eagle. Boasting narrower tyres and a lot more speed then he had previously been used to, the new car took some learning, although a Lotus 49 would be in pole position for a further nine successive World Championship races. Clark was unluckier, suffering rear wheel bearing and brake troubles on his introduction to the 49. Taking time to adjust his

seating position, he was less than happy with the car's handling. The DFVs possessed 50bhp more than the 360bhp of their rivals but problems, such as oil scavenging, made Ford's technicians less than confident about the outcome of the race.

Hill led the first ten laps of the Dutch GP until his timing-gear teeth failed and he was forced to coast and push his car into retirement. Secretly, he was worried that he might have knocked the cut-out off, but luckily this was not the case! Clark played himself in gently whilst learning about the DFV's 6,500rpm burst of power and he eventually won, despite fading brakes, much to the pleasure of Ford's Walter Hayes and Harley Copp, who had taken their début Grand Prix just two months after the first DFV had been fired up. Quietly the Team were worried as one engine had blown and the winning car had also suffered from timing-gear, clutch and brake maladies. Teeth were also found to be missing from its cam gears – a DFV problem that would take some years to cure.

Both 49s filled the front of the grid at Spa with lap speeds in excess of 150mph (240kph) and terminal velocities of more than 190mph (305kph) at Burnenville. Small nose aerofoils intended to help high-speed stability were removed by Chapman before the race, during which Hill was last away before retiring after only three laps and two pitstops (to examine his clutch and gearbox). He had starting problems on the grid and had needed a new battery. Plagued by spark plug breakages that had caused him two pitstops, the first of which took two minutes and lost him his 30-second lead, Clark came sixth.

The French GP at Le Mans saw both Lotuses retire with similar crown-wheel and pinion failures. Having been delayed at French Customs and thus missed initial

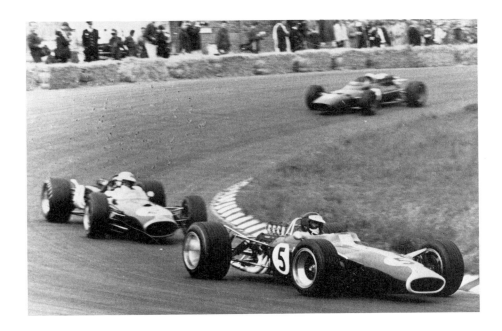

The dream début for the Lotus 49 and the Ford Cosworth DFV engine. Clark, pictured here, seized the lead at Zandvoort and won despite failing brakes. Hill had taken pole, and having initially led, retired with timing gear failure.

qualifying, Hill took pole, but Clark was in fuel-injection trouble. This was sorted out on the adjacent main road overnight! In the race both Hill and Clark led before the former dropped out, having tried in vain to warn Clark, who suffered identical transmission failure on lap 22, robbing him of potential victory. The curious Bugatti circuit had highlighted the DFV prob-

lem of abrupt power and the track's slow corners put enormous pressure on the gearbox, causing the crown-wheels and pinions to strip under the strain. Before leaving the circuit Chapman worked out some modifications, and these were hurriedly engineered at ZF's base in Friedrichshafen.

Engine troubles returned at Silverstone and then a faulty weld on a rear radius arm mounting viciously pitched Hill right into the wall as he entered the pits at Woodcote Corner. A frantic rush – involving the mechanics being flown back to Norfolk by Chapman – followed to build a third chassis overnight, and Hill rewarded everyone's efforts by leading the race for twenty-nine laps. Unfortunately, a suspension screw then worked loose – giving him a big fright at Becketts – but once replaced he was off again until a camshaft broke up. Clark, in the background of all this drama, took a well-deserved fifth British GP win in six years, keeping the crowd enthralled with numerous power-on slides.

Relief greeted this result, but prior to visiting the Nurburgring, Walter Hayes convinced Chapman that the DFV should be offered to other teams from 1968 onwards.

Hill firstly encountered a seized gearbox in Germany – it hadn't contained any oil! – and then, thanks to unfamiliarity with his new solid brake discs, he got his braking distances wrong and crashed badly. Having done a wall of death along a bank approaching Adenau, his 49 was badly damaged and without seat belts he had been lucky to stay in his cockpit. Hill had only done

At Silverstone Jim Clark took his fifth British Grand Prix win in six seasons, but Graham Hill had suffered all kinds of troubles including a practice crash at Woodcote corner, which required a replacement 49 to be built up.

TEAM LOTUS AND PRIVATE LOTUS ENTRY RESULTS 1967

Drivers:
Jim Clark: British; Graham Hill: British; Eppie Weitzes: Canadian; Ginacarlo Baghetti: Italian; Moises Solana: Mexican
Car:
Lotus 43 Engine: BRM H-16 3-litre
Lotus 33 T   BRM H-16 3-litre/Climax V8 2-litre
Lotus 49   Ford Cosworth DFV 3-litre

CAR	CHASSIS	DRIVER	PRACTICE SESSION	GRID	RACE	LAPS	%	REASON	CHAMPIONSHIP POSITION	POINTS
S AFRICAN GP, Kyalami – 2nd January – 80 L, 203.51 miles (372.52km) (81)										
43	1	Hill	1m 32.6s 3	15th	R	7	8.7	Accident	–	–
43	2	Clark	1m 29.0s 3	3rd	R	23	28.7	Engine	–	–
25 P	R13★★	Courage	1m 33.8s –	18th	R	52	65.0	Fuel system	–	–
MONACO GP, Monte Carlo – 7th May – 100 L, 195.42 miles (314.50km) (82)										
33 T	R11	Hill	1m 29.9s 2	8th	2nd	99	99.0	–	3rd=	6
33 T	R14★	Clark	1m 28.8s 3	5th	R	43	43.0	Accident	–	–
Fastest Lap: 1m 29.5s – 78.605mph (126.502km/h) on lap 38										
DUTCH GP, Zandvoort – 4th June – 90 L, 234.49 miles (377.37km) (83)										
49	R2	Clark	1m 26.8s 2	8th	1st W	90	100.0	–	3rd	9
Fastest Lap: 1m 28.08s – 106.487mph (171.375km/h) on lap 67										
49	R1	Hill	1m 24.6s 4	1st P	R	11	12.2	Camshaft	6th=	6
25 P	R1★★	Irwin	1m 27.5s –	13th	7th	88	97.7	–	–	–
BELGIAN GP, Spa – 18th June – 28 L, 245.32 miles (394.80km) (84)										
49	R2	Clark	3m 28.1s 2	1st P	6th	27	96.4	–	4th	10
49	R1	Hill	3m 29.2s 1	3rd	R	3	10.7	Gearbox	7th=	6
FRENCH GP, Le Mans – 2nd July – 80 L, 219.82 miles (353.76km) (85)										
49	R2	Clark	1m 37.5s 2	4th	R	23	28.7	Final drive	5th=	10
49	R1	Hill	1m 36.2s 2	1st P	R	14	17.5	Gearbox	8th=	6
Fastest Lap: 1m 36.7s – 102.293mph (164.624km/h) on lap 7										
BRITISH GP, Silverstone – 15th July – 80 L, 234.16 miles (376.81km) (86)										
49	R2	Clark	1m 25.3s 3	1st P	1st W	80	100.0	–	2nd=	19
49	R3	Hill	1m 26.0s 3	2nd	R	65	81.2	Engine	8th=	6
49	R1	(Spare)								
GERMAN GP, Nurburgring – 6th August – 15 L, 212.84 miles (342.53km) (87)										
49	R2	Clark	8m 04.1s 3	1st P	R	4	26.6	Suspension	3rd	19
49	R1	Hill	8m 31.7s 2	13th	R	8	53.3	Suspension	9th=	6
49	R3	(Spare)								
CANADIAN GP, Mosport Park – 27th August – 90 L, 221.29 miles (356.13km) (88)										
49	R3	Hill	1m 22.7s 2	2nd	4th	88	97.7	–	8th	9
49	R2	Clark	1m 22.4s 2	1st P	R	69	76.6	Ignition	4th	19
Fastest Lap: 1m 23.1s – 106.544mph (171.466km/h) on lap 54										
49	R1	Weitzes	1m 30.8s 2	16th	DSQ	69	76.6	–	–	–
33 F	R11★★	Fisher	1m 31.9s –	17th	11th	81	90.00	–	–	–
ITALIAN GP, Monza – 10th September – 68 L, 242.96 miles (391.00km) (89)										
49	R2	Clark	1m 28.5s 1	1st P	3rd	68	100.0	–	–	–
Fastest Lap: 1m 28.5s – 145.337mph (233.899km/h) on lap 26										
49	R3	Hill	1m 29.7s 1	8th	R	59	86.7	Engine	9th	9
49	R1	Baghetti	1m 35.2s 2	17th	R	51	75.0	Engine	–	–
US GP, Watkins Glen – 1st October – 108 L, 248.40 miles (399.71km) (90)										
49	R2	Clark	1m 06.07s 2	2nd	1st W	108	100.0	–	3rd	32
49	R3	Hill	1m 05.48s 2	1st P	2nd	108	100.0	–	6th	15
Fastest Lap: 1m 06.0s – 125.455mph (201.899km/h) on lap 81										
49	R1	Solana	1m 07.88s 2	7th	R	8	7.4	Ignition	–	–
MEXICAN GP, Mexico – 22nd October – 65 L, 201.94 miles (325.00km) (91)										
49	R1	Clark	1m 47.56s 2	1st P	1st W	65	100.0	–	3rd	41
Fastest Lap: 1m 48.13s – 103.437mph (166.466km/h) on lap 52										
49	R3	Hill	1m 48.74s 2	4th	R	18	27.6	D/shaft	6th=	15
49	R2	Solana	1m 50.52s 2	9th	R	13	20.0	Suspension	–	–
33 F	33★★	Fisher	1m 57.41s –	18th	DNS	–	–	–	–	–

four of the five mandatory qualifying laps so he had to borrow a concerned Clark's car for a final tour. In the race, having been pushed on to the grass and then having had a wobbling wheel repaired, the 'loose screw' problem returned, causing his retirement. Clark had led but, retired too on lap 4 with collapsed front suspension as he returned to the pits with a rear puncture. The front rocker arms were beefed up as a result of these suspension problems.

Canada's first-ever Grand Prix was a sodden affair, and in learning the circuit Clark spun into a bank. The car was repaired for local racer Eppie Weitzes as a third Team Lotus entry. The Mosport rain caused ignition failure for Clark when he was well in the lead and revelling in the conditions. Hill suffered clutch trouble causing him to spin; he jumped out and push started his car to finish fourth. Weitzes drove at the back of the field before his electrics expired.

Before the United States GP Lotus transferred to Europe and Monza. Practice for the Italian GP was fouled up when the circuit's electronic timing gear failed and Hill was sure he had gone quicker than his third-row place. A chaotic start was followed by an action-packed race as Clark swept into the lead from pole, chased for three laps by a fast-starting Hill as well as Brabham and Gurney. Clark then suffered a puncture when an experimental Firestone arrangement of a tubeless tyre containing a tube deflated, and having been warned by the following Jack Brabham, a tyre change ensued after only twelve laps. He rejoined just behind the cars he had been leading a lap previously, but now in a lowly sixteenth place. In a great record-breaking drive, many would say his best, not only did Clark fight through the slipstreaming battle for the lead but he made up a whole lap. When the Brabhams both dropped back and Hill's engine blew at the Parabolica on lap 59, Clark was back in front on lap 61. With bitter irony his car then let him down with two laps to go as it wouldn't drain the last two gallons of fuel because of some experimental foam filling. He coasted across the line in third behind Surtees's winning Honda and Brabham.

So dominant were the 49s at Watkins Glen that Hill and Clark tossed a coin to see who would win, should they end up vying for the lead. This tactic was insisted upon by Ford, who didn't want the two drivers fighting

In Mexico Clark equalled Fangio's record of twenty-four Grand Prix wins and took his fourth win of the season. Brabham's (pictured behind Clark here) challenge failed and the Scot was assured of the crown.

each other and risking taking one another off after they had, it was suggested, been less than mature in their pole fight. Hill won the toss and did in fact lead away, but they eventually finished in reverse order for a one-two result. Only after the race, on close examination of the cars, which were in a sorry state, was it realized how lucky Lotus had been. Clark had seized the early lead before allowing Hill past as agreed only for the latter's transmission to fail. Clark was quickly back into the lead as the Ferrari of Amon closed in. The Scot's suspension broke with two laps to go and the right rear tyre was at a strange angle as a result. Hill, now lacking gears and a proper clutch, as well as suffering strong vibration and low oil pressure, took a well-earned second place. Clark did in fact subsequently apologize to Hill for going back on their wager!

Clark won again in Mexico whilst both Hill and Solana encountered suspension troubles. A hesitant Clark, thanks to an ambiguous starter, was rammed by Gurney, terminally damaging the American's Eagle. Clark suffered no ill effects and after three laps forced past Hill to eventually win, and thus equal Fangio's record of twenty-four Grand Prix victories. Hill had retired.

The final race on the 1967 calendar was the non-championship Madrid GP at Jarama, which was won by Clark with Hill second.

═══════ **1968** ═══════

Lotus's exclusive use of the DFV ended in South Africa with Matra and McLaren now also running the £7,500 engines. The problematic ZF gearboxes would be replaced by a Hewland alternative early in the season and the rear suspension sub-frames were also strengthened. The main trouble spots would be the transmission as well as the wheels, although reliability improved greatly.

On New Year's Day at Kyalami both 49s were still in 1967 specification but sharing the front row of the grid: this was the eleventh successive time that a Lotus 49 had taken a Grand Prix pole position. In practice Clark had busily researched rubber wear eventually to choose Firestones rather than the Dunlop alternatives.

Whilst the Matra of Stewart briefly snatched the lead at the start, Clark was soon back in front on lap 2 and eleven laps later Hill had taken third. He passed Stewart's Matra, which subsequently blew its DFV spectacularly on lap 43, and Lotus took the two premier

WORLD CHAMPIONSHIP RESULTS 1967

Position	Driver	Points
1	Denny Hulme	51
2	Jack Brabham	46
3	**Jim Clark**	**41**
4=	John Surtees	20
	Chris Amon	20
6=	**Graham Hill**	**15**
	Pedro Rodriguez	15
8	Dan Gurney	13
9	Jackie Stewart	10
10	Mike Spence	9
11=	John Love	6
	Jochen Rindt	6
	Jo Siffert	6
14=	Bruce McLaren	3
	Jo Bonnier	3
16	**Chris Irwin**	**2**
	Bob Anderson	2
	Mike Parkes	2

CONSTRUCTORS' CUP 1967

Position	Constructor	Points
1	Brabham-Repco	63
2	**Lotus-Ford**	**44**
3	Cooper-Maserati	28
4=	Honda	20
	Ferrari	20
6	BRM	17
7	Eagle-Weslake	13
8=	**Lotus-BRM**	**6**
	Cooper-Climax	6

New Year's Day 1968. In the South African sunshine of Kyalami, Jim Clark took his twenty-fifth Grand Prix win using Firestone tyres. A slow-starting Graham Hill made it a Lotus one-two finish.

The Lotus 63 benefited from Jim Clark's research during the 1968 South African Grand Prix. Pictured here winning that race, his Lotus 49 was fitted with a tube above his legs to simulate a four-wheel-drive shaft!

positions as Clark raced on to his record twenty-fifth Grand Prix win: one more than Juan Manuel Fangio.

Unbeknown to many, Clark had run with a tube above his legs to see whether this would hamper his driving, because Chapman had been researching potential routes for future four-wheel drive-shafts.

Kyalami was the last race for the traditional green and yellow Team Lotus colours, as full-blooded sponsorship was about to take over the sport. Lotus set off for the Tasman series where the distinctive new red, white and gold Players/Gold Leaf colour scheme would début on Clark's car in the Lady Wigram Trophy race in New Zealand. The new colours controversially illustrated Chapman's ability to move with the times, as this was the first time tobacco company sponsorship money was harnessed, at a time when the funds from other traditional motor sport backers, such as Esso, were on the decline. The deal had been done mainly through personal contacts, which had led to Chapman and the chairman of Players, Geoffrey Kent, meeting and hitting it off immediately. Kent was later to join the board of Lotus.

The CSI wisely relaxed their previous rules by allowing the Gold Leaf colours to appear on Grand Prix cars (as opposed to Tasman cars) at the Brands Hatch Race of Champions, although the 'mobile advertisement' caused a furore amongst both traditionalists and the BBC as well as creating a lot of publicity for its originators! Before it retired, Hill's car was run on wide tyres, which caused handling problems including the generation of 'aerodynamic lift'. The poor result prompted an immediate post mortem of the 49 concept. With the relatively minor F2 races at Barcelona and Hockenheim on the horizon, Chapman took a family holiday in Switzerland, only to be recalled urgently to Germany in the wake of the tragic event that occurred there.

Jim Clark's Accident

That a comparatively minor F2 race – The Hockenheim Deutschland Trophy – should claim Jim Clark's life has always seemed tragically unfair. Indeed, he should not have been racing there at all, having already been asked to race Alan Mann's sports car in the Brands Hatch BOAC 500 on the same day. When arrangements for that drive were slow in being confirmed Clark instead fatefully decided to go to Hockenheim. On the fifth lap of a damp race his Lotus 48 left the track at high speed – about 140mph (225kph) – and hit a strong sapling sideways, killing Clark instantly. Clark was on his own and the most likely cause of the tragedy was subsequently alleged to have been a deflating rear tyre coming off its rim.

Whatever the cause, the racing world had been robbed of a great talent. Clark had competed in seventy-two Grands Prix, attaining thirty-three pole positions, twenty-eight fastest laps and twenty-five wins. It will always seem supremely ironic that having safely led over 6,000 miles of Grand Prix races, such talent should be squandered in a comparatively trivial event in a foreign field miles away from his Borders home of Duns and Chirnside.

A shattered Team Lotus returned to F1 at Silverstone's International Trophy but Hill retired at Abbey after eleven laps when a fuel line split. During May, Lotus interest turned to Indianapolis, where they were running four Lotus 56 Indy turbine cars. Following Clark's death, Mike Spence joined the driver line-up of Greg Weld and Graham Hill in Indiana. Spence set a series of very fast times in practice only to later lose control of Weld's car and strike the wall in an accident in which two wheels were torn off. One of these struck Spence's helmet and he died from his injuries some hours later.

An even more devastated Chapman left Indianapolis threatening to quite motor racing, and no doubt wondering what Lotus had done to be dealt two such cruel blows within a calendar month.

Lotus 49B

In a state of shock, Team Lotus's next Grand Prix was to be the Spanish at Jarama, where the spare car, R5, was kept hidden. Having been very heavily involved with Indianapolis, as well as extremely upset by the deaths of both Clark and Spence, Chapman declined to attend; as a result, the intended début of the updated 49 would not take place, as he wanted to oversee its first race personally.

The 49B in fact took much more notice of the air-flow around and over a racing car than its predecessors. Outwardly there seemed very little different about it but it had sprouted airflow-harnessing fins on the nose and a sweeping engine cover. The wings had evolved out of Clark's Tasman series experiments in trying to cure the problems of the wider racing tyres as well as the 'lift' identified in tests at Indianapolis. The wheel-base was longer, the suspension modified to cure bump-steer and an adaptable Hewland DG300 gearbox was employed initially rather than the 2F. The brake discs and new callipers were returned to within the wheels, which were themselves now conical in design, and the oil radiator and tank were located over the gearbox.

Meanwhile Chapman loaned Rob Walker 49/R2 for Jo Siffert to drive after their existing car had been wrecked in Brands Hatch practice.

During Jarama practice Hill's engine played up and for the first time since Zandvoort in 1967 a Lotus 49 was not in pole position. The fine weather of the Spanish GP allowed Hill to move through the field from sixth place on the grid as the number of retirements mounted. The most significant was that of Amon in the pole position Ferrari when it was over 20 seconds ahead; after that Hill only had Hulme's very determined McLaren to fight off in order to hold the lead. This he managed and it was not only Hill's first Grand Prix win for Lotus but also his first win since the USA in 1965. The whole Team desperately needed this result to raise their spirits; their new no. 1 driver had delivered magnificently.

ZF transmission failures were prevalent in Monaco practice, whilst Hill's pole position 49B escaped such problems thanks to its Hewland system. Hill was to achieve a well-earned win having headed the field from lap 4 and kept Attwood's BRM at bay. The second successive win by the Englishman following Clark's death continued to restore Team Lotus's faith

Providing a much needed boost to morale, Graham Hill won his first Grand Prix for Lotus at Jarama. Lotus 49/R1 now boasted the new Gold Leaf Team Lotus colours and was victorious, having been forced past Hulme's determined McLaren.

in itself, raising morale tremendously. It was also Hill's fourth win at Monaco, which in itself constituted a record.

Newly promoted Lotus Team driver Jackie Oliver suffered a first lap collision at the Chicane but this didn't detract from the fact that Lotus were on the winners' rostrum again. Chapman did not see things the same way, being livid with Oliver and dismissing him instantly, only for Jim Endruweit to successfully plead for his reinstatement.

In truth Chapman was still earnestly searching for a Clark replacement, and at Spa his attention would turn

Complete with a reliable Hewland gearbox, Graham Hill shows off the sleek lines of the 49B on the way to his fourth win at Monaco, this time from pole position.

Graham Hill didn't have it all his own way at Monaco; here he fends off Siffert's Rob Walker Lotus 49 and Surtees's Honda early in the race on the plunge down from the Mirabeau.

to the young Austrian Jochen Rindt, although at the time he was more intent on courting and signing American Mario Andretti. In Belgium, Team Lotus qualified badly as firstly Hill's 49B suffered from myriad gearbox and oil pressure problems – he had only managed one lap on the first day of practice – whilst Oliver's new 49B didn't even appear until the second day when the weather in the Ardennes was particularly inclement. Nobody fancied his job of running-in a virgin car complete with the new science of wings in the wet on this particular track!

In the Belgian GP Hill ran without wings feeling that they slowed the 49B on the long straights. Both cars experienced CV joint failures in the wet race, Hill's failing after just five laps and Oliver's after a fuel pitstop on lap 26, when he was fifth.

Pre-Holland testing revealed that the wings were indeed effective, which surprised the previously sceptical drivers. Hill's ignition was to be a problem in official Dutch practice, when the rains affected proceedings at Zandvoort again. The 49Bs raced for the last time with the rear bodywork extended; Hill also had to cope with a sand-induced jamming throttle slide. This caused two excursions. Then, having led the first lap, his second spin removed a wheel at Tarzan. Oliver had similar throttle troubles to add to a soaked ignition, and he therefore spent much of the race stopped either in the pits or on the circuit. Chapman was again furious, giving his driver no credit for the fact that the Lotus's Firestone rain tyres were no match for Dunlop's products as fitted to the winning Matras.

Ferrari, Brabham and McLaren had all appeared at Spa with fully fledged wings, and Chapman realized he needed to do the same. He therefore sent both 49s to the French GP at Rouen with a full set of aerofoils. These large 'wings' were fitted to the rear suspension instead of the chassis and produced downward pressure in excess of 400lb (180kg) at 150mph (240kph). The intention was to increase cornering speeds in exchange for a slight increase in drag along the straights.

Rouen brought a number of troubles for Lotus all of which could be indirectly or directly attributed to the new 'wings', of which Oliver possessed larger versions than Hill. Their unpredictability caused Oliver to crash violently in race-morning practice. Having pulled out of Attwood's slipstream at about 130mph (210kph) he found himself a passenger heading for a substantial gatepost. How he survived unharmed is still not clear as the aftermath resembled an aircraft accident. It was later recognized that the large 'wing' had momentarily lost its effect, unbalancing the car. Hill had broken drive-shafts in practice and would do the same in the damp race, thanks to a drive train that was fighting against the Firestone tyres, which in turn were being squashed on to the track much more than previously. Hill was fourth at the time of his retirement.

Wing modifications were undertaken before the British GP: they were mounted much higher to try to avoid turbulence, although overtaking was still uncomfortable. Mario Andretti had finally declined overtures from Chapman for 1969 so attention was turned back to Brabham driver Jochen Rindt. A deal was provisionally agreed only for Andretti to reverse his decision later in the year, causing Lotus to run three cars on occasions in 1969. Rindt's wife, Nina, was never keen on her husband driving for Lotus as she thought Brabham's cars were much safer.

Back in April Siffert had written off the new Walker 49 only for the remains to be completely destroyed in a severe workshop fire. The blaze very nearly finished the Walker team off, but thanks to the generosity of businessman Sir Val Duncan, Walker's brother-in-law, the organization kept afloat. The second-hand ex-Tasman 49/R2 was then loaned by the works team and pressed into service before a new chassis (49B /R7) was completed just in time for the British GP.

Lotus cars captured most of the front row of the grid, and in the race both works drivers led before Hill's drive-shafts went on lap 26. Oliver's crown-wheel and pinion broke on lap 43. Siffert then went on to distinguish himself by winning the race for Rob Walker after a fraught battle with Amon's Ferrari. These two were never more than 4 seconds apart and it was Walker's first World Championship win since Moss's 1961 German GP victory.

The major event of German GP practice was Oliver's wheel-removing trip into the Adenau undergrowth. In the extraordinarily inclement race conditions Hill came second to Stewart, who had made excellent use of his unique narrow Dunlop wet tyres. Following a long dice with Amon on lap 12, Hill aquaplaned off the circuit only to dismount, push start himself and return to the fray unabashed in what was a gritty drive to second overall. Oliver was eleventh, having nearly taken a lapping Stewart out at Adenau as the race drew to a close. Stewart was now only 4 points behind Hill in the Championship.

The Team returned to Oulton Park's Gold Cup where Oliver came third and Hill retired. A new nose for the 49B was revealed at a demonstration for Ford at Mallory Park before, in anticipation of Monza, the Team's DFVs were given new exhaust systems, which gave another 15bhp at top speed.

During pre-Italian GP testing at Monza, Andretti ran faster than Amon's Ferrari, turning in the quickest time of all with 1 minute 27 seconds. He was most impressed by F1 although his car was blessed with less power than his normal USAC mount.

After recording the eighth-fastest practice time at Monza, Andretti was precluded from continuing as the rules stated that he could not complete in two major races within 24 hours – that same weekend he had been trying to dovetail in a USAC race in America. Andretti maintains to this day that agreement had been reached to waive this rule but for whatever reason, maybe Ferrari-applied pressure, the promise was rescinded.

Following a spate of practice engine failures, both Hill and Oliver ran well in the Grand Prix, the former getting as high as second, until he crashed out at the second Lesmo corner when a wheel came off. His drive train yet again failed Oliver. Siffert – running without any wings of consequence – looked set to take second until his suspension gave out.

Throughout the season, circuits with tight turns were feared by Lotus because of the fragility of the transmissions. Mont Tremblant, the Canadian venue, was just such a circuit and Chapman had been experimenting with different wings. All the works cars were found to have warped drive-shafts after the warm-up which necessitated a hasty replacement session. Hill's car was given preferential treatment, which was probably reflected in the results as his team mates fell by the

Swiss driver Jo Siffert won the British Grand Prix at Brands Hatch in the new 49B/R7 owned by Rob Walker's private team. Both works Lotuses had led but dropped out, and victory came after the Ferrari of Chris Amon had been repulsed.

wayside while he came fourth, spurred on by his chase of Rodriguez. He might have come higher had he not been subjected to a series of inexplicable shudders and judders. It turned out that the reason for these was that his DFV was not attached at the top as the mountings had parted. His car had literally been bending in the middle on the bumpy circuit!

At least for Watkins Glen the Team said goodbye to their 'old' and weak drive-shafts. In the Championship, Hill was now equal on points with Hulme's McLaren at the top of the table. Andretti was drafted back into the Team and promptly rewarded Chapman's enthusiasm – and the mechanics' many engine changes – by taking pole position for his first ever Grand Prix!

Oliver crashed heavily in practice when a wheel collapsed and he became a non-starter.

Andretti led away but his nose cone collapsed just after Stewart got past him. This was taped up but a promising drive was subsequently ruined by clutch failure. Chapman decided there and then to continue pursuing the talented American, but it would be some time before he succeeded in finally signing him. Hill's car sprayed out fuel from its breather pipe and momentarily the engine stopped, dropping him to fourth, only to luckily pick up again. For 108 laps he also had to cope with a loose steering wheel – which early on trapped his fingers knocking the switches off and stalling his engine – but he still came in second. The stage

What a difference a year makes. In his 49 Clark won his final 1967 Grand Prix in Mexico in the British racing green colours. He had also taken pole position and fastest lap.

In 1968 Lotus again won in Mexico but this time Graham Hill was behind the wheel. The winged 49B now boasted the Gold Leaf Team Lotus colours as well as the very visible oil cooler, which was part of the improved design.

was set for the Championship finale as Hill, Stewart and Hulme all had mathematical chances of taking the title.

Stewart managed some unofficial practice in Mexico the week before the Grand Prix, unlike Lotus. The 1968 Mexico Olympics having just finished, Hill had the luxury of a choice of cars, one of which (49B/R6) had an adjustable rear wing activated by a fourth foot pedal mounted above the clutch. The idea was that the wing could be angled for the corners and feathered on the straights. The car's rear brakes were set up on the assumption that the download would be provided by the wing. In a classic piece of gamesmanship Chapman left the spare car on open view without any wings at all so that the opposition would waste time experimenting with such a set-up!

The patriotic locals were more concerned that Moises Solana's car depended totally on Hill who, as Championship contender, took precedence in choosing his car. The impatient Mexican and his boiling supporters were later appeased when Oliver agreed to share a car with him in practice.

After Hill had made a meteoric start, the race saw three leaders, including pole-sitter Siffert, but in the end Hill's 49B was the most reliable and he held on to the flag as both Hulme and Stewart fell by the wayside. Hill later admitted that he couldn't have caught Stewart so the Scot's retirement was very timely.

TEAM LOTUS AND PRIVATE LOTUS ENTRY RESULTS 1968

Drivers:
Jim Clark: British; Graham Hill: British; Jackie Oliver: British; Mario Andretti: USA; Bill Brack: Canadian; Moises Solana: Mexican
Car:
Lotus 49 Engine: Ford Cosworth DFV 3-litre
Lotus 49B   Ford Cosworth DFV 3-litre

CAR	CHASSIS	DRIVER	PRACTICE	SESSION	GRID	RACE	LAPS	%	REASON	CHAMPIONSHIP POSITION	POINTS
SOUTH AFRICAN GP, Kyalami – 1st January – 80 L, 204.012 miles (328.32km) (92)											
49	R4	Clark	1m 21.6s	3	1st P	1st W	80	100.0	–	1st	9
Fastest Lap and Record: 1m 23.7s – 109.682mph (176.516km/h) on lap 73											
49	R3	Hill	1m 22.6s	3	2nd	2nd	8	100.0	–	2nd	6
SPANISH GP, Jarama – 12th May – 90 L, 190.38 miles (306.39km) (93)											
49	R1	Hill	1m 28.4s	1	6th	1st W	90	100.0	–	1st	15
49	R5	(Spare)									
49 W	R2	Siffert	1m 29.7s	3	10th	R	63	70.0	Transmission	–	–
MONACO GP, Monte Carlo – 26th May – 80 L, 156.34 miles (215.60km) (94)											
49 B	R5	Hill	1m 28.2s	2	1st P	1st W	80	100.0	–	1st	24
49	R1	Oliver	1m 31.7s	1	13th	R	1	1.25	Accident	–	–
49 W	R2	Siffert	1m 28.8s	2	3rd	R	12	15.0	Transmission	–	–
BELGIAN GP, Spa – 9th June – 28 L, 245.32 miles (394.80km) (95)											
49 B	R6	Oliver	4m 30.8s	2	15th	5th NR	26	92.8	D/shaft	15th	2
49 B	R5	Hill	4m 06.1s	1	14th	R	6	21.4	D/shaft	1st	24
49 W	R2	Siffert	3m 39.0s	1	9th	7th NR	26	92.8	Engine	–	–
DUTCH GP, Zandvoort – 23rd June – 90 L, 234.49 miles (377.37km) (96)											
49 B	R5	Hill	1m 23.84s	2	3rd	9th NR	81	90.0	Accident	1st	24
49 B	R6	Oliver	1m 25.48s	2	10th	10th NC	80	88.8	–	15th=	2
49 W	R2	Siffert	1m 25.86s	2	13th	R	56	62.2	Gears	–	–
FRENCH GP, Rouen – 7th July – 60 L, 243.90 miles (392.52km) (97)											
49 B	R5	Hill	1m 59.1s	2	9th	R	15	25.0	D/shaft	1st	24
49 B	R6	Oliver	2m 00.2s	2	DNS	–	–	–	Accident	–	–
49 W	R2	Siffert	2m 00.3s	2	11th	11th	54	90.0	–	–	–
BRITISH GP, Brands Hatch – 20th July – 80 L, 212.00 miles (341.20km) (98)											
49 B	R5	Hill	1m 28.9s	3	1st P	R	27	33.7	D/shaft	1st	24
49	R2	Oliver	1m 29.4s	3	2nd	R	44	55.0	Transmission	18th=	2
49 B W	R7	Siffert	1m 29.7s	3	4th	1st W	80	100.0	–	7th=	9
Fastest Lap: 1m 29.7s – 106.354mph (171.161km/h)											
GERMAN GP, Nurburgring – 4th August – 14 L, 198.65 miles (319.69km) (99)											
49 B	R5	Hill	9m 46.0s	1	4th	2nd	14	100.0	–	1st	30
49 (B)	R2	Oliver	10m 18.7s	3	13th	11th	13	92.8	–	18th=	2
49 W	R7	Siffert	10m 03.4s	1	9th	R	7	50.0	Ignition	7th=	9

ITALIAN GP, Monza – 8th September – 68 L, 242.96 miles (391.00km) (100)

49 B	R6*	Hill	1m 26.57s	1	5th	R	11	16.1	Accident	1st	30
49 B	R5	Oliver	1m 27.40s	2	11th	R	39	57.3	Transmission	20th=	2

Fastest Lap: 1m 26.5s – 148.698mph (239.306km/h) on lap 7

49 B	R5	Andretti	1m 27.20s	1	(10th)	DSQ	–	–	–	–	–
49 W	R7	Siffert	1m 26.96s	1	9th	R	59	86.7	Suspension	8th=	9

CANADIAN GP, Mt Tremblant – 22nd September – 90 L, 238.50 miles (383.85km) (101)

49 B	R6	Hill	1m 34.8s	1	5th	4th	86	95.5	–	1st	33
49 B	R2	Oliver	1m 35.2s	2	9th	R	33	36.6	D/shaft	20th=	2
49 B	R5	Brack	1m 41.2s	2	20th	R	19	21.1	D/shaft	–	–
49 W	R7	Siffert	1m 34.5s	2	3rd	R	30	33.3	Oil system	9th=	9

Fastest Lap: 1m 35.1s – 100.315mph (161.442km/h) on lap 22

US GP, Watkins Glen – 6th October – 108 L, 248.40 miles (399.71km) (102)

49 B	R6	Hill	1m 04.28s	2	3rd	2nd	108	100.0	–	1st	39
49 B	R5	Andretti	1m 04.20s	2	1st P	R	33	30.5	Clutch	–	–
49 B	R2	Oliver	1m 07.46s	1	16th	DNS	–	–	Accident	21st	2
49 B W	R7	Siffert	1m 06.17s	1	12th	5th	105	97.2	–	8th=	11

MEXICAN GP, Mexico – 3rd November – 65 L, 201.94 miles (325.00km) (103)

49 B	R6	Hill	1m 46.01s	1	3rd	1st W	65	100.0	–	1st	48
49 B	R5	Oliver	1m 48.44s	1	14th	3rd	65	100.0	–	13th=	6
49 B	R2	Solana	1m 47.67s	1	11th	R	15	23.0	Rear wing	–	–
49 W	R7	Siffert	1m 45.22s	2	1st P	6th	107	99.0	–	7th=	12

Fastest Lap: 1m 44.23s – 107.307mph (172.695km/h) on lap 52

Key:
- ★ = New monocoque
- DNS = Did Not Start
- NC = Not Classified
- NR = Not Running
- R = Retired
- L = Laps
- P = Pole
- W = Win

Private Lotus Entries:
W = R.R.C. Walker

Rodriguez, meanwhile, fought with Oliver, and the Mexican very nearly took a passing Hill out when he locked up his wheels, but again Hill's luck held. Oliver came home a lapped third and the Team successfully took both the 1968 Drivers' and Constructors' Championships thereby silencing those who thought Lotus would collapse completely after Clark's death. It was to be said, though, that Hill's win was completed literally 'on a wing and a prayer' as one half of the adjustable aerofoil linkage had broken early in the race: had the other side let go Hill would have been sunk.

So successful had the 1968 season been for Lotus-Ford that Walter Hayes was concerned about the DFV's dominance. His fears that either the opposition could be perceived as being too weak or that Ford would be accused of virtually buying out Grand Prix racing, were to prove groundless.

During October Lotus Cars Ltd became a public company and throughout the year Chapman had been deeply involved in the 'politics' of the flotation, as if the racing season hadn't been hectic enough! Oliver left Lotus to join BRM leaving behind a Team that now possessed a Grand Prix record second only to Ferrari, with thirty-four wins and three world titles.

WORLD CHAMPIONSHIP RESULTS 1968

Position	Driver	Points
1	**Graham Hill**	**48**
2	Jackie Stewart	36
3	Denny Hulme	33
4	Jacky Ickx	27
5	Bruce McLaren	22
6	Pedro Rodriguez	18
7=	**Jo Siffert**	**12**
	John Surtees	12
9	Jean-Pierre Beltoise	11
10	Chris Amon	10
11	**Jim Clark**	**9**
12	Jochen Rindt	8
13=	**Jackie Oliver**	**6**
	Richard Attwood	6
	Johnny Servoz-Gavin	6
	Ludovico Scarfiotti	6

CONSTRUCTORS' CUP 1968

Position	Constructor	Points
1	**Lotus-Ford**	**64**

═══ **1969** ═══

Jochen Rindt

Over the winter Lotus sent cars to the Tasman series for Hill, who now boasted an OBE, and new equal no. 1 driver Jochen Rindt, who promptly won at Wigram and Warwick Farm, so starting a rivalry between the two.

The new GP season was to be pressured for Lotus as wings were to be closely examined after a series of spectacular Lotus accidents in Spain. Whilst Chapman was coping with this he was also working on the four-wheel drive project (Lotus 63). It had been intended that the Lotus 63 would be Lotus's main weapon during the year but as technical problems mounted the 49B remained in use much longer than anticipated. The Indy cars the team were running would prove troublesome, and with Lotus entries in many other minor Formulae the development of the 49B would not be as swift as the drivers would have liked. They in turn would openly express their dissatisfaction on a number of occasions during what would be a disappointing year for Team Lotus.

Following the Tasman Series, in which Rindt had been second and Hill fifth, the GP season opened at Kyalami, where there were three pristine Gold Leaf Team Lotus 49Bs sporting adjustable 'biplane' wings attached to both the front and rear suspensions. Hill and Andretti were works drivers accompanied by an aggrieved Rindt, whose 49B didn't have an up-to-date exhaust manifold and had a DFV borrowed from Alan Mann. He was not keen either on Andretti being the third driver but took second on the grid, as ironically his old team Brabham snatched pole position. The tall wing stays fouled the wheels around Kyalami's twists and turns and both Rindt and Andretti had complete failures; the rear stays were consequently shortened for the race, making them less effective. In the race, having passed Brabham, Stewart's Matra-Ford led the field, and whilst the 49Bs of Hill, Siffert, Rindt and Andretti – who had made a bad start – tried to give chase, the Scot was not to be headed. Unsurprisingly, Rindt's borrowed engine failed after forty-four laps. Hill's adjustable wings became less effective as the race progressed, but having wisely selected dry tyres, he finished second as the threatened rain held off.

Back in Europe for the Brands Hatch Race of Champions, Hill came second again whilst Rindt retired, complaining that Hill hadn't let him overtake. Chapman intervened and the simmering feud was forgotten. A fortnight later at Silverstone's International Trophy, Rindt kept the crowd on their toes in the wet conditions with a memorable run to second place, with

Hill this time coming in seventh. Rindt's worst moment had been in practice when at top speed in the wet he had abruptly run out of fuel in the middle of the old Woodcote corner. The resulting moment was somehow recovered but not before onlookers had mentally taken cover!

Rindt was now very vociferous in the press about his dislike of 'wings' and before the Spanish GP feelings were mounting that they should be banned. The Austrian had also inspected the Barcelona circuit on behalf of the GPDA making his views known about the newly installed barriers.

Rindt finally signed his Lotus contract in Spain having quietly expected Brabham to put in a counter bid. Barcelona's parkland track was another tight and twisty venue and Chapman modified the 49B's wings by adding an elevated tab to the rear edge, thereby increasing pressure by about 50 per cent. There were doubts, though, that the struts could cope although Rindt took pole, despite hitting a dog, breaking a shock absorber and cracking a brake disc! Hill was third in what was now a two-year-old design. Rindt took the lead in the beautiful Spanish sun but after nine laps of the race Hill had his rear wing collapse at about 150mph (240kph) when his suspension dropped as the car jumped the hump immediately after the pits. The Englishman continued at undiminished pace through the air and twisted sideways before ricocheting down the road from barrier to barrier.

Hill examined his wreck only to realize that his accident had not, after all, been caused by a wheel coming off but by a collapsing rear wing. Spotting a ripple appearing in his team-mate's wing he tried to warn Rindt, but shortly afterwards exactly the same fate befell the Austrian at the identical spot at about 140mph (225kph). Rindt's 49B ended up banana-shaped and inverted in a pool of fuel, having slammed sickeningly along the barriers and then crashed into and over Hill's 49B. Mercifully both drivers escaped relatively unharmed, considering the impacts, although Rindt – having been released by Hill – was taken away to the local hospital with a skull fracture as well as a broken nose and jaw. Considering he had had the top of his helmet worn away as the car slid upside-down along the tarmac he was lucky indeed. A shocked Chapman had sprinted to the accident scene to be left to examine the wreckage of his two cars, caused by wing failures. Elsewhere, his Austrian driver was to express his dislike of wings forcibly to the press.

Hill was fit to drive almost immediately whilst Rindt – who initially blamed Hill for not warning him of the risk of a wing failure – would take some time to recover fully at his Geneva home; he was therefore replaced by circuit lap-record holder Richard Attwood

In the confusion over the regulations surrounding wings, Hill's 49B boasted the contrived gearbox cover in Monaco. The car had started practice with full wings but these had been banned by the CSI.

at Monaco. A possible Lotus withdrawal from Monaco did not happen.

For Monaco two ex-Tasman cars were readied as replacements for the Spanish wrecks. Hill only arrived in Monte Carlo from Indianapolis half an hour before practice commenced to find that nobody knew whether wings were legal or not. After the first practice the CSI introduced some interim rules effectively ban-

With all the cars looking somewhat naked, Graham Hill, here seen fending off Beltoise's Matra, drove sensibly to take his fifth Monaco win. Rindt watched proceedings on his television as Richard Attwood stood in for him.

ning wings, but some team managers were annoyed at having their initial times deleted. Modified nose fins and a hastily contrived gearbox-mounted 'cover', or tail, were allowed as a wing replacement on the 49Bs. Throughout all this Chapman was still at Indianapolis, but he did arrive for the race itself before returning to the United States with Hill. The 49Bs now felt strange and Hill drove conservatively to take his fifth win at Monaco – watched by Rindt on TV at Jo Bonnier's – having a definite knack where the circuit was concerned, and Attwood did well too to come in fourth, even though his gear lever had come loose. Three Lotuses had finished in the first four positions.

The wing situation was still not entirely clear and a variety of solutions were employed for the Dutch race. Hill's car sprouted a deep aerofoil between the rear wheels, whilst Siffert's Walker car had a sheet aluminium tail.

Lotus 63

The four-wheel drive Lotus 63 was somewhat stillborn, thanks to the CSI rules on wings, as the design was reliant on substantial downforce. Hill always regarded the 63 as one of the best thought-through of designs and was as disappointed as anyone when the eventual outcome was failure. The overweight 63 housed a substantial transmission to deliver power to both sets of wheels and the DFV was reversed. The off-set gearbox and clutch were connected to the drive, which ran down the left of the driver and uncomfortably over his ankles so he was located on the right-hand side of the monocoque.

Much had been learned about the final drive from the abortive Lotus 56 design; the drive percentage between front and rear could be altered from 50/50 to 40/60 and on to 30/70. Gradually the car was balanced until it became similar to a conventional F1 car and the need for four-wheel drive disappeared! Andretti didn't like the car as it was 'bog-slow on the straightaway' and he tried to convince Chapman that it was not agile enough and 'was not the required ticket'. The development of F1 tyres had in fact overtaken the need for four-wheel drive.

Following Lotus's withdrawal from Indianapolis, a number of operational problems resulted with Firestone but two 63s were taken to Zandvoort for their intended début, becoming the centre of attention. Hill undertook some damp exploratory laps, which he felt showed no speed advantage in the very conditions for which the 63 was designed. Rindt simply refused even to drive the 63 – which was well off the pace – arguing that it shouldn't be race tested. He further fuelled the situation by placing a 'For Sale' sign on the 63 in the pits! Chapman was outraged at his driver's attitude as they returned to their trusty 49Bs, the wings on which now attracted protests from Matra and Ferrari. Chapman flew back to Norfolk to fetch some old wings, which were mounted directly on to the chassis overnight. Rindt promptly took pole, with Hill too joining him on the front row in third, sandwiching Stewart.

Both Lotus drivers scrapped early on before each led the race. Rindt humbled Stewart in the process but was to have a drive-shaft break, and Hill was pushed down the field after an abortive pitstop to rectify his car's unusual handling. He attributed this to the new wings and the lack of stiffer rear springs to combat the downforce. Siffert took second place.

Immediately after the Dutch GP the CSI agreed new regulations, which henceforth would require wings to be fixed, much reduced in size and fitted solely to the sprung parts of the car. This upset Chapman, who was coping with the floundering 63 design and the negative attitude of his drivers. For the fast-approaching French GP he decided that John Miles would be the first driver of a 63 in a race. Development of the 49Bs was to be shelved and Chapman's attention turned exclusively to the 63; or, at least, that was the intention.

On the hilly French Charade circuit ineffective new rear wings on the 49Bs were abandoned, whilst Rindt only managed two successive practice laps between bouts of motion sickness, thanks to continuing symptoms of post-Barcelona concussion. Both Lotuses developed cracks in their steering, which required Dick Scammell's welding expertise.

Miles arrives to drive the 63 but the car retired after only two understeering laps, when the belt drive to the fuel pump gave out; to replace this meant removing the engine, which was out of the question. Rindt retired feeling most unwell on the tortuous circuit and Hill came sixth, despite the persistence of the Dutch ill-handling symptoms, having watched Siffert crash through the straw bales trying to overtake him.

Prior to the British GP, Chapman sold 49Bs to both Jo Bonnier and John Love, leaving the works team with only one 49B; he was effectively trying to force either Hill or Rindt into a 63 – a prospect that didn't please either. 'Discussions' took place behind the scenes and eventually one 49B was 'borrowed back' for Hill to drive and Bonnier was 'loaned' the 63 prototype, thereby keeping the majority of those involved 'happy'. Privateer Bonnier can hardly have been ecstatic with his uncompetitive 63 in front of a Swedish TV company especially there to film him. Rindt was more sorry for the overworked mechanics trying to cope as best they could with four cars.

All the discussions had effectively denied the Team Lotus drivers the opportunity to take advantage of the first Silverstone official practice session. Hill had therefore tested a Brabham and had thoroughly enjoyed himself, whilst creating all sorts of gossip! He then had a couple of laps in the 63 before reverting to a 49B, which then required replacement hubs that Chapman had to fly back to Norfolk to collect. Rindt, though, took pole in his single qualifying opportunity. Two great friends, Rindt and Stewart, dominated the event until the Lotus's aerodynamics intervened in a most unexpected way. Chapman had added end plates to the 49B's rear wing and the left-hand version bent back under pressure, fouling a rear tyre and forcing Rindt into the pits, leaving Stewart in the lead. Silverstone's right-handed sweeps affected fuel pick-up on all the 49Bs and both team cars as well as Siffert's needed urgent top-ups. Drivers were supposed to dismount whilst refuelling but Lotus forgot this (Rob Walker didn't!). Rindt eventually came fourth having traded lap records with Stewart on a day when the Austrian was obviously faster. Poor preparation had cost Rindt the race, and both he and his wife were not amused – leaving immediately by helicopter – as both felt that Rindt was jinxed at Lotus.

Hill – whose big party at his Mill Hill home that evening Rindt missed – had oversteered to seventh thanks to a bent aerofoil, and Miles plugged on in the 63 to a clutchless and jammed third-gear tenth, whilst Bonnier lasted only seven laps before his engine failed. A young Brazilian driver by the name of Emerson Fittipaldi was an enthralled paying spectator that day, particularly admiring Rindt's talents.

Before the Nurburgring the 49B's fuel system was reworked. Chapman had meanwhile asked four-wheel

New regulations somewhat strangled the four-wheel-drive Lotus 63 and it fell to John Miles, pictured during the British Grand Prix at Silverstone, to undertake the development. Here he is coping with his 63, not only jammed in third gear but also lacking a clutch!

drive advocate Mario Andretti to race the 63 in an apparent attempt to show up his regular drivers. In Germany Rindt and Chapman confronted the increasing rift between them and the Austrian was promised total no. 1 treatment for 1970. Rindt considered this scenario, whilst also discussing creating his own team in conjunction with Robin Herd and Bernie Ecclestone (when Rindt's discussions failed, the March team was what emerged).

Andretti coped with a broken crankshaft in Nurburgring practice before crashing at the Karussel on the race's first lap, so Chapman's trump card could not be fully played. The accident severely damaged the 63 and involved Vic Elford's McLaren, breaking that driver's arm in three places. Hill was in fourth position with a failing gearbox, and during the meeting it was decided that he would be found a drive with Rob Walker for the following year. Rindt retired yet again thanks to both sickness and ignition problems, being particularly upset by the practice accident in which Gerhard Mitter had died. Siffert crashed into the trees and Bonnier retired with a leaking fuel bag on a day when Ickx's Brabham had dominated.

Chapman and Rindt patched up their differences in time for Oulton Park's Gold Cup, where the Austrian was actually to drive a 63. Rindt took second place, complaining publicly that the power split between front and rear axles was not right. Bonnier seriously damaged his 49B against a tree in practice but once again the strength of the Lotus 49B tub protected its driver from serious injury.

Rindt's concession in driving the 63 in the Gold Cup meant that by the time of Monza the atmosphere

in the Team had notably improved. There the 49Bs ran without significant aerofoils and this tweek enabled Rindt to gain pole. Rindt and Hill had discovered the extra 300rpm that could be so generated on the main straight, and they decided to keep the idea secret from the rival teams, although Stewart had spotted it. (Undoubtedly this successful experiment gave Rindt and the Team the encouragement to do the same again a year later.)

The entire Italian GP provided an enthralling slip-streaming battle, which was only settled on the line when Stewart took the flag 0.08 seconds ahead of Rindt – as the Lotus was momentarily delayed by its rev-limiter – to become World Champion. The first four drivers, which included Beltoise and McLaren, were covered by a mere 0.19 seconds! Hill had pitched in there too, having already lost one exhaust pipe (it struck Surtees's helmet at 160mph (258kph)!), and then a half-shaft let go just as he was poised in the leading bunch for the final frantic five laps. The Lotus 63 of Miles only lasted for four laps before his camshaft broke.

On the finishing line in Italy, Rindt had decided that 1970 must be his make-or-break year where the World Championship was concerned. By the time of Canada he had already discussed his future with McLaren and Matra and then Alan Rees made him a huge financial offer (rumoured to be £100,000), whilst Brabham was convinced he would return to them.

Rindt initially tried a 63 in Canadian practice, but returned to his regular car to take third on the grid and in the race. Firestone tyres were generally at a disadvantage at Mosport and the Lotus cars were therefore

During Watkins Glen practice Rindt felt that he was never going to win a Grand Prix, even though he did take his fifth pole position of the season in the 49B.

battling against heavy Goodyear-shod Brabham odds. Hill had been fighting with Brabham before a camshaft broke, forcing him to park just behind Miles's 63, which had suffered gearbox failure.

The Brabhams had ironically finished in the first two positions in Canada just as Rindt had decided not to race with them in 1970. At this time he finally signed for Lotus, lured not only by the financial agreement but also by the parallel F2 programme that Chapman offered.

After forty-eight Grands Prix the pessimistic Rindt went to Watkins Glen with the feeling that the combination of his '1969 luck' and Lotus's reliability record would deny him the opportunity to win. He did prove his speed by taking his seventh pole position – his fifth in 1969 – and the $2,000 reward. He led the race too for eleven laps, before Stewart swept past only to be retaken by the Austrian. Stewart's engine blew and

Lotus displayed a 'STEW OUT' pit signal to tell Rindt the good news. He had beaten Stewart fair and square to win his first World Championship GP ahead of Courage's Brabham.

Hill had suffered a nasty accident to take the Team's enjoyment away. On worn tyres he had spun on some oil at The Loop on lap 89 and had dismounted from his stalled car to give it a push. In getting going again he omitted to fasten his seat belts, and on lap 91, when intending to come in to change his tyres, a deflating rear caused his car to leave the track where it overturned, throwing him out. He suffered a broken right knee, a dislocated left knee and torn ligaments, from which he would only slowly recover after treatment at University College Hospital. Andretti had given the 63 another abortive outing at the Glen but it was now apparent that the concept was getting nowhere and the design was discarded.

A titanic battle ensued between Rindt and Stewart. Rindt lost the lead to Stewart after eleven laps, but regained it before the Matra's engine blew and the Austrian went on to score his maiden Grand Prix victory.

TEAM LOTUS AND PRIVATE LOTUS ENTRY RESULTS 1969

Drivers:
Graham Hill: British; Mario Andretti: USA; Jochen Rindt: Austrian; Richard Attwood: British; John Miles: British; Bill Brack: Canadian;
Moises Solana: Mexican
Car:
Lotus 49B Engine: Ford Cosworth DFV 3-litre
Lotus 63   Ford Cosworth DFV 3-litre

CAR	CHASSIS	DRIVER	PRACTICE	SESSION	GRID	RACE	LAPS	%	REASON	CHAMPIONSHIP POSITION	POINTS
S AFRICAN GP, Kyalami – 1st March – 80 L, 204.01 miles (328.32km) (104)											
49 B	R6 801★	Hill	1m 21.1s	–	7th	2nd	80	100.0	–	2nd	6
49 B	R11 818★	Andretti	1m 20.8s	–	6th	R	32	40.0	Transmission	–	–
49 B	R9 816★	Rindt	1m 20.2s	–	2nd	R	44	55.0	Engine	–	–
49 B W	R7 809★	Siffert	1m 22.2s	–	12th	4th	80	100.0	–	3rd	3
49 L	R3 705★	Love	1m 22.1s	–	10th	R	31	38.7	Ignition	–	–
SPANISH GP, Barcelona – 4th May – 90 L, 211.95 miles (341.10km) (105)											
49 B	R6 934★	Hill	1m 26.6s	3	3rd	R	9	10.0	Accident	4th	6
49 B	R9 929★	Rindt	1m 25.7s	3	1st P	R	20	22.2	Accident	–	–
Fastest Lap: 1m 28.3s – 96.023mph (154.535km/h) on lap 15											
49 B W	R7 932★	Siffert	1m 28.2s	3	6th	R	31	34.4	Engine	6th	3
MONACO GP, Monte Carlo – 18th May – 80 L, 156.34 miles (251.60km) (106)											
49 B	R10 811★	Hill	1m 25.8s	2	4th	1st W	80	100.0	–	2nd	15
49 B	R8 818★	Attwood	1m 26.5s	3	10th	4th	80	100.0	–	8th	3
49 B W	R7 809★	Siffert	1m 26.0s	3	5th	3rd	80	100.0	–	5th	7
DUTCH GP, Zandvoort – 21st June – 90 L, 234.49 miles (377.37km) (107)											
49 B	R10 811★	Hill	1m 22.01s	1	3rd	7th	88	97.7	–	2nd	15
49 B	R6★★ 818★	Rindt	1m 20.85s	2	1st P	R	17	18.8	D/shaft	–	–
63	2 –	Hill	(Spare)								
63	1 801★	Rindt	(Spare)								
49 B W	R7 932★	Siffert	1m 23.94s	2	10th	2nd	90	100.0	–	3rd	13
FRENCH GP, Charade – 6th July – 38 L, 190.19 miles (306.09km) (108)											
49 B	R10 934★	Hill	3m 05.9s	3	8th	6th	37	97.3	–	2nd	16
49 B	R6 929★	Rindt	3m 02.5s	3	3rd	R	23	60.5	Driver ill	–	–
63	2 811★	Miles	3m 12.8s	3	12th	R	2	5.2	Fuel pump	–	–
49 B W	R7 928★	Siffert	3m 06.3s	2	9th	9th	34	89.4	–	3rd=	13
BRITISH GP, Silverstone – 19th July – 84 L, 245.86 miles (395.68km) (109)											
49 B	R6 945★	Rindt	1m 20.8s	3	1st P	4th	83	98.8	–	10th=	3
49 B	R8 929★	Hill	1m 23.6s	3	12th	7th	82	97.6	–	3rd	16
63	2 821★	Miles	1m 25.1s	3	14th	10th	75	89.2	–	–	–
63	1★★★ 934★	Bonnier	1m 28.2s	3	16th	R	7	8.3	Engine	–	–
49 B W	R7 932★	Siffert	1m 22.7s	3	9th	8th	81	96.4	–	4th=	13
GERMAN GP, Nurburgring – 3rd August – 14 L, 198.65 miles (319.69km) (110)											
49 B	R10 934★	Hill	7m 57.0s	3	9th	4th	14	100.0	–	4th	19
49 B	R6 945★	Rindt	7m 48.0s	3	3rd	R	11	78.5	Ignition	10th	3
63	2 929★	Andretti	8m 15.4s	3	12th	R	1	7.1	Accident	–	–
49 B W	R7 932★	Siffert	7m 50.3s	2	4th	5th NR	12	85.7	Accident	5th	15
49 B JB	R8 –	Bonnier	8m 35.0s	–	14th	R	5	35.7	Fuel system	–	–
ITALIAN GP, Monza – 7th September – 68 L, 242.96 miles (391.00km) (111)											
49 B	R6 921★	Rindt	1m 25.48s	2	1st P	2nd	68	100.0	–	9th	9
49 B	R10 934★	Hill	1m 27.31s	1	9th	9th NR	63	92.6	H/shaft	4th	19
63	1 932★	Miles	1m 30.56s	2	14th	R	4	5.8	Engine	–	–
49 B W	R7 809★	Siffert	1m 27.04s	2	8th	8th NR	64	94.1	Engine	6th	15
CANADIAN GP, Mosport – 20th September – 90 L, 221.29 miles (356.13km) (112)											
49 B	R6 921★	Rindt	1m 17.9s	1	3rd	3rd	90	100.0	–	7th	13
49 B	R10 934★	Hill	1m 18.3s	1	7th	R	43	47.7	Camshaft	4th=	19
63	2 911★	Miles	1m 20.0s	2	11th	R	41	45.5	Gearbox	–	–
49 B W	R7 920★	Siffert	1m 18.5s	1	8th	R	41	45.5	D/shaft	6th	15
49 B PL	R11 –	Lovely	1m 22.9s	–	16th	7th	81	90.0	–	–	–

US GP, Watkins Glen – 5th October – 108 L, 248.40 miles (399.71km) (113)

49 B	R6 921★	Rindt	1m 03.62s	2	1st P	1st W	108	100.0	–	4th	22
Fastest Lap: 1m 04.34s – 128.691mph (207.108km/h) on lap 69											
49 B	R10 929★	Hill	1m 04.05s	2	4th	R	91	84.2	Accident	5th=	19
63	2 911★	Andretti	1m 06.52s	2	13th	R	4	3.7	Accident	–	–
49 B W	R7 932★	Siffert	1m 04.06s	2	5th	R	4	3.7	Drivebelt	8th	15
49 B PL	R11 –	Lovely	1m 07.55s	–	16th	R	26	24.0	D/shaft	–	–

MEXICAN GP, Mexico – 19th October – 65 L, 201.94 miles (325.00km) (114)

49 B	R6 921★	Rindt	1m 43.94s	2	6th	R	22	33.8	Suspension	4th	22
63	2 934★	Miles	1m 47.76s	2	11th	R	4	6.1	Fuel pump	–	–
49 B W	R7 909★	Siffert	1m 43.81s	1	5th	R	5	7.6	Accident	9th	15
49 B PL	R11 –	Lovely	1m 50.34s	–	16th	9th	62	95.3	–	–	–

Key:
			Lotus Private Entries:	
★	= Ford Cosworth DFV engine number		JB	= Jo Bonnier
★★	= new monocoque		W	= R.R.C. Walker/Durlacher
★★★	= on loan to Ecurie Bonnier		L	= John Love
NR	= Not Running		PL	= Pete Lovely
R	= Retired			
L	= Laps			
P	= Pole			
W	= Win			

A recuperating Hill was most upset to miss only the second GP of his career but Lotus was represented by Rindt and Miles in Mexico; both retired early in the race, as did Siffert. Over the winter, Rindt put his mind to running his Viennese *Jochen Rindt Show*, which fast became the most successful European racing-car exhibition.

WORLD CHAMPIONSHIP RESULTS 1969

Position	Driver	Points
1	Jackie Stewart	63
2	Jacky Ickx	37
3	Bruce McLaren	26
4	**Jochen Rindt**	**22**
5	Jean-Pierre Beltoise	21
6	Denny Hulme	20
7	**Graham Hill**	**19**
8	Piers Courage	16
9	Jo Siffert	15
10	Jack Brabham	14
11	John Surtees	6
12	Chris Amon	4
13=	**Richard Attwood**	**3**
	Vic Elford	3
	Pedro Rodriguez	3

CONSTRUCTORS' CUP 1969

Position	Constructor	Points
1	Matra-Ford	66
2	Brabham-Ford	49
3	**Lotus-Ford**	**44**

1970

Lotus 49C

In 1970 the 49s were intended solely for testing, but when the replacement 72s were held up, they were pressed back into action again as 49Cs with new front suspension for the 13in front wheels, and new hubs. Rindt and Miles remained and Hill was back, partly recovered from his injuries, in Walker's 49C after several winter months in hospital.

In South Africa the new suspension cured the 49C's lack of braking stability after research had taken 600 laps of Kyalami tyre testing. Despite all this mileage, the Firestones caused endless qualifying problems because of vibrations and the fact that they ran too hot. Rindt was worried about the pressure of tyre competition on safety standards after Brabham had a failure. Indeed, eventual winner Brabham rammed Rindt from behind in the race's first corner, throwing the Lotus into the air and off the circuit. Rindt fought back tenaciously to finish fifth from seventeenth although engine failure terminated his race with eight laps to go.

Miles, too, shone at Kyalami taking fifth place sitting in a pool of petrol for seventy-seven laps, thanks to a split fuel tank! Hill returned to racing but his weakened legs impaired his braking capabilities; Walker had Brian Redman standing by just in case a replacement driver were needed.

Brands Hatch's Race of Champions, in which Rindt came second, should have been the 49's last race, but events ensured that this would not be the case.

CHAPTER 4

The Old Faithful: Lotus 72

Lotus 72

When in mid-1969 it became evident that the 63 was a failure, Chapman and Phillipe began work on a re-placement to be known as the 72, not guessing that this design would race for six seasons and gain twenty GP wins!

Chapman's priority was to use Firestone's tyres to best effect with a flexible-rising rate torsion bar suspension and inboard front brakes to reduce unsprung weight. The car's wedge shape provided excellent aerodynamic penetration, at a time when wing regulations were still embryonic, with the side-mounted radiators improving the driver's coolness and comfort. Weight distribution was biased 70 per cent towards the rear, and the monocoque was constructed out of magnesium alloy, as were the 13in front and 15in rear wheels. Rindt was very impressed by the car's appearance but had reservations about the safety of the Citroen-like suspension.

The 72 was run in at a wet Snetterton before débuting at Jarama, where it disappointed. The meeting started badly when both Team Lotus and Rob Walker had fallen foul of the Spanish Customs. In practice Rindt was caught out by the heat build-up in his in-board brakes in the pits, which caused his solid left brake disc to part company from its retaining bolts. He spun off in a cloud of dust, and replacement ventilated discs were hurriedly fitted, as was larger radiator ducting to cope with the Spanish heat. Spaniard Alex Soler-Roig also ran a 49 with Chapman's assistance, because of the help the driver's surgeon father had given to Rindt the previous year at Barcelona.

At the last minute the organizers decided that only twenty cars could start, leaving Soler-Roig out of his home event as well as Miles; Hill was nearly dragged out of his car when he was undiplomatic towards the police! The eventual results were disappointing as Rindt – with a down-on power engine that had proved difficult to start – retired after ten laps with ignition failure. Rindt thought too that the race should have been stopped after Oliver and Ickx's fiery accident on the first lap, which he had only just avoided.

Ignition and engine failure caused Rindt's and Miles's retirements at Silverstone's International Trophy, where the 72s wouldn't handle in the long

The Lotus 72 would be pressed into service for no less than six seasons, during which twenty Grand Prix successes would be recorded. Initially the radical design (seen here winning in 1970 in France) would be problematic.

Complete with a 72 triplane rear wing, Rindt gives chase to Brabham at Monaco. He would force the Australian into a final lap mistake, taking a fine win in his four-year-old Lotus 49C. This was the fifth Lotus win at Monaco.

corners. Hill's ninth-placed 49C was the highest-placed Lotus, resplendent in its new Brooke Bond Oxo Racing-Rob Walker livery.

Chapman now embarked on a complete redesign of the 72's suspension geometry and the four-year-old 49Cs were pressed back into service for Monaco. Possessing a 72 'triplane' rear wing, Rindt was the only Team qualifier and was very pessimistic, accusing his team-mate of holding him up in the wet. Miles's 49C was repainted and lent to Hill, who had crashed twice in practice. Following a mediocre start, Rindt's worries subsided as retirements mounted, and with twenty laps to go he found himself only 14 seconds behind the leader. In a stirring charge he pulled Brabham into sight with three laps to go, forcing the Australian into a mistake at the final Gasworks hairpin, whilst lapping Courage. Rindt streaked past to take the flag first, giving Lotus their fifth win at Monaco and a new lap record set on his final lap just to illustrate how hard he had driven!

In 'sensational' Silverstone testing, the 72 was found to be faster using 400rpm less than the 49, although Rindt regarded the new rear suspension as too fragile for Spa, a circuit he disliked intensely.

Soler-Roig was again given a chance to race a Lotus at Spa, where he only completed three practice laps after engine troubles and so failed to qualify. Rindt's 72 lacked the rear anti-squat and front anti-dive suspension, but his left rear wheel seized, forcing him into the 49C. His car's oil temperature rose alarmingly in the warm-up and Chapman had the start delayed as a 72 wing was bolted on. Rindt led away, but at the end of the first lap he dropped to third place, retiring after only eleven laps at Malmedy with piston failure, like rivals Stewart and Brabham. Miles suffered two flat tyres as well as fuel system and gear-change troubles.

Lotus tested intensively for 500 miles at Silverstone before going to Zandvoort for a week, where Rindt was happier without the anti-dive as it gave him more feel. He was 5 seconds inside Stewart's record at 1 minute 17.6 seconds, although cracks appeared in the rear frames in the process.

The best official times were set in the misty final Dutch qualifying session. Earlier Rindt had stopped at the Hunzerug before spinning off at Tarzan when a front brake locked. Worryingly, the monocoque had bent around the suspension mountings, but he took pole being much happier without the anti-dive system. He was to go on to win the first of four successive races, having overtaken early leader Ickx after two laps. His close friend, Piers Courage, perished on lap 22 in a fiery accident and for fifty-six laps Rindt had his suspicions, but continued to drive to the flag to beat Stewart by 30 seconds. The deflated Austrian was unable to enjoy his third win and that evening seriously considered quitting the sport. His wife, Nina, wanted him to do just that, but he decided to continue to the end of the season as the World Championship was in sight . . .

A more safety-conscious Rindt went to the French GP one point behind Stewart. In between Zandvoort and Clermont-Ferrand he had raced in F2 at Rouen, where young French F3 driver, Jean-Luc Salomon, died following an accident, thereby cruelly denying him the chance of taking up his Team Lotus entry in the forthcoming French GP.

In France Rindt was happier with his strengthened but understeering 72, but he was gashed on his cheek by a large stone thrown up by Beltoise's car. To combat car sickness, he had decided to use an open-face helmet exposing him to his injury, which was patched up by Soler-Roig. Chapman predicted the retirements of the leading Ferraris and Matras and Rindt eventually drew away, knowing just how to deal with Amon's March, to take the chequered flag 7.61 seconds ahead, although it had not been as easy a victory as that in Holland. Miles was eighth.

Now knowing that Rindt would retire at season's end, Chapman recruited Brazilian F3 star Emerson

Rindt scored a fine win in Holland (here he is pursued by Pescarolo's Matra).

Fittipaldi for the forthcoming British GP. His impressive testing time at Silverstone in preparation was 1 minute 22.6 seconds as against Rindt's 1 minute 22.8 seconds!

Rindt captured the British GP pole in first practice – 0.8 seconds ahead of his nearest rival – in a 'perfect' car

A devastated Jochen Rindt stands atop the podium at the end of the 1970 Dutch Grand Prix. Having just learned that his close friend Piers Courage had died he very nearly quit racing on the spot; fatefully, he continued, only to die tragically himself and become the posthumous 1970 World Champion.

and retained it, despite Brabham having equalled the time using Goodyears, which were better suited to Brands Hatch than Lotus's Firestones. The Austrian inherited first place in the race itself when Brabham ran out of fuel on the last lap – it was later admitted that the Australian's chief mechanic, one Ron Dennis, had turned the mixture up too much! Early leader had been Ickx's Ferrari, which retired after seven laps shortly after Rindt had passed Brabham for second place. With twelve laps to go the Lotus's handling went off and at Clearways Brabham got the lead back. His tyres deteriorating, Rindt settled for a safe second place 13 seconds behind the leader, only to be presented with a slowing Brabham on the final lap at Stirlings and the opportunity to nip past and take the chequered flag. Team Lotus started their champagne celebrations – having sent a case to Brabham out of sympathy – only for Rindt's 72 to be disqualified because a rear wing was higher than the 80cm maximum. After two hours it was calculated that on one side it was 76.7cm and on the other 80.2cm giving an average of 79.9cm – 1 cm within the requirement! A controversial bracing stay was blamed, which had probably been leaned on during the lap of honour on a packed trailer. When straightened it left the aerofoil legal by 2mm and a climbdown was agreed. Miles had retired with engine failure and Fittipaldi came eighth, despite being reduced to seven cylinders and suffering a broken exhaust.

During 1970 Rindt was a track safety inspector for the Grand Prix Drivers' Association and it was he who caused the German GP to be moved from the Nurburgring. At Hockenheim, Rindt was initially happy

Jochen Rindt swoops down Paddock Hill at Brands Hatch in second place, his Firestones not as good as Brabham's Goodyears. When the Australian ran out of fuel on the last lap Rindt won, only to be disqualified and then reinstated!

aiming for a good placing but Chapman (suffering from severe food poisoning) was insistent that he should try to win. The Team lost three engines as Rindt was bumped off pole at the last minute by Ickx's Ferrari. The two drivers privately agreed on overtaking places prior to the race in the interests of safety. In practice Miles used an adjustable Lucas rev-limiter to take his DFV over the normal 10,200rpm. By contrast Rindt did not use his at all during the 1970 season, taking a much more relaxed practice attitude.

Ickx led at the start only to be overtaken by the Austrian after six laps, who lost out again three laps later. A challenge from Regazzoni's Ferrari faded when his engine seized so the race was then down to a two-car duel. In an F2-type scrap they swapped places endlessly – the Lotus getting on to the grass two laps from the end – only for Rindt to cleverly calculate his way past in time for the final lap, much to the pleasure of the cap-throwing Chapman. The lengthy race-long duel was truly one of the Lotus's great wins, showing the 72 off to best effect. Later the mechanics poignantly placed what were to be Rindt's last victory laurels on the spot where Clark had died two years previously.

Rindt was now 20 points ahead of Brabham and he looked increasingly uncatchable, so he decided to forget retirement and continue racing in 1971.

During Austrian practice Ken Tyrrell spotted that the 72 was half an inch wider than the rules permitted, and an angry Chapman initiated modifications before an official protest materialized; ironically the slimmer car was then faster down the straights! Rindt was under immense pressure from his fellow countrymen, who recognized the possibility of an Austrian World Champion. Dominant in practice, he took pole and was initially third in the race, before he dropped three places avoiding an oil slick. Sadly he retired with engine failure after twenty-one laps as Ferrari took a one-two. Significantly, Miles had retired with front brake-shaft

Having reached an agreement with Ickx, Rindt mastered Hockenheim's slipstreaming to slingshot past the Ferrari and win the German Grand Prix. This would be his last victory as the fateful Monza race meeting would follow Austria.

failure casting doubt over the part's structural integrity. All the brake-shafts were examined in minute detail before going to Italy but Miles was already reconsidering his position as mechanical breakages were becoming increasingly regular.

Lotus 56B

Since November 1967 Chapman had built several turbine-powered four-wheel drive Lotus 56 cars for Andy Granatelli to run in Indy racing for Team Lotus-STP. The venture was unsuccessful but the design was revived as the 56B for F1 following Hill's successful experimental 1968 road race at Mosport. Boasting Ferguson four-wheel drive the major difference from its predecessor was the 'pregnant' bulge for the fuel tankage.

In August Miles crashed the prototype 56B at Hethel and plans to go to Monza were scrapped. United Aircraft successfully produced a 3-litre F1 limit equivalent turbine and the car underwent many hundreds of miles of testing in the hands of Miles, Fittipaldi and Dave Walker. Braking efficiency was a concern because of the turbine's overrun. The controversy about the gas turbine (Pratt & Whitney ST96/76) surrounded the equivalence formula for what was basically a helicopter engine. Without a gearbox the 56B boasted just a brake and accelerator pedal, which required judicious use of the left foot to brake as the right foot maintained the revs!

Having taken second place in the Oulton Park Gold Cup in his 72, Rindt went to Monza with the Championship pressure mounting on him. A win in Italy would secure the crown, and there was still the possibility that this might precipitate his retirement . . .

Brabham had originally intended to race in the USA on the day of the Italian GP but he gave preference to the World Championship, knowing he must finish higher than fifth to deny Rindt the Championship.

At Monza Rindt was obsessively determined in practice and on Chapman's advice he repeated the previous year's tactics by not only running without the rear wing but also by using a more powerful engine and upping the gear ratios by two steps. Other drivers, such as Stewart and Hulme, were to emulate this technique, but significantly Miles tried it and then reverted to using wings, having found his Lotus unstable without.

Rindt's Accident

A new car (72/5) had been built for Rindt in time for Monza with modified fuel tankage and front brakes. Fittipaldi was to run the car in and Rindt would take it over should he prefer it, though he never got the chance as Fittipaldi crashed it early on. In first practice, Rindt's fuel system played up and then the engine refused to give enough power, a problem rectified by a plug change. He was, though, way down the grid in a lowly twenty-second place, having run with the triple rear wing. This was then removed releasing another 700rpm-plus on the straights and elevated Rindt to being one of the fastest on the track. He eagerly anticipated Cosworth's latest engine, which would be at his disposal on Saturday.

The Lotus 56B was another example of Chapman innovation. Powered by a Pratt & Whitney ST96/76 gas turbine the car, modified from the Indy version, lacked a gearbox and required mastery of left-foot braking. At Monza, in 1971, Fittipaldi raced it in Worldwide Racing colours.

The young Brazilian Emerson Fittipaldi passes Gethin's McLaren at Watkins Glen to win the US Grand Prix and to ensure that Jochen Rindt became F1's first posthumous World Champion. A fitting end to a tragic season.

The Saturday afternoon practice session commenced late in the day and Rindt started to circulate with increasing speed for four laps using Hulme's McLaren for his slipstreaming 'tow'. Rindt disposed of the McLaren after Lesmo and headed at top speed down the straight towards the 180-degree Parabolica corner. At about 185mph (300kph) the Lotus entered the 200m braking area and was seen to weave and then turn sharp left into the barriers, striking a substantial supporting post, before rebounding into the sand-trap. The violence of the accident tore off the front of the car, fatally injuring Rindt, who was transferred by ambulance to the Niguarda Clinic in Milan where he was found to be dead on arrival. All the other Lotus cars entered for the Grand Prix were immediately withdrawn.

Following the accident the car's wreckage was impounded, although the Team were allowed to return a week later to collect the undamaged DFV engine. Amongst the mechanics was a disguised Phillipe, who was unconvinced that the broken brake-shaft had been the accident's cause. His view was that the instability of the wingless vehicle was much more likely to have been responsible. Under Italian law Chapman was accused of homicide, and although the charge was subsequently dropped, he was intent on clearing the allegation that Lotus cars were dangerous. Both Tony Rudd and Peter Jowett of the RAC conducted a detailed investigation as did former Ferrari engineer Dr Sandro Colombo, a local magistrate, and it was officially established that an inboard brake-shaft failure was what had precipitated the accident to the unstable

car. For later races the hollow shafts were replaced with larger solid versions.

As Chapman retreated reclusively to his home, Team Lotus withdrew their entries from the Canadian GP as a mark of respect. Whilst Hill was unclassified, Ickx won for Ferrari, which meant that if he were to win the final two races he would end up 1 point ahead of Rindt and Champion.

Miles left Lotus, being devastated by the series of accidents in 1970, including that to his close friend Paul Hawkins. Swede Reine Wisell joined the driving strength in time for the US GP so for the first time Team Lotus lacked a British driver.

As a relative newcomer in only his fourth GP, Fittipaldi went extremely well in Watkins Glen practice to take third place, despite an engine low on oil pressure. In the race he ran in eighth before retirements promoted him up to second behind Rodriguez's BRM. As the Mexican's car consumed fuel at a faster rate, Fittipaldi was able to get past when it made a final pitstop and won, thereby securing the World title posthumously for Rindt. Wisell acquitted himself well by finishing third. The Team were elated that they had snatched back the Championship when lesser teams might have capitulated.

The farcical Mexican 'race' saw the drivers trying to avoid the mass of spectators flooding the circuit and Wisell finished in last place. Lack of oil pressure affected all of the other Lotuses in the high altitude in an unsatisfactory conclusion to a victorious yet sad season.

TEAM LOTUS AND PRIVATE LOTUS ENTRIES RESULTS 1970

Drivers:
John Rindt: Austrian; John Miles: British; Alex Soler-Roig: Spanish; Emerson Fittipaldi: Brazilian; Reine Wisell: Swedish
Car:
Lotus 49C Engine: Ford Cosworth DFV 3-litre
Lotus 72   Ford Cosworth DFV 3-litre

CAR	CHASSIS	DRIVER	PRACTICE	SESSION	GRID	RACE	LAPS	%	REASON	CHAMPIONSHIP POSITION	POINTS
S AFRICAN GP, Kyalami – 7th March – 80 L, 204.01 miles (328.32km) (115)											
49 C	R 10	Miles	1m 21.0s	3	14th	5th	79	98.7	–	5th	2
49 C	R 6	Rindt	1m 19.9s	3	4th	13th NR	72	90.0	Engine	–	–
49 C W	R 7	Hill	1m 21.6s	2	19th	6th	79	98.7	–	6th	1
		Redman	(T-car)								
49 GU	R 3	Love	1m 23.1s	–	22nd	8th	78	97.5	–	–	–
49 C SS	R 8	Charlton	1m 20.9s	–	13th	12th NR	73	91.2	Engine	–	–
SPANISH GP, Jarama – 19th April – 90 L, 190.38 miles (306.39km) (116)											
72	2	Rindt	1m 24.80s	1	8th	R	10	11.1	Ignition	–	–
72	1	Miles	1m 25.3s	NS	DNQ	–	–	–	–	8th=	2
49 C	R 6	(Spare)									
49 C W	R 7	Hill	1m 25.54s	3	15th	4th	89	98.8	–	5th=	4
49B GA	R 10	Soler-Roig	1m 25.8s	–	DNQ	–	–	–	–	–	–
MONACO GP, Monte Carlo – 10th May – 80 L, 156.34 miles (251.60km) (117)											
49 C	R 6	Rindt	1m 25.9s	1	8th	1st W	80	100.0	–	3rd=	9
Fastest Lap: 1m 23.2s – 84.557mph (136.081km/h) on lap 80!											
49 C	R 10	Miles	1m 27.4s	NS	DNQ	–	–	–	–	10th=	2
72	1	(Spare)									
49 C W	R 10*	Hill	1m 26.8s**	1	16th	5th	79	98.7	–	5th=	6
BELGIAN GP, Spa – 7th June – 28 L, 245.32 miles (394.80km) (118)											
49 C	R 6	Rindt	3m 30.1s	2	2nd	R	11	39.2	Engine	4th=	9
72	1	Miles	3m 33.8s	3	13th	R	13	46.4	Fuel	13th=	2
72	2	Soler-Roig	3m 52.7s	3	DNQ	–	–	–	–	–	–
49 C W	R 7	Hill	3m 37.0s	3	16th	R	20	71.4	Engine	7th=	6
DUTCH GP, Zandvoort – 21st June – 80 L, 208.43 miles (335.44km) (119)											
72	2	Rindt	1m 18.50s	3	1st P	1st W	80	100.0	–	2nd	18
72	1	Miles	1m 20.24s	3	8th	7th	78	97.5	–	15th=	2
49 C W	R 7	Hill	1m 21.75s	3	20th	12th NC	71	88.7	–	7th=	6
49 B L	R 11	Lovely	1m 23.37s	–	DNQ	–	–	–	–	–	–
FRENCH GP, Charade – 5th July – 38 L, 190.19 miles (306.09km) (120)											
72	2	Rindt	2m 59.74s	3	6th	1st W	38	100.0	–	1st	27
72	1	Miles	3m 04.16s	3	18th	8th	38	100.0	–	15th=	2
49 C WW	R 6	Soler-Roig	3m 14.49s	2	DNQ	–	–	–	–	–	–
49 C W	R 7	Hill	3m 07.84s	3	20th	10th	37	97.3	–	9th=	6
49 B L	R 11	Lovely	3m 15.58s	–	DNQ	–	–	–	–	–	–
BRITISH GP, Brands Hatch – 18th July – 80 L, 212.00 miles (341.20km) (121)											
72	2	Rindt	1m 24.8s	1	1st P	1st W	80	100.0	–	1st	36
72	1	Miles	1m 25.9s	2	7th	R	16	20.0	Engine	15th=	2
49 C	R 10	Fittipaldi	1m 28.1s	1	21st	8th	78	97.5	–	–	–
49 C W	R 7	Hill	1m 28.4s	1	22nd	6th	77	98.7	–	8th=	7
49 B L	R 11	Lovely	1m 30.2s	–	23rd	10th NC	69	86.2	–	–	–
GERMAN GP, Hockenheim – 2nd August – 50 L, 210.92 miles (339.45km) (122)											
72	2	Rindt	1m 59.7s	2	2nd	1st W	50	100.0	–	1st	45
49 C	R 10	Fittipaldi	2m 02.0s	3	13th	4th	50	100.0	–	15th=	3
72	3	Miles	2m 01.6s	2	10th	R	25	50.0	Engine	17th=	2
49 C W	R 7	Hill	2m 03.0s	3	20th	R	38	76.0	Engine	10th	7
AUSTRIAN GP, Österreichring – 16th August – 60 L, 220.38 miles (354.67km) (123)											
72	2	Rindt	1m 39.23s	2	1st P	R	22	36.6	Engine	1st	45
72	3	Miles	1m 41.6s	3	10th	R	5	8.3	Brakes	17th=	2
49 C	R 10	Fittipaldi	1m 41.86s	2	16th	15th	55	91.6	–	15th=	3

ITALIAN GP, Monza – 6th September – 68 L, 242.96 miles (391.00km) (124)

72	2	Rindt	1m 25.71s	2	DNS***	–	–	–	–	1st	45
72	3	Miles	1m 26.51s	2	DNS***	–	–	–	–	17th=	2
72	5	Fittipaldi	1m 28.39s	2	DNS***	–	–	–	–	15th=	3
72 W	4	Hill	1m 26.38s	1	DNS***	–	–	–	–	12th	7

US GP, Watkins Glen – 4th October – 108 L, 248.40 miles (399.71km) (125)

72	5	Fittipaldi	1m 03.67s	2	3rd	1st W	108	100.0	–	10th	12
72	3	Wisell	1m 04.79s	2	9th	3rd	108	100.0	–	15th=	4
72 W	4	Hill	1m 04.81s	1	10th	R	73	67.5	Clutch	13th	7
49B	R11	Lovely	1m 07.45s	–	DNQ	–	–	–	–	–	–

MEXICAN GP, Mexico – 25th October – 65 L, 201.94 miles (325.00km) (126)

72	5	Fittipaldi	1m 48.13s	1	18th	R	2	3.1	Engine	10th	12
72	3	Wisell	1m 44.59s	2	12th	10th NC	56	86.1	–	15th=	4
72 W	4	Hill	1m 44.13s	2	8th	R	5	7.6	Engine	13th	7

Key:

*	= Borrowed
**	= Time set in R7
***	= All Lotus cars withdrawn due to Rindt's fatal practice accident
DNQ	= Did Not Qualify
NC	= Not Classified
NR	= Not Running
R	= Retired
L	= Laps
P	= Pole
W	= Win
NS	= Non-Seeded

Private Lotus Entries:

GA	= Garvey Team Lotus
GU	= Team Gunston
L	= Pete Lovely Volkswagen Inc
SS	= Scuderia Scribante
W	= Brooke Bond Oxo/Rob Walker
WW	= Worldwide Racing

WORLD CHAMPIONSHIP RESULTS 1970

Position	Driver	Points
1	**Jochen Rindt**	**45**
2	Jackie Ickx	40
3	Clay Regazzoni	33
4	Denny Hulme	27
5=	Jack Brabham	25
	Jackie Stewart	25
7=	Pedro Rodriguez	23
	Chris Amon	23
9	Jean-Pierre Beltoise	16
10	**Emerson Fittipaldi**	**12**
11	Rolf Stommelen	10
12	Henri Pescarolo	8
13	**Graham Hill**	**7**
14	Bruce McLaren	6
15=	**Reine Wisell**	**4**
	Mario Andretti	4
17=	Ignazio Giunti	3
	John Surtees	3
19=	**John Miles**	**2**
	Johnny Servoz-Gavin	2
	Jackie Oliver	2

CONSTRUCTORS' CUP 1970

Position	Constructor	Points
1	**Lotus-Ford**	**59**

1971

Maurice Phillipe left to go to America and during 1971 Team Lotus fielded both Fittipaldi and Wisell but they failed to take any wins with the 72C/D which featured new low profile Firestone-friendly suspension. Much time was wasted too on the 56B turbine car, but all season there was uncertainty over the financial future of the Team, thanks to a single-year contract with John Player.

In the non-championship Argentine GP at Buenos Aires, Wisell took a lowly seventh place with Wilson Fittipaldi ninth in a 49B as his younger brother, Emerson, was unclassified, having lost oil pressure at the start of the second heat.

In deference to the posthumous World Champion, no car carried No 1 in South Africa, where Fittipaldi was unable to challenge Stewart's pole-sitting Tyrrell even though he possessed some demon Firestone qualifiers. He was only fifth on the grid and he retired in the race, despite having briefly held second early on, when after fifty-eight ill-handling laps, his engine blew. By contrast Wisell hauled himself up from fourteenth to fourth to gain three valuable points.

Tony Trimmer débuted for Lotus in the non-championship Brands Hatch Race of Champions, but like Wisell retired with engine failure. Fittipaldi drove the 56B turbine, qualifying an encouraging second, but in the race the car bottomed so heavily the rear suspension broke. After two heats of the Questor GP at California's Ontario Motor Speedway, Fittipaldi was twenty-first and Wisell twenty-seventh, following engine problems. Back at Oulton Park for the Rothmans International Trophy a promising Trimmer took sixth in a 49C as Fittipaldi came last! Following a sudden puncture, Wisell retired the turbine when the suspension failed.

After the heavy schedule of three non-championship races, Lotus possessed only two serviceable DFVs to take to the Spanish GP! During Barcelona practice the 72s refused to handle and in the race Wisell was unclassified, having had gear selection difficulties and a consequent fourteen-lap pitstop; Fittipaldi retired when he lost his brakes just before his rear suspension collapsed. The Silverstone International Trophy saw Wisell come thirteenth, again after engine failure, whilst Fittipaldi got the 56B on to the front row of the grid only to have another suspension breakage after only two laps of the first heat; in the second heat he came third, giving the 56B its best-ever result.

In Monaco, Fittipaldi had modified rear suspension with some anti-squat, creating the 72D variant, but after practice he was at the rear of the field and Wisell, who liked the circuit, was in mid-grid. The Swede ran in seventh until a contretemps with Regazzoni's Ferrari on lap 21 damaged his suspension. Fittipaldi drove without a clutch to take fifth, giving him his first two points of the season.

Fittipaldi broke two ribs in a road accident, and for the Jochen Rindt Memorial Race at Hockenheim he was replaced by Australian Dave Walker, who finished ninth with Wisell tenth. Whilst in Walker's hands the 56B suffered an engine fire in practice; it had probably not been rebuilt properly after Silverstone.

With Fittipaldi still unwell, Dave Charlton was recruited by Chapman to take his place at Zandvoort, but his intended car was crashed by Walker leaving him without a vehicle. Walker reverted to the 56B but missed his braking point as he attempted to overtake Hill at Tarzan on lap 5 of the race; he hurtled off the track to damage his car's front severely, but luckily not himself. He had been going well on Firestone's excellent wet-weather tyres with the four-wheel drive and Chapman was not amused knowing full well that he could have won had he kept up his momentum. Shortly afterwards Wisell felt a peculiar sensation from the back of his car as he passed the pits; he stopped beyond the pit exit and reversed back to have two loose rear wheel nuts tightened. The stewards subsequently disqualified him for his reversing manoeuvre.

Fittipaldi recovered in time for the French GP although his ribs were still heavily bandaged. The impressive purpose-built Paul Ricard hosted its first GP in 1971, where both Lotus drivers qualified in the back half of the field. Fittipaldi was spurred on in the race by his fight with Schenken's Brabham and the two towed each other up through the pack. Fittipaldi eventually finished third on a day when the Elf Tyrrells led home in a classic one-two result for the Surrey team. Wisell came in a fighting sixth to boost Lotus morale considerably.

Silverstone seemed curiously primitive after Paul Ricard, and during the British GP Fittipaldi's injuries precluded his driving the turbine – which was handled by Wisell – so he was in his usual car with Charlton racing the 72D he was about to buy. Fittipaldi sparkled, pushing the fastest drivers, Regazzoni and Stewart, throughout practice and ending up fourth fastest, knowing that he could have gone faster had an engine fastening not given out. The start of the GP was indecisive, with Fittipaldi making a slow getaway; at the end of the first lap Charlton's smoking car headed for retirement only just missing Hill's Brabham, which was straddling the pit entrance. Fittipaldi started to drive through the field from eleventh place but had difficulty shaking off Peterson's March and Schenken's Brabham. He took a fine third at the flag as his handling deteriorated. 'Rene Whistle', as the spectators had dubbed Wisell, was plagued by a lack of power and spent so much time in the pits that he was unclassified.

Ferrari and Tyrrell were the teams to beat at the Nurburgring, where Wisell's brand new 72D/6, which had only been completed in the pits, had a loose radiator, which terminated his practice. At the start of the race, the Swede was stranded without fuel pressure whilst Fittipaldi's suspension broke. Wisell finished a lowly eighth and Fittipaldi had his engine blow on the eighth lap.

Brake troubles afflicted both Lotuses in Austrian practice but both drivers made excellent starts, and by mid-race they were dicing with the Brabhams of Schenken and Hill. Chapman encouraged Fittipaldi to chase after Stewart and the extra pressure caused the Tyrrell to shear a drive-shaft and spin off. The Brazilian then found himself hot on the heels of Cevert's second-placed Tyrrell, only for that car's engine to blow, leaving him in second place behind eventual winner Jo Siffert (BRM). This was both Lotus's and Fittipaldi's best result of the season, and Wisell, too, scored a personal best with fourth. In the paddock, Geoffrey Kent committed Players to three more years of support, thereby giving the Team the much-needed financial security it deserved.

The continuing investigations following Rindt's accident meant that Gold Leaf Team Lotus could not attend the Italian GP in case the cars were impounded

TEAM LOTUS AND PRIVATE LOTUS ENTRIES RESULTS 1971

Drivers:
Emerson Fittipaldi: Brazilian; Reine Wisell: Swedish; Dave Walker: Australian; Dave Charlton, South African
Car:
Lotus 72C/D Engine: Ford Cosworth DFV 3-litre
Lotus 56B   Pratt & Whitney

CAR	CHASSIS	DRIVER	PRACTICE	SESSION	GRID	RACE	LAPS	%	REASON	CHAMPIONSHIP POSITION	POINTS
S AFRICAN GP, Kyalami – 6th March – 79 L, 201.45 miles (324.21km) (127)											
72 C	3	Wisell	1m 19.9s	3	14th	4th	79	100.0	–	4th	3
72 C	5	Fittipaldi	1m 19.1s	2/3	5th	R	58	73.4	Engine	–	–
SPANISH GP, Barcelona – 18th April – 75 L, 176.62 miles (284.25km) (128)											
72 C	3	Wisell	1m 28.6s	2	16th	12th NC	58	77.3	–	6th=	3
72 C	5	Fittipaldi	1m 27.9s	2	14th	R	54	72.0	Suspension	–	–
MONACO GP, Monte Carlo – 23rd May – 80 L, 156.34 miles (251.60km) (129)											
72 D	5	Fittipaldi	1m 27.7s	2	17th	5th	79	98.7	–	10th	2
72 C	3	Wisell	1m 26.7s	2	12th	R	22	27.5	Hub	8th=	3
DUTCH GP, Zandvoort – 20th June – 70 L, 182.38 miles (293.51km) (130)											
56 B	1	Walker	1m 21.83s	3	22nd	R	5	7.1	Accident	–	–
72 D	3	Wisell	1m 18.70s	1	6th	DSQ	17	24.2	Backing	9th	3
72 D	5	Walker	1m 35.36s	1	DNQ★	–	–	–	–	–	–
FRENCH GP, Ricard – 4th July – 55 L, 198.56 miles (319.55km) (131)											
72 D	5	Fittipaldi	1m 54.22s	2	17th	3rd	55	100.0	–	8th	6
72 D	3	Wisell	1m 53.75s	2	15th	6th	55	100.0	–	11th=	3
BRITISH GP, Silverstone – 17th July – 68 L, 199.03 miles (320.31km) (132)											
72 D	5	Fittipaldi	1m 18.3s	3	4th	3rd	68	100.0	–	4th	10
56B	1	Wisell	1m 20.6s	4	19th	13th NC	57	83.8	–	11th=	4
72 D	3	Charlton	1m 20.05s	3	13th	R	1	1.4	Engine	–	–
GERMAN GP, Nurburgring – 1st August – 12 L, 170.27 miles (274.02km) (133)											
72 D	6	Wisell	7m 39.96s	3	17th	8th	12	100.0	–	11th=	4
72 D	5	Fittipaldi	7m 27.5s	3	8th	R	8	66.6	Engine	7th	10
AUSTRIAN GP, Österreichring – 15th August – 54 L, 198.34 miles (319.19km) (134)											
72 D	5	Fittipaldi	1m 37.90s	3	5th	2nd	54	100.0	–	4th	16
72 D	6	Wisell	1m 38.95s	3	10th	4th	54	100.0	–	11th	7
ITALIAN GP, Monza – 5th September – 55 L, 196.51 miles (316.25km) (135)											
56 B WW	1	Fittipaldi	1m 25.18s	3	18th	8th	54	98.1	–	4th	16
CANADIAN GP, Mosport – 19th September – 64 L, 157.36 miles (253.25km) (136)											
72 D	6	Wisell	1m 16.3s	3	7th	5th	63	98.4	–	9th=	9
72 D	5	Fittipaldi	1m 16.1s	3/4	4th	7th	62	96.8	–	5th	16
69 L	5★★	Lovely	1m 21.1s	–	25th	18th NC	55	85.9	–	–	–
US GP, Watkins Glen – 3rd October – 59 L, 199.25 miles (320.66km) (137)											
72 D	5	Fittipaldi	1m 42.659s	2	2nd	19th NC	49	83.0	–	6th	16
72	6	Wisell	1m 44.024s	2	9th	R	5	8.4	Accident	9th=	9
69 L	5★★	Lovely	1m 52.140s	–	29th	20th NC	49	83.0	–	–	–

Key:
★   = car crashed by Walker in first practice, denying Dave Charlton a drive
★★   = powered by Ford Cosworth DFV 3-litre
DSQ = Disqualified
NC   = Not Classified
WW = Worldwide Racing
R   = Retired
L   = Laps

Private Lotus Entries:
L = Pete Lovely Volkswagen Inc

and team members arrested. The 'Worldwide Racing' name, originally used for Indianapolis, was rekindled, enabling the turbine car to be run at Monza, which was ideally suited to its concept. Its gold and yellow colour scheme was prophetically not unconnected with the John Player Special cigarette brand but unfortunately the meeting was to be run in high temperatures. This didn't suit the turbine's power characteristics and Fittipaldi could manage only eighth, thanks largely to its brakes. He was more successful at Hockenheim the following weekend where the turbine turned in the fastest lap of the non-championship Preis de Nationen and took second overall, but the 56B disappeared soon afterwards as Chapman terminated the project.

In Canada Wisell practised intensively to learn the circuit, and in the dank race the Lotuses circulated for eleven laps in fifth and sixth place before an understeering Fittipaldi fell back. Eventually Wisell took fifth and Fittipaldi seventh place. Interestingly Pete Lovely had built a Lotus special utilizing the rear of his 49B/R11 grafted on to the front of the ex-Rindt F2 Lotus 69/5, but it did not feature significantly in this race or the following United States GP.

At Watkins Glen Fittipaldi slotted on to the front row for the first time in 1971 despite both wheel and tyre vibrations. He praised the practice modifications made to his 72, but his optimism turned sour when, after a bad start, he fell back to eighth following a series of pitstops (jammed throttle, damaged suspension, puncture and burst fuel line). Wisell crashed because of brake failure thereby rounding off a less than perfect season for Lotus.

.The final F1 race of 1971 was the Rothmans World Championship Victory Race at Brands Hatch to celebrate Stewart's title, but tragically the race was cut short when Siffert crashed his BRM fatally; Fittipaldi was second and took fastest lap too (1 minute 24.0 seconds).

The year had seen Lotus trying to recover from the previous season's Monza tragedy, and it had been the first time that the Team had not taken a victory in an entire season since 1959. On the home front, too, Lotus Racing had been in financial trouble, and the production of customer racing cars for other Formulae was terminated, bringing to an end an era that had started with Lotus Components. It was just as well that a complete change in image would take place in 1972.

1972

Lotus morale was lifted in 1972 by a novel F1 marketing arrangement by which Players promoted their new John Player Special brand through motor racing; even

WORLD CHAMPIONSHIP RESULTS 1971

Position	Driver	Points
1	Jackie Stewart	62
2	Ronnie Peterson	33
3	François Cevert	26
4=	Jacky Ickx	19
	Jo Siffert	19
6	**Emerson Fittipaldi**	**16**
7	Clay Regazzoni	13
8	Mario Andretti	13
9=	**Reine Wisell**	**9**
	Peter Gethin	9
	Pedro Rodriguez	9
	Chris Amon	9
	Denny Hulme	9

CONSTRUCTORS' CUP 1971

Position	Constructor	Points
1	Tyrrell-Ford	73
2	BRM	36
3=	Ferrari	33
	March-Ford	33
5	**Lotus-Ford**	**21**

the cars themselves were renamed. The idea was that should cigarette advertising be banned, the cars could still be called John Player Specials! In a truly successful year Fittipaldi won five races, making him Chapman's fourth World Champion. The Lotus 72Ds, with their distinctive new oil cooler/side-plated rear wing design, appeared in their new colours for the first time in Argentina, where Texaco became the fuel sponsor.

The Buenos Aires Autodrome had not been used for a World Championship F1 race since 1960; now, in the intense heat, local man Carlos Reutemann stirred the spectators' patriotic emotions by capturing pole for Brabham. Walker had brake fade at the end of the main straight, which concentrated his mind! In the race Fittipaldi revelled in the conditions making a better tyre choice (he was the fastest Firestone runner) than Reutemann although it was to be Stewart's Tyrrell that led away. Once Fittipaldi had disposed of Reutemann he closed in on Stewart, demonstrating the competitiveness of the 72D, but an 'old' part of the rear suspension failed on lap 60 causing the Brazilian's retirement. The dusty circuit had claimed Walker on the opening lap when his new air box sucked dirt into the throttle slides and jammed them; having obtained tools to effect a repair he was excluded for receiving outside assistance!

Kyalami testing resulted in the gear changes being modified in a nearby aircraft repair shop; 900 miles of

Powered by his favourite 12-series DFV, Emerson Fittipaldi won the Spanish Grand Prix at Jarama even though his fire extinguisher had emptied itself over him early in the race. He managed to maintain his lead when rain fell.

running followed, during which Fittipaldi thoroughly learned the car with its new 'Surtees' magnesium wheels. During the South African GP meeting the 72Ds performed excellently on full tanks, but in practice Fittipaldi frighteningly lost a wheel and Walker coped with a recalcitrant gearbox. Having taken a mid-race lead for twelve laps the handling of Fittipaldi's car deteriorated as the fuel load lightened, and Hulme's McLaren got back past with sixteen laps to go. The severe understeering of the Lotus was also caused, according to Warr, by worn rear tyres. Walker finished tenth.

On their return to Britain, the Team visited Brands Hatch's Race of Champions, which Fittipaldi won with Walker ninth; the intelligent Brazilian would build on this victory to win the British GP at the same venue later in the year. Brazil was next on the schedule, where Interlagos hosted the non-championship Brazilian GP, in which Walker came fifth on a day when Fittipaldi inappropriately retired with suspension failure. Silverstone's International Trophy was then won by Fittipaldi, in the absence of Tyrrell and Ferrari, with Walker not qualifying, having crashed heavily at Club Corner in practice.

At Jarama, Fittipaldi chose to race 72D/7, which had his favourite 12-series DFV, after the spare suffered both engine and gear failures. On race day he selected slicks for the drying track only to find himself sitting in a pool of petrol from a leaking supplementary tank. On Chapman's instructions it was drained and the remaining tanks topped up, but Warr calculated that there would be barely sufficient fuel to complete the race! On the run to the first corner Fittipaldi had too much wheelspin and dropped to fifth; on the next lap he slipstreamed past Regazzoni's wild Ferrari only for his fire extinguisher to go off accidentally covering him in freezing extinguishant. By lap 7 he had stopped shivering sufficiently to slipstream past both Ickx (Ferrari)

and Hulme (McLaren) before, on lap 9, Stewart's Tyrrell was similarly disposed of. The rain then started and Fittipaldi's slicks allowed Ickx to close in as the team became increasingly concerned about the fuel situation. Extra was kept handy, but as the track dried again, Fittipaldi maintained his lead and eventually came home first, allowing Chapman to throw his cap in the air for the first time since October 1970. Ironically Walker ran out of fuel two laps from the end!

The next race was in Monaco, where initially practice was fine, with Fittipaldi being pleased to take pole although he thought he could have gone quicker. Times did not improve later in the then wet qualifying session, and race day, too, was unusually inclement for what Fittipaldi would describe as the most dangerous race he had ever driven in! In a ball of spray he was demoted to fourth on the first lap as Ickx, Beltoise and Regazzoni stormed away apparently oblivious to the conditions. Ickx got out of shape approaching the tunnel, and Fittipaldi seized third before gluing his eyes on to Regazzoni's gearbox tail-light. Fittipaldi blindly followed the light down the chicane escape road and in the mêlée Ickx got back past again. Whilst trying to lap Beuttler, the Lotus fell further behind on the treacherous track, which was so slippery that Fittipaldi kissed the Mirabeau guard rails in trying to pass Hill's Brabham. Eventually Fittipaldi took third place and a slender championship lead whilst having to hold his helmet's visor open! Walker was fourteenth.

Fittipaldi came second in Oulton Park's Gold Cup behind Hulme, whilst Walker retired with gearbox failure.

Following many complaints about Spa, the Belgian GP moved to the new track of Nivelles. This featureless circuit suited Lotus, with Fittipaldi being consistently fastest on his way to pole, during what was to be the Team's best race meeting of the season. Some of the success could be attributed to the 72D's rear wing,

At Nivelles for the Belgian Grand Prix, Lotus had its best race of 1972. Having disposed of Hulme and Regazzoni, the pole-sitting Emerson Fittipaldi made the most of the fact that his Lotus 72 was ideally suited to the circuit and won.

which had been moved further back with a reduced angle of attack. An extra oil cooler had also cured the previous high lubricant temperatures. Before the start, the mechanics fastidiously swept the track in front of Fittipaldi to help reduce wheelspin, but when the flag dropped Regazzoni and Hulme were still slightly faster away. The latter went wide and Fittipaldi was soon second behind the Ferrari, which fought him off several times at the hairpin. Under pressure from an approaching Ickx, Fittipaldi slipped past on lap 9 and promptly drove away from the Italian cars to win. Walker came fourteenth, having collided with De Adamich's Surtees and briefly spun out.

Much to the annoyance of the Roman spectators, Ferrari drove straight to Austria to test, ignoring Vallelunga's non-championship Gran Premio Republica Italiana, which Fittipaldi won with his rear wing mounted even further back and now bolted to the conical oil tank. Lotus then joined Ferrari in Austria.

Lotus fell from the pedestal of Nivelles and despaired during qualifying at Clermont-Ferrand for the French GP. Losing two engines, the Team were worried about their Firestone tyre choice and Fittipaldi felt that he needed more than four hours to learn the circuit. Stewart (Tyrrell), he felt, was better prepared, with extensive local knowledge. Rain prevented Fittipaldi from improving on his eighth place, and in the race the Goodyear-shod Amon, Hulme and Stewart headed the field. The better handling 72 benefited from retirements through punctures and Fittipaldi was second at the end, just managing to fend off the inspired Amon who was only 4.2 seconds behind. Walker had retired because of his gearbox.

On his return, Chapman contacted March driver Ronnie Peterson to set up a dinner appointment to discuss his driving for Lotus in 1973. Lotus had pursued the Swede before but this time there was competition from not only March, but also from BRM and the embryonic Shadow. Chapman was convinced that if he could sign Peterson he would be World Champion within two years.

Rumours of Trimmer, Graham McRae or Jody Scheckter joining the driver strength at Brands Hatch came to nothing and the usual pairing appeared in Kent for the European GP. For the first time the race was sponsored by John Player and it was opportune that Fittipaldi should take the 72's fourth victory in beautiful sunny conditions. The same sponsorship of both Team and event put a lot of pressure on Lotus, who won thanks to superior Firestone tyres. In practice Ferrari's modified suspension improved their competitiveness with Ickx taking pole. At the start Ickx's Ferrari accelerated better, but soon smoke appeared from the engine's left-hand side causing Fittipaldi to sit back and wait whilst hoping that there would be no repetition of the cracked brake discs that had occurred in practice. Meanwhile Stewart's Tyrrell was closing up to make a trio of drivers fighting for the lead. Unwittingly Walker was part of a confusion at Druids that made Ickx go wide, but Fittipaldi couldn't take advantage and in fact dropped back. It took six laps for the trio to regroup and the battle continued for another 20 tours. In lapping Wilson Fittipaldi, Stewart slid wide and Emerson Fittipaldi was now through to second, which he held until Ickx retired, leaving the Brazilian a clear road right through to Chapman's cap-throwing victory

The British Grand Prix at Brands Hatch was appropriately backed by John Player, and Fittipaldi won the fight with Ickx (Ferrari) and Stewart (Tyrrell) for the lead.

welcome. There was much relieved celebration in Kent, especially as the winning car's front tyre deflated as it was wheeled into the transporter!

Before the German GP Lotus tested tyres at the Nurburgring only to suffer gearbox troubles, with Fittipaldi even having vibration pain in his teeth! In official qualifying he excelled, taking third grid position. Both 72s had been jacked up to minimize bottoming, but Walker still damaged his rear suspension during a rain shower. Fittipaldi made a flying start only to be usurped by Ickx, Regazzoni and Peterson. Exiting Brunnchen on lap 2, Fittipaldi slipped past again, only for the wild Regazzoni and the even wilder Peterson to

get even a little later. At this point, Fittipaldi's gearbox played up and he lost both third and top gear. Passing the pits on lap 11 the Team appeared agitated and Fittipaldi realized that the rear of his car was ablaze. The gearbox had inexplicably seized, exploded and caught fire, leaving Fittipaldi to abandon ship and supervise the extinguishing of the conflagration. Walker's broken oil tank had already caused his retirement.

In Austria, Fittipaldi had handling problems, but the spare was smooth enough to give him pole. He subsequently raced the spare, which had exactly the same chassis and engine that he had used the previous year in Austria! Stewart's Tyrrell was quickest away and the Scot led the first twenty-three laps. Regazzoni's Ferrari also beat Fittipaldi away, but the 72 handled better with a full fuel load, and after five laps the Brazilian got past and was able to set off after Stewart. The Tyrrell understeered approaching the Bosch corner, and Fittipaldi seized the advantage to get past and draw away from his opponent's deteriorating car. Hulme's McLaren started to threaten towards the end, especially when Fittipaldi had trouble overtaking Galli's Tecno, but all was well for Lotus to win and put the Championship in sight. Walker had blown up one of the Team's two 12-series DFVs after only six laps and he was rested until Watkins Glen.

Before the next GP, Lotus entered Fittipaldi in the Brands Hatch Rothmans 50,000 Libre Race, which he won, thereby bringing a very handy £10,000 prize back to Hethel. On the same day Chapman finally signed Peterson as no. 2 driver for 1973. The final reason that the Swede signed was his observation of the immaculate organization of Lotus.

The World Championship came that much closer after Emerson Fittipaldi won in Austria. Using the same car as the previous year, he fought off Hulme's late-charging McLaren, having passed Stewart and Regazzoni.

Fittipaldi's Championship

Monza was critical for Fittipaldi, and he didn't need the news that the Lotus transporter had crashed just outside Milan. Whilst one mechanic, Steve Gooda, was rushed to hospital, the inverted lorry revealed Fittipaldi's severely damaged race car – it had a hole gouged right through it. A replacement 72 was rushed to Monza to enable Fittipaldi to mount his challenge after all; he was again entered by Worldwide Racing for fear of a second car being impounded by the police. The race would almost certainly decide the Championship and Fittipaldi could become the youngest-ever World Champion. Would, though, Monza's bitter-sweet relationship with Lotus continue?

Mathematically, for Hulme and Stewart to be champion, they would have to win all the remaining races, and additionally Fittipaldi would have to finish lower than fourth in Italy. He only managed sixth in practice, and in the race day warm-up a brake disc caused the front brakes to vibrate, requiring a lengthy change on Girling's advice. An hour before the start a fuel leak was found and the offending tank was replaced just in time! Stewart's clutch gave out at the start so Hulme was then the only challenger. The Brazilian initially ran in third place behind the two Ferraris, only for Regazzoni's to spin out in flames having collided with Pace's March. Whilst planning his attack on leader Ickx, Fittipaldi conserved his tyres only to be confronted by the Ferrari slowing with electrical gremlins nine laps short of the flag. An interminable series of laps followed until Fittipaldi was able to breathe again, when he passed the chequered flag and finally knew that he was the first Brazilian World Champion. The entire Team were elated as were the several thousand Brazilian spectators in the Italian park.

Firestone announced their withdrawal from F1 at Monza but the Team still went tyre-testing in Canada. Now the World Champion Fittipaldi confidently travelled to Mosport for the Labatt's 50 GP and Wisell returned for the North American races. In practice the much repaired 72D didn't perform as well as the Goodyear runners, such as McLaren. A race-morning mist halted the proceedings and in the race Fittipaldi's car lacked speed on the straight. After a bad and confused start, his gearbox started to lose second and third gears and the front wing broke – giving him a nasty moment to gather up – and he was relegated to a lowly eleventh-place finish. A defective fuel hose brought Wisell's race to a premature halt even though Ron Tauranac had been trying to sort out the Swedish driver's handling problems.

The US GP was abysmal for Lotus as the highest finisher of the three cars was to be Wisell in tenth

After the transporter had crashed, Fittipaldi's replacement Lotus 72 carried him both to Italian victory and the 1972 World Championship. He had cleverly conserved his tyres, much to the delight of his Brazilian fans!

position, even though he didn't possess fourth gear. Lotus was criticized for running three cars by those who thought the team's efforts were being dissipated, but Warr strenuously denied this. Firestone produced unsuitable tyres, having ceased production some time before, and Lotus practice times were well behind the Goodyear-contracted teams. Fittipaldi recorded his worst qualifying performance of the year and a calculated risk was taken to run him on unscrubbed qualifiers in the race. This didn't work and wheel imperfections (16in rear wheels replaced the 17in versions, which were cracking) affected performance too. A series of pitstops for tyres resulted in Fittipaldi retiring in an untypical end to his World Championship year.

Brands Hatch hosted the John Player Victory Meeting in which Fittipaldi took pole but retired after a bad tyre choice and engine failure.

At season's end Fittipaldi complimented his mechanics – Eddie Dennis, Steve Gooda, Jim Pickles and Trevor Seaman – who had prepared cars to a very high standard in very difficult situations against impossible schedules. Walker left wishing that he had had the same reliability as the no. 1 driver. Over five seasons John Player had spent half a million pounds on Lotus and Geoffrey Kent said that, 'as a public company you have to be able to justify that sort of expenditure to your shareholders. We have proved over the years that our involvement is well justified.'

In November Australian Ralph Bellamy arrived at Lotus to assist Chapman with design matters. In December Peterson tested the 72 and was immediately impressed by the rear weight bias as compared with his old March.

TEAM LOTUS AND PRIVATE LOTUS ENTRIES RESULTS 1972

Drivers:
Emerson Fittipaldi: Brazilian; Dave Walker: Australian; Reine Wisell: Swedish
Car:
Lotus 72D Engine: Ford Cosworth DFV 3-litre

CAR	CHASSIS	DRIVER	PRACTICE	SESSION	GRID	RACE	LAPS	%	REASON	CHAMPIONSHIP POSITION	POINTS
ARGENTINE GP, Buenos Aires – 23rd January – 95 L, 197.46 miles (317.78km) (138)											
72 D	5	Fittipaldi	1m 13.28s	2	5th	R	60	63.1	Suspension	–	–
72 D	6	Walker	1m 15.55s	2	20th	DSQ	8	8.4	Out/Assist	–	–
S AFRICAN GP, Kyalami – 4th March – 79 L, 201.45 miles (324.21km) (139)											
72 D	5	Fittipaldi	1m 17.4s	2/3	3rd	2nd	79	100.0	–	3rd	6
72 D	6	Walker	1m 18.7s	3	19th	10th	78	98.7	–	–	–
SPANISH GP, Jarama – 1st May – 90 L, 190.38 miles (306.39km) (140)											
72 D	7	Fittipaldi	1m 19.26s	2	3rd	1st W	90	100.0	–	1st=	15
72 D	5	Walker	1m 22.74s	2	24th	9th NR	87	96.6	Fuel	–	–
		Fittipaldi	1m 20.64s	2							
MONACO GP, Monte Carlo – 14th May – 80 L, 156.34 miles (251.60km) (141)											
72 D	7	Fittipaldi	1m 21.4s	2	1st P	3rd	79	98.7	–	1st	19
72 D	5	Walker	1m 24.0s	2	14th	14th	75	93.7	–	–	–
BELGIAN GP, Nivelles – 4th June – 85 L, 196.69 miles (316.54km) (142)											
72 D	7	Fittipaldi	1m 11.43s	3	1st P	1st W	85	100.0	–	1st	28
72 D	6	Walker	1m 12.76s	3	12th	14th	79	92.9	–	–	–
72 D	5	(Spare)									
FRENCH GP, Charade – 2nd July – 38 L, 190.19 miles (306.09km) (143)											
72 D	7	Fittipaldi	2m 58.1s	2	8th	2nd	38	100.0	–	1st	34
72 D	6	Walker	3m 04.7s	2	22nd	R	34	89.4	Transmission	–	–
72 D	5	(Spare)									
72D	3	Charlton	3m 11.6s	–	DNS	–	–	–	–	–	–
BRITISH GP, Brands Hatch – 15th July – 76 L, 201.40 miles (324.12km) (144)											
72 D	7	Fittipaldi	1m 22.6s	4	2nd	1st W	76	100.0	–	1st	43
72 D	6	Walker	1m 24.4s	4	15th	R	59	77.6	Suspension	–	–
72 D	5	(Spare)									
72 D LS	3	Charlton	1m 25.6s	–	24th	R	21	27.6	Gears	–	–
GERMAN GP, Nurburgring – 30th July – 14 L, 198.65 miles (319.69km) (145)											
72 D	6	Walker	7m 29.5s	3	23rd	R	6	42.8	Oil tank	–	–
72 D	7	Fittipaldi	7m 09.9s	3	3rd	R	10	71.4	Fire	1st	43
72 D	5	(Spare)									
72 D LS	3	Charlton	7m 34.1s	–	26th	R	4	28.5	Driver ill	–	–
AUSTRIAN GP, Österreichring – 13th August – 54 L, 198.34 miles (319.19km) (146)											
72 D	5	Fittipaldi	1m 35.97s	1	1st P	1st W	54	100.0	–	1st	52
72 D	6	Walker	1m 38.81s	2	19th	R	6	11.1	Engine	–	–
72 D	7	(Spare)									
ITALIAN GP, Monza – 10th September – 55 L, 197.36 miles (317.62km) (147)											
72 D WW	5	Fittipaldi	1m 36.29s	1	6th	1st W	55	100.0	–	1st	61
CANADIAN GP, Mosport – 24th September – 80 L, 196.70 miles (316.56km) (148)											
72 D	7	Fittipaldi	1m 14.4s	3	4th	11th	78	97.5	–	1st	61
72 D	6	Wisell	1m 16.0s	3	16th	14th NR	65	81.2	Fuel line	–	–
72 D	5	(Spare)									
US GP, Watkins Glen – 8th October – 59 L, 199.25 miles (320.66km) (149)											
72 D	6	Wisell	1m 43.543s	1	15th	10th	57	96.6	–	–	–
72 D	5	Fittipaldi	1m 42.400s	1	8th	R	17	28.8	Suspension	1st	61
72 D	7	Walker	1m 50.600s	1	29th	R	44	74.5	Oil loss	–	–

Key:
DNS = Did Not Start
DSQ = Disqualified
NR = Not Running
WW = Worldwide Racing
R = Retired
L = Laps
P = Pole
W = Win

Private Entries:
LS = Lucky Strike Racing

WORLD CHAMPIONSHIP RESULTS 1972

Position	Driver	Points
1	**Emerson Fittipaldi**	**61**

CONSTRUCTORS' CUP 1972

Position	Constructor	Points
1	**JPS (Lotus-Ford)**	**61**

1973

Fittipaldi and Peterson

Fittipaldi and Peterson were now team-mates with the Swede, who brought his trusty mechanic Keith Leighton with him from March. Even though he knew the problem of being a Lotus no. 2 driver, Peterson was confident about his Championship chances with Lotus. Peter Warr had promised a joint no. 1 arrangement, and as reigning Champion Fittipaldi had largely 'achieved' already, Peterson became the Team's charger. There was an agreement, too, that if the situation arose, both drivers would allow each other to win their home races. Peterson's move was to prove most beneficial as he was to take nine of the season's pole positions and never qualified lower than fourth.

Now using Goodyear tyres, Lotus and particularly Peterson, were plagued by unreliability in South America. In practice in the heat of Buenos Aires, Peterson was spectacular as he opposite-locked and kerb-hopped whilst establishing the correct tyre mixture for his 72D, which now had a slightly wider rear track. The consistent Fittipaldi, though, qualified second just behind Regazzoni's BRM, and the latter led the first twenty-eight laps before falling back. The two Lotuses now trailed Cevert's Tyrrell with Fittipaldi leading Peterson, but the Swede kept in touch until, on lap 67, he retired with failing oil pressure. Stewart's Tyrrell had begun to harry Fittipaldi, but on lap 75 the Scot slowed with tyre trouble and the Lotus was promoted to second, before ten laps from the finish, Fittipaldi forced past Cevert at the hairpin. A cascade of thousands of balloons were released as Fittipaldi finally crossed the line in first place as a South American winner, if not an Argentinian!

The media made much of the perceived rivalry between Fittipaldi and Peterson, claiming the former was desperate to win his home event in Brazil; as outsiders they were unaware of the agreement between the two drivers.

The Lotus v. Tyrrell battle continued on the 'new' Interlagos circuit where Fittipaldi appeared for the first time as reigning World Champion in front of his adoring home crowd. The Team's intensive testing paid off, as in practice both drivers (Peterson overcoming an old neck injury to take pole) dominated with the new suspension proving unbeatable. Fittipaldi led the Brazilian GP from flag to flag and finished 13 seconds

Emerson Fittipaldi drove more conservatively than Peterson in Argentina and reaped the reward. He caused the South American crowd to release thousands of balloons when he passed Cevert for the lead, ten laps from the flag.

ahead of Stewart to the particular pleasure of his father, who was commentating for the Brazilian media. The crowd exploded with joy at the home win as fireworks were released everywhere. Peterson started badly and retired with a broken rear wheel rim after only five laps.

At Kyalami a variety of wheel types were on offer after Peterson's Brazilian failure, and the rear wings were flattened off for more speed. Stewart had a brake failure at Crowthorne and smote the wall very hard indeed; the Tyrrell challenge wilted as the McLarens proved very quick, Scheckter taking pole with Fittipaldi second. The Lotus momentarily led the first few yards before the McLarens regained the advantage. On lap 3 Charlton's Lucky Strike Lotus 72D spun at Crowthorne, triggering a nasty incident in which Regazzoni's BRM caught fire. The Swiss was rescued by Mike Hailwood, but Stewart took the lead he was not to lose in an allegedly opportunistic way from Hulme as the debris was being cleared. Both McLaren and Lotus vainly protested Stewart's actions. Peterson's throttle linkage broke whilst he was in fifth place on lap 49, causing his retirement as Fittipaldi salvaged fastest lap on his way to third.

A fortnight later at the Brands Hatch Race of Champions, JPS suffered a double retirement with Fittipaldi falling victim to his fuel metering unit and Peterson to his gearbox. The 72s were now in 'E' specification to conform with the new 'deformable structure' regulations, which increased their weight by about 30lb

(13.5kg) whilst reducing fuel tankage to 55 gallons (250 litres). Their rear uprights were now also cast and in overall dimensions they were 0.8in (20mm) wider, with the radiator intakes slightly more sculptured.

In testing prior to Silverstone's International Trophy, Peterson had an altercation with an F3 car and 72E/6 was shunted heavily in an accident that had commenced at Maggots and ended at Becketts. Back in Norfolk 72E/8 was hurriedly prepared for Peterson, who would take second in the race whilst Fittipaldi retired with flywheel failure.

Zolder testing of a new large low-drag rear wing was undertaken on the way to Barcelona, and this considerably helped Fittipaldi in scoring Lotus's 50th World Championship win. The narrow-track 72 was the intended race configuration, but Fittipaldi disliked the new rear suspension and reverted to the spare. Peterson was nearly 2 seconds faster than Fittipaldi and 1.7 seconds clear of the rest of the field in taking pole! The mechanics, though, found that his gearbox internals were breaking up under the stress. On the rev-limiter in the race Peterson tore into the lead but pressurized his gearbox too much, so it let him down at two-thirds distance. This critical retirement subsequently affected his Championship aspirations. Fittipaldi had fought off Cevert before picking up a puncture, which meant that when Stewart and Peterson retired he was promoted to the front with a left rear tyre that was virtually flat! To his credit he held off Cevert and Reutemann to win. This result had taken Lotus past Ferrari's total number

His left rear tyre almost flat, Fittipaldi wins Barcelona's Spanish Grand Prix. This was the fiftieth World Championship win for Team Lotus, beating Ferrari's previous record. A new rear wing had helped considerably.

of wins, which was a remarkable feat: Chapman's cars had won no less than 24 per cent of the 213 World Championship races to date. Amongst many other ac-colades the BARC awarded Chapman one of their coveted gold medals to mark the achievement.

Zolder's European GP was full of political intrigue because of the poor track surface, which caused great controversy amongst the drivers and team owners. The 72s had identical fuel pick-up problems and Fittipaldi insisted that this might have been cured had there not been two equal no. 1 drivers. He felt he could other-wise have won rather than taken third place, as the Tyrrells of Stewart and Cevert finished one and two. Peterson crashed three times in Belgium; firstly, in practice he crashed the T-car at the chicane when his brakes failed, and secondly whilst allowing Oliver's Shadow to pass. On race day he forced himself into the lead on the first lap in the repaired 72E/6 but crashed for the third time at the same spot as another five cars! Chapman was very displeased even though the race crash had been caused by the gravel-like track surface. The introverted Swede was also suffering from flu.

At the end of May the Italian authorities announced that they were to charge Chapman with manslaughter for Rindt's death at Monza three years previously. This was despite the wreckage of 72/2 never having been shown to a member of the Team.

Stewart's Tyrrell dominated Monaco, with only Fit-tipaldi remotely challenging him, even though the 72's gearbox broke off at one point! Fittipaldi climbed from fifth to second place by lap 5, where he remained until the flag as Stewart dictated the race from the front. The Brazilian tried everything he knew, getting to within 1.3 seconds at the line, but could not usurp the leader as the crowd urged him on. Peterson had led the first seven laps and eventually took third, which was

the boost he needed as the next race was his home Swedish GP, for which he had that agreement with Fittipaldi . . .

Peterson promptly took pole at Anderstorp in char-acteristic oversteering style whilst actually complaining of understeer! For the first sixty-nine laps, a home win seemed a virtual certainty as both Peterson and Fit-tipaldi headed the two Tyrrells. With only ten laps to go Peterson had every right to expect to win his first GP, and he was to lead all but the last two laps as behind him Fittipaldi dutifully fended off Stewart's Tyrrell. The Brazilian's brakes and gearbox then played up, only for Stewart, too, to lose his brakes as he was about to try to pass Peterson. The Swede cruelly suf-fered an eleventh-hour puncture on lap 79, which per-mitted Hulme's McLaren to snatch the lead. A shattered Peterson saw his potential victory snatched from him literally within sight of the flag and he could only battle on to second in front of the equally deflated crowd.

At Paul Ricard the 72s had their rear aerofoils, com-plete with oil tank and radiator, mounted ten inches further back, where the air flow provided much greater downforce. Myriad mechanical troubles hindered practice, openly raising stress levels within the Team. Fittipaldi was the faster, with Peterson very worried about his fuel system after the warm-up. Chapman forecast a Lotus win and Peterson duly delivered by a margin of 40 seconds over Cevert's Tyrrell. Scheckter's McLaren led the early laps, the M23 being quicker down the long Mistral straight than the 72E. When Peterson's down-on power engine wouldn't let him make an impression, Fittipaldi took over, but during a potential overtaking manoeuvre at Virage du Pont on lap 41, he and Scheckter collided, causing both their retirements. Peterson nipped through to cruise for

The rear wing now ten inches further back, Peterson holds off Stewart's Tyrrell at Paul Ricard. Even though he had a down-on-power engine he won, but for the last thirteen laps his heart was in his mouth.

thirteen laps to the flag. Remembering his Swedish puncture he had his heart in his mouth in the last few laps as worrying noises came from both his gearbox and engine, but on this occasion everything held together.

Having at last achieved his first win, a much more relaxed Peterson almost perceptibly started to mature. At Silverstone the British GP was halted after two laps when Scheckter's McLaren had almost wiped out most of the following field in front of the pits. Luckily neither Lotus was directly involved although a slow-away Fittipaldi – he had been baulked by Reutemann – had had a lucky escape whilst threading through the carnage. Chapman had taken over the Team's management in Warr's absence – he was suffering from a slipped disc – and Peterson had been on pole despite fuel-pump troubles, with Fittipaldi fifth. Before the crash Stewart had slipped past Peterson on the inside of Becketts in a surprise move before the red flags came out. Peterson did not fall for this at the restart, and he led for another 37 laps, pressurized all the time by Stewart. After the Scot missed a gear and had gone grass-cutting at Stowe, Peterson continued, only to run into severe oversteer; Fittipaldi almost reeled him in only to retire with a broken constant-velocity joint. Revson's McLaren took up the chase, getting past the ill-handling JPS and leaving Peterson to come home second.

At Silverstone an Italian judge had discussions with the Formula One Constructors regarding the legal position surrounding their competing in Italy and in particular at Monza. Reassurance was wanted that the legal problems still affecting Chapman three years after Rindt's death would not involve them. No such assurance was given.

The Lotus 72Ds boasted enlarged air intakes for Zandvoort's Dutch GP. In Saturday practice Fittipaldi and Peterson circulated in formation until the Brazilian felt a momentary vibration milliseconds before the centre of his left front wheel pulled out on the entry to Pullevelt. The ensuing mighty collision with the Armco wrote off 72/5 and trapped Fittipaldi in the car. Luckily Mike Hailwood stopped at the scene and with the help of a spectating Tyrrell mechanic the young Brazilian was freed. Amazingly, after a quick check-up he went out again to take a subdued sixteenth on the grid, whilst Peterson annexed pole using a controversial set of Goodyear tyres.

Fittipaldi, who felt unable to last seventy-two laps as a result of his foot injuries, only drove two laps before retirement in a race now widely remembered for the tragic death of Roger Williamson, and David Purley's heroic rescue attempts. Peterson extended his lead for sixty-three laps before he slowed with handling and brake problems to see his championship hopes effectively evaporate. Having lost gears with only six laps to go, his DFV blew, leaving Stewart and Cevert to take a Tyrrell one-two on a very sad day.

The Nurburgring's German GP was another Tyrrell one-two, although Lotus had been hopeful when Peterson took second-fastest practice lap; Fittipaldi was

That rear aerofoil moved even further back as Peterson handed the lead in Austria to Fittipaldi; he inherited it back again when the Brazilian's fuel system failed. Peterson had driven maturely for his second Grand Prix win.

way down in fourteenth place. On lap one Peterson retired from third place at Adenau with a broken distributor and Fittipaldi never really featured, thanks to an engine with fuel pressure trouble; he finished sixth, behind his brother.

Austria was to be the first of two mature races for Peterson. Whilst the rear wings of the 72s were mounted even further back than previously, it had been agreed in advance that if the Swede found himself leading he would let Fittipaldi through to win, as the Brazilian had the better chance of taking the title. In the event Peterson fulfilled his obligations to the letter as, having headed the field and fended off Hulme's McLaren, he let Fittipaldi through on lap 16. He was, though, to get the lead back on lap 49 (six laps from the end) when the Brazilian's fuel system pulled apart and he frustratedly ground to a halt at the Texaco chicane. Peterson's fortuitous win meant that only Cevert and Fittipaldi (who would have to win all the following races to stand a chance) could now challenge Stewart for the title. The Scot only needed to come fourth at

Monza to take the Championship. The Italian GP, though, would be full of controversy, especially where Brazil was concerned . . .

Before Monza it had again been agreed that should he be leading, Peterson would let Fittipaldi through to win in a seemingly obvious tactic. When combined with an ill-handling car, Fittipaldi's foot troubles in practice left him in fourth place as Peterson took his season's seventh pole position. In the race the two Lotuses led the field into the Curva Grande and they were never to be headed, although Hulme tried briefly, before spinning. Stewart drove through the field after a puncture to capture that much required fourth place and the Championship, as Lotus scored their first one-two in a GP since Kyalami in 1968. The winner, though, was Peterson with Fittipaldi a few feet behind! During the race Chapman had apparently made the controversial decision to let Peterson win. Fittipaldi was furious. Chapman and Warr knew that he needed not only to win at Monza, but also at Mosport and Watkins Glen to snatch the title, and as this seemed

Controversially Chapman permitted Peterson to win at Monza, and having started from pole he led home a Lotus one-two. Stewart took the Championship with fourth, but in the background a furious Fittipaldi decided to leave Lotus.

TEAM LOTUS AND PRIVATE LOTUS ENTRY RESULTS 1973

Drivers:
Emerson Fittipaldi: Brazilian; Ronnie Peterson: Swedish
Car:
Lotus 72D/E Engine: Ford Cosworth DFV 3-litre
Lotus 16   Coventry Climax 1.9-litre

CAR	CHASSIS	DRIVER	PRACTICE	SESSION	GRID	RACE	LAPS	%	REASON	CHAMPIONSHIP POSITION	POINTS
ARGENTINE GP, Buenos Aires – 28th January – 96 L, 199.53 miles (321.12km) (150)											
72 D	7	Fittipaldi	1m 10.84s	4	2nd	1st W	96	100.0	–	1st	9
Fastest Lap: 1m 11.22s – 105.078mph (169.107kph) on lap 79											
72 D	8	Peterson	1m 11.06s	4	5th	R	67	69.7	Oil	–	–
BRAZILIAN GP, Interlagos – 11th February – 40 L, 197.84 miles (318.40km) (151)											
72 D	7	Fittipaldi	2m 30.7s	4	2nd	1st W	40	100.0	–	1st	18
Fastest Lap*: 2m 35.0s – 114.877mph (184.877kph) on lap 20											
72 D	8	Peterson	2m 30.5s	2	1st P	R	5	12.5	Wheel	–	–
S AFRICAN GP, Kyalami – 3rd March – 79 L, 201.45 miles (324.21km) (152)											
72 D	7	Fittipaldi	1m 16.41s	3	2nd	3rd	79	100.0	–	1st	22
Fastest Lap: 1m 17.10s – 119.071mph (191.626kph) on lap 76											
72 D	8	Peterson	1m 16.44s	2	4th	11th	73	92.4	–	–	–
72 D L	3	Charlton	1m 18.92s	–	13th	R	3	3.7	Bodywork	–	–
SPANISH GP, Barcelona – 29th April – 75 L, 176.62 miles (284.25km) (153)											
72 E	5	Fittipaldi	1m 23.7s	3	7th	1st W	75	100.0	–	1st	31
72 E	8	Peterson	1m 21.8s	3	1st P	R	57	76.0	Gears	–	–
Fastest Lap: 1m 23.8s – 101.186mph (162.844kph) on lap 13											
72 D	7	(Spare)									
EUROPEAN GP, Zolder – 20th May – 70 L, 183.55 miles (295.40km) (154)											
72 E	7	Fittipaldi	1m 23.44s	3	9th	3rd	70	100.0	–	1st	35
72 E	6	Peterson	1m 22.46s	3	1st P	R	42	60.0	Accident	–	–
72 D	5	(Spare)									
72 D	8	(Spare)									
MONACO GP, Monte Carlo – 3rd June – 78 L, 158.87 miles (255.68km) (155)											
72 E	7	Fittipaldi	1m 28.1s	2	5th	2nd	78	100.0	–	1st	41
Fastest Lap: 1m 28.1s – 82.231mph (133.947kph) on lap 78											
72 E	6	Peterson	1m 27.7s	2	2nd	3rd	77	98.7	–	9th	4
72 D	5	(Spare)									
SWEDISH GP, Anderstorp – 17th June – 80 L, 199.73 miles (321.44km) (156)											
72 E	6	Peterson	1m 23.081s	2	1st P	2nd	80	100.0	–	6th	10
72 E	7	Fittipaldi	1m 24.084s	3	4th	12th NR	76	95.0	Gearbox	1st	41
72 D	5	(Spare)									
72 D	8	(Spare)									
FRENCH GP, Ricard – 1st July – 54 L, 194.95 miles (313.74km) (157)											
72 E	6	Peterson	1m 49.45s	1	5th	1st W	54	100.0	–	4th=	19
72 E	5	Fittipaldi	1m 49.36s	3	3rd	R	41	75.9	Accident	2nd	41
72 D	7	(Spare)									
72 D	8	(Spare)									
BRITISH GP, Silverstone – 14th July – 67 L, 196.11 miles (315.60km) (158)											
72 E	6	Peterson	1m 16.3s	2	1st P	2nd	67	100.0	–	4th	25
72 E	5	Fittipaldi	1m 16.7s	2	5th	R	36	53.7	CV-joint	2nd	41
72 D	7	(Spare)									
72 D	8	(Spare)									
DUTCH GP, Zandvoort – 29th July – 72 L, 189.06 miles (304.27km) (159)											
72 E	6	Peterson	1m 19.47s	4	1st P	11th NR	66	91.6	Engine	4th	25
Fastest Lap: 1m 20.31s – 117.710mph (189.435kph) on lap 42											
72 E	7	Fittipaldi	1m 22.24s	4	16th	R	2	2.7	Illness	2nd	41
72 D	5	(Spare)									
GERMAN GP, Nurburgring – 5th August – 14 L, 198.65 miles (319.69km) (160)											
72 E	7	Fittipaldi	7m 19.7s	1	14th	6th	14	100.0	–	3rd	42
72 E	6	Peterson	7m 08.3s	1	2nd	R	0	0.0	Distributor	4th	25
72 D	8	(Spare)									

AUSTRIAN GP, Österreichring – 19th August – 54 L, 198.34 miles (319.19km) (161)

72 E	6	Peterson	1m 25.37s	2	2nd	1st W	54	100.0	–	4th	34
72 E	7	Fittipaldi	1m 34.98s	4	1st P	R	48	8.8	Fuel	3rd	42
72 D	8	(Spare)									

ITALIAN GP, Monza – 9th September – 55 L, 197.36 miles (317.62km) (162)

72 E	6	Peterson	1m 34.8s	4	1st P	1st W	55	100.0	–	4th	43
72 E	7	Fittipaldi	1m 35.68s	4	4th	2nd	55	100.0	–	2nd	48
72 D	8	(Spare)									

CANADIAN GP, Mosport – 23rd September – 80 L, 196.70 miles (316.56km) (163)

72 E	7	Fittipaldi	1m 15.035s	3	5th	2nd	80	100.0	–	2nd	100.0
Fastest Lap: 1m 15.496s – 117.256mph (188.706kph)											
72 E	6	Peterson	1m 13.697s	2	1st P	R	16	20.0	Accident	4th	43
72 D	8	(Spare)									

US GP, Watkins Glen – 7th October – 59 L, 190.25 miles (320.66km) (164)

72 E	7	Peterson	1m 39.657s	2	1st P	1st W	59	100.0	–	3rd	52
72 E	6	Fittipaldi	1m 40.393s	2	3rd	6th	59	100.0	–	2nd	55
72 D	8	(Spare)									

Key:
★ = Shared with Denny Hulme
NR = Not Running
W = Win
P = Pole
R = Retired

Private Lotus Entries:
L = Scribante – Lucky Strike Racing

unlikely they had allowed Peterson to remain ahead. This action gave credence to those who felt that Chapman favoured the Swede, but whatever the truth, Fittipaldi decided to leave Lotus.

The Canadian race at Mosport Park was very confused, involving both tyre stops and a pace-car period that were a result of the wet conditions. After eighty laps it was widely assumed that Fittipaldi had won but the result was given to Revson, with even McLaren unable to substantiate his premier place. The two drivers were both ushered into the winner's paddock only for the American to be selected; various protests were lodged and rejected. Peterson, who had again started from pole, retired on the sixteenth lap with broken suspension after he had jumped the kerbs and glanced the barriers because of a slow puncture. This was a race to forget. In Canada Fittipaldi continued discussions about the 1974 season. He required an acknowledgement from Chapman that he had been wrong in permitting Peterson to win at Monza, and

Badly shocked by Cevert's death in practice, the pole-sitting Peterson took a flag-to-flag victory at Watkins Glen and his fourth win of 1973. Lotus also won the Constructors' Cup for a record sixth time.

whilst this was apparently given, no overall agreement was reached.

At Watkins Glen Peterson was particularly affected by the death in practice of François Cevert, as the two had been friendly rivals throughout their respective racing careers. Peterson had been one of the first to try and rescue his friend, who was sadly beyond help. Practice was not a cheerful procedure after the accident and Chapman appreciated that Peterson was unable to concentrate on improving his car. On 12in wheels, this was transformed overnight by Chapman thereby enabling 'Super-Swede' to take both pole and his fourth victory of the year. Peterson led from start to finish, coming under pressure from Hunt for fifty-six laps, whilst the oversteering Fittipaldi eventually came in sixth to conclude his racing career with Lotus.

Lotus won the Constructors' Cup for a record sixth time and Warr was to receive the award from Prince Metternich at the FIA prize-giving in December. By the time Chapman had made a large financial bid to keep Fittipaldi along with a promise that he could be no. 1 driver, it was too late. The apparent favouritism shown Peterson had irritated him, and he felt too that the Team's mechanical expertise had been overstretched in 1973 with two no. 1 drivers. His move to McLaren would yield him the 1974 World Championship.

Both the Team and Warr had confidence in Peterson, particularly was he was such a good tester. In October, to back him up, Belgian Jacky Ickx – who had eight Grand Prix wins to his credit already with both Brabham and Ferrari – signed for the Team to establish a very strong driver line-up for 1974.

Meanwhile two 72s were sold to John Love's Team Gunston and would be raced in the 1974 South African F1 Championship by Ian Scheckter and John Love. The two cars would join that of Dave Charlton, which had been in South Africa since the end of 1971.

WORLD CHAMPIONSHIP RESULTS 1973

Position	Driver	Points
1	Jackie Stewart	71
2	**Emerson Fittipaldi**	**55**
3	**Ronnie Peterson**	**52**

CONSTRUCTORS' CUP 1973

Position	Constructor	Points
1	**JPS (Lotus-Ford)**	**92**

━━━━ 1974 ━━━━

The start of the new season was overshadowed by the worldwide fuel crisis, which caused some commentators to criticize the apparent squandering of valuable fossil fuels by motor sport. Amidst fears that the sport might be curtailed completely, F1 escaped largely unscathed as Lotus fell back on the faithful 72s.

In Argentina, an oversteering Peterson snatched pole in the last few seconds of practice; the 72's rear wing had been moved inwards to satisfy new regulations, but brake, tyre and trailing battery problems in the race meant that, having led the opening two laps, he had to stop and dropped right back. Ickx learned his new car and had a complicated practice, but got as high as third in the race only to retire with a failed transmission.

The fanatical Brazilian crowd applauded Fittipaldi's home win for McLaren. An unwell Peterson suffered from both the high temperatures as well as from a stomach disorder and he finished the day in hospital, having been sixth at the time the rain-affected race was prematurely halted. Reutemann had led at the start, only for Fittipaldi and Peterson to lock horns and for the latter to take the lead after three laps. Fittipaldi drove round the outside of Peterson twelve laps later whilst the late-starting Merzario was being lapped. Shortly afterwards Peterson's right rear tyre punctured and he dropped out of contention, as Ickx drove carefully to third on the flooded track.

Lotus 76 – JPS Mk 1

For some time Chapman had wanted to try automatic transmission in F1 and the clutch part of this system was to be tried in the 76, which was also the first design to be entirely created around the colours of John Player Special. It was therefore to be known as the JPS Mk 1.

The 76 was unveiled publicly in mid-February 1974, having been tested by Peterson on St. Valentine's Day, which was his thirtieth birthday. The Bellamy and Chapman design was initially 100lb (45kg) lighter than its predecessor and considerably stronger, but it later gained much more weight. The innovative car incorporated electrics and hydraulics to allow the option of two-pedal control, with the conventional clutch pedal being needed only to pull away before a gear-lever switch actuated a hydraulic substitute. The Borg and Beck two-place automatic clutch was then operated by an AP control system with 800psi hydraulics. The driver's left foot was left free for braking and the right foot for accelerating. The distinctive feature of the 76 was the biplane rear wing, which was so designed to allow the lower of the two wings to be removed to reduce drag on faster circuits.

With its distinctive 'Pinocchio' nose and removable biplane rear wing, the Lotus 76 was a brave step forward. Two-pedal control was also an option but Peterson, seen here at Silverstone's International Trophy, lost faith in the 76, which was later junked.

It should have débuted at the Brands Hatch Race of Champions but the three-day week affecting the country meant that there were neither sufficient spares nor engines available. After the toss of a coin Ickx drove the 72E and in fact won, proving to be the master of the wet conditions; he pulled an audacious overtaking manoeuvre when he had coolly driven around the outside of Lauda's Ferrari at Paddock Hill.

The South African GP was where the 76 would in fact début, and after intensive private testing the multi-foot pedal system was revised for Kyalami, although both drivers were building up a dislike of the car. The 76's promise was not maintained at Kyalami, as a combination of electrics, engines and fire extinguishers ruined Lotus's qualifying, leaving the cars stranded way down the grid. Things got worse in the race as Peterson suffered from a sticking throttle on the run down to Crowthorne; this played its part in a collision between the two Lotuses at the first corner. The Swede retired after one more lap with damaged steering and Ickx used the balance of the race as an intermittent test session!

Back at Silverstone's International Trophy the 76 disappointed again as Peterson retired. So concerned were Lotus by now, that they remained behind to test the following day. The product of this research was seen in Spain.

With the twin débâcles of both Kyalami and Silverstone fresh in his mind, Chapman desperately wanted to right the situation at Jarama, but a double retirement was the reward after Peterson had led the first twenty laps – thanks to a single and much larger rear wing and the scrapping of the electronic clutch

system. Such was the progress being made that Lotus was the only team to get near the bench-mark Ferraris. Peterson lost his early lead when a stop for dry tyres took a disastrous 90 seconds. The unsettled Team then almost let Ickx go again before his right rear had been completely tightened; as the situation was retrieved, Ickx then mistakenly pressed the fire extinguisher button covering himself in extinguishant and embarrassment. Race winner was the virtually unknown Austrian Niki Lauda, whom Peterson had already tipped as being destined for the top. The Swede himself had retired on lap 23 when his over-heating engine had finally boiled dry and expired.

Ickx suffered a nasty accident in private practice at Nivelles, which finally knocked his faith in Lotus's mechanical reliability; a front brake-shaft had apparently broken. All Zolder's Belgian GP could produce for Lotus was another double retirement, as well as a painful soaking in petrol for Peterson when his fuel tank ruptured. Ickx had an oil pipe split, his engine overheat and brake problems, and did not finish either.

Pressure was now on Chapman to get the 76 right. The major problem was a lack of road-holding and back in Norfolk a remedy was sought. In the meantime the 72E was pressed back into service for its fifth season, but now running on Goodyear tyres for which it was not designed.

At Monaco the situation was curiously reminiscent of 1970, when the 49 had been brought out of retirement as the 72 had not been considered sufficiently reliable. In Monte Carlo, Ferrari flags waved as that team took the entire front row with Lauda on pole and Regazzoni alongside. Meanwhile, at Lotus gear

Peterson started from third place on the grid at Monaco behind the two Ferraris. He had an eventful race having to reverse back on to the circuit after a lap 6 indiscretion. His 72E eventually won, much to Chapman's pleasure.

troubles in practice distracted both third-placed Peterson and Ickx in their 72s. Ickx had had no luck at all with JPS 10, which had a particularly weak engine. Being well ahead of an eight-car multiple accident on the run-up to the Casino on lap 1, in which Ickx suffered nose-cone damage, Peterson proved all the pundits wrong by winning. He chased the Ferraris hard, having fought back past Jarier's presumptuous Shadow, only to plunge off line at Rascasse on lap 6. Whilst reversing backwards he collected Reutemann's Brabham, ending the Argentinian's race with broken suspension, and found himself in fifth. He tore after the leaders, passing both Scheckter and Jarier only for Regazzoni to spin out and Lauda's ignition to fail. He seized the lead on lap 33 and the reliable 72E did the rest, giving JPS and Chapman a timely cap-throwing win. Ickx had retired with gearbox failure.

Most of the top F1 teams then went to Dijon to Goodyear tyre-test; Lauda's Ferrari was fastest with 59.4 seconds. Ickx's Lotus 72E was a promising third with 60.1 seconds, just behind Championship leader Fittipaldi's McLaren (59.6 seconds). The Swedish Grand Prix was eagerly anticipated, especially by Peterson.

In order to cure over-heating problems, the 76 was modified for Anderstorp, but the car's engine seized in practice and the 72 was dug out again; Peterson took fifth in this car, complete with cracked rear suspension.

Having outmanoeuvred Lauda at the start of the race, Peterson got alongside Scheckter into the first corner only to have a drive-shaft fail after eight laps; the frustrated Swede hurled his helmet to the ground when he retired. The Tyrrells went on to take a one-two whilst Ickx had long since retired with low oil pressure.

During tyre-testing at Zandvoort, Peterson had a heavy accident when a brake pad broke up, hurling his car through a number of catch fences; a pole struck his helmet knocking him unconscious for half an hour. After examination back in London he was pronounced fit enough to race, once a severe headache had subsided. In the Dutch GP itself the two Lotuses qualified in mid-grid and actually finished the race. The 76 had its radiators moved forward to both help cooling and to address front end lack of grip, but the straight line handling was still unpredictable. Peterson persevered with the 72E only to have a rear wing collapse; he took fastest lap, however, finishing eighth with Ickx eleventh.

Tyre-testing at Dijon had been particularly successful for Lotus, indicating that JPS might actually perform well in the French GP; Peterson was to find that his 72 handled 'perfectly' after only a few racing laps. Peterson and Lauda shared the front row and the start was eagerly awaited. Lauda arrived at the first corner ahead; Peterson's 72 turned sideways, thereby losing some ground. The Swede quickly caught up and after sixteen laps slipped past into the long Courbe de Pouas,

Thoroughly at home on the switchback Dijon-Prenois circuit, Peterson put in a virtuoso display of ten-tenths driving. Having humbled Lauda here, he plunged downhill at S. de Sablieres . . .

. . . and then pulled uphill to maintain the lead he took on lap 16. On this day he described his car as 'perfect' and one can see his response in the attitude of his 72E in both photos.

and drove away to take another well-deserved win.

Mathematically Peterson could now win the Championship and went to the British GP at Brands Hatch as a firm crowd favourite; again, both he and Lauda shared the front row. Ickx complained about his tyres – which later turned out to have been badly constructed – which were then given to Peterson. Thanks to this mistake the Swede dropped back in the race as the handling deteriorated, following a tyre stop, caused by a puncture, a new tyre blistered, dropping him to tenth. His remote Championship chances had now evaporated, whilst Ickx had gone well again, coming home third with non-existent brakes.

At the Nurburgring, Peterson had a big practice accident when the left rear Melmag wheel failed; although the car was badly damaged, he got away without major injuries. The Team promptly changed from 15in to 13in rims, which were not ideal. Hurriedly the front of JPS 10 was attached to the rear of the damaged 72E/8 by the mechanics, and it was this configuration that was to take an eventual fourth place in Peterson's hands. The two Lotuses provided much of the race spectacle as they battled with Mass and Hailwood. Ickx was fifth.

The 76s were used as spares in Austria as the favoured 72s were plagued by understeer. Peterson's proved difficult to start, and when he joined the grid, it was at such speed that he got away very quickly indeed! By lap 42 he was in second place, before retiring just nine laps from the end when a universal joint failed. Ickx had suffered a collision with Depailler's Tyrrell as Reutemann went on to win.

Despite overtures from other teams, Peterson signed a two-year contract with Lotus just before he set off for Monza. He preferred the spare at Monza, and once it had been fitted with the narrower front track there was no holding the Swede. Ickx, for once, found his JPS 10 satisfactory, although he still only achieved a sixteenth grid position. Peterson was seventh. The Ferraris of Lauda and Regazzoni set the pace and for two-thirds of the Italian GP they led, only to abruptly retire with identical engine failures. Peterson was promoted into the lead ahead of the McLaren of Fittipaldi, and after an excellent fight Chapman could again hurl his cap high into the Monza air.

After the long trip to Canada Peterson came in third behind Fittipaldi and Regazzoni, even though he had a nose wing bent back in a minor incident. He had started tenth on the Mosport grid, having cured a severe balance problem, whilst Ickx was well back, finishing thirteenth.

At Watkins Glen all eyes were on the Championship fight between Scheckter, Regazzoni and Fittipaldi, with the Brazilian in the end taking the crown. Peterson retired with engine failure whilst the sole 76 driver, Australian recruit Tim Schenken, couldn't even get up enough steam to qualify any better than second reserve. When Andretti failed to start on the grid, Schenken stepped in, only to later be disqualified when the American did eventually cover four laps. Ickx had an accident after seven laps.

1974 had been a dire season for Lotus, which had only been enlivened by Peterson's three wins in the old 72, and had been characterized by mechanical failures.

TEAM LOTUS AND PRIVATE LOTUS ENTRY RESULTS 1974

Drivers:
Ronnie Peterson: Swedish; Jacky Ickx: Belgian; Tim Schenken: Australian
Car:
Lotus 72E Engine: Ford Cosworth DFV 3-litre
Lotus 76　　　　　Ford Cosworth DFV 3-litre

CAR	CHASSIS	DRIVER	PRACTICE	SESSION	GRID	RACE	LAPS	%	REASON	CHAMPIONSHIP POSITION	POINTS
ARGENTINE GP, Buenos Aires – 13th January – 53 L, 196.55 miles (316.31km) (165)											
72 E	8	Peterson	1m 50.78s	4	1st P	13th	48	90.5	–	–	–
72 E	5-2	Ickx	1m 51.70s	4	7th	R	35	66.0	Transmission	–	–
BRAZILIAN GP, Interlagos – 27th January – 32 L, 158.28 miles (254.73km) (166)											
72 E	5-2	Ickx	2m 34.64s	3	5th	3rd	31	96.8	–	6th	4
72 E	8	Peterson	2m 32.82s	2	4th	6th	31	96.8	–	9th=	1
S AFRICAN GP, Kyalami – 30th March – 78 L, 198.90 miles (320.10km) (167)											
76 JPS	10	Ickx	1m 17.18s	1	10th	R	31	39.7	Brakes	8th=	4
76 JPS	9	Peterson	1m 18.00s	2	16th	R	2	2.5	Accident	12th=	1
72 E	8	(Spare)									
72 E G	6	Scheckter	1m 18.56s	–	22nd	13th	76	97.4	–	–	–
72 E G	7	Driver	1m 19.49s	–	26th	R	6	7.6	Clutch	–	–
SPANISH GP, Jarama – 28th April – 84 L, 177.69 miles (285.96km) (168)											
76 JPS	10	Ickx	1m 19.28s	3	5th	R	26	30.9	Brakes	9th=	4
76 JPS	9	Peterson	1m 18.47s	2	2nd	R	23	27.3	Engine	13th=	1
BELGIAN GP, Nivelles – 12th May – 85 L, 196.69 miles (316.54km) (169)											
76 JPS	10	Ickx	1m 12.42s	4	16th	R	72	84.7	Brakes	10th=	4
76 JPS	9	Peterson	1m 11.21s	3	5th	R	56	65.8	Fuel	13th=	1
72 E	8	(Spare)									
MONACO GP, Monte Carlo – 26th May – 78 L, 158.87 miles (255.67km) (170)											
72 E	8	Peterson	1m 26.8s	2	3rd	1st W	78	100.0	–	6th=	10
Fastest Lap: 1m 27.9s – 83.421mph (134.25kph) on lap 57 – RECORD											
72 E	5-2	Ickx	1m 29.5s	3	19th	R	34	43.5	Gearbox	11th=	4
76 JPS	10	(Spare)									
SWEDISH GP, Anderstorp – 9th June – 80 L, 199.73 miles (321.43km) (171)											
72 E	5-2	Ickx	1m 25.650s	3	7th	R	27	33.7	Oil	13th=	4
72 E	8	Peterson	1m 25.390s	4	5th	R	8	10.0	D/shaft	6th=	10
76 JPS	9	(Spare)									
DUTCH GP, Zandvoort – 23rd June – 75 L, 196.94 miles (316.94km) (172)											
72 E	8	Peterson	1m 20.22s	1	10th	8th	73	97.3	–	8th=	10
Fastest Lap: 1m 21.44s – 116.077mph (186.80kph) on lap 63											
72 E	5-2	Ickx	1m 21.21s	2	18th	11th	71	94.6	–	13th=	4
76 JPS	10	(Spare)									
FRENCH GP, Dijon – 7th July – 80 L, 163.49 miles (263.11km) (173)											
72 E	8	Peterson	59.08s	4	2nd	1st W	80	100.0	–	5th	19
72 E	5-2	Ickx	1m 0.00s	4	13th	5th	80	100.0	–	11th=	6
76 JPS	10	(Spare)									
BRITISH GP, Brands Hatch – 20th July – 75 L, 198.75 miles (319.86km) (174)											
72 E	5-2	Ickx	1m 21.2s	3	12th	3rd	75	100.0	–	9th=	10
72 E	8	Peterson	1m 19.7s	4	2nd	10th	73	97.3	–	5th	19
GERMAN GP, Nurburgring – 4th August – 14 L, 198.65 miles (319.69km) (175)											
76 JPS	10	Peterson	7m 9.0s★	1	8th	4th	14	100.0	–	5th	22
72 E	5-2	Ickx	7m 9.1s	1	9th	5th	14	100.0	–	7th=	12
72 E	8	(Spare)									
AUSTRIAN GP, Österreichring – 18th August – 54 L, 198.34 miles (319.19km) (176)											
72 E	8	Peterson	1m 36.0s	4	6th	R	45	83.3	U/joint	6th	22
76 JPS	10	Ickx	1m 38.14s	3	22nd	R	43	79.6	Accident	8th=	12
76 JPS	9	(Spare)									
72 E	5-2	(Spare)									

ITALIAN GP, Monza – 8th September – 52 L, 186.76 miles (300.56km) (177)

72 E	8	Peterson	1m 34.24s	2	7th	1st W	52	100.0	–	5th	31
76 JPS	10	Ickx	1m 35.19s	3	16th	R	30	57.6	Throttle	8th=	12
76 JPS	9	(Spare)									

CANADIAN GP, Mosport – 22nd September – 80 L, 196.72 miles (316.59km) (178)

72 E	8	Peterson	1m 14.340s	4	10th	3rd	80	100.0	–	5th	35
72 E	5-2	Ickx	1m 15.661s	3	21st	13th	78	97.5	–	9th	12
76 JPS	9	(Spare)									

US GP, Watkins Glen – 6th October – 59 L, 199.24 miles (320.64km) (179)

72 E	8	Peterson	1m 41.195s	4	19th	R	52	88.1	Engine	5th	35
72 E	5-2	Ickx	1m 40.876s	2	16th	R	7	11.8	Accident	10th=	12
76 JPS	9	Schenken	1m 43.243s	3	27th	DSQ	6	10.1	–	–	–

Key:
*   = Time achieved in 72/8 before accident – best 76/10 time 7m 11.3s in ses
DSQ = Disqualified
R   = Retired
L   = Laps
P   = Pole
W   = Win

Private Lotus Entries:
G   = Team Gunston

The 76 had failed, and despite all his efforts Peterson had only finished seven of the fifteen races.

In October, the *Daily Express* carried an article suggesting that Players were about to pull the plug on their F1 sponsorship. Players had indeed decided to quit motor racing but they only made up their minds shortly before the 1975 season started, and they were eventually persuaded to remain, having been told that their departure would finish Team Lotus. The sponsorship budget was to be much reduced, but at least it pulled Team Lotus back from the brink.

WORLD CHAMPIONSHIP RESULTS 1974

Position	Driver	Points
1	Emerson Fittipaldi	55
2	Clay Regazzoni	52
3	Jody Scheckter	45
4	Niki Lauda	38
5	**Ronnie Peterson**	**35**
6	Carlos Reutemann	32
7	Denny Hulme	20
8	James Hunt	15
9	Patrick Depailler	14
10=	**Jacky Ickx**	**12**
	Mike Hailwood	12

CONSTRUCTORS' CUP 1974

Position	Constructor	Points
1	McLaren-Ford	73 (75)
2	Ferrari	65
3	Tyrrell-Ford	52
4	**John Player Special/ Lotus-Ford**	**42**

1975

Lack of finance combined with the 76's failure meant that the now uncompetitive 72 would incredibly be raced for a fifth season. Tyre technology had overtaken the 72's original concept and much of the year was spent changing suspension set-ups – dictated somewhat by the fragility of brake-shafts – and trying to move weight forward on to the front tyres to cure the almost terminal power understeer. There were to be no wins at all in 1975, and whilst Peterson would remain with Lotus for the whole season, Ickx left after the French GP to be replaced at various times by John Watson, Brian Henton and Jim Crawford. In midsummer, Peter Warr was involved in a nasty car accident and he was temporarily replaced by former Firestone man Nigel Bennett.

With lack of money being the major preoccupation for Lotus, Peterson was the centre of much controversy. Although possessing a two-year contract, rumours were to persist in Argentina that he would be swapped for Shadow's Tom Pryce. Rumour turned to fact as both Shadow and Hesketh openly courted the Swede, and Warr agreed to his early departure. Most people therefore anticipated that Brazil would be his last Lotus drive.

In Argentina the narrow-front track 72s boasted more powerful front brakes, the balancing of which caused Peterson some trouble because of a sticking calliper. He collided with Wilson Fittipaldi in practice and retired in the race – after what looked like a jump start – when his brakes weakened. Ickx plugged on to eighth place on a day when Emerson Fittipaldi took the honours for McLaren.

Prior to Brazil, Players were persuaded both to stay

and to come up with sufficient money to retain Peterson. Ironically the Swede was disappointed, as he had lost faith in the organization and in Chapman in particular, who had not to date – as apparently agreed previously – delivered him a 'new car' capable of winning the Championship. The Swede was also very concerned about driving the 72E, which he privately perceived to be most dangerous. Through all this the mechanics worked hard in Brazil to complete a new rear suspension for the 72Es. Peterson was bedevilled in Interlagos practice by an unbalanced front brake disc and both 72s suffered from unpredictable high-speed handling; the Swede's new engine wouldn't run cleanly either. He changed from unsuitable soft tyres to a harder compound, only to be rewarded by an engine that wouldn't start. When it was eventually coaxed into life he was soon back in the pits to have the mixture adjusted, and then commenced an uncharacteristically slow race to a vibrating last place. Not daring to drive flat out, Ickx drove safely to ninth place.

Peterson received a brand new 72E(9) in time for South Africa in an attempt to rectify his many previous mechanical troubles. Some thought this was Chapman's tongue-in-cheek way of providing the Swede with the much promised 'new car'! Both Lotuses boasted new front suspension with replacement uprights, but they still suffered from understeer. Peterson's fuel lines parted twice, and then an oil pipe burst at Barbeque and flooded the track. This caught out both Hill's Lola, which struck the barriers without personal damage, and Tunmer's private 72/7. Having initially run in third place, Peterson was soon afflicted by recurrent understeer and Ickx never featured at all, ending up a lowly twelfth as Scheckter won his home event for Tyrrell.

The South African went on to win the Brands Hatch Race of Champions too, with Peterson third, followed home by Ickx in fourth. Unfortunately at Silverstone's International Trophy, both Peterson and Crawford were rendered non-starters thanks to engine seizures; accusations of sabotage were subsequently aired.

Back in Norfolk, despite working day and night, Lotus were unable to ready the new F1 car for Barcelona and it would be many months before it finally appeared. For the Spanish GP, Barcelona's Montjuich circuit was the centre of a political storm as the drivers, represented by the Grand Prix Drivers Association (GPDA), objected to the installation of the safety barriers. Peterson recalled the accidents that had befallen both Cevert and Koinigg and joined the GPDA in their stance, whilst non-member Ickx was one of only two drivers to practice, controversially, on the Friday afternoon. Eventually full practice got under way, but Peterson suffered from low fuel pressure. The race was

tragically stopped after twenty-nine laps when Stommelen's Hill vaulted the barriers killing a number of onlookers. Peterson had already retired after a clash with Migault's Hill, whilst Ickx came second in all the confusion surrounding the accident; he had actually led the race for a single lap. Ickx, amongst a number of drivers, was subsequently unsuccessfully protested after Brabham accused him of apparently overtaking under the yellow flags.

In Monte Carlo both Lotuses were fielded with wide track front suspension, and in the warm-up Peterson was second quickest after Lauda's Ferrari. He ran strongly in an early second place behind the Ferrari and as the damp track quickly started to dry he decided to change to slicks. Stopping on lap 25 he had a bad pitstop, during which a mechanic dropped a wheel retaining nut under the car, so he fell to fourth place. Both Peterson and Chapman were livid with the mechanic concerned who left the Team immediately. Ickx did well having gambled that the wet conditions would dry out, but he could only manage eighth place. The two Lotus drivers now drew level: each had 3 points in joint tenth place in the Championship as they headed for Belgium.

Ickx excelled in Zolder's wet Saturday practice but at the end of qualifying both Lotuses were well down the grid. Peterson was much happier after the warm-up but he admitted that he needed more testing time to get the car handling correctly. The race saw him battle with Pace's Brabham, in one of the highlights of the GP, but this was rudely halted when he crashed heavily at the chicane because of sudden brake failure. He later revealed that a jammed throttle had been distracting him too. A lonely Ickx had his front left brake-shaft break on lap 52 and he narrowly avoided being pitched headlong into the barriers. Zolder had produced a double Lotus retirement.

At Anderstorp, Peterson was unhappy as he had to take to the chicane escape road in practice, as well as spinning violently on his way to a lowly ninth place. A troubled Ickx was way back in eighteenth place. Dirt jammed the throttle slides of several cars in the race itself, but with a pair of Anne Murphy's tights covering his air-intakes, Peterson avoided such problems on his way to ninth place with bad brake balance. An oversteering Ickx, who had helped Alan Jones's Hesketh off the road at one point, could only manage a lowly fifteenth-place finish.

New brake shafts permitted the wide-track configuration at Zandvoort and the car batteries were relocated to the nose, but the cars still proved virtually impossible to balance. The race started wet, but as the track dried Peterson made a swift pitstop on lap 11 to change tyres; as he hurriedly left the pits, he knocked

over Ferrari's Luca Montezemolo, luckily without seriously hurting him. Ickx's engine blew after only seven laps and on a day when James Hunt took his first GP victory for Hesketh, Peterson climbed from fourteenth to fourth, only to run out of petrol frustratingly at Tarzan six laps from the flag. The last churn of fuel had apparently not been put into the car before the start.

At Paul Ricard, the wheelbase of the 72Es was made five inches longer, with new 76 oil tanks inserted between the back of the tub and the front of the engine. The rear suspension was now narrow track and the front wide track in order to place another 25lb (11kg) on the understeering front tyres. Peterson's car was still in standard wheelbase trim, but thanks to other problems he was unable to make any valid comparisons. Whilst Lauda went on to win the French GP, Peterson fought with Laffite (in a dice for tenth and eleventh place!) just beating the Frenchman to the flag. Ickx had long since retired with a broken front brake-shaft. Having despaired at waiting for promises to be fulfilled, Peterson summarily gave in his notice after the race. Warr consequently took on a couple of promising up-and-coming drivers in the shape of Brian Henton and Jim Crawford to see how they would cope with F1.

New Blood

For the John Player Grand Prix, Silverstone now wisely boasted a chicane in the middle of the fearsome old Woodcote corner. Within Lotus the search continued for not only a half-reasonable balance but also an understeer cure; to this end, Peterson's 72 had been

returned to 1973 specification! The two new drivers – Henton and Crawford – took over the long-wheelbase cars from Paul Ricard. Following practice all three of the Team's cars were in the back half of the grid led, on experience, by the fearless Peterson in sixteenth place.

Peterson's race ended in retirement again when a valve let go after only seven laps, but the rains were still to come, much to the chagrin of the two remaining Lotus apprentices. By lap 20 the track was decidedly wet and yet five laps later the horizontal rain had let up, and there was even a hint of sun! Crawford had already retired because of an accident, but at around the fifty-lap mark the rain returned, to Stowe and Club in particular, and by lap 56 it was coming down with a vengeance. Most of the front runners succumbed to the catch fences at the southern end of the track and, whilst Fittipaldi was credited with the win, the last remaining JPS of Henton was amongst those that crashed heavily at the flooded Club corner.

John Watson was released by Surtees to drive for Lotus at the Nurburgring in the long-wheelbase car previously driven by Crawford. Peterson had his 'old' spec car but was caught out in practice when he overlooked a warning pit signal and ran out of fuel, only for a spectating fan to give the Swede sufficient from his car to get the 72 back to the pits! Watson ended up faster than Peterson and 2 seconds ahead on the grid. In the race the Swede's clutch went after only a single lap and Ulsterman Watson visited the scenery at high speed when a torsion-bar lever gave way. Reutemann won for Brabham.

Peterson was furious at the Nurburgring, as by then he had been expecting to be driving the promised new

In common with many drivers, Brian Henton left the circuit at Club Corner and rammed into the sleepers. Here his 72 is joined by the Hesketh of James Hunt, which was another victim of the sudden rainstorm. Henton had been as high as thirteenth before he crashed.

Lotus F1 car. He confronted Chapman and was promised his new steed for Austria, but as history now shows, it didn't appear there either . . .

Henton returned to the Team at the Österreichring in the 'long' car, but in practice he was caught out by an oil slick. Up to that moment, apart from a suspension breakage, the car had been performing much better than usual, but on the slick at the Jochen Rindt corner, it sailed off into the barriers rendering its driver a non-starter. Peterson had already had a big accident

when cut up at one of the fastest corners by a less-experienced driver. The car was damaged but was repairable, and Peterson reverted to his original steed.

Sadly Mark Donohue's Penske March was to suffer an even bigger accident in the pre-race warm-up, which would later claim the American driver's life. In the race Peterson's 'old' 72 went surprisingly well and he took fifth place, having been as high as fourth. In the very wet conditions he had had to stop after twenty-two laps for his helmet visor to be exchanged.

At Monza, Crawford (pictured at Silverstone) started from the back of the grid, wishing that he could have raced the short-wheelbase 72. Bad handling caused him to spin several times and he eventually finished thirteenth.

TEAM LOTUS AND PRIVATE LOTUS ENTRY RESULTS 1975

Drivers:
Ronnie Peterson: Swedish; Jacky Ickx: Belgian; Brian Henton: British; Jim Crawford: British; John Watson: British
Car:
Lotus 72E/F Engine: Ford Cosworth DFV 3-litre

CAR	CHASSIS	DRIVER	PRACTICE	SESSION	GRID	RACE	LAPS	%	REASON	CHAMPIONSHIP POSITION	POINTS
ARGENTINE GP, Buenos Aires – 12th January – 53 L, 196.55 miles (316.31km) (180)											
72 E	5-2	Ickx	1m 52.90s	4	18th	8th	52	98.1	–	–	–
72 E	8	Peterson	1m 51.44s	4	11th	R	15	28.3	Gearbox	–	–
BRAZILIAN GP, Interlagos – 26th January – 40 L, 197.84 miles (318.39km) (181)											
72 E	5-2	Ickx	2m 33.20s	2	12th	9th	40	100.0	–	–	–
72 E	8	Peterson	2m 33.90s	4	16th	15th	38	95.0	–	–	–
S AFRICAN GP, Kyalami – 1st March – 78 L, 198.90 miles (320.10km) (182)											
72 E	9	Peterson	1m 17.14s	4	8th	10th	77	98.7	–	–	–
72 E	5-2	Ickx	1m 18.68s	4	21st	12th	76	97.4	–	–	–
72 E GU	6	Keizan	1m 19.01s	–	22nd	13th	76	97.4	–	–	–
72 GU	7	Tunmer	1m 19.52s	–	25th	11th	76	97.4	–	–	–
SPANISH GP, Barcelona – 28th April – 29 L, 68.31 miles (109.93km) (183)											
72 E	5-2	Ickx	1m 26.3s	3	16th	2nd	29	100.0	–	10th	3★
72 E	9	Peterson	1m 25.3s	3	12th	R	23	79.3	Accident	–	–
MONACO GP, Monte Carlo – 11th May – 75 L, 152.76 miles (245.84km) (184)											
72 E	9	Peterson	1m 27.40s	3	4th	4th	75	100.0	–	10th=	3
72 E	5-2	Ickx	1m 28.28s	3	14th	8th	74	98.6	–	10th=	3
BELGIAN GP, Zolder – 25th May – 70 L, 185.38 miles (298.34km) (185)											
72 E	5-2	Ickx	1m 27.40s	4	16th	R	52	74.2	Brakes	10th=	3
72 E	9	Peterson	1m 27.17s	4	14th	R	38	54.2	Accident	10th=	3
SWEDISH GP, Anderstorp – 8th June – 80 L, 199.73 miles (321.43km) (186)											
72 E	9	Peterson	1m 26.012s	2	9th	9th	79	98.7	–	10th=	3
72 E	5-2	Ickx	1m 27.320s	2	18th	15th	77	96.2	–	10th=	3
72 E	8	(Spare)									
DUTCH GP, Zandvoort – 22nd June – 75 L, 196.94 miles (316.94km) (187)											
72 E	9	Peterson	1m 21.46s	4	16th	15th NR	69	92.0	Fuel	10th=	3
72 E	5-2	Ickx	1m 23.20s	1	21st	R	6	8.0	Engine	10th=	3
FRENCH GP, Ricard – 6th July – 54 L, 194.95 miles (313.74km) (188)											
72 E	9	Peterson	1m 50.04s	4	17th	10th	54	100.0	–	11th=	3
72 E	5-2	Ickx	1m 50.94s	4	19th	R	17	31.4	Brakes	11th=	3
72 E	8	(Spare)									
BRITISH GP, Silverstone – 19th July – 56 L, 164.19 miles (264.23km) (189)											
72 E	5-2	Henton	1m 21.36s	3	21st	16th NR	53	94.6	–	–	–
72 E	8	Crawford	1m 21.86s	2	25th	R	28	50.0	Accident	–	–
72 E	9	Peterson	1m 20.58s	1	16th	R	7	12.5	Engine	12th=	3
GERMAN GP, Nurburgring – 3rd August – 14 L, 198.65 miles (319.69km) (190)											
72 F	8	Watson	7m 9.4s	3	14th	R	2	14.2	Suspension	–	–
72 E	9	Peterson	7m 11.6s	3	18th	R	1	7.1	Clutch	14th=	3
AUSTRIAN GP, Österreichring – 17th August – 29 L, 106.52 miles (171.43km) (191)											
72 E	9	Peterson	1m 37.61s	1	13th	5th	29	100.0	–	14th=	4
72 F	8	Henton	1m 38.72s	3	22nd	DNS	–	–	Accident	–	–
ITALIAN GP, Monza – 7th September – 52 L, 186.76 miles (300.56km) (192)											
72 F	8	Crawford	1m 37.14s	4	25th	13th	46	88.4	–	–	–
72 E	9	Peterson	1m 34.22s	4	11th	R	1	1.9	Engine	14th=	4
US GP, Watkins Glen – 5th October – 59 L, 199.24 miles (320.64km) (193)											
72	9	Peterson	1m 43.570s	3	14th	5th	59	10.0	–	12th=	6
72 F	5-2	Henton	1m 45.244s	3	19th	NC	49	83.0	–	–	–

Much to everyone's surprise, Vittorio Brambilla (Beta March) slithered to a win in the thoroughly inclement weather.

Before Monza the first Swiss Grand Prix since 1954 was held, at Dijon-Prenois. Swiss driver Regazzoni appropriately won for Ferrari, and Peterson was fourth in the only Lotus entry.

At the last moment, lack of appropriate rims stopped the new Lotus going to Monza, so yet again the trusty 72s were wheeled out. To show that some progress at least had been made in the intervening year, Peterson was actually slightly faster than he had been the previous season.

Crawford, all the while, was at the back of the grid with a car that would neither handle nor brake properly, and he was wishing that he could have the shorter-wheelbase version of the 72. The race-morning flooding was replaced, by mid-afternoon, with dry conditions. Crawford was hit by another car almost before he had left the grid, and after but one lap Peterson was also struck by Brise's Hill, which in turn had been swiped by Andretti's Parnelli at the first chicane; the 72's throttle had jammed open in this incident and the Swede swiftly retired. Crawford plugged on to an eventual thirteenth place after several 'refusals' at the first chicane, thanks to locking front brakes.

Whilst the new car was still promised the venerable Lotus 72's final race was to be at Watkins Glen, where Henton was in a long version; again he and Peterson ruined their suspensions by kerb-hopping in practice. On lap 6 Henton and Brise collided in Turn 1, breaking the Lotus's suspension, which took six laps to repair. Peterson spent much of the race fighting with Mass, and with only three laps to go the Swede flat-spotted his front tyres when he locked his wheels; shortly afterwards Hunt caught up and overtook, dropping Peterson to fifth.

At season's end, the 72 at last bowed out, having achieved twenty GP wins and three Constructors' Cups for Lotus. Whilst by now the cars looked very tired, it has to be recognized that the design to the present day is the most successful to have been produced by Lotus for racing.

WORLD CHAMPIONSHIP RESULTS 1975

Position	Driver	Points
1	Niki Lauda	64.5
2	Emerson Fittipaldi	45
3	Carlos Reutemann	37
4	James Hunt	33
5	Clay Regazzoni	25
6	Carlos Pace	24
7=	Jochen Mass	20
	Jody Scheckter	20
9	Patrick Depailler	12
10	Tom Pryce	8
11	Vittorio Brambilla	6.5
12=	**Ronnie Peterson**	**6**
	Jacques Laffite	6
14	Mario Andretti	5
15	Mark Donohue	4
16	**Jacky Ickx**	**3**

CONSTRUCTORS' CUP 1975

Position	Constructor	Points
1	Ferrari	72.5
2	Brabham-Ford	54 (56 gross)
3	McLaren-Ford	53
4	Hesketh-Ford	33
5	Tyrrell-Ford	25
6	Shadow-Ford	9.5
7	**John Player Special/ Lotus-Ford**	**9**

CHAPTER 5

Ground Effect

Lotus 77 (JPS Mk 2)

The long-awaited 77 was launched in September 1975 fresh from the Lotus design group pens of Martin Ogilvie, Mike Cooke and Geoff Aldridge. Peterson wanted to race it in the United States GP in October, but Chapman insisted that it should be properly tested first. The car featured 'variable geometry' suspension so that the track and wheelbase could be tailored, by using different sub-frames, to suit different circuits. Early season experiments showed that the 77 performed best in the wide-track, long-wheelbase configuration. Ogilvie placed the twin-calliper brakes in the air stream to help cooling and the fuel was placed immediately behind the driver in Aldridge's narrow aluminium tub.

In November, testing at Paul Ricard proved promising, although reliability and stiffness were questionable. The test was subsequently marred by the fatal air crash that wiped out the fledgling Embassy Hill Racing Team, including Graham Hill. Peterson should have been on that flight but at the last moment had decided to fly home with Chapman.

Over the winter Peterson had become a father, which helped him to forget his previous disastrous season. Sponsorship for the Team was still tight and even Peterson's contract was up for sale to the right bidder.

Peterson's position was still uncertain, especially as there was a vacancy at McLaren. He was disgruntled with Chapman over his payment, but hiding his annoyance he set off for Brazil, where he was joined by Parnelli-driver Mario Andretti. Andretti, who was completely unaware that he was about to lose his Parnelli drive, was pleased to be able to accept Lotus's offer.

Andretti described his introduction to the short-wheelbase, narrow-track 77 as 'terrible' and 'frightening'. He said the car scared him but he tried his best at Interlagos. Peterson decided that it was time to quit when, after only three practice laps, a ruptured water pipe made him skid into the Ferradura fences. Whilst fighting off the Brabhams in the race, a misunderstanding caused the two Lotus drivers to collide on lap 6. The accident was attributed to a misjudgement by Andretti, who retired with mangled suspension, whilst Peterson did four more laps before his damaged suspension and high water temperatures forced him out too.

Peterson relished leaving Lotus as he had found it difficult to communicate with Chapman for some time. Andretti, too, would have been quite happy never to have seen the 77 again as his car had been unable to heat its front tyres properly.

Andretti initially described the Lotus 77 as both 'terrible' and 'frightening'. By season's end he had transformed the car and in the dry Japanese GP practice seen here, he took pole. He went on to win the race in torrential rain.

Having lost faith in Chapman's cars, Peterson, with the help of his personal benefactor Count Zano, returned to March, only to look back enviously shortly afterwards as Lotus found more funds and personnel and better motivation.

A spectating Gunnar Nilsson casually visited the Lotus pit at Interlagos only to shortly become a Lotus driver, when he was in effect swapped with March for 'Super Swede'. Bob Evans briefly joined the Team too but was quickly replaced full-time by Andretti.

The new drivers tested in South Africa, covering more than six Grand Prix distances between them; the stiffened chassis handled better on this occasion. The testing was largely trouble-free, so it was ironic that after only one lap of official practice at Kyalami, Nilsson's car caught fire when his rear brakes jammed on. Following gearbox maladies he was slowest, with the oversteering Evans two places ahead. The rear of both cars' tubs came apart because of the heavy suspension loadings; urgent reinforcement was required. On his Lotus début, Nilsson had an ill-handling car and a cracked engine, and after only eighteen laps his clutch gave out as well. Evans drove steadily to tenth.

In Brands Hatch's Race of Champions Nilsson was eighth, two laps behind winner Hunt's McLaren, and Evans was ninth and last. The 77s now had strengthened rear radius rod fixings in preparation for Long Beach.

In California Nilsson qualified last again. During practice a rear wheel bearing gave out, causing him to glance a wall; he later hit a barrier again, badly damaging the rear suspension. On his last appearance for Lotus Evans failed to qualify because of engine maladies. On lap 1, whilst driving flat out (in excess of 170mph (275kph), Nilsson's car struck the wall along Shoreline Drive and caught fire; miraculously he leapt out unharmed. It appeared that the right rear suspension had failed and Lotus hadn't even recorded one lap!

Chapman accepted that the 77 had to be modified to outboard brake specification to suit the Goodyear tyres. Freelancer Len Terry was commissioned to design a new suspension kit, which he did in a mere eleven days! The brakes were moved into the wheels, saving unsprung weight as well as heating the tyres better. At Silverstone's International Trophy, Nilsson finished a competitive sixth and Andretti, driving for Wolf-Williams, was so impressed when the Swede lapped him that he soon signed a Lotus contract.

A week later Tony Southgate was taken on as both a designer and as Nilsson's race engineer. At Jarama, new air box and wing regulations were introduced to reduce overall speeds and it was hoped that the 77 would benefit. Thanks to a 5in spacer the cars were longer in Spain, with half-inch aluminium honeycomb foot-

wells. Nilsson outqualified Andretti for seventh place as the two drivers befriended each other, which considerably lightened the atmosphere. Nilsson fought off Brambilla for third place, his hands blistered from heavy gear changing. For thirty-three laps Andretti followed Nilsson but then retired with a failed gear linkage, allowing Regazzoni's Ferrari through. The Swiss suffered fuel pressure troubles and the Lotus's low-power engine just got Nilsson to the line behind Hunt and Lauda. The winner's McLaren failed post-race scrutineering and Nilsson thought he might have been second, but the disqualification was annulled after the French GP.

Belgium was better, although both Lotuses were plagued by their engines and gearboxes in practice; however, a new reverse-vee leading-edge rear wing proved effective. After a successful warm-up Nilsson started twenty-second but he climbed through the field until lap 7, when sand caused his throttle to stick open, spinning him off. Andretti's similarly affected throttles cleared and he was in eighth place on lap 14 when a CV joint failed, putting him out; like Nilsson, he was nevertheless much happier with his steed now.

Only Nilsson was entered for Monaco as Lotus were simultaneously testing in Sweden, and Chapman was very annoyed when the Swede collided with Regazzoni early in practice. Nilsson later admitted guilt, but replacement parts still had to be flown from Norfolk. Despite being ordered to go easily in the race, he stubbornly pushed so hard that his engine blew at half distance.

Nilsson went to Sweden needing to get back into Chapman's good books; he was worried about his first home GP, which was also the 200th to be contested by Team Lotus. Angry to be hampered by a misfire early on he ran out of fuel in final practice; once replenished, his adrenaline gained him the sixth-best time. Andretti, now recovered from a big testing accident, fought for pole only to have third gear strip. The mechanics reckoned he was the fastest, but Scheckter's Tyrrell was given pole! In the race Andretti received a one-minute penalty whilst leading for jumping the start. As Nilsson was running in fifth place on lap 3, he crashed into the pit wall at a furious Chapman's feet whilst being pressurized by Lauda. Andretti turned up the pace, putting his oval racing experience to good effect in Anderstorp's constant-radius corners, but his engine failed at around thirty laps, just when he was apparently in a safe lead on the road. He retired fifteen laps later and Lotus were glad to leave Sweden.

In Paul Ricard practice Andretti's 77 collapsed as the engine pulled away from the tub just before he got up to top speed on the Mistral straight! Nilsson went through three gearboxes and managed only eight race laps as Andretti took fifth place to finish his first GP with the 77.

The John Player GP of Great Britain saw Andretti third fastest; Nilsson's transmission played up, yielding only fourteenth place. The race itself only lasted a few hundred yards before the Ferraris of Regazzoni and Lauda touched at Paddock Hill and Andretti only just avoided becoming involved. When the race recommenced, Andretti stalled and was terrified that the newly refuelled cars would hit him. He started several laps later but retired after only five with an electrical fault. Nilsson, by contrast, held fourth place for twenty-seven laps as he fought with Pryce's Shadow in the best dice of the race. Unfortunately his engine blew within nine laps of the flag, but he received great acclaim from the grandstands.

At the Nurburgring, Andretti's car sported an air starter for the first time; it also had its oil cooler relocated in the nose. A driver-adjustable rear roll bar was being tested, too, before Andretti suffered another engine-mount failure. The race was stopped after Lauda's Ferrari crashed in flames at Bergwerk; for Nilsson this was the first experience of a driver being seriously hurt, and he was deeply shocked. In the re-started race Nilsson held off Andretti for four laps only for a damper to fail. The American got past just before his engine gave out and the Swede subsequently took fifth place.

The two Lotus drivers had a hair-raising flight with Chapman to the Österreichring, where the Team tested prior to the Austrian GP meeting. Using very little rear wing, Nilsson qualified fourth and Andretti ninth, the latter's side-pods now containing the car's water radiators. Nilsson had his first wet F1 race, and as the track dried he fought past Peterson before attacking race winner Watson until his oil pressure dropped. The engine eventually blew up as he crossed the finishing line in third, with Andretti fifth.

Nilsson couldn't make his 77 handle in Holland, and after only ten race laps he missed the waved oil-warning flags at Schievelak and spun into the catch fencing. By contrast, a happy Andretti came third – complete with his preferred differential – only 2 seconds behind Hunt's McLaren. A high-speed misfire occurred, thanks to a fuel pick-up problem, and he couldn't wrest the lead.

Behind the scenes the 78 was now complete and Andretti wanted it for Monza, but Chapman, who didn't want any copies built, decreed that it would début in 1977. In Italy, Lauda miraculously returned for Ferrari but the 77s were just too slow to feature. Andretti had his rear brakes lock on in practice as the stub axles expanded, and Nilsson was only just ahead on the sixth row. During the race, Nilsson's front wing

worked loose and the ensuing pitstop dropped him down the field to finish thirteenth. Andretti collided with Stuck at the damp first chicane and both drivers retired in the sand trap after twenty-three laps.

The 77s appeared with nylon brush skirts for the first time at Mosport; Andretti found these very effective. In the first session Nilsson crashed at Turn 2 whilst learning the tricky circuit, to be joined shortly afterwards by Andretti, when one of his wheels worked loose. The American had apparently already had this problem rectified in the pits, but it was later discovered that a stub axle had been weakened and had sheared. Nilsson was stranded on the warm-up lap as his engine wouldn't start; when the mechanics coaxed it back he took his place, but could only manage to finish twelfth. Andretti was third, having fought with Scheckter's six-wheeled Tyrrell, touched wheels with Peterson and been forced off on to the dirt by a tail-ender! He had again run with very little wing, and as a consequence his 77 was really competitive.

Nilsson and Peterson holidayed at Andretti's Nazareth home after the Mosport race, before going on to United States GP. Much of Watkins Glen practice was wet, but race day turned dry and very cold. Nilsson's smoking engine forced him to retire after only thirteen laps, and Andretti joined him ten laps later with damaged suspension, having attacked a kerb too energetically; he also had a misfire.

Andretti took pole position in Japan (his first since Watkins Glen in 1968!) after a battle with Hunt's McLaren. He ran the 77 in the dry with minimal wing and the narrow-track arrangement, which gave a substantial power advantage on the straight. Whilst practice had been dry, the race itself was very wet. The world watched the Lauda v. Hunt Championship battle. Nilsson kept on the road, unlike many more experienced colleagues, and finished sixth, whilst Andretti powered through the puddles to take a well-deserved win. He had carefully passed both Depailler and Hunt to take the lead on lap 64 as he preserved his wet tyres on the drying track. Ironically, as Chapman had already recognized, it was the fact that the car's ground-effect chassis wasn't working properly that stopped those very soft wet tyres from destroying themselves! Andretti eventually won by a whole lap, showing his complete mastery of the conditions, although his front left tyre was worn right down to the canvas.

During 1976, the 77 become Chapman's 78 test-bed, and the two cars' rear suspension would be identical. Andretti had raised the Team's spirit and Nilsson was regarded as the most pleasant of new recruits. During the year Peterson had expressed his desire to return to Lotus, where he had enviously observed the visible improvement in the cars.

TEAM LOTUS RESULTS 1976

Drivers:
Ronnie Peterson: Swedish; Mario Andretti: USA; Bob Evans: British; Gunnar Nilsson: Swedish
Car:
Lotus 77 Engine: Ford Cosworth DFV 3-litre

CAR	CHASSIS	DRIVER	PRACTICE	SESSION	GRID	RACE	LAPS	%	REASON	CHAMPIONSHIP POSITION	POINTS
BRAZILIAN GP, Interlagos – 25th January – 40 L, 198.75 miles (319.86km) (194)											
77 2/JPS	12	Peterson	2m 37.19s	4	18th	R	10	25.0	Accident	–	–
77 1/JPS	11	Andretti	2m 36.01s	4	16th	R	6	15.0	Accident	–	–
S AFRICAN GP, Kyalami – 6th March – 78 L, 198.90 miles (320.10km) (195)											
77 2/JPS	12	Evans	1m 19.35s	2	23rd	10th	77	98.7	–	–	–
77 1/JPS	11	Nilsson	1m 22.70s	4	25th	R	18	23.0	Clutch	–	–
US GP **WEST**, Long Beach – 28th March – 80 L, 161.60 miles (260.07km) (196)											
77 1/JPS	11	Nilsson	1m 25.277s	4	20th	R	0	0.0	Accident	–	–
77 2/JPS	12	Evans	1m 25.890s	4	DNQ	–	–	–	–	–	–
SPANISH GP, Jarama – 2nd May – 75 L, 158.65 miles (255.32km) (197)											
77 2/JPS	12	Nilsson	1m 19.35s	1	7th	3rd	75	100.0	–	7th=	4
77 1/JPS	11	Andretti	1m 19.59s	4	9th	R	34	45.3	Gearbox	14th=	1★
BELGIAN GP, Zolder – 16th May – 70 L, 185.38 miles (298.34km) (198)											
77 1/JPS	11	Andretti	1m 27.75s	4	11th	R	28	40.0	D/shaft	15th=	1★
77 2/JPS	12	Nilsson	1m 28.99s	4	22nd	R	7	10.0	Accident	8th=	4
MONACO GP, Monte Carlo – 30th May – 78 L, 160.52 miles (258.34km) (199)											
77 2/JPS	12	Nilsson	1m 32.10s	4	16th	R	39	50.0	Engine	9th=	4
SWEDISH GP, Anderstorp – 13th June – 72 L, 179.76 miles (289.30km) (200)											
77 1/JPS	11	Andretti	1m 26.008s	4	2nd	R	45	62.5	Engine	16th=	1★
Fastest Lap: 1m 28.002s – 102.134mph (164.369kph) on lap 11											
77 2/JPS	12	Nilsson	1m 26.570s	4	6th	R	2	2.7	Accident	9th=	4
FRENCH GP, Ricard – 4th July – 54 L, 194.95 miles (313.74km) (201)											
77 1/JPS	11	Andretti	1m 49.19s	4	7th	5th	54	100.0	–	13th=	3★
77 2/JPS	12	Nilsson	1m 49.83s	4	12th	R	8	14.8	Gearbox	10th=	4
77 3/JPS	14	(Spare)									
BRITISH GP, Brands Hatch – 18th July – 76 L, 198.63 miles (319.67km) (202)											
77 2/JPS	12	Nilsson	1m 20.67s		14th	R	67	88.1	Engine	11th=	4
77 1/JPS	11	Andretti	1m 19.76s	4	3rd	R	4	5.2	Engine	14th=	3★
77 3/JPS	14	(Spare)									
GERMAN GP, Nurburgring – 1st August – 14 L, 198.65 miles (319.69km) (203)											
77 2/JPS	12	Nilsson	7m 23.0s	2	15th	5th	14	100.0	–	11th=	6
77 3/JPS	14	Andretti	7m 16.1s	1	11th	12th	14	100.0	–	14th=	3★
77 1/JPS	11	(Spare)									
AUSTRIAN GP, Österreichring – 15th August – 54 L, 198.29 miles (319.11km) (204)											
77 2/JPS	12	Nilsson	1m 36.46s	1	4th	3rd	54	100.0	–	9th	10
77 3/JPS	14	Andretti	1m 36.68s	1	9th	5th	54	100.0	–	13th	5★
77 1/JPS	11	(Spare)									
DUTCH/EUROPEAN GP, Zandvoort – 29th August – 75 L, 196.94 miles (316.95km) (205)											
77 1/JPS	11	Andretti	1m 21.88s	2	6th	3rd	75	100.0	–	11th	9★
77 2/JPS	12	Nilsson	1m 22.16s	3	13th	R	10	13.3	Accident	9th=	10
77 3/JPS	14	(Spare)									
ITALIAN GP, Monza – 12th September – 52 L, 187.41 miles (301.60km) (206)											
77 2/JPS	12	Nilsson	1m 43.30s	3	12th	13th	51	98.0	–	9th=	10
77 3/JPS	14	Andretti	1m 43.34s	3	14th	R	23	44.2	Accident	12th	9★
77 1/JPS	11	(Spare)									
CANADIAN GP, Mosport – 3rd October – 80 L, 196.72 miles (316.59km) (207)											
77 1/JPS	11	Andretti	1m 13.028s	3	5th	3rd	80	100.0	–	9th	13★
77 2/JPS	12	Nilsson	1m 14.397s	3	15th	12th	79	98.7	–	10th=	10
77 3/JPS	14	(Spare)									

US GP, Watkins Glen – 10th October – 59 L, 199.24 miles (320.65km) (208)

77 1/JPS	11	Andretti	1m 45.311s	2	11th	R	23	38.9	Suspension	9th	13★
77 2/JPS	12	Nilsson	1m 46.776s	2	20th	R	13	22.0	Engine	10th=	10
77 3/JPS	14	(Spare)									

JAPANESE GP, Fuji – 24th October – 73 L, 197.72 miles (318.21km) (209)

77 1/JPS	11	Andretti	1m 12.77s	3	1st P	1st W	73	100.0	–	6th	22★
77 2/JPS	12	Nilsson	1m 14.35s	3	16th	6th	72	98.6	–	10th	11

Key:
★ = Single point scored in Parnelli-Ford in South Africa
DNQ = Did Not Qualify
R = Retired
L = Laps
P = Pole
W = Win

WORLD CHAMPIONSHIP RESULTS 1976

Position	Driver	Points
1	James Hunt	69
2	Niki Lauda	68
3	Jody Scheckter	49
4	Patrick Depailler	39
5	Clay Regazzoni	31
6	**Mario Andretti**	**22★**
7=	John Watson	20
	Jacques Laffite	20
9	Jochen Mass	19
10	**Gunnar Nilsson**	**11**

★ One point scored in Parnelli-Ford in South Africa

CONSTRUCTORS' CUP 1976

Position	Constructor	Points
1	Ferrari	83
2	McLaren-Ford	74 (75)
3	Tyrrell-Ford	71
4	**John Player Special/ Lotus-Ford**	**29**

Lotus 78 – JPS Mk 3

The 78 commenced testing in August 1976 and was recognized immediately as a major breakthrough, harnessing as it did the air flow under the car in the form of 'ground effect'. Andretti felt from day one that it was something special.

Chapman's concept had been dreamed up during his 1975 Ibiza holiday, and on his return Tony Rudd and aerodynamicist Peter Wright (who had identified ground effect whilst he was at BRM), were given the 'reverse wing research project'. Additionally, Ralph Bellamy and Charlie Prior created negative lift under the 78 model in Imperial College's wind tunnel. This sucked the model on to the ground, improving adhesion and cornering speeds with an inverted wing shape within the car's pannier side-pods. The slim tub, which was trimmed using the wings and fins, was reinforced with aluminium honeycomb. The driver had an adjustable rear roll bar, and fuel take-up could be used to balance the car, which was only slightly heavier than its predecessor. The 78's centre of gravity was much further forward, which heated the front tyres up better, and Andretti relished the thought of applying his Indy-honed car trimming techniques to it.

Chapman was furious when pictures of the 78 were published in September because he didn't want any competition from copies in 1977. The design was kept under wraps until officially launched at London's Royal Garden Hotel in late December. The year then ended sadly for Lotus when Stan Chapman died in a pre-Christmas road accident.

1977

The 'ground-effect' drag factor initially slowed the 78 on the straights, but before this was understood Andretti mistakenly blamed Cosworth. They initiated development work, causing unreliability, and Andretti regretted his criticisms when it also became apparent that the oil tank assembly had contributed to the problems. The 78 concept was so good that it didn't need the extra power that Cosworth's experiments sought. Andretti preferred the short-wheelbase, wide-front-track version of the 78, nicknamed the 'Black Rocket' and Nilsson was also eventually converted to this specification, which really bit into corners.

Andrew Ferguson returned as Team manager and Bob Dance as chief racing mechanic in time for the 78 to be briefly tested at Paul Ricard before being rushed to Argentina, where Chapman negotiated a $4m insurance

The Lotus 78 fully harnessed ground effect. With the driver situated further forward than was the norm, the centre of gravity was improved to raise front tyre temperatures. Andretti is seen here winning at Jarama.

policy against kidnapping for his drivers, such was the political instability! Nilsson's car was 4in (10mm) longer than Andretti's in Argentina; both suffered early engine failures. Andretti had a big fright when the intense heat caused his extinguisher bottle to explode approaching the fast first corner. The front of the car was blown off and Andretti was showered with oil, losing his pedals as he plunged off the circuit, luckily escaping serious injury. JPS 16's destruction meant that Andretti, as no. 1 driver commandeered Nilsson's car, in which he ran third for most of the race. Andretti was rudely chopped by Ribeiro, damaging his front wing, when he had got as high as second, but with only two laps to go he frustratedly dropped to fifth as a special wheel bearing assembly broke up.

Before Brazil JPS 16 was completely repaired in Norfolk but Ferguson had great difficulty getting it back through Customs. Despite a gearbox already having returned as 'hand luggage', it took a lot of diplomacy to free the chassis itself. In qualifying third at Interlagos, Andretti baled out at relatively low speed because of a fuel fire; the car continued into the barriers! Nilsson gave his singed team-mate a lift back, worried that his car might be taken over again. To his relief JPS 16 was repaired after an all-nighter by the mechanics. An exhausted Nilsson came fifth in the race after two tyre changes and after taking on extra fuel, as one of his tanks had been cannibalized for Andretti. The latter attacked eventual winner Reutemann's Ferrari until a shorting battery and ignition switch caused his retirement on lap 19.

During testing at Kyalami, fixed skirts replaced the brushes, and the benefit of ground effect was illustrated when a wingless 78 was only 2 seconds slower than the normal set-up! Andretti lost two engines, partly because of the circuit's altitude; even so, both cars were in the top ten on the grid. Andretti spent most of the South African GP dicing with Reutemann's Ferrari,

which he could drop in the corners but which would then power away on the straight. They eventually touched at Clubhouse, damaging Andretti's front suspension and causing his retirement. Nilsson's Lotus struck some of the accident debris from Tom Pryce's ill-fated Shadow, damaging his car's nose and puncturing both rear tyres. A blocked pit lane greeted him on his first attempt to stop, so by the time he did he was way behind. He finished a shocked twelfth with a weak engine, which lacked at least 600rpm.

In Brands Hatch's Race of Champions Andretti was denied an easy win when his ignition switch shorted out again.

Andretti used a Nicholson-McLaren DFV and the new short-wheelbase JPS 17 in Long Beach, where he scored the 78's first win whilst also becoming the first American F1 driver to win a GP in the USA. He had been fastest after first practice, and his delicate driving style was obvious as were his very short braking distances, although Lauda just pipped him for pole. Having avoided Reutemann's Ferrari at the first turn, a lucky Andretti fought off Lauda's Ferrari too, and overtook Scheckter's Wolf for the last four laps to win. Nilsson spent all weekend taming the short-wheelbase 78 and had yet another puncture, the fourth in four races; he felt sufficiently aggravated to remonstrate with Goodyear. Before this he had had a superb fight with Jarier only to struggle across the line in eighth place.

Nilsson couldn't understand why in Spain he was twelfth fastest and his team-mate was on pole. Chapman gave him a pep talk, and a new flowing driving style emerged to take him to fifth place in the race. Andretti's JPS 17 performed perfectly at Jarama, being visually smoother than the opposition and using a new locked differential to give Andretti his second victory of the year. Rivals accused Lotus of using better tyres than everyone else: only Ken Tyrrell recognized that

A new locked differential enabled Andretti to win the Spanish Grand Prix smoothly at Jarama. Such was his performance advantage that the opposition accused him of using 'trick' tyres, and only Ken Tyrrell realized the truth.

ment engine. Nilsson overcame huge understeer to qualify thirteenth. In the race Andretti followed Mass's McLaren for sixty-seven laps, ending up fifth overall. Nilsson retired after three stops failed to cure the gear problems of the 'reliable' five-speed box. Inexplicably, Monaco never suited the 78.

Having blown his engine at Zolder, Nilsson used the spare to take third for his highest-ever qualifying position. The Nicholson-propelled Andretti took pole, being fastest in both the wet and dry sessions by a margin of 1.5 seconds; Chapman had wanted him to sand-bag. On the damp race day, Nilsson remained on wets unlike most of the opposition. During the first lap, Andretti and race leader Watson collided, when under braking for the chicane and thus eliminated themselves; Nilsson luckily avoided the mêlée and continued. An annoyed Andretti honestly admitted responsibility for the accident, during which Scheckter had nipped past. Both Reutemann and Mass would breathe down Nilsson's neck for twenty laps before the track started to dry. Nilsson changed on to slicks in a pitstop, a process that was agonizingly slow compared with Lauda's 18 seconds, and he returned to the race in eighth place. Nilsson now charged through the field to second behind Lauda's Ferrari as the rain started to fall again. Piling on the pressure he eventually overtook to pull away by 2 seconds a lap, ignoring Chapman's 'hold it' signal when he was 15 seconds ahead! In the end an ecstatic Nilsson won his first GP to become a Swedish hero.

Nilsson couldn't repeat his Belgian success at home

the 78 was simply making better use of its Goodyears! Andretti's 78 just wouldn't handle at all in Monaco and he struck the Casino Square barriers; after repairs, the car felt even worse so he decided to risk a develop-

Having been lectured by Chapman at Jarama, Gunnar Nilsson altered his driving style and promptly took his sole Grand Prix win at Zolder. In doing so he ignored Chapman's pleas to go steady and finished 15 seconds ahead of Niki Lauda.

because of a jamming throttle in practice. A first-lap collision saw his aviating Nicholson-powered 78 loosen its nose cone, which necessitated a stop. He emerged right in front of, but a lap behind, pole-sitter Andretti, and Chapman ordered him to stay behind the American, who had a chance of winning both the race and the championship. Nilsson eventually retired when a wheel bearing gave out, much to the crowd's dismay. With a win seemingly assured, Andretti ran out of fuel when his development Cosworth DFV's metering unit switched itself to rich, allowing Laffite through at the last minute. With three laps to go, Andretti charged into the pits to refuel, failed to kill his engine and also missed the red light as he charged out again! He was subsequently fined, to crown a meeting that had seen enormous effort being devoted to setting Andretti's car up only for a furious Chapman to be informed that it had all the time been on the incorrect tyres!

In France, Watson's Brabham ran out of fuel and a lucky Andretti nipped through to win on the final lap. A happy Nilsson quietly came home fourth pleased with the progress he was making, having started third. Practice had been an Andretti demonstration as he swooped around the newly extended Dijon-Prenois circuit in a smooth unflustered style, in stark contrast to the unrefined efforts of his opposition. Andretti took pole with Hunt's McLaren alongside, but at the start the Lotus lagged, dropping to third behind the charging Watson. Hunt was disposed of but Watson was more difficult: it took most of the race to overcome the Ulsterman. Just as Andretti planned a banzai manoeuvre on the final lap the Ulsterman's car ran short of fuel and the relieved American was able to score another victory.

Andretti was fastest in Silverstone testing before the British GP, but in qualifying the opposition had caught up, and the eventual winner, Hunt, seized pole.

Andretti blamed his sixth place partly on a poor engine and partly on the fact that he had been blinded and forced off the track by smoke at Chapel from Brambilla's blown engine. His favourite Nicholson engine was fitted for the race, which he started immediately behind Nilsson, who was getting to grips with his 78. In the dry event an oil-covered Nilsson came third, having obediently trailed Andretti and his smoking 78 for forty-eight laps before the American's engine eventually failed. On lap 62 Andretti disconsolately parked at Woodcote, realizing how slow he was on the straights.

By mid-season Peterson, who was feeling media pressure in Sweden because of Nilsson's progress, secretly negotiated with Chapman. When Nilsson later signed for Shadow the Lotus drive was freed for Peterson. At this time Nilsson discovered that he was showing the first symptoms of cancer.

In early Hockenheim practice, Andretti's 78 wouldn't handle after its suspension had been banged across a kerb. He later improved to seventh place as Nilsson took ninth. Following an engine blow-up, he raced the troublesome spare, but the 78s were still slow on the long straights while being spectacularly fast through the Stadium corners. The engines of both Lotuses failed, with Andretti's development Cosworth blowing seven laps from the end and being parked alongside its sister, which had only lasted for thirty-one laps. Andretti had fought a long (thirty-four lap) vain battle with Reutemann, which had included some hair-raising slides on oil dropped in the Stadium.

On Chapman's advice, in Austria Goodyear used a softer compound, which heated up more quickly, and the 78's handling was transformed: it was regarded as the 1977 F1 chassis that was most sympathetic towards its tyres. An immediate 2.5 second benefit ensued, making Andretti third fastest, although Nilsson was

In the French Grand Prix, Watson's Brabham seemed destined to win until the final lap. The Ulsterman unexpectedly ran out of fuel and Andretti slipped past. Andretti had been on pole, having easily out-performed Hunt's McLaren.

only sixteenth thanks to an ill-performing damper and an engine blow-up. Again twin engine failures plagued Lotus in the Austria GP itself. Firstly Andretti's Nicholson blew at the Bosch corner after just eleven laps as he was leading and trying to cruise home; then Nilsson's engine failed whilst he was circulating exceedingly quickly after a pitstop for slicks. His development Cosworth objected to being revved to well above 11,000rpm during a number of fastest laps and blew as he passed the pits.

Zandvoort was ideal for the 78s and they performed perfectly, yielding pole for Andretti; provided his Nicholson engine held together, he was the hot favourite for victory. His tactic was to take the race easy by changing gear gently; this gave Hunt the opportunity to snatch the lead going into Tarzan, the first corner. Hunt obstinately stayed in front until Andretti tried to go round the outside, again at Tarzan, on lap 5. Hunt wouldn't give way and the two collided on the exit with Hunt retiring on the spot and Andretti spinning off. He recovered in fourth place and clawed his way up the field again, passing the Ferraris of both Reutemann and Lauda before yet another engine blow-up on lap 14 put him out. He then underwent a verbal assault from a furious Hunt. From fifth on the grid, Nilsson had collided with Reutemann in a self-inflicted accident, which spun him into retirement.

Having suffered four successive race engine failures, gossip suggested that Andretti would move to Ferrari for 1978, but in fact he had already signed a letter of intent with Lotus. Prior to Monza, contracts were drawn up, but significantly not signed, only for Lauda's surprise departure from Ferrari to be announced.

The new political situation caused both Andretti and Chapman some thought during the Italian GP meeting. In Monza practice, an over-confident Lauda overtook Nilsson's ill-handling 78 around the outside of the Parabolica, gesticulating as he went, only to spin into the barriers, allowing the nineteenth-placed Swede to wave back! Both Lotuses used unmodified DFVs, so worried were the Team by the spate of engine failures. Andretti finished third fastest. Early in the race Nilsson broke his shock absorbers after a tangle with Jabouille's Renault; by then all eyes were on Andretti, who took the lead from Scheckter after ten laps around the outside of the Parabolica. In Italy it was assumed that Andretti would join Ferrari for 1978, so even though he won the race for Lotus, the *Tifosi* went wild. He had used an excellent Cosworth development engine; had it blown, he almost certainly would have gone to Ferrari. Despite a large financial inducement and the temptation of engine reliability, he remained loyal to Lotus, only to express concern that Peterson would be joining him; he was unsure of the Team's ability to support two top-line drivers. Andretti's contract, though, very definitely stated that he would be no. 1 driver.

At Watkins Glen Andretti was bemused because he was comparatively slow on the straights even though his car was unchanged; even the engine was identical, yet he could only achieve fourth on the grid. Nilsson was twelfth. In the wet race Peterson and Nilsson clashed on lap 17 during the latter's unsuccessful overtaking manoeuvre ended up in the fencing. Eventual winner Hunt held off Andretti throughout the United States GP as a mismatched rear tyre handicapped him.

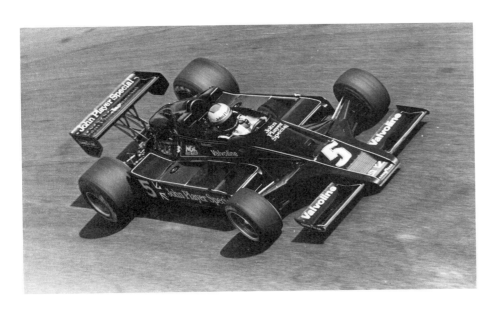

Andretti, who was preoccupied with the possibility of driving for Ferrari in 1978, won at Monza, having overtaken Scheckter around the outside of the Parabolica (pictured here) in a most audacious manoeuvre.

TEAM LOTUS RESULTS 1977

Drivers:
Mario Andretti: USA; Gunnar Nilsson: Swedish
Car:
Lotus 78 Engine: Ford Cosworth DFV 3-litre

CAR	CHASSIS	DRIVER	PRACTICE	SESSION	GRID	RACE	LAPS	%	REASON	CHAMPIONSHIP POSITION	POINTS
ARGENTINE GP, Buenos Aires – 9th January – 53 L, 196.55 miles (316.31km) (210)											
78 1/JPS	15	Andretti	1m 50.13s	4	8th	5th	51	96.2	–	5th	2
78 2/JPS	16	Nilsson	1m 50.66s	2	10th	DNS			(car raced by Andretti)		–
BRAZILIAN GP, Interlagos – 23rd January – 40 L, 197.85 miles (318.42km) (211)											
78 1/JPS	15	Nilsson	2m 32.14s	3	10th	5th	39	97.5	–	7th=	2
78 2/JPS	16	Andretti	2m 30.35s	3	3rd	R	19	47.5	Ignition	7th=	2
S AFRICAN GP, Kyalami – 5th March – 78 L, 198.90 miles (320.10km) (212)											
78 1/JPS	15	Nilsson	1m 16.65s	4	10th	12th	77	98.7	–	8th=	2
78 2/JPS	16	Andretti	1m 16.38s	4	6th	R	43	55.1	Accident	8th=	2
US GP WEST, Long Beach – 3rd April – 80 L, 161.60 miles (260.07km) (213)											
78 3/JPS	17	Andretti	1m 21.868s	4	2nd	1st W	80	100.0	–	4th	11
78 2/JPS	16	Nilsson	1m 23.384s	4	16th	8th	79	98.7	–	9th=	2
SPANISH GP, Jarama – 8th May – 75 L, 158.65 miles (255.32km) (214)											
78 3/JPS	17	Andretti	1m 18.70s	1	1st P	1st W	75	100.0	–	2nd	23
78 2/JPS	16	Nilsson	1m 20.38s	1	12th	5th	75	100.0	–	10th	4
MONACO GP, Monte Carlo – 22nd May – 76 L, 156.41 miles (251.71km) (215)											
78 3/JPS	17	Andretti	1m 31.50s	4	10th	5th	76	100.0	–	4th	22
78 2/JPS	16	Nilsson	1m 32.37s	4	13th	R	51	67.1	Gearbox	10th	4
78 1/JPS	15	(Spare)									
BELGIAN GP, Zolder – 5th June – 70 L, 185.38 miles (298.34km) (216)											
78 2/JPS	16	Nilsson	1m 26.45s	4	3rd	1st W	70	100.0	–	5th	13
78 3/JPS	17	Andretti	1m 24.64s	4	1st P	R	0	0.0	Accident	4th	22
78 1/JPS	15	(Spare)									
SWEDISH GP, Anderstorp – 19th June – 72 L, 179.76 miles (289.30km) (217)											
78 3/JPS	17	Andretti	1m 25.404s	4	1st P	6th	72	100.0	–	4th	23
Fastest Lap: 1m 27.607s – 102.594mph (165.110kph)											
78 2/JPS	16	Nilsson	1m 26.227s	4	7th	R	64	88.8	Wheel	6th	13
FRENCH GP, Dijon – 3rd July – 80 L, 188.99 miles (304.00km) (218)											
78 3/JPS	17	Andretti	1m 12.21s	4	1st P	1st W	80	100.0	–	2nd=	32
Fastest Lap and Record: 1m 13.75s – 115.259mph (185.492kph) on lap 76											
78 2/JPS	16	Nilsson	1m 12.79s	4	3rd	4th	80	100.0	–	5th	16
BRITISH GP, Silverstone – 16th July – 68 L, 199.38 miles (320.88km) (219)											
78 2/JPS	16	Nilsson	1m 18.95s	4	5th	3rd	68	100.0	–	6th	20
78 3/JPS	17	Andretti	1m 19.11s	2	6th	14th NR	62	91.1	Engine	2nd=	32
78 4/JPS	18	(Spare)									
GERMAN GP, Hockenheim – 31st July – 47 L, 198.27 miles (319.08km) (220)											
78 3/JPS	17	Andretti	1m 53.99s	4	7th	R	34	72.3	Engine	3rd	32
78 4/JPS	18	Nilsson	1m 54.44s	4	9th	R	31	65.9	Engine	6th	20
78 2/JPS	16	(Spare)									
AUSTRIAN GP, Österreichring – 14th August – 54 L, 199.39 miles (320.89km) (221)											
78 2/JPS	16	Nilsson	1m 41.24s	1	16th	R	38	70.3	Engine	6th	20
78 3/JPS	17	Andretti	1m 39.74s	4	3rd	R	11	20.3	Engine	4th	32
78 4/JPS	18	(Spare)									
DUTCH GP, Zandvoort – 28th August – 75 L, 196.94 miles (316.95km) (222)											
78 4/JPS	18	Nilsson	1m 19.57s	4	5th	R	34	45.3	Accident	6th	20
78 3/JPS	17	Andretti	1m 18.65s	4	1st P	R	14	18.6	Engine	4th	32
78 2/JPS	16	(Spare)									
ITALIAN GP, Monza – 11th September – 52 L, 187.41 miles (301.60km) (223)											
78 3/JPS	17	Andretti	1m 38.37s	4	4th	1st W	52	100.0	–	3rd	41
Fastest Lap and Record: 1m 39.1s – 130.920mph (210.696km) on lap 31											
78 2/JPS	16	Nilsson	1m 39.85s	4	19th	R	4	7.6	Suspension	7th	20

US GP, Watkins Glen – 2nd October – 59 L, 199.24 miles (320.55km) (224)

78 3/JPS	17	Andretti	1m 41.481s	2	4th	2nd	59	100.0	–	2nd	47
78 4/JPS	18	Nilsson	1m 42.815s	2	12th	R	17	28.8	Accident	7th	20

CANADIAN GP, Mosport – 9th October – 80 L, 196.72 miles (316.59km) (225)

78 3/JPS	17	Andretti	1m 11.385s	2	1st P	9th NR	77	96.2	Engine	3rd	47
Fastest Lap and Record: 1m 13.299s – 120.771mph (194.362kmh) on lap 56											
78 4/JPS	18	Nilsson	1m 12.975s	2	4th	R	17	21.2	Accident	7th	20

JAPANESE GP, Fuji – 23rd October – 73 L, 197.72 miles (318.21km) (226)

78 4/JPS	18	Nilsson	1m 13.66s	1	14th	R	63	86.3	Gearbox	8th	20
78 3/JPS	17	Andretti	1m 12.23s	1	1st P	R	1	1.3	Accident	3rd	47

Key:
DNS = Did Not Start
NC = Not Classified
NR = Not Running
P = Pole
W = Win
R = Retired
L = Laps

Andretti's 78 was easily the most balanced chassis at Mosport, and he easily took a damp pole again with Nilsson on the row behind. Andretti started perfectly, only to fight hard with Hunt again; this time the Lotus had the advantage. Hunt's team-mate Jochen Mass blocked Andretti so well when he was being lapped that Andretti nearly took to the grass at Turn 5; Hunt closed up and got past. The two McLarens promptly collided at Turn 3, causing Hunt's retirement and leaving Andretti perfectly positioned. Unbelievably, whilst a lap ahead and with only three laps left to go, his Cosworth development engine exploded! On lap 17 Nilsson had slammed head-on into a bank as his throttle jammed open.

Andretti claimed his seventh pole in Japan with a Nicholson DFV, but he was swamped at the start, and on the second lap he collided with Laffite's Ligier, swiped the barriers and retired. Nilsson's car unusually carried the red livery of the Imperial Tobacco Corporation; It was not strictly a JPS being referred to instead as the 'Imperial International Lotus 78/4'. Having qualified a lowly fourteenth because of oil pressure troubles, he went well in the race, climbing to fourth (for fourteen laps) before his gearbox failed after a long struggle. In posting his seventh successive retirement, Nilsson was sorry to finish his last race for Lotus in such a way before his intended departure to Shadow.

At the year's end Chapman expressed his anger at a points system that rewarded finishes rather than wins. Andretti had won four events as against Lauda and Scheckter's three. Andretti had led more race laps in 1977 than any other driver, despite suffering five engine failures. As the year closed, Ralph Bellamy left to join Copersucar and Tony Southgate went to Shadow.

WORLD CHAMPIONSHIP RESULTS 1977

Position	Driver	Points
1	Niki Lauda	72
2	Jody Scheckter	55
3	**Mario Andretti**	**47**
4	Carlos Reutemann	42
5	James Hunt	40
6	Jochen Mass	25
7	Alan Jones	22
8	**Gunnar Nilsson**	**20**

CONSTRUCTORS' CUP 1977

Position	Constructor	Points
1	Ferrari	95 (97 gross)
2	**John Player Special/ Lotus-Ford**	**62**

1978

Peterson was ecstatic after sampling the 78 for the first time, and he was to regard both it and the 79 as the best cars he had ever driven. The 78 in fact had a lot of life left in it, and Chapman decreed that whilst it maintained it's superiority the 79 would not be used. He anticipated a fully competitive season and began to enjoy his racing again.

Mexican privateer Hector Rebaque ran two 78s during the year even though he was somewhat out of his element. He would at least manage a fighting sixth place at Hockenheim, which was no mean feat.

From the Buenos Aires pole position Andretti dominated the 1978 Argentinian Grand Prix. A considered use of soft tyres enabled Lotus to out-perform both Reutemann's Ferrari and Watson's Brabham-Alfa.

Andretti claimed pole in Buenos Aires, having only been rivalled by Reutemann's Michelin-shod Ferrari 312T2. Both Lotuses boasted Hewland gearboxes, as the home-grown version was still unreliable. From the very start of the Argentinian GP, Andretti drew away to dominate utterly with his soft tyres countering Watson's Brabham-Alfa. Peterson drove carefully and tactically on harder tyres, fighting both understeer and a red-hot accelerator pedal. He had to lift his blistered right foot completely off the pedal at times.

Featureless Jacarepagua – the Brazilian GP's new venue – suited the Lotuses, after Peterson's hire car crashed as he learned the circuit. He still took pole, but after a slow start was savaged by Villeneuve's Ferrari puncturing a tyre and badly damaging his rear suspension. Reutemann's Michelin-shod Ferrari then led and won easily, whilst Andretti understeered. He had taken second place only to be overtaken by both Fittipaldi and Lauda when he was left with just fourth gear. This is where he stayed on an afternoon that was exhausting for everyone, as Goodyear were unhappy that Michelin had won.

Before the South African GP Kyalami testing saw Andretti collecting data for the evolving new 79, which would not run before Silverstone's International Trophy; Goodyear took along 3,000 tyres, including radials. Peterson took twelfth place thanks to his gearbox and an unhappy Andretti, who had suffered a steering breakage, was on the front row alongside Lauda. Immediately prior to the start Chapman, concerned about weight, significantly reduced Andretti's fuel by three gallons. After an argument over the location of pole position, Andretti took the lead, only to blister his left front tyre, allowing Scheckter to lead for six laps as he pitted. Riccardo Patrese then got past but

his Arrow's engine failed him on lap 63 handing the lead to Depailler's Tyrrell. Almost within sight of the flag Andretti's challenge faded as his small fuel load reduced and he was forced to refill; on his return his car failed him again. Depailler's leading Tyrrell had a similar problem as it drained its tanks and Peterson caught him up on the final lap seizing the lead at the Esses – after a few wheel banging moments – amid a great cheer. This was both a superb victory for Peterson and the 78's swan-song.

Lotus 79 – JPS Mk 4

Ground effect was fully harnessed by the Lotus 79 with its interchangeable venturi side-pods, containing the water radiator on the right and the oil cooler on the left. This design became feasible because a new regulation required that the fuel tankage be behind the driver, which permitted improved aerodynamics. The slim aluminium sheet tub only used honeycomb materials in the floor, but the lightweight Lotus/Gertrag gearbox proved unreliable and the Hewland alternative was preferred. The 79 proved sophisticated to set up, requiring a number of small adjustments, such were the cornering forces generated; ride height and tyre stagger suddenly became very important.

Following testing at Paul Ricard in December, the 79 was modified to make it easier to balance, as Andretti realized that he had been given the best possible steed in which to chase the Championship. The 79's official launch was at Silverstone's International Trophy, where it was dominant in practice until its gearbox blew. Andretti sailed off the waterlogged track at Abbey and retired; the car so damaged that its World Championship début would be postponed until the US

In a memorable South African GP Peterson grabbed a superb victory on the last lap when Depailler's Tyrrell started to run short of fuel. Side-by-side around the final lap, the two touched wheels before the Swede forced past.

GP West. Poledriver Peterson had crashed his 78 at Woodcote in the warm-up.

Andretti used some specially grooved Goodyears to try to cure the handling at Long Beach and Peterson had an engine fail. After Watson's optimistic first lap attack at the Queen Mary hairpin, Villeneuve's Ferrari seized the lead, with Andretti powerless to catch him because of his narrow 9.5in front tyres. Reutemann subsequently led before Jones (Williams) passed Andretti on lap 18, only to drop back again, leaving the American securely in second place at the flag. Peterson tortured his tyres on his way to fourth place as Andretti now shared the Championship lead with Reutemann.

Andretti went tyre-testing at Jarama before his 79 was rebuilt for Monaco, where it sported the Hewland gearbox and a completely redesigned back end. Chapman celebrated his fiftieth birthday in Monaco, and during dinner he significantly met American oil dealer

David Thieme for the first time. On the track Andretti raved about the 79's improved rear grip, although in the event he opted to race the proven 78. Peterson had crashed out in Thursday practice and in the race his gearbox seized on lap 56. Whilst in fourth place, and fighting with Scheckter, Andretti's fuel gauge blew up on lap 44 and blinded him with spraying petrol just as he emerged from the tunnel. He managed to gather everything together but had to make a total of three pitstops.

Whilst Andretti headed for Indianapolis, Peterson was fastest during Anderstorp testing although minor problems meant that the Team expected to run the 78s at Zolder. In Belgium, Andretti, who had sacrificed Indy 500 qualifying, surprisingly raced his 79 and easily took pole. Avoiding a number of first-lap accidents, Andretti pulled away pursued only by Villeneuve, who eventually had a puncture allowing Peterson into

The Lotus 79 made full use of ground effect now that the fuel tank was immediately behind the driver. The side-pods contained the radiators, but the sensitive machine, seen here at Jarama, was initially difficult to set up.

Andretti qualified a second faster than anyone else at Jarama, having been hoodwinked by his team-mate! In the race he soon overtook Hunt, out of necessity where his engine was concerned, and easily won.

second place. The Swede had to make a quick pitstop for a new left front tyre – incurring a 250-franc fine for ignoring the red exit light – and then pass Laffite to take station for the first Lotus one-two since Monza in 1973. Andretti, now leading the Championship, was ecstatic but poignantly, having recently visited his seriously ill friend in hospital, dedicated the race to Gunnar Nilsson.

Andretti's Jarama pole time was more than a second faster than the opposition's with his now Olympus-sponsored 79! Peterson had been fastest in the first session but had missed the trackside gesticulations for more fuel from his stranded team-mate! As the Swede's main competitor was impotently parked, the first hint of a feud between Andretti and Chapman on one side and Peterson on the other surfaced. Fearing a damaging shoot-out between his two drivers, Chapman decided that Andretti alone would use qualifying tyres.

Peterson was slow starting, being ninth at the first corner. As Hunt led, Peterson turned up the pressure, passing firstly Laffite and then both Watson and Keegan at the Virage Nuvolari with a memorable manoeuvre. Chapman was concerned, but Peterson knew exactly what he was doing as he targeted Hunt; he finished second behind Andretti. Earlier in the race Andretti had run side by side with Hunt's McLaren into the first corner before maturely deciding to settle for second place. His water temperature then rose in the dead air behind the McLaren, and so after five laps he seized the lead, which he held to the flag. The Lotus one-two was repeated in Spain, when Peterson too got past Hunt on lap 52, vindicating the Team's choice of hard-compound Goodyears to combat the intense heat.

Before Anderstorp Peterson injured his heel racing a

BMW at the Nurburgring, but the Swedish press objected to the notion that 'team orders' might force him to give way to Andretti should he be leading the forthcoming Swedish GP. Much to his credit Peterson accepted his supporting role without complaint. The controversial Brabham BT46 'sucker' car arrived in Sweden providing temporary competition for the 79. The BT46 possessed a rear-facing fan, which allegedly cooled its engine but also sucked out air from underneath, thereby gaining a huge amount of adhesion. Following cars were pelted with grit and Andretti dreaded what might happen in a wet race. Chapman was convinced that the Brabhams were illegal and, encouraged by fellow FOCA members, he protested officially, something he hadn't done for some considerable time; he was rejected only because he had exceeded the time limit for protests.

The apparently sand-bagging Brabhams were thus permitted to race from their second (Lauda) and third (Watson) grid positions. Andretti held pole but the crowd cheered 'their' Peterson, who was only fourth fastest because sheared engine bolts affected the handling. Early in the race he passed both Watson and Patrese, but then pitted with a puncture and a damaged screen. There being no radios, he mistakenly signalled concern about the wrong tyre and valuable seconds were lost, dropping him to seventeenth. He recovered brilliantly as early leader Andretti found he could keep ahead of Lauda, being faster on the straights. Andretti then made a mistake at Laktar, letting Lauda past, only for the Lotus to retire with piston failure on lap 46.

Peterson only failed to overtake Lauda and Patrese because the Italian stubbornly held his line, despite the marshals furiously waving blue flags. An enraged Peterson failed to pass him by a mere hundredth of a second

Following a heavy practice shunt at Paul Ricard, Andretti took second place on the grid. Having made a slow start he rectified this on the Mistral straight and took the lead in what was to become a Lotus one-two victory.

and was not amused at having been blocked; unusually he openly articulated his anger. A week later the BT46 'sucker' was banned, but secretly Chapman had designed a twin-fan 79, just in case!

Paul Ricard practice was damp, and Andretti made a mistake and flew off the road at the fast 'S' de Laverrerie. The repaired car was far from perfect; still, despite worrying about the critical ground-effect set-up, Andretti took second behind Watson's now fanless Brabham, which was suddenly the fastest car in a straight line. On the grid Andretti had more wing added but momentarily lagged at the start with his rear wheels spinning on his own cooling water; he then fought off Hunt for second place behind Watson. Hunt was not amused. Once on the Mistral straight for the first time, Andretti towed past Watson to lead another Lotus one-two finish. The oversteering Peterson had coped with a bent front wing and only Hunt had challenged, but he failed when he was sick and spun-out on the last lap.

The two Lotuses jousted for pole in qualifying for Brands Hatch. When Andretti took Peterson's fastest time away using qualifiers, Chapman ordered the Swede to come in, but before he returned he promptly recaptured pole by a substantial margin using race tyres. This led to a lengthy 'discussion' with Chapman. The very unwell Gunnar Nilsson returned to see his friends, making the Team's mobile home his base with Mike and Ann Murphy. Pole-holder Peterson could decide on which side he wanted to start and he avoided Brands Hatch's downhill position, where a hollow can catch the occupant out. His uphill choice backfired, as Andretti was quicker away, disappearing into the distance once Scheckter had been repulsed. Neither

Lotus, though, lasted long: Peterson retired after six laps when his fuel system failed at Graham Hill bend and Andretti's engine blew on lap 28 following a tyre stop. The anticipated Lotus demonstration run had collapsed as Reutemann's Ferrari won to become Lotus's only real challenger. Hockenheim was therefore to be vitally important.

In Germany Peterson deliberately aimed to impress other teams and, having become the fastest Lotus qualifier, Chapman decided to slow him. In the second qualifying run, Peterson was again the faster on race tyres and 'coincidentally' he was then picked for full tank tests. Bennett filled the 79 up with more fuel than necessary and Peterson knew he was being handicapped. He promptly maintained his dominance and only a spin caused by a rear suspension top-link breakage allowed Andretti to snatch pole back. In the race Peterson planned to go fast initially and then to back off and let Andretti through. This he did, letting Andretti past on lap 5, only for his gearbox to break thirty-one laps later, allowing the no. 1 driver to take his fifth win. Andretti was 23 points ahead of Reutemann with Peterson 18 points behind and supposedly no threat. Any complacency, however, would be wiped out in Austria.

At the Österreichring Peterson was constantly fastest despite being denied qualifiers. In the final session he tricked Andretti into waiting in the pits for the track to dry, when in fact he anticipated the session would indeed be washed out. By his actions he had quietly avenged his lack of qualifiers. Andretti changed his car back to the standard suspension, which improved its handling and even after all this gamesmanship, Lotus comfortably occupied the front row. In the drizzle

At Hockenheim, Peterson let Andretti through as pre-arranged and the American cruised on to his fifth win of the season. Peterson had proved exceedingly fast in practice only to be ordered to undertake full tank tests!

In Austria Peterson, who still had a mathematical chance of snatching the title, was quickest without qualifiers! Having won by a margin of 40 seconds he was now perceived as a threat by Andretti.

Peterson got away best as Andretti spun his tyres before trying to pass Reutemann at the Sebring corner, where they took each other off and Scheckter's Wolf joined the mêlée, severely damaging the Lotus. The race was red-flagged after seven laps, and only after crossing the line first did Peterson spin into a morass of mud. The restarted event was again wet, but the track soon dried and Peterson scored a 40-second victory, having overtaken both Reutemann and Villeneuve despite stopping for slicks, to finish within nine points of Andretti . . .

Before Zandvoort Peterson made it plain that he wasn't going to accept another year as understudy. Andretti didn't accept the conditions that were put to him and from that moment Peterson decided to move, quickly signing for McLaren for 1979.

Lotus hogged the front row in Holland, where Team orders were implemented for another Lotus one-two result. Andretti was considerably relieved, knowing that if Peterson had won again they would have tied for the Championship lead. Following a first-lap accident, Patrese's wrecked Arrows lay in the middle of the track, and on lap 2 the Lotuses dived either side as onlookers held their breath! Peterson had forced Andretti to speed up at one point, when the latter came under pressure from Lauda, and the Swede seemed a lot faster than his team leader. He later admitted that he could easily have overtaken even though he had brake troubles. Ten laps from the finish Andretti's exhaust broke, worryingly changing his engine note, but he still kept ahead of Peterson. Only a Lotus driver could now win the Championship.

Peterson's Accident

Peterson unusually couldn't challenge Andretti for pole at Monza because his engine blew up and the spare 78 had a tired engine. Sporting a fresh engine in his 79 on Saturday, he had brake troubles; finally a gearbox seal leaked fluid on to his clutch, forcing him to sit out most of final qualifying. With minutes to go he returned to the track in a cloud of aggressive tyre smoke but could get no higher than fifth, vowing to avenge his low placing in the race. Andretti took pole with ease although Villeneuve gave spirited chase. Sunday's warm-up was again troublesome for Peterson as brake failure – allegedly caused by a missing split pin – made him plough through the second chicane's catch fencing, bruising his legs, to come to rest against a tree. He would have to drive the 'old' 78 in the race.

The premature race start was a complete disaster. As Villeneuve and Andretti led the funnelling field towards the first chicane, at a point where the very wide pit straight narrows, a number of cars tangled whilst still accelerating heavily.

Amid the chaos Peterson's slow-starting 78 was punted heavily into the barriers, having been hit or struck by a number of other cars, rebounding in a fireball. Patrick Depailler, Clay Regazzoni and James Hunt, with the aid of a quick-thinking fire marshal, courageously waded into the conflagration and pulled Peterson free, but the obviously badly hurt Swede had to be stabilized on the track before being rushed by helicopter to the Niguarda hospital in Milan, his legs severely injured.

The race was stopped with Vittorio Brambilla, too, being unconscious in his Surtees. Eventually the GP was restarted but many drivers did not really want to continue. The race was 3 hours late after Scheckter had crashed in the warm-up, and the Lesmo barriers had had to be repaired. Andretti won on the road, having been unable to resist chasing an over-zealous Villeneuve, who had left the grid somewhat early. The two were therefore given a penalty for jumping the second highly charged start, but Andretti did not know his official position as the electronic score-board was not altered to cater for the penalty. In the end Lauda's Brabham won; Andretti's eventual sixth place, however, gave both him and Lotus the Championship, which was just reward for a dominant season.

All this was achieved under the cloud of Peterson's accident. On the day of the race news from Milan was that Peterson's life was not in danger but overnight, following emergency operations, his condition worsened as a result of a series of embolisms. On Monday morning he succumbed to his injuries, devastating the

racing world, Team Lotus and its new World Champion in particular.

Monza's bitter-sweet relationship with Team Lotus had continued, and Chapman was furious that Peterson had been forced to drive the 78 – there being no spare 79 available – as the newer car had a much stronger footbox and might have protected its driver more. Peterson's death led to Jean-Pierre Jarier being brought into the Team for last two races of the season.

A depressed Team Lotus set off for North America with Andretti insisting that a spare 79 be provided as stipulated in his contract. Exactly a decade after taking his first F1 pole at Watkins Glen, Andretti did the same again but this time as World Champion. He performed faultlessly, as did the 79, which absorbed the ripples on the unusually bumpy circuit. In the warm-up he dropped the car into the barriers when a rear wheel loosened and was forced to commandeer Jarier's mount. The Frenchman had been coping exceedingly well with his 79 even though it had a split exhaust system. Initially Andretti seemed set to walk away from the Ferraris but his car developed understeer as well as fading brakes. Dropping down the field his engine finally blew, much to the disappointment of his home crowd. In the unfamiliar spare Jarier seemed set for third place – having recovered from an early tyre stop – but after setting a new lap record his fuel ran out within three laps of the flag. When one realizes that his bad seating position had caused him to pull some muscles, Jarier's drive seems even more meritorious.

The Canadian GP was run at the former Expo 67 site in Montreal on the Circuit Ile de Notre-Dame. In pain from his back, Jarier took an impressive pole on the tight new venue, which was rain-afflicted during practice; Andretti's car, twisted as a result of its USA GP accident, was only on row five, and had the wrong set-up. In the race, Andretti went well before colliding with Watson's Brabham on lap 6; they were both push-started with the American eventually salvaging tenth place. Jarier starred by leading for forty-nine laps only for his brakes to let him down, allowing Villeneuve through for a popular local win. With this result Jarier's brief but successful period at Lotus concluded.

At thirty-eight years of age Andretti had become World Champion in only his second complete season of F1. He followed in Phil Hill's footsteps to become America's second World Champion F1 driver. John Player Team Lotus too had convincingly won the Constructors' Cup, which was a fitting way for Players to temporarily end their sponsorship.

Sadly, in the early hours of 20 October Gunnar Nilsson died in Charing Cross Hospital, having lost his brave fight against cancer.

TEAM LOTUS AND PRIVATE LOTUS ENTRY RESULTS 1978

Drivers:
Mario Andretti: USA; Ronnie Peterson: Swedish; Jean-Pierre Jarier: French
Car:
Lotus 78 Engine: Ford Cosworth DFV 3-litre

CAR	CHASSIS	DRIVER	PRACTICE SESSION	GRID	RACE	LAPS	%	REASON	CHAMPIONSHIP POSITION	POINTS
ARGENTINE GP, Buenos Aires – 15th January – 52 L, 192.84 miles (310.35km) (227)										
78 3/JPS	17	Andretti	1m 47.75s 3	1st P	1st W	52	100.0	–	1st	9
78 2/JPS	16	Peterson	1m 48.39s 3	3rd	5th	52	100.0	–	5th	2
78	4/JPS	18	(Spare)							
78 R	1	Rebaque	1m 52.52s –	DNQ	–	–	–	–	–	–
BRAZILIAN GP, Jacarepagua – 29th January – 63 L, 196.95 miles (316.95km) (228)										
78 3/JPS	17	Andretti	1m 40.62s 3	3rd	4th	63	100.0	–	1st	12
78 2/JPS	16	Peterson	1m 40.45s 3	1st P	R	15	23.8	Accident	7th=	2
78 R	1	Rebaque	1m 43.86s –	20th	R	40	63.4	Exhaustion	–	–
S AFRICAN GP, Kyalami – 4th March – 78 L, 198.90 miles (320.10km) (229)										
78 2/JPS	16	Peterson	1m 15.94s 2	12th	1st W	78	100.0	–	2nd	11
78 3/JPS	17	Andretti	1m 14.90s 1	2nd	7th	77	98.7	–	1st	12
Fastest Lap: 1m 17.09s – 119.082mph (191.650kmh) on lap 2										
78 4/JPS	18	(Spare)								
78 R	1	Rebaque	1m 17.50s –	21st	10th	77	98.7	–	–	–
US GP **WEST**, Long Beach – 2nd April – 80 L, 162.61 miles (261.70km) (230)										
78	3	Andretti	1m 21.188s 3	4th	2nd	80	100.0	–	1st=	18
78	2	Peterson	1m 21.474s 3	6th	4th	80	100.0	–	3rd=	14
78	4	(Spare)								
78 R	1	Rebaque	1m 26.128s –	DNQ	–	–	–	–	–	–
MONACO GP, Monte Carlo – 7th May – 75 L, 154.35 miles (248.40km) (231)										
78	3	Andretti	1m 29.10s 2	4th	11th	69	92.0	–	2nd=	18
78	2	Peterson	1m 29.23s 3	7th	R	56	74.6	Gearbox	5th	14
79	2	(Spare)								
78 R	4	Rebaque	1m 34.95s –	DNQ	–	–	–	–	–	–
78 R	1	(Spare)								
BELGIAN GP, Zolder – 21st May – 70 L, 185.38 miles (298.34km) (232)										
79	2	Andretti	1m 20.90s 3	1st P	1st W	70	100.0	–	1st	27
78	2	Peterson	1m 22.62s 3	7th	2nd	70	100.0	–	4th	20
Fastest Lap and Record: 1m 23.13s – 144.685mph (184.569kmh) on lap 66										
78	3	(Spare)								
78 R	4	Rebaque	1m 25.10s –	DNQ	–	–	–	–	–	–
SPANISH GP, Jarama – 4th June – 75 L, 158.65 miles (255.31km) (233)										
79	3	Andretti	1m 16.39s 3	1st P	1st W	75	100.0	–	1st	36
Fastest Lap and Record: 1m 20.06s – 95.119mph (153.080kmh) on lap 6										
79	2	Peterson	1m 16.68s 1	2nd	2nd	75	100.0	–	2nd	26
78	2	(Spare)								
78	3	(Spare)								
78 R	1	Rebaque	1m 20.21s –	20th	R	21	28.0	Exhaust	–	–
78 R	4	(Spare)								
SWEDISH GP, Anderstorp – 17th June – 70 L, 175.33 miles (282.17km) (234)										
79	2	Peterson	1m 23.120s 3	4th	3rd	70	100.0	–	2nd	30
79	3	Andretti	1m 22.058s 2	1st P	R	46	65.7	Engine	1st	36
78	2	(Spare)								
78	3	(Spare)								
78 R	4	Rebaque	1m 27.139s –	21st	12th	68	97.1	–	–	–
78 R	1	(Spare)								
FRENCH GP, Ricard – 2nd July – 54 L, 194.95 miles (313.74km) (235)										
79	3	Andretti	1m 44.46s 2	2nd	1st W	54	100.0	–	1st	45
79	2	Peterson	1m 44.98s 3	5th	2nd	54	100.0	–	2nd	36
78	2	(Spare)								
78	3	(Spare)								
78 R	4	Rebaque	1m 50.40s –	DNQ	–	–	–	–	–	–
78 R	1	(Spare)								

BRITISH GP, Brands Hatch – 16th July – 76 L, 198.63 miles (319.67km) (236)

79	3	Andretti	1m 17.06s	3	2nd	R	28	36.8	Engine	1st	45
79	2	Peterson	1m 16.80s	3	1st P	R	6	7.8	Fuel	2nd	36
78	3	(Spare)									
79	1	(Spare)									
78	2	(Spare)									
78 R	4	Rebaque	1m 20.24s	–	21st	R	15	19.7	Gearbox	–	–
78 R	1	(Spare)									

GERMAN GP, Hockenheim – 30th July – 45 L, 189.83 miles (305.51km) (237)

79	3	Andretti	1m 51.90s	3	1st P	1st W	45	100.0	–	1st	54
79	2	Peterson	1m 51.99s	3	2nd	R	36	80.0	Gearbox	2nd	36

Fastest Lap and Record: 1m 55.62s – 131.349mph (211.386kmh) on lap 26

79	1	(Spare)									
78	2	(Spare)									
78 R	4	Rebaque	1m 55.57s	–	18th	6th	45	100.0	–	–	–
78 R	2	(Spare)									

AUSTRIAN GP, Österreichring – 13th August – 54 L, 199.39 miles (320.89km) (238)

79	2	Peterson	1m 37.71s	1	1st P	1st W	54	100.0	–	2nd	45

Fastest Lap: 1m 43.12s – 128.906mph (207.454kmh)

79	3	Andretti	1m 37.76s	2	2nd	R	0	0.0	Accident	1st	54
79	1	(Spare)									
78	2	(Spare)									
78 R	4	Rebaque	1m 40.84s	–	18th	R	1	1.8	Clutch	–	–
78 R	1	(Spare)									

DUTCH GP, Zandvoort – 27th August – 75 L, 196.94 miles (316.95km) (239)

79	4	Andretti	1m 16.36s	3	1st P	1st W	75	100.0	–	1st	63
79	2	Peterson	1m 16.97s	1	2nd	2nd	75	100.0	–	2nd	51
79	1	(Spare)									
78	3	(Spare)									
78 R	4	Rebaque	1m 20.02s	–	20th	11th	74	98.6	–	–	–

ITALIAN GP, Monza – 10th September – 40 L, 144.16 miles (232.00km) (240)

79	4	Andretti	1m 37.52s	3	1st P	6th*	40	100.0	Penalty	1st	64

Fastest Lap and Record: 1m 38.23s – 132.080mph (212.562kmh) on lap 33

78	3	Peterson	1m 38.256s	1	5th	R	0	0.0	Accident	2nd	51
79	1	(Spare)									
79	3	(Spare)									
78 R	4	Rebaque	1m 41.063s	–	DNQ	–	–	–	–	–	–
78	2	(Spare)									

US GP, Watkins Glen – 1st October – 59 L, 199.24 miles (320.55km) (241)

79	1	Jarier	1m 40.034s	3	8th	15th	55	93.2	–	–	–

Fastest Lap and Record: 1m 39.557s – 122.113mph (196.521kmh) on lap 55

79	3	Andretti	1m 38.114s	3	1st P	R	27	45.7	Engine	1st	64
79	4	(Spare)									
78 R	2	Rebaque	1m 43.028s	–	23rd	R	0	0.0	Clutch	–	–
78 R	1	(Spare)									

CANADIAN GP, Montreal – 8th October – 70 L, 195.72 miles (314.98km) (242)

79	4	Andretti	1m 39.236s	3	9th	10th	69	98.5	–	1st	64
79	3	Jarier	1m 38.015s	3	1st P	R	49	70.0	Brakes	–	–
79	1	(Spare)									
78 R	2	Rebaque	1m 42.413s	–	DNQ	–	–	–	–	–	–
78 R	1	(Spare)									

Key:

★	= First on road
DNQ	= Did Not Qualify
NC	= Not Classified
NR	= Not Running
R	= Retired
L	= Laps
P	= Pole
W	= Win

Private Lotus Entries:

R   = Team Rebaque

WORLD CHAMPIONSHIP RESULTS 1978

Position	Driver	Points
1	**Mario Andretti**	**64**
2	**Ronnie Peterson**	**51**
3	Carlos Reutemann	48
4	Niki Lauda	44
5	Patrick Depailler	34
6	John Watson	25
7	Jody Schekter	24
8	Jacques Laffite	19
9=	Emerson Fittipaldi	17
	Gilles Villeneuve	17
11=	Alan Jones	11
	Riccardo Patrese	11
13=	James Hunt	8
	Patrick Tambay	8
15	Didier Pironi	7
16	Clay Regazzoni	4
17	Jean-Pierre Jabouille	3
18	Hans-Joachim Stuck	2
19=	**Hector Rebaque**	**1**
	Vittorio Brambilla	1
	Derek Daly	1

CONSTRUCTORS' CUP 1978

Position	Constructor	Points
1	**Lotus-Ford**	**86**

═══ 1979 ═══

Peter Collins joined the now Martini-sponsored Team as assistant competitions manager, in a year dominated by both Ligier and Williams. Reutemann arrived too, allegedly at the request of Goodyear, even though Villeneuve had been on the short list. Inconceivably, though, in 1979 the reigning Constructor would not win a single GP.

Even though design and production effort went into the new 80, the ageing 79s were still retained. Further development of the 79 would be undertaken to counter the Williams's FW07, as the 80 proved to be a blind alley.

In Argentina the new Goodyear cross-ply tyres boasted stiffer side-walls than previously, which improved not only the times of the 79s but also of Laffite's Ligier, which took pole. The Martini-Lotuses struggled, the setting-up of the taller Goodyears leaving them lower on the grid (third and seventh) than usual.

The Argentinian crowd greeted Reutemann's appearance with acclaim but the first attempt at a race lasted only a few yards as a chain reaction accident saw Tambay's McLaren aviating over Andretti's 79. An hour later the race was restarted with Andretti in the unfamiliar spare and Reutemann being encouraged by the crowd to chase the Ligiers. He was hampered by a broken exhaust but he took second with nine laps to go, unable to close the final gap to winner Laffite. Andretti struggled through to fifth in his understeering and out-paced 79.

For Brazil the 79s had replacement rear uprights to try to accommodate the 'new' tyres, but the new ride height affected the whole car's set-up. The Lotuses shared the second row, having juggled tyres to good effect. Andretti's car caught fire twice on the parade lap disappearing in extinguishant on the grid and Reutemann's wouldn't start: it had to be pushed in what in theory was an illegal manoeuvre! The Lotus drivers then touched on the opening lap at Curva 3, before Andretti pitted on lap 2 as a recurring fuel leak caused yet another fire. Reutemann settled for third place on lap 2 and held this for the entire race, being powerless to catch the Ligiers. His push-start was analysed afterwards and he was lucky that the result was ratified, much to Pironi's chagrin.

The Martini-Lotuses were well down the grid at Kyalami with Reutemann complaining that his large rear wing slowed him on the straights. Rain fell after two laps of the South African GP causing a stoppage; once restarted on a quickly drying track, the Lotuses stopped for slicks, rejoined and then threaded their way through the field. Andretti, with both brake troubles and a mismatched rear tyre, came fourth as the competition dropped by the wayside and a virtually brakeless Reutemann was fifth as the Ferraris dominated.

Spanish tyre-testing followed before the United States GP West in Long Beach, where Reutemann seemed assured of pole only inopportunely to lose a drive-shaft, allowing Villeneuve's Ferrari past. Andretti was inexplicably slower on the third row. At the start Reutemann was stranded with electrical failure, and once he did get going he only lasted for twenty-one laps before his third drive-shaft failed. Andretti fought with Depailler and Jones before settling for fourth, as both his brakes and his engine started to desert him in front of another disappointed home crowd.

In Brands Hatch's Race of Champions the pole-sitting Andretti came third in what was intended to be the 79's last race before the 80 took over.

CHAPTER 6

Essex Man

Lotus 80

The Lotus 80, with Martini sponsorship as well as an increasing influence from David Thieme's Essex Petroleum, was launched at Brands Hatch, where it was explained that the design would produce sufficient downforce to remove the need for wings, as well as reduce drag. Downforce was to be created entirely by the under-car wing configuration; for a time skirts even appeared around the nose but they were soon to be removed. Although very long, the 80 was much lighter than the 79, with a considerable quantity of aluminium honeycomb in the tub and a transverse Hewland FGA gearbox.

Following Paul Ricard testing, the design had been considerably modified for Jarama: the car now boasted both wings and much reduced skirts. The titanium

Essex Petroleum's larger-than-life supremo, David Thieme, became an increasingly high-profile sponsor of Team Lotus, sharing a kindred spirit with Chapman.

suspension rocking arms had suffered weld problems and had been replaced by conventional steel versions. The skirts proved to be the main problem as they sealed and unsealed, creating downforce that could suddenly be lost; the drivers were very concerned about their unpredictability. The 80 was the fastest Ford-powered car at Jarama, with Andretti on the second row saying there was plenty of development potential to come. Reutemann was further back thanks to a leaking water radiator, and he took second place on lap 16 of the GP to hold off attacks from Scheckter's Ferrari successfully, despite numerous small mechanical problems. Andretti had momentarily taken the lead on the run to the first corner but dropped to fifth as he hit the rev-limiter. He then took fourth until lap 43 when his front wing was clipped by Tambay, letting Lauda's Brabham through. As the fuel load reduced the car's handling improved, and Andretti passed Scheckter on lap 67 to seize third place, which remained his. The Team was now thoroughly optimistic about the Lotus 80, but sadly it was flattering to deceive.

The 79s were fielded in the Belgian GP at the resurfaced Zolder circuit after Andretti had clashed with Mass in qualifying, badly damaging the 80's monocoque in the process. Overnight repairs were wasted when the car's engine gave out in the warm-up. Andretti had also had a confrontation with Chapman in practice when, after a suspension collapse, the frustrated American decided he would continue running the new car against the wishes of the Lotus boss. After the accident Andretti transferred to the unpractised 79/5, which suffered complete front brake failure on lap 27 after a steady run in fifth place. The gearbox was actually used to stop at the pit! Having replaced a worn front tyre after eleven laps, dropping from sixth to twenty-first in the process, Reutemann clawed his way back to fourth at the finish. He would put on a similar display in Monte Carlo.

A year after being on pole for Ferrari at Monaco, Reutemann was now driving for a team in the second division. He was eleventh fastest, having hit the swimming-pool barriers with his preferred 79/2, and like Andretti – who was giving Indianapolis a miss – complaining of a lack of grip. The previous year Andretti had been fourth fastest in the 78 but now he was

Andretti's third place in the 1979 Spanish Grand Prix was the sole good result for the Lotus 80 before it was junked. Ironically, Reutemann's Lotus 79 was second and the Team would fall back on this 'old' car when the 80 proved less than successful.

thirteenth in the 80, which he stuck with, only for a rear rocker arm to break after only twenty-one laps: he must have wondered why he hadn't gone to Indiana! Reutemann, by contrast, had one of his best races of the year, complete with a broken exhaust, no second gear and a failing left front tyre. He fended off Piquet's Brabham, which terminally severed a drive-shaft, to come home a splendid third. Reutemann's luck, though, would change, for these four points were the last he was to score during 1979.

Whilst France celebrated an all-French victory on Renault's adopted test track of Dijon-Prenois, Lotus could only boast a double retirement. The second 80 chassis, with different side-pods, was practised by Andretti, but he preferred his original car's configuration. This couldn't cope with the fast corners and neither could Reutemann's 79. In the race the Argentinian plugged on but failing brakes induced a terminal collision with Rosberg's Wolf three laps before the end. The 80 was put through an extended test session in the race but Andretti retired after fifty-one laps with a persistent brake problem.

The French weekend sounded the death knell of the 80, and it was not to be seen again, although it was tested further at Snetterton during the summer. Its aerodynamic problems were too complex to sort out in the middle of the season and the Team was forced to revert to the 79.

In testing before the British GP, the 79, which had previously been unsuited to the year's new tyre sizes, was fitted with modified geometry; this showed promise as Reutemann put in a best Silverstone lap of 1 minute 13.90 seconds. Ligier experienced grip problems during the GP meeting at Silverstone; as a result

the 79s suddenly became more competitive, but the Williams FW07s of both Alan Jones, who took pole, and Clay Regazzoni who would win, benefited most. Reutemann qualified in eighth place although he struggled to repeat his testing time, possessing, he thought, inferior rubber. Andretti discarded the 80 as a lost cause and put the 79 into ninth place. At the start of the British GP, Andretti jumped into sixth on the first lap but was forcibly repelled by Lauda's Brabham at Abbey, only for his left rear hub to cause his premature retirement on lap 3. Reutemann finished after a battle with Jarier, Mass and Rosberg and a pitstop for a new left front tyre. He finished in eighth place with damaged skirts, thanks to having had to make use of the kerbs.

During a lull in F1 practice Peters Collins and Windsor had persuaded Chapman to watch up-and-coming Unipart F3 racer Nigel Mansell, as he was looking to establish a British driver in F1 on the assumption that Reutemann would probably leave. Shortly afterwards, in the knowledge that a test drive was in the offing, Mansell joined the engineering staff of Lotus to look after liaison with the Team's suppliers.

Hockenheim was a disaster for Lotus as the two drivers managed only seventeen laps of racing between them! Lack of grip was again the problem in practice, as Reutemann had two shunts, firstly at slow speed on oil and then following a clash with Scheckter. Whiplash from these incidents caused the Argentinian's driving to become most erratic in the warm-up, and having been advised not to race, he crashed on the opening lap at the first chicane where he was pushed off by an Arrows. Andretti climbed to seventh, only to have a drive-shaft coupling break, terminating his race. He parked and joined Reutemann to spectate for the rest of the race at the first chicane.

In the Austrian race the two Lotus drivers at least managed twenty-two laps of racing between them! According to a still unwell Reutemann, his 79 was uncontrollable at the Österreichring, but Chapman insisted that no changes should be made that had not already been tested. In the end a different undertray, and what was in effect the rear of the 80, was tried, but it was ineffective; Nigel Bennett, amongst others, was embarrassed for the driver, who couldn't be blamed for the lack of performance. Andretti persevered with a virtually standard 79 specification, but his clutch let go at the start and he managed only a few yards of the GP. Reutemann waged an unequal battle with his car, only to have a slow tyre stop on lap 20 and to retire two laps later as the handling became impossible.

Before Zandvoort Andretti tested a revised 80 at Snetterton, but the machine was still too slow. The Team was optimistic after wet practice in Holland, as the two 79s were initially very well placed in these conditions; infuriatingly, as soon as the track later dried, they were reduced to being uncompetitive again. On race day Andretti had his ground-effect skirts fitted to his car on the grid and he would manage only nine laps before a breakage at the rear of the car (whilst he was in eleventh place) damaged his oil tank. By this time Reutemann had long since disappeared into the pits with damaged suspension following an 'argument' with Jarier at the new chicane. Lotus had completed ten laps of racing this time.

By the time of Monza Alan Jones was looking for his fourth consecutive win for Williams. In stark contrast to recent races Andretti was much happier, as the 79s seemed more suited to the circuit; whilst both cars were in mid-grid – Reutemann having suffered another failure of the rear sandwich plate – there was great hope of an improved result. This was achieved as both cars finished (in fifth and seventh positions) with the reigning World Champion ending his run of five consecutive retirements. This result totally escaped the Italian crowd who only really had eyes for Scheckter, who took a Ferrari victory just ahead of the similarly mounted Villeneuve.

Lotus only sent one car to the non-championship Dino Ferrari Grand Prix at Imola on 16 September, where Reutemann was able to take second behind Lauda's Brabham.

Andretti was the better qualifier in Montreal, coming in tenth with his 79 boasting larger brakes, whilst Reutemann pulled in immediately behind despite clutch and suspension troubles. The Argentinian initially impressed the most as he climbed up to fifth place by lap 15, but then the infamous sandwich plate broke

After no less than five consecutive retirements, Andretti finished fifth at Monza in the martini-liveried Lotus 79. This was in stark contrast to a year previously when he had become World Champion in the very same Italian park.

again, causing the rear of the car to be covered in oil. Andretti had gear problems, but spent thirty-six laps in fifth place, seeming destined for some more valuable points; he then ran out of fuel, having already lost two gears.

Back in the United States at Watkins Glen, Reutemann had a wheel bearing break up, but still qualified well for sixth place on the third row complete with a necessarily strengthened rear suspension. Andretti's practice was punctuated by an engine failure, but he decided to risk slick tyres in the GP when he guessed that the damp track would dry out. The wet race came to a premature end for Reutemann as a sensor worked loose and fell round his feet: this was sufficient to take away his concentration and he spun out of third place on lap 6 as a consequence. Andretti did at least last another ten laps, although he had stopped on lap 9 for his dry tyres to be changed to wets when his gamble failed. His retirement was eventually caused by the disappearance of two gears, followed by fourth jamming in. The 1979 United Stated GP was therefore disappointing although typical of Martini-Lotus's difficult year.

By the end of the season the venerable 79s were visibly wilting under the downforce they were creating; even though they had been strengthened, they could not keep up with the progress being made, by Williams in particular. The 79 design was to bow out

TEAM AND PRIVATE LOTUS RESULTS 1979

Drivers:
Mario Andretti: USA; Carlos Reutemann: Argentinian
Car:
Lotus 79 Engine: Ford Cosworth DFV 3-litre
Lotus 80   Ford Cosworth DFV 3-litre

CAR	CHASSIS	DRIVER	PRACTICE	SESSION	GRID	RACE	LAPS	%	REASON	CHAMPIONSHIP POSITION	POINTS
ARGENTINE GP, Buenos Aires – 21st January – 53 L, 196.548 miles (316.31km) (243)											
79	2	Reutemann	1m 45.34s	3	3rd	2nd	53	100.0	–	2nd	6
79	4	Andretti	1m 45.96s	3	7th	5th	52	98.1	–	5th	2
70	3★	(Spare)									
79 R	1	Rebaque	1m 49.36s	–	18th	R	46	86.7	Suspension	–	–
78 R	4	(Spare)									
BRAZILIAN GP, Interlagos – 4th February – 40 L, 197.85 miles (318.42km) (244)											
79	2	Reutemann	2m 24.15s	3	3rd	3rd	40	100.0	–	2nd	10
79	4	Andretti	2m 24.28s	3	4th	R	2	5.0	Misfire	6th=	2
79	3	(Spare)									
79 R	1	Rebaque	2m 32.66s	–	DNQ	–	–	–	–	–	–
78 R	4	(Spare)									
S AFRICAN GP, Kyalami – 3rd March – 78 L, 198.90 miles (320.10km) (245)											
79	5	Andretti	1m 12.36s	1	8th	4th	78	100.0	–	6th	5
79	2	Reutemann	1m 12.75s	1	11th	5th	78	100.0	–	2nd	12
79	4	(Spare)									
79 R	1	Rebaque	1m 16.15s	–	23rd	R	71	91.0	Engine	–	–
US GP WEST, Long Beach – 8th April – 80 L, 162.61 miles (261.70km) (246)											
79	5	Andretti	1m 19.454s	3	6th	4th	80	100.0	–	5th	8
79	2	Reutemann	1m 18.886s	3	2nd	R	21	26.2	D/shaft	4th	12
79	4	(Spare)									
79 R	1	Rebaque	1m 22.990s	–	23rd	R	71	88.7	Accident	–	–
SPANISH GP, Jarama – 29th April – 75 L, 158.65 miles (255.31km) (247)											
79	2	Reutemann	1m 15.67s	1	8th	2nd	75	100.0	–	3rd=	18
80	1	Andretti	1m 15.07s	2	4th	3rd	75	100.0	–	6th	12
79	4	(Spare)									
79	5	(Spare)									
79 R	1	Rebaque	1m 18.42s	–	23rd	R	58	77.3	Engine	–	–
BELGIAN GP, Zolder – 13th May – 70 L, 185.38 miles (298.34km) (248)											
79	2	Reutemann	1m 22.56s	2	10th	4th	70	100.0	–	5th	19★★
79	5	Andretti	1m 21.83s	2	5th	R	27	38.5	Brakes	6th	12
80	1	(Spare)									
79	4	(Spare)									
79 R	1	Rebaque	1m 23.63s	–	15th	R	13	18.5	D/shaft	–	–
78 R	4	(Spare)									
MONACO GP, Monte Carlo – 27th May – 76 L, 156.408 miles (251.714km) (249)											
79	4	Reutemann	1m 27.99s	2	11th	3rd	76	100.0	–	3rd=	20★★
80	1	Andretti	1m 28.23s	2	13th	R	21	27.6	Suspension	6th	12
79	2	(Spare)									
79	5	(Spare)									
FRENCH GP, Dijon – 1st July – 80 L, 188.88 miles (304.00km) (250)											
79	4	Reutemann	1m 09.36s	3	13th	13th NR	77	96.2	Accident	4th=	20★★
80	1	Andretti	1m 09.35s	3	12th	R	51	63.7	Brakes	6th	12
80	2	(Spare)									
79	5	(Spare)									
79 R	1	Rebaque	1m 11.97s	–	23rd	12th	78	97.5	–	–	–
78 R	4	(Spare)									
BRITISH GP, Silverstone – 14th July – 68 L, 199.38 miles (320.88km) (251)											
79	5	Reutemann	1m 13.87s	2	8th	8th	66	97.0	–	4th=	20★★
79	4	Andretti	1m 14.20s	2	9th	R	3	4.4	Bearing	8th	12
80	1	(Spare)									
79	3	(Spare)									
79 R	1	Rebaque	1m 17.25s	–	24th	9th	66	97.0	–	–	–
78 R	4	(Spare)									

GERMAN GP, Hockenheim – 29th July – 45 L, 189.83 miles (305.51km) (252)

79	5	Andretti	1m 50.68s	2	11th	R	16	35.5	C-V joint	10th	12
79	3	Reutemann	1m 50.94s	1	13th	R	1	2.2	Accident	5th=	20★★
79	4	(Spare)									
79 R	1	Rebaque	1m 55.86s	–	24th	R	22	58.8	Handling	–	–
78 R	4	(Spare)									

AUSTRIAN GP, Österreichring – 12th August – 54 L, 199.37 miles (320.89km) (253)

79	4	Reutemann	1m 37.32s	2	17th	R	22	40.7	Balance	6th=	20★★
79	5	Andretti	1m 37.11s	1	15th	R	0	0.0	Clutch	10th	12
79	2	(Spare)									
79 R	1	Rebaque	1m 41.16s	–	DNQ	7th	73	97.3	–	–	–
78 R	4	(Spare)									

DUTCH GP, Zandvoort – 26th August – 75 L, 196.94 miles (316.95km) (254)

79	2	Andretti	1m 18.452s	2	17th	R	9	12.0	Rear plate	10th	12
79	4	Reutemann	1m 18.001s	2	13th	R	1	1.3	Accident	6th=	20★★
79	5	(Spare)									
79 R	1	Rebaque	1m 21.344s	–	24th	7th	73	97.3	–	–	–

ITALIAN GP, Monza – 9th September – 50 L, 180.197 miles (290.00km) (255)

79	5	Andretti	1m 36.655s	2	10th	5th	50	100.0	–	8th=	14
79	4	Reutemann	1m 37.202s	2	13th	7th	50	100.0	–	6th=	20★★
79	2	(Spare)									
79 R	1	Rebaque	1m 42.769s	–	DNQ	–	–	–	–	–	–

CANADIAN GP, Montreal – 30th September – 72 L, 197.28 miles (317.52km) (256)

79	5	Andretti	1m 32.651s	2	10th	10th NR	66	91.6	Fuel	8th=	14
79	3	Reutemann	1m 32.682s	1	11th	R	23	31.9	Suspension	6th=	20★★
79	4	(Spare)									

US GP, Watkins Glen – 7th October – 59 L, 199.243 miles (320.650km) (257)

79	5	Andretti	1m 40.144s	2	17th	R	16	27.1	Gearbox	6th=	20★★
79	3	Reutemann	1m 37.872s	2	6th	R	6	10.1	Accident	10th=	14
79	4	(Spare)									

Key: Private Lotus Entries:
★   = Car used by Andretti in re-started race   R   = Team Rebaque
★★   = Best four results counted
DNQ = Did Not Qualify
NR   = Not Running
R   = Retired
L   = Laps

of racing service and would eventually go into history as the only Lotus to carry the colours of three prime sponsor displays – John Player (1978), Martini (1979) and then Essex, which would take over in 1980 when the 79 was used for development work.

In October, Lotus tested at Paul Ricard with the aim of finding both a test driver and a replacement for Reutemann, who had moved to Williams. Mansell was one of those invited along, but his very attendance was an achievement in itself. David Phipps had contacted him whilst he was lying in bed recuperating after a nasty F3 accident. Having fixed himself up with painkillers from his disapproving specialist, Mansell set off for the south of France, to return with the test contract. Although Elio De Angelis was fastest, Mansell was selected as the new full-time driver – largely on the insistence of David Thieme – having beaten off competition from Eddie Cheever, Jan Lammers and

WORLD CHAMPIONSHIP RESULTS 1979

Position	Driver	Points
1	Jody Scheckter	51
2	Gilles Villeneuve	47
3	Alan Jones	40
4	Jacques Laffite	36
5	Clay Regazzoni	29
6=	**Carlos Reutemann**	**20**
	Patrick Depailler	20
8	Rene Arnoux	17
9	John Watson	15
10	**Mario Andretti**	**14**

CONSTRUCTORS' CUP 1979

Position	Constructor	Points
1	Ferrari	113
2	Williams-Ford	75
3	Ligier-Ford	61
4	**Lotus-Ford**	**39**

Stephen South. South was Chapman's original choice but when legal problems arose, Mansell was later taken aboard and was additionally offered three races.

In a last-ditch attempt to cure the 80 Stephen South briefly drove it at Paul Ricard in November with very stiff springs. He was shaken around violently in the cockpit, but Chapman was already toying with the concept of a twin-chassis F1 car. The philosophy was that such a design might make life more comfortable for the driver whilst still making maximum use of ground effect.

As 1979 closed, Martini sponsorship faded and Essex Petroleum took over completely; over the following season their high-profile hospitality became the norm.

1980

Lotus 81

At Essex's lavish Paris launch in December, the 81 was revealed to be 79-style bodywork on a 79/80 chassis with an 80 gearbox! The car was intended to fill the gap until the revolutionary twin-chassis 86 was fielded. Complete with new suspension on an aluminium honeycomb chassis, the car suffered both from traction and rigidity problems, and unexpectedly had to last the entire 1980 season.

Elio De Angelis

Reutemann's replacement was Italian hotshot Elio De Angelis, who left Shadow to test for Lotus whilst still under contract for another two seasons. The ensuing confrontation with Shadow's Don Nichols was settled out of court.

In Argentina's first meeting of the season, brake failure caused Andretti to plunge through a crowd of trackside onlookers during Buenos Aires practice, as he vainly tried to better De Angelis's fifth-fastest time. He finished up just behind his young team-mate, who had also been off the track. Andretti's metering unit played up during the warm-up, but was supposedly fixed before the race. De Angelis apparently had a minor collision with Patrese's Arrows on the opening lap; a damper fixing point was damaged, causing his retirement on lap 7. Thirteen laps later Andretti – who had fought with Piquet, Laffite and Reutemann – also retired as his fuel-metering unit problem recurred; during the second pitstop he dismounted. Alan Jones scored his first victory of his Championship year.

De Angelis was seventh fastest in Brazil and praised his car which, like Andretti's, had new dampers and strengthened mounting points. Andretti, who, plagued by electrical gremlins and a misfire, was slightly slower, lost his car and spun off early in the race. De Angelis quickly climbed from an early sixth to fourth, only for his tyres to go off. Sensibly he conserved them to inherit second place behind Arnoux's Renault; Chapman was very pleased with his new driver and their mutual regard was from that moment firmly cemented.

Lotus travelled to South Africa knowing that the turbo Renaults would like Kyalami's high altitude (5,000ft/1,500m). Lotus's bad weekend started when three engines controversially seized, having been over-polished on the instructions of Essex; the Team would rather have traded appearance for performance. On the track, not even removing his rear wing completely could improve Andretti's performance. An embarrassed De Angelis sat in his 81 as it refused to fire for the warm-up lap. He eventually got away from the

Intended as a stopgap design, the Lotus 81 unexpectedly had to last the entire 1980 season. At Watkins Glen, Elio de Angelis benefited from modified rear suspension to come home a fighting fourth.

The immaculate cockpit of the Lotus 49 with the characteristic red leather steering wheel. (The car may now be seen at the National Motor Museum at Beaulieu.)

By 1969 Lotus displayed the John Player colours of Gold Leaf Team Lotus. This is Graham Hill's Monaco-winning 49B R10 complete with its strange gearbox cover-cum-rear wing.

Reine Wisell's Lotus 56B turbine car would show promise but eventually proved to be a dead end. In the 1971 Woolmark Grand Prix at Silverstone, engine troubles meant the 'Rene Whistle' would finish an unclassified thirteenth.

In the 1974 Race of Champions, Belgian Jacky Ickx pulled off a once-in-a-lifetime manoeuvre when he took his 'borrowed' 72E around the outside of Lauda's Ferrari at Paddock in the pouring rain.

Swede Ronnie Peterson generated an enthusiastic following from those who admired an extroverted driving style. At Brands Hatch in 1978 his Lotus 79 is being tailed by the private Lotus 78 of Hector Rebaque.

Mario Andretti won the World Championship in 1978 with the sleek Lotus 79, after Chapman and the Team had fully harnessed ground effect. Six times the design would cross the line first during the season.

The Lotus 79 was pulled out of retirement in 1979 when the Lotus 80 proved uncompetitive. Andretti is pictured here at Hockenheim, where his Martini Racing 79 retired early after a drive-shaft coupling failed.

In the 1981 British Grand Prix the 88B had been banned, Mansell had non-qualified, and De Angelis drove like lightning from twenty-second to sixth with his 87 on Goodyears for the first time . . .

The two Lotus 91s in the Brands Hatch pit lane. The design was prone to porpoising and handled much better on fast circuits; it desperately needed a turbo engine to be competitive during the 1982 season.

Nigel Mansell gets his first taste of turbo power on a hardly ideal, damp Brands Hatch track surface! The 1983 Lotus 93T possessed unusually long side-pods, but Martin Ogilvie's design was uncompetitive and would be replaced mid-season.

At Brands Hatch's 1983 European Grand Prix, Mansell was threatened with replacement, so he promptly tigered to Lotus's best result of the season – third overall with a fastest lap of 126.563mph (203.683kph).

By 1984 the 95T was widely regarded as the best-handling chassis in F1. A huge amount of testing was undertaken and here Mansell pushes his car to the limit, demonstrating understeer.

From Team Lotus's 100th pole position Senna won the 1986 Spanish GP in his 98T by the amazingly small margin of 0.014 seconds from Mansell (pictured).

Senna detested Detroit but still won the 1986 race from another 98T pole, but only after Mansell had slipped back on lap 39.

In the garage at Silverstone the 102B shows its parentage, and the quest was already on for more powerful engines, which would lead to Ford in 1992.

The 1993 Lotus, the 107B, frequently frustrated its talented young driver Johnny Herbert. In truth the Briton deserved better and in 1994 he would come close to signing for McLaren, but his contract kept him with Team Lotus. (Photo reproduced by courtesy of L.A.T. Photographic)

back of the grid and with his adrenalin pumping collided with Watson at Leeukop and retired. Andretti's engine was down on power, thanks to a crumbling exhaust system, and he circulated towards the rear of the field, finishing a bad day in twelfth place.

The two 81s boasted a 3in-longer wheelbase and an improved rear suspension for the disastrous US GP West at Long Beach. De Angelis was second fastest in first practice but slipped back to twentieth; Andretti was fifteenth in his 'standard' 81. In their total of three racing laps Andretti drove over Jarier's Tyrrell at the start, damaging his steering, and De Angelis struck the back of Cheever's Osella, mauling his 81's front.

Mansell surprised everyone in his first test at Silverstone with a 1 minute 12.5 seconds lap, which was the fastest a Lotus had ever negotiated the circuit, and was even quicker than Prost's McLaren! De Angelis later bettered this time, only to drive slower than Mansell in the next Brands Hatch tests. As a result Chapman offered Mansell a drive in the Austrian GP.

In Belgium the Lotuses lasted longer but the results were again uninspiring. De Angelis was eighth fastest, following an engine failure, whilst Andretti was on the ninth row! Pironi won for Ligier – having complained of ill-treatment as he lapped Andretti – before the American retired with a collapsed gear linkage. De Angelis finished tenth, having spun into the fences at the back chicane whilst trying to pass Villeneuve for sixth place.

Despite prominent Essex sponsorship in Monaco, the 81s were again way down the grid. Lack of grip caused Andretti to hit the swimming-pool wall in practice, severely damaging 81/4 and gaining the penultimate grid position; De Angelis was fourteenth. The two Lotuses avoided Daly's spectacular first-lap accident; then, as spots of rain dropped, De Angelis spun, restarted after a push, stopped quickly at the pits and finished ninth. Andretti was seventh after a pitstop when his gear linkage let him down again.

All season the sport's administration had been criticized and a simmering FISA (Jean-Marie Balestre) versus FOCA (Bernie Ecclestone) confrontation boiled over at Jarama's Spanish GP meeting. Some drivers missed the official briefing and subsequently refused to pay their FISA-imposed fines; the race was then removed from the World Championship. Turbo teams such as Alfa Romeo, Ferrari and Renault, who had aligned themselves with FISA, did not take part whilst the normally aspirated FOCA teams, including Lotus, did. In the race, De Angelis encouragingly came third whilst Andretti retired when his engine blew; sadly no points would be awarded. Prior to the French GP, Chapman tried to mediate, but in the end the 'war' between FOCA and FISA broke out with the latter summarily banning 'skirts' for 1981.

De Angelis spun several times in Paul Ricard practice to take fourteenth on the grid, two places behind Andretti in the other ill-handling 81. Clutch problems were frequent at the start and De Angelis crept away to manage only three laps, which included a pitstop, before retiring. Andretti fought with Patrese for eighteen laps, only for his gear linkage to force him out too.

Continued Snetterton testing addressed the 81's handling, and strengthened, taller cockpit sides were introduced for Brands Hatch's British GP. There, De Angelis had a side-pod give way, causing him to plough ino the barriers, luckily without major injury. He took fourteenth place as Andretti worked hard on his suspension to claim ninth. Both cars broke in the race: De Angelis's rear suspension cross-member gave way after sixteen laps, shortly after a tyre stop, while Andretti, who had run in fifth for twenty-two laps, was denied a good finish by a failed gearbox bearing.

The 81's top-speed deficiency was highlighted at Hockenheim, where De Angelis had a frightening wheel failure at the Ostkurve – where a testing tragedy had claimed the life of Patrick Depailler a week earlier. Andretti was the best Lotus qualifier in ninth. In the race, De Angelis climbed through the field to fifth by lap 28. As he held off Giacomelli and Watson a wheel bearing failed, putting him out within three laps of the flag. Andretti plugged on to an eventual seventh place, being overtaken by Villeneuve just before the end.

Lotus 81B

In Hockenheim's paddock, the longer-wheelbase 81B had been hurriedly completed, but it wasn't to be raced by Mansell until the Austrian GP a week later. The design's length improved its handling, but it by no means cured all the problems, which showed up in the fast Österreichring sweeps.

De Angelis had another fright in Austria when he lost his 81 in the Boschkurve and rebounded off the barriers. He still qualified in ninth place with the spinning Andretti eight places behind. Mansell was at the back of the grid in the 81B, having seemed unlikely to qualify; Chapman, however, was absolutely sure that his protégé was prepared for F1. Just before the start some petrol was spilled into Mansell's seat burning him badly. An ineffectual bucket of water was thrown over him and he suffered for forty laps before engine failure caused his retirement and considerable relief. He returned to Birmingham Accident Hospital for full treatment. Andretti's Cosworth expired after seven laps, but De Angelis finished sixth after a solid drive.

Andretti was tenth, and the fastest Lotus qualifier in Holland, driving with new side-pods. A wheel breakage delayed De Angelis but he was eleventh fastest,

Having impressed in testing, Nigel Mansell was entrusted with the Lotus 81B in the Austrian Grand Prix. He just squeezed on to the grid and then sat in a painful pool of petrol until mercifully his engine failed, and he could retire for medical treatment.

while weak suspension fixing points afflicted the sixteenth-placed Mansell in the 81B. His burns gradually healing, Mansell had qualified easily but a complete lack of brakes caused his retirement after fifteen race laps, when he dramatically slid sideways, to scrub off speed approaching the Panoramabocht. De Angelis had already crashed there after ramming Pironi's Ligier on lap 3. Andretti had an excellent race, finding his 81 brilliant, and under-braking as he fended off Jones's Williams; the latter was particularly upset by the American's tactics. Having run in fourth place for twelve laps, before Reutemann forced past, Andretti dropped from fifth with three laps to go as his fuel ran out; eighth was poor reward. The 81's improved performance came too late, however, as he had already determined to leave Lotus at season's end.

For Imola's Italian GP, Mansell did not qualify, while De Angelis had a superb drive. In practice he used the new 'Dutch' side-pods but was only eighteenth because of a mysterious misfire; Andretti was tenth fastest. In the race itself, Villeneuve had a big accident at Tosa and Andretti had a wheel hub give out at just over half distance, terminating his day. De Angelis climbed aggressively higher as the race progressed to take a fine fourth; even though he was a lap behind the leaders, this was the best Lotus finish since Jarama.

In Montreal a CV-joint failure caused Andretti to slow so abruptly in practice that Thackwell's Tyrrell brushed the Lotus at over 160mph (258kph)! Both drivers were very lucky . . . De Angelis found his 81 impossible to balance. Andretti's woe continued in the race, which was restarted after Piquet and Jones – the World title protagonists – collided. In the ensuing accident Andretti's 81 went over the top of and then embedded itself in the side of Daly's Tyrrell. Using the spare, the American's engine failed after eleven laps, whilst De Angelis eventually finished tenth.

Mansell's promised final Watkins Glen race did not occur as his intended car had been severely damaged in Canada; the remaining 81s possessed modified rear suspension, which much improved their handling. De Angelis's 81 ran very smoothly over the track's undulations, securing him a second row position. Andretti was slower, having luckily got off with minimal damage, as there was no spare! Both cars ran well in the GP: De Angelis fought with Reutemann and Laffite and Andretti shadowed Keegan before sparring with Villeneuve. De Angelis finished fourth and when Watson slowed, Andretti overtook to take sixth and his sole championship point of the season!

TEAM LOTUS RESULTS 1980

Drivers:
Mario Andretti: USA; Elio de Angelis: Italian; Nigel Mansell: British
Car:
Lotus 81 Engine: Ford Cosworth DFV 3-litre
Lotus 81B   Ford Cosworth DFV 3-litre

CAR	CHASSIS	DRIVER	PRACTICE	SESSION	GRID	RACE	LAPS	%	REASON	CHAMPIONSHIP POSITION	POINTS
ARGENTINE GP, Buenos Aires – 13th January – 53 L, 196.548 miles (316.31km) (258)											
81	2	Andretti	1m 45.78s	1	6th	R	20	37.7	Fuel	–	–
81	1	De Angelis	1m 45.46s	2	5th	R	7	13.2	Suspension	–	–

BRAZILIAN GP, Interlagos – 27th January – 40 L, 195.70 miles (314.95km) (259)

81	1	De Angelis	2m 22.40s	2	7th	2nd	40	100.0	–	3rd=	6
81	2	Andretti	2m 23.46s	1	11th	R	1	2.5	Accident	–	–

S AFRICAN GP, Kyalami – 1st March – 78 L, 198.90 miles (320.10km) (260)

81	2	Andretti	1m 12.93s	2	15th	12th	76	97.4	–	–	–
81	1	De Angelis	1m 12.74s	1	14th	R	1	1.2	Accident	5th=	6
81	3	(Spare)									

US GP WEST, Long Beach – 30th March – 80 L, 192.61 miles (261.70km) (261)

81	3	De Angelis	1m 20.830s	1	20th	R	3	3.7	Accident	6th=	6
81	2	Andretti	1m 19.763s	2	15th	R	0	0.0	Accident	–	–
81	1	(Spare)									

BELGIAN GP, Zolder – 4th May – 72 L, 190.656 miles (306.864km) (262)

81	3	De Angelis	1m 20.96s	1	8th	10th NR	69	95.8	Accident	6th=	6
81	1	Andretti	1m 23.50s	1	17th	R	41	56.9	Gears	–	–
81	2	(Spare)									

MONACO GP, Monte Carlo – 18th May – 76 L, 156.406 miles (251.712km) (263)

81	2	Andretti	1m 27.514s	2	19th	7th	73	96.0	–		
81	3	De Angelis	1m 26.930s	2	14th	9th NR	68	89.4	Accident	8th	6
81	1	(Spare)									
81	4	(Spare)									

FRENCH GP, Ricard – 29th June – 54 L, 194.95 miles (313.74km) (264)

81	1	Andretti	1m 41.56s	2	12th	R	18	33.3	Gearbox	–	–
81	3	De Angelis	1m 41.66s	1	14th	R	3	5.5	Clutch	8th	6
81	2	(Spare)									

BRITISH GP, Brands Hatch – 13th July – 76 L, 198.63 miles (319.67km) (265)

81	1	Andretti	1m 13.400s	2	9th	R	57	75.0	Gearbox	–	–
81	3	De Angelis	1m 13.859s	2	14th	R	16	21.0	Suspension	8th=	6
81	2	(Spare)									

GERMAN GP, Hockenheim – 10th August – 45 L, 189.832 miles (305.505km) (266)

81	1	Andretti	1m 48.45s	2	9th	7th	45	100.0	–	–	–
81	3	De Angelis	7m 48.59s	2	11th	16th NR	43	95.5	Wheel	8th=	6
81	2	(Spare)									

AUSTRIAN GP, Österreichring – 17th August – 54 L, 199.368 miles (320.890km) (267)

81	3	De Angelis	1m 33.76s	2	9th	6th	54	100.0	–	8th=	7
81	1	Andretti	1m 35.21s	2	17th	R	6	11.1	Engine	–	–
81B	B1	Mansell	1m 35.71s	2	24th	R	40	74.0	Engine	–	–
81	2	(Spare)									

DUTCH GP, Zandvoort – 31st August – 72 L, 190.228 miles (306.144km) (268)

81	1	Andretti	1m 18.60s	1	10th	8th NR	70	97.2	Fuel	–	–
81 B	B1	Mansell	1m 18.97s	2	16th	R	15	20.8	Accident	–	–
81	3	De Angelis	1m 18.74	2	11th	R	2	2.7	Accident	8th=	7
81	2	(Spare)									

ITALIAN GP, Imola – 14th September – 60 L, 186.410 miles (300.000km) (269)

81	3	De Angelis	1m 36.919s	2	18th	4th	59	98.3	–	7th	10
81	1	Andretti	1m 36.084s	2	10th	R	40	66.6	Engine	–	–
81	2	Mansell	1m 37.661s	–	DNQ	–	–	–	–	–	–
81 B	B1	(Spare)									

CANADIAN GP, Montreal – 28th September – 70 L, 191.82 miles (308.70km) (270)

81	2	De Angelis	1m 30.316s	2	17th	10th	68	97.1	–	7th	10
81	3	Andretti	1m 30.59s	2	18th	R	11	15.7	Accident	–	–
81	1	(Spare)									

US GP, Watkins Glen – 5th October – 59 L, 199.243 miles (320.650km) (271)

81	2	De Angelis	1m 34.185s	2	4th	4th	59	100.0	–	7th	13
81	3	Andretti	1m 25.343s	2	11th	6th	58	98.3	–	20th=	1

Key:
DNQ = Did Not Qualify
R = Retired
L = Laps

For 1981 Andretti moved to Alfa Romeo and Mansell was appointed as no. 2 driver to De Angelis. Mansell's promotion by Chapman was felt to be unwise by some, but the Lotus boss was to be vindicated.

WORLD CHAMPIONSHIP RESULTS 1980

Position	Driver	Points
1	Alan Jones	67★
2	Nelson Piquet	54
3	Carlos Reutemann	42★
4	Jacques Laffite	34
5	Didier Pironi	32
6	Rene Arnoux	29
7	**Elio de Angelis**	**13**
8	Jean-Pierre Jabouille	9
9	Riccardo Patrese	7
10=	Derek Daly	6
	Jean-Pierre Jarier	6
	Keke Rosberg	6
	Gilles Villeneuve	6
	John Watson	6
15=	Emerson Fittipaldi	5
	Alain Prost	5
17=	Jochen Mass	4
	Bruno Giacomelli	4
19	Jody Schekter	2
20=	**Mario Andretti**	**1**
	Hector Rebaque	1
	Patrick Gaillard	1

★ Best five results in last half of season.

CONSTRUCTORS' CUP 1980

Position	Constructor	Points
1	Williams	120
2	Ligier	66
3	Brabham	55
4	Renault	38
5	**Lotus-Ford**	**14**

1981

During 1981 Chapman personally supervised De Angelis's car, which led to some disagreements between the two, but politics ruled at Kyalami, where FISA defeated FOCA. The non-championship race was ignored by the major manufacturer teams and although De Angelis was third and Mansell tenth, the lack of spectators, owing to the non-appearance of Ferrari, Renault and others, caused several sponsors to threaten to pull out of F1. A compromise 'Concorde Agreement' was reached, agreeing that the Championship would recommence at Long Beach. New regulations also required that a car's under-surface must not come within 6cm of the ground; the loophole was that this could only be checked when a car was stationary! The FOCA teams had therefore lost their battle to retain 'skirts' and Lotus more than most were to feel the adverse effects.

Lotus 86

The banning of skirts would eventually improve safety by reducing cornering speeds, but in the short term designers sought ways around the 6cm clearance rule: Lotus was not alone in being caught with an outdated car. The revolutionary 86 never actually appeared at a race meeting. Conceived in October 1979 and completed a year later it was run in the Jarama tests in November 1980. It utilized two separate chassis and moving skirts; one chassis carried the aerodynamic bodywork and a few mechanical ancillaries whilst the second, inner chassis contained the driver and engine, which were given a 'soft ride' by a separate springing system. The new regulations meant that it was stillborn, but it would still become the basis of the 88.

Lotus 88

Secret testing of the refined and lightened 86, now called the 88, was undertaken at Jarama and Paul Ricard. The car, publicly launched at the Albert Hall in February, possessed a Du Pont Chemicals carbon-fibre Kevlar tub. All new Chapman designs were perceived as a threat by the opposition and they immediately looked for ways to have the 88 banned. Chapman knew that it would be controversial, so the car's US début was approached with some trepidation.

The 88, which was entrusted to technicians Nigel Stepney and Geoff Hardacre, was tested by De Angelis at Riverside, where he learned about the twin-chassis concept. The bodywork 'floated' above the base chassis, which held the wheels, tub and engine. At speed the bodywork pushed down on its attaching springs (which joined on to the suspension uprights) and sealed the fixed skirts on to the track creating ground effect. The driver's tub was left free from much of the normal buffeting. Just in case the design proved too controversial, a conventional car (the 87) was wisely created around the 88 tub as an insurance policy.

Before Long Beach, Chapman held a press conference at London Airport to explain the 88 concept, but when it appeared in the pit road, arguments arose about whether or not the primary chassis suspension went rigid when the car was in motion. The scrutineers confirmed that it was legal and permitted it to practice whilst the opposition prepared their protests, only for fuel pump failure to cut the car's lappery short.

The Lotus 88 would have a brief and controversial history. Seen here during practice at Long Beach the novel twin-chassis design would throw the scrutineers and officials into an unprecedented turmoil.

Chapman was told that the car could race provided he accept that any points achieved would be removed if any protests were upheld.

After a spring change De Angelis recorded several encouraging laps, only to be recalled; under the threat by some other teams of a race boycott, the 88 was excluded, much to Chapman's great disgust. He was angry about the way Lotus had been summarily dealt with and he appealed directly to the ACCUS (Automobile Competition Committee of the US), who after some days declared the 88 legal. Mansell, meanwhile, continued in his 81, being seventh fastest while De Angelis, now in an 81, could manage only thirteenth. In both the warm-up and the race Mansell struck walls. The first Queens hairpin collision deranged his suspension, and then on lap 25 of the race he struck the Pine Avenue wall, retiring with a damaged rear wheel. De Angelis had similarly hit a wall twelve laps earlier, so neither Lotus finished as Jones took another Williams win.

The 88 was shipped to Rio in the knowledge that FISA had disowned the ACCUS decision. It was tested, but high-speed cornering stability problems were identified when the two chassis halves diverged. Piquet won in Rio with the hydraulically suspended Brabham BT49, which FISA controversially declared legal. The uncertain Portuguese-speaking scrutineers (who should have been applying the rules in English!) initially declared the 88 eligible but the stewards disagreed when, amongst others, Ferrari and Williams protested. De Angelis had already briefly practised the 88 but on legal advice Chapman, feeling Lotus was being victimized, decided to refer everything to the Parisian FIA Court of Appeal. In an 81 De Angelis was tenth fastest and Mansell, with brakes and engine troubles, was thirteenth. In the race, Mansell posted his first finish, coming in eleventh, whilst De Angelis was

an excellent fifth despite a slow puncture and a broken damper!

The Argentinian scrutineers turned the 88 down, provoking Chapman to miss his first GP in twenty-two years! He put out a critical press release provoking a $100,000 fine (later revoked) from FISA. The race was ironically won by the hydraulically suspended Brabham, and as if that were not enough, Essex's finances collapsed over the same weekend as Thieme was arrested for alleged malpractice. Chapman organized bail of £70,000 and Essex stickers optimistically remained on the cars. De Angelis spun on lap 2, only to find his ill-handling cured, and he proceeded to claw his way back to an excellent sixth-place finish. Mansell held his gear lever in place whilst coping with severe understeer, but only lasted for three laps before his engine expired.

The FIA Court of Appeal declared the 88 illegal, leaving Chapman devastated; Lotus missed the first GP since 1958, since there was 'less than enough time to get two replacement race-worthy cars to Imola'.

Lotus returned for the Belgian GP in May where it was not singled out in all the arguments. The 81s understeered badly and Mansell was the faster qualifier as the organization creaked: a mechanic died following a pit lane accident and then another was struck on the start line. An upset and flu-ridden Mansell had to be persuaded to race but he eventually scored his first points, in only his eighth GP, finished third after fighting with Villeneuve's Ferrari. His race was subsequently recognized as one of the season's great performances. De Angelis, having been slowed by both Cheever and Villeneuve, took a meritorious fifth place. Ensign's Mo Nunn tried to lure Mansell to his team but was firmly refused by Chapman, who recognized the talent that Lotus possessed.

CHAPTER 7

Chapman's Swan-Song

Lotus 87

For Monaco, two conventional 87s were pressed into service, built around 88 tubs with new body panels. They were something of a compromise and of necessity lacked ground effect, although they were about 60lb (27kg) lighter than the 81s. Chapman had realized that a fall-back situation, in the shape of a back-up model, might be needed should the controversial 88 concept falter, and this was why the 87 was developed. The construction of these conventional cars was put in hand in early 1980, with 88 running gear inside an 87 body. The car had its own development research programme until the 88 took precedence, but it was resurrected after the political problems encountered by the 88, and was initially intended to be a fully skirted car to comply with the 1980 World Federation of Motor Sport regulations. The 87s, lacking as they did the development being lavished on the 86 and the 88, were sadly never competitive, although they suited circuits with tight corners, and they debuted at just such a venue.

In Monaco Chapman was extremely impressed by Mansell's competent third place in qualifying, when he had managed to keep up with the front-runners despite having swiped the swimming-pool barriers lightly. Immediately the times were known, discussions started that ensured that Mansell's retainer was increased! De Angelis was somewhat annoyed that he couldn't match his new team-mate's success, but gear troubles as well as an inability to run with a consistent ride height, slowed him down to sixth after a mere nine practice laps.

In the race Mansell's hopes were dashed when a rear suspension top link gave out after only sixteen laps; this was particularly galling as he was easily holding down third place at the time. The cause of the breakage was either an incident with Reutemann at the Station hairpin or a brush with the barriers. Whichever, the damage was located in a stop for tyres two laps later and the Team diplomatically decided it was more likely to have been caused by metal fatigue. De Angelis had climbed up to fourth place by lap 30 but two laps later, as Piquet went on to win, the Italian had his engine blow and parked disappointedly by the harbour.

In a major boost to morale, John Player returned as sponsors (for two years) in time for the Spanish GP, as it became apparent that Essex Petroleum was going to be unable to continue – several million dollars of sponsorship money were still outstanding. Curiously, though, it was obvious that the saga was not over: later in the season Essex stickers would continue to appear and then disappear at various times.

At Jarama the black and gold John Player Special livery was back, but certain necessary parts, including the nose cone for Mansell's wide-track 87, were stuck in Customs. The Briton took provisional sixth grid place, just avoiding an engine blow-up, but eventually dropped to eleventh with De Angelis, who had fallen off the track as he adjusted his brake balance, just in front in tenth. The Spanish race saw De Angelis push Reutemann's Williams for all he was worth, although he could not get higher than fifth place at the end. Mansell came in sixth, having had a tough race, but at least he had gained another point on a day when Villeneuve's Ferrari triumphed.

The Team's revival continued in the French GP at Dijon-Prenois. De Angelis was eighth on the grid once engine troubles had been sorted out, whilst Mansell had initially been fastest of all only for his understeering car to catch fire later in practice, dropping him to thirteenth. In France, Michelin offered Lotus a single set of special practice tyres, which De Angelis regarded as his by right as no. 1 driver. Chapman controversially split the tyres equally between his two charges as a way, it was perceived, of chastising the Italian for not having attended a private practice session! The French GP itself was stopped after fifty-eight laps, thanks to a downpour; at this point De Angelis was running in eighth place, a lap down on the leader (Piquet), with Mansell two places behind. As the track dried the final twenty-two laps were run in the order that the drivers had earlier finished. A frenzy of activity preceded the second start as drivers made their tyre choices, and that set of Michelins was still certainly on the mind of at least one Lotus driver. The second part of the race featured a no-holds-barred fight between the two JPS drivers for ninth place, which was settled on the road in Mansell's favour; when the times of the two races were combined, however, De Angelis was sixth and Mansell seventh. Alain Prost had won for Renault.

Lotus 88B

Following encouragement from the RAC in advance of Silverstone, Chapman modified the Lotus 88 design slightly: the windscreen and gearbox oil cooler were moved to the outer sprung structure, and panelling was added to ensure that the external airstream could not lick the inner sprung structure. This modified car was called the 88B. The car was shown to the RAC's scrutineers before the British GP and it was approved. The executive of the FIA, though, overruled the decision after official practice, thanks to the somewhat controversial intervention of FISA president Jean-Marie Balestre at Silverstone. Balestre was also involved in the FISA presidential election campaign, for which the RAC's Basil Tye had already announced his intention to stand and many thought the banning of the 88B to be a complete disgrace.

Controversy started at Silverstone from the moment the JPS transporter disgorged the pair of 88Bs. Following protests from a number of teams, Balestre summarily banned the cars. Having gone well in France, Mansell was particularly looking forward to his first British GP and it was therefore very galling for him to find the Lotus 88Bs outlawed once again – after De Angelis had managed a number of practice laps – and a rush was initiated to convert the cars back to 87s in time to qualify. Unfortunately the efforts went unrewarded as Mansell couldn't wrestle the 'new' machine

to a representative time, and so failed to qualify. Second practice was the first time that the Team had run the 87 on Goodyears and there wasn't time to gain sufficient set-up knowledge. Both Chapman and Mansell were bitterly upset about the latter's non-qualification and later it would often be suggested that Chapman never again felt the same way about motor racing after the 88 dispute.

De Angelis scraped through in twenty-second place only for controversy to recur when, after an electric drive up to sixth, he was reported for overtaking Laffite under the yellow flags surrounding Piquet's accident at Becketts. He was given the black flag and on arrival in the pit lane he received a dressing down from the RAC's Robin Langford. He could have returned to the race, but thinking he had been disqualified, he abandoned his car and marched off.

An improvement in fortune was desperately needed at Hockenheim, where the two drivers were more confident about their 87s on the straights, but had trouble with the handling in and out of the chicanes. Mansell, in particular, did well to be just behind De Angelis, especially as much practice time had been wasted trying Goodyear's 15in 'qualifiers'. On race day Mansell suffered from the after-effects of gastroenteritis, but he still entered into the spirited fight to overtake Villeneuve's twelfth-placed Ferrari along with De Angelis and Derek Daly (March). Mansell had made contact with both the March, damaging its wheel

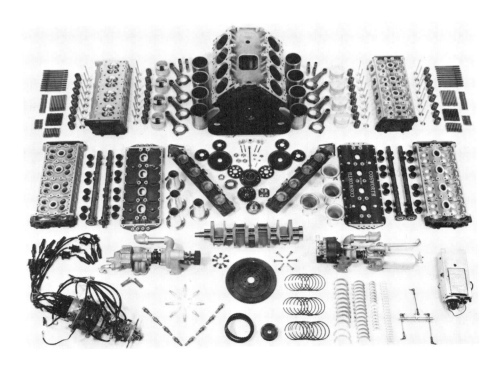

The inner-most workings of a Ford Cosworth DFV engine. Since the Dutch Grand Prix in 1967 and including Austria in 1982, this engine gave Team Lotus forty-seven Grand Prix victories. A marvellous tribute to its design.

rim, and with the rear of the Ferrari, severely bending the Lotus's nose. After twelve laps Mansell shot into the pits, leapt out of his car and tugged at his overalls. Fuel had leaked into the cockpit to give him some nasty burns. Rather less frantically, De Angelis took seventh place at the end of a much better race for JPS.

In Austria De Angelis again finished seventh and Mansell raced for twenty-three laps before he retired. The cars had visibly handled very badly over the notorious bumps of the Styrian track during practice, and that De Angelis ended up the faster of the two was almost certainly down to the fact that his car had less worn dampers than Mansell's. In the paddock and motor-home the Italian's future within the Team was the subject of a full debate between himself and Chapman; the case cannot have been helped by the damage inflicted on his 87 in a spin through the notorious Hella Licht corner. On race day Mansell put in a creditable performance before retiring from seventh place, whilst De Angelis bravely took on Pironi's Ferrari, which was proving very wide for all those following. The two shook fists at each other until the Lotus eventually got past on lap 33, was retaken on laps 34 and 35, and finally headed the rogue Frenchman on the thirty-sixth tour.

Boasting its long straight, Zandvoort suited the turbos and at the end of the day Renault, with Alain Prost at the helm, would take their second race win of the year. Mansell only completed a single race lap because of electrical failure, which stopped him out on the circuit after a practice made troublesome by ill-handling, down-on-power engines and inoperative brakes! Both cars had modified side panniers and De Angelis made best use of these to take ninth on the grid. In the race he fought again with Patrese, and then tried unsuccessfully to cope with Rebaque's Brabham on his way to a hard-earned fifth place.

De Angelis was to go one better at Monza to finish fourth in a race that saw leader Prost's Renault lead from flag to flag. For Mansell practice had been his first sight of the daunting Monza Autodrome and he had quickly learned not only the line but where the worst of the undulations were located. He didn't quite catch De Angelis, who had virtually grown up at the parkland circuit, but the 87s still occupied eleventh and twelfth places on the grid. Mansell was bedevilled by progressively deteriorating handling as his car's skirts gradually destroyed themselves, whilst the maximum fuel load weighed the car down further. As a result he was forced to retire after only twenty-one laps. De Angelis had a brief fight with Daly but circulated steadily to gain his best result of the season at flag fall.

Montreal was very wet and the cars were again a horrifying handful for their drivers in the thankfully dry practice. This time the brave Mansell (fifth) qualified ahead of De Angelis (seventh) after the Italian had escaped from a top-speed spin when his rear suspension broke. Early in the Canadian GP, De Angelis ran in a strong fourth place, but after four laps he dropped away to ninth. He had collided with Villeneuve's Ferrari at the Hairpin at mid-distance, which did nothing to help his concentration, although he did get back to sixth by the end. Mansell had also had an accident at the Hairpin with Prost's Renault.

Such had been his performance over the last few races that Williams investigated the possibility of signing Mansell to replace Alan Jones in 1982, but was to be yet another team to be refused by Chapman.

For the final race of the year, the car-park of Caesar's Palace in Las Vegas was to be the venue! Whilst Piquet clinched the World Championship, following the demise of Reutemann and his Williams, Lotus very nearly got Mansell on to the podium. He had been plagued in practice by a less than powerful engine, but he was still ahead of De Angelis, who had broken his front anti-roll bar. The race started badly as De Angelis was out on the second lap, after a pitstop to cure his car's terminal handling revealed a cooling system leak.

TEAM LOTUS RESULTS 1981

Drivers:
Elio de Angelis: Italian; Nigel Mansell: British
Car:
Lotus 81 Engine: Ford Cosworth DFV 3-litre
Lotus 88   Ford Cosworth DFV 3-litre
Lotus 87   Ford Cosworth DFV 3-litre

CAR	CHASSIS	DRIVER	PRACTICE	SESSION	GRID	RACE	LAPS	%	REASON	CHAMPIONSHIP POSITION	POINTS
US GP, Long Beach – 15th March – 80 L, 162.61 miles (261.70km) (272)											
81	2	Mansell	1m 20.573s	2	7th	R	25	31.2	Accident	–	–
81	3	De Angelis	1m 20.928s	2	13th	R	13	16.2	Accident	–	–
88	1	(Spare)									

BRAZILIAN GP, Jacarepagua – 29th March – 62 L, 193.82 miles (311.922km) (273)

81	3	De Angelis	1m 37.734s	2	10th	5th	62	100.0	–	7th=	2
81	2	Mansell	1m 38.003s	2	13th	11th	61	98.3	–	–	–
88	1	(Spare)									

ARGENTINE GP, Buenos Aires – 12th April – 53 L, 196.548 miles (316.31km) (274)

81	3	De Angelis	1m 45.065s	2	10th	6th	52	98.1	–	6th=	3
81	2	Mansell	1m 45.369s	1	15th	R	3	5.6	Engine	–	–
88	1	(Spare)									

BELGIAN GP, Zolder – 17th May – 54 L, 143.007 miles (230.148km) (275)

81	1	Mansell	1m 24.44s	1	10th	3rd	54	100.0	–	7th=	4
81	3	De Angelis	1m 24.96s	1	14th	5th	54	100.0	–	6th	5
81	2	(Spare)									

MONACO GP, Monte Carlo – 31st May – 76 L, 156.406 miles (251.712km) (276)

87	2	De Angelis	1m 26.259s	2	6th	R	32	42.1	Engine	7th=	5
87	1	Mansell	1m 25.815s	2	3rd	R	16	21.0	Suspension	10th=	4
81	2	(Spare)									

SPANISH GP, Jarama – 21st June – 80 L, 164.64 miles (264.96km) (277)

87	2	De Angelis	1m 15.399s	1	10th	5th	80	100.0	–	7th	7
87	1	Mansell	1m 15.562s	2	11th	6th	80	100.0	–	8th=	5
81	2	(Spare)									

FRENCH GP, Dijon – 5th July – 80 L, 188.88 miles (304.00km) (278)

87	2	De Angelis	1m 07.52s	2	8th	6th	79	98.7	–	9th	7
87	1	Mansell	1m 07.72s	2	13th	7th	79	98.7	–	11th=	5
81	2	(Spare)									

BRITISH GP, Silverstone – 18th July – 68 L, 199.38 miles (320.88km) (279)

87	3	De Angelis	1m 15.971s	2	22nd	R	25	36.7	Driver Error	9th=	8
87 (88 B)	2 (2)	Mansell	1m 16.432s	2	DNQ	–	–	–	–	12th=	5
			(1m 15.992s)		1	TD	–	–	–		
88 B	4	De Angelis	1m 16.029s		1	TD	–	–	–		
88 B		(Spare)									

GERMAN GP, Hockenheim – 2nd August – 45 L, 189.832 miles (305.505km) (280)

87	3	De Angelis	1m 50.74s	2	14th	7th	44	97.7	–	10th=	8
87	4 (88 B/4)	Mansell	1m 50.86s	2	15th	R	12	26.6	Fuel Leak	13th=	5
87	2	(Spare)									

AUSTRIAN GP, Österreichring – 16th August – 53 L, 195.699 miles (314.947km) (281)

87	3	De Angelis	1m 35.294s	1	9th	7th	52	98.1	–	11th=	8
87	4	Mansell	1m 34.569s	2	11th	R	23	43.3	Engine	14th	5
87	2	(Spare)									

DUTCH GP, Zandvoort – 30th August – 72 L, 190.228 miles (306.144km) (282)

87	3	De Angelis	1m 19.738s	2	9th	5th	71	98.6	–	10th=	10
87	4	Mansell	1m 20.633s	2	17th	R	1	1.3	Electrics	14th	5
87	2	(Spare)									

ITALIAN GP, Monza – 13th September – 52 L, 187.403 miles (301.600km) (283)

87	3	De Angelis	1m 36.158s	1	11th	4th	52	100.0	–	8th	13
87	4	Mansell	1m 36.210s	2	12th	R	21	40.3	Handling	14th	5
87	2	(Spare)									
87	5	(Spare)									

CANADIAN GP, Montreal – 27th September – 63 L, 172.62 miles (277.83km) (284)

87	3	De Angelis	1m 30.231s	2	7th	6th	62	98.4	–	8th	14
87	5	Mansell	1m 29.997s	2	5th	R	45	71.4	Accident	14th	5
87	2	(Spare)									

CAESARS PALACE GP, Las Vegas – 17th October – 75 L, 170.1 miles (273.75km) (285)

87	5	Mansell	1m 19.044s	1	9th	4th	75	100.0	–	14th	8
87	3	De Angelis	1m 19.562s	2	15th	R	2	2.6	Cooling	8th	14
87	2	(Spare)									

Key:
DNQ = Did Not Qualify
TD = Time Disallowed
R   = Retired
L   = Laps

WORLD CHAMPIONSHIP RESULTS 1981

Position	Driver	Points
1	Nelson Piquet	50
2	Carlos Reutemann	49
3	Alan Jones	46
4	Jacques Laffite	44
5	Alain Prost	43
6	John Watson	27
7	Gilles Villeneuve	25
8	**Elio de Angelis**	**14**
9=	Rene Arnoux	11
	Hector Rebaque	11
11=	Riccardo Patrese	10
	Eddie Cheever	10
13	Didier Pironi	9
14	**Nigel Mansell**	**8**

CONSTRUCTORS' CUP 1981

Position	Constructor	Points
1	Williams	95
2	Brabham	61
3	Renault	54
4	Ligier	44
5	Ferrari	34
6	McLaren	28
7	**Lotus-Ford**	**22**

Mansell perceptively conserved his tyres but dropped to eleventh in the process, speeding up again after twenty-five laps. At this time both his clutch and engine started to play up as did a trapped nerve in his left leg. He could have backed off, but his eventual fourth place was a true testimony to both his determination and his intelligent driving. His reward was confirmation of a three-year contract with Lotus.

In Milan during November, a court found Patrese guilty of 'culpable manslaughter' with regard to the death of Peterson three years previously. Closer to home, Peter Warr replaced Peter Collins as team manager, having returned to Lotus after four years with both the Fittipaldi and Wolf teams. Dave Scott was taken on as a test driver.

═══════ **1982** ═══════

In his second season with Lotus the Team were pleased that Mansell was starting to rival De Angelis much more, although the Italian himself was not so keen. De Angelis disliked the cars of this particular era intensely, and proved unpredictable as his moods were reflected in his results. When his car felt well set-up he responded, but at other times his performances were

somewhat lacklustre as his enthusiasm evaporated.

For 1982 the unenforceable 6cm ground clearance rule was dispensed with, along with the need for the cars to possess variable ride heights. Sliding skirts were to be replaced by the flexible variety, but political attention was to turn firstly to the terms of the drivers' new 'super licences', which provoked a strike at Kyalami. All year too the Cosworth-powered non-turbo teams, such as Lotus, would try to find ways to keep pace with the likes of Ferrari and Renault, and an uneasy peace would often be rudely shattered by dispute.

Lotus 87B

The wider-track 87 design had been modified to B specification by the insertion of a spacer between the gearbox and engine, which added an extra 3in to the wheelbase, thereby altering the weight distribution. The side-pods, too, were wider than those of its predecessor, but in reality the 87B was never anything more than an interim car created in anticipation of the introduction of the Lotus 91, which itself would be largely 87-based.

Extensive pre-race testing was undertaken in South Africa although political arguments would catch the limelight as the drivers objected to their new FISA 'super licences', which they feared would tie them too tightly to teams. For some time the race looked threatened, indeed first practice was cancelled, but eventually agreement was reached. As negotiations had continued the drivers spent the night in their hotel conference room being entertained by, amongst others, De Angelis playing classical music on the piano. The only light-hearted moment of practice came when De Angelis apparently started his engine up in the pits in anticipation of going out to practice; in reality it was Clive Hicks dressed up in the Italian's race suit and helmet who caught everyone out with his practical joke, which had been aided and abetted by the JPS mechanics!

The threat of a drivers' strike eventually averted, Mansell – who had not personally been in favour of the industrial action – and De Angelis were therefore left with but a single session in which to make their mark with their 87Bs. A leaking brake system afflicted Mansell, whilst De Angelis could not conquer a mysterious handling problem. On race day Mansell retired without completing a lap, when an electrical fault both stranded him out on the circuit and inadvertently forced Jarier's Osella into the fences at Ford as he slowed. De Angelis still had an ill-handling car and could only manage eighth after a day of wrestling with his 87B.

Lotus 91

Peter Wright's intention as chief engineer was for the 91 to be 10 per cent lighter than its predecessor. The result was a car that either ran perfectly or diabolically, preferring the fast circuits, where it desperately needed a turbo engine, whilst slower tracks produced understeer. 'Colin's weight-watcher' was launched in February with its infamous yet fashionable water-cooled brakes, fixed skirts and variable track and wheelbase options, which would cause it to porpoise on uneven tracks. Martin Ogilvie reworked the aerodynamics of the attractive bodywork successfully.

Water-cooled brakes gained notoriety when Ferrari and Renault perceived their reservoirs to be a way of overcoming the minimum weight regulations: having drained during the race, they could be replenished afterwards, thereby restoring the car's correct weight for post-race scrutineering. Legal arguments continued all season and Lotus would replace theirs with lead ballast.

Mansell endured a vicious practice spin in Brazil when his bodywork lifted, creating positive lift, and De Angelis fought off the attentions of Winkelhock to join his team mate in mid-grid. The Italian's woes continued in the race when he collided with Baldi, who had missed his overtaking manoeuvre, sending the fourteenth-placed Lotus off the road after twenty-one laps. Mansell was physically battered by his solid 91 but managed to avoid the carnage to take fifth on lap 34, which he held to the end. Controversy surrounded the water-cooled brakes of the two leading cars: Renault and Ferrari un-

successfully protested, although the results were correctly interpreted by many as provisional.

Mansell was bruised in a heavy accident at Willow Springs while testing for the US GP at Long Beach. He found California grip elusive and was just out-qualified by his team-mate, who used the short wheelbase option. De Angelis confused his grid position and reversed into Mansell's 91 as he rectified his error, incurring a substantial fine. When the race actually commenced Mansell was in reverse! De Angelis unsuccessfully fought with Patrese's Brabham to finish in fifth place after Villeneuve's disqualification. Lauda's Ferrari took the honours and Mansell came seventh.

A month later Piquet (Brabham) and Rosberg (Williams) were disqualified by an FIA Appeal Tribunal for possessing water-cooled brakes in Brazil. The ruling promoted Mansell to third place, but had other repercussions: the San Marino GP took place with a skeleton field when the FOCA-allied non-turbo teams, including Lotus, boycotted the race. The turbo-powered FISA teams did participate and Pironi's Ferrari won, much to the annoyance of Villeneuve.

Villeneuve's denied victory at Imola contributed greatly to the Zolder qualifying accident that claimed his life. Mansell was particularly shocked as the two had been close friends. The 91s were better balanced and Lotus were hopeful when Mansell was initially fastest, but he could not repeat this in official qualifying, ending up seventh. De Angelis was hampered by engine failures. Clutchless Mansell had to be push-started against the rules, causing both Salazar and Giacomelli

De Angelis was unexpectedly fourth in the Belgian Grand Prix at Zolder in the Lotus 91. The design proved unpredictable throughout the season and was in desperate need of a turbo engine to make it competitive.

to crash whilst dodging him; he only lasted nine laps before his clutch failed completely. The lonely De Angelis spectacularly climbed up to fifth, having spun off at one point, as Watson went on to win for McLaren; Lauda's subsequent disqualification from third promoted him to fourth.

Suspension testing was undertaken at Croix-en-Ternois before Monaco, where Mansell came close to winning. The chaotic race was rain afflicted but Mansell eventually finished fourth, having fallen out with Warr; their relationship would never be quite the same again. Understeer and lack of grip had affected practice, and this, combined with the difficulty of passing, placed both Lotuses well down the grid. At the start De Angelis passed Piquet but was furious at having been slowed, and throughout the race he steadfastly held his line come what may. Pironi knocked his nose cone off against the back of the Lotus at Rascasse before Prost forced his way past at Ste Devote by banging wheels. A series of incidents occurred in the last few laps, eliminating most of the leaders except Patrese and Mansell, who was unaffected by the oil haze he trailed, and eventually overtook De Angelis for fourth place having unknowingly come amazingly close to winning. The Lotus drivers were now level in the Championship.

The 91s ran without their rear bodywork at Detroit to help cooling and Mansell yet again excelled on a street circuit, being the faster Lotus driver. In the race De Angelis collided with Guerrero on lap seven, bending his steering and damaging a side-pod in a collision, and Patrese crashed in avoidance, thereby stopping the race. In the interval Mansell's skirts were repaired and a damaged wheel replaced, and De Angelis's steering was rebuilt. At the restart De Angelis's gearbox failed and Mansell's skirts induced understeer before his engine blew. Watson went on to win.

At the renamed Circuit Gilles Villeneuve in Montreal, Mansell was afflicted by understeer and a weak engine as De Angelis busily blistered his tyres on his way to tenth fastest. The first start was marred by a tragic fatal accident, which befell Riccardo Paletti when he struck the rear of Pironi's stalled Ferrari. Once the highly charged race eventually got under way, Mansell involuntarily ran over the back of Giacomelli's slowing Alfa, breaking his steering wheel and damaging his left arm sufficiently to be taken to hospital. De Angelis, meanwhile, drove carefully to fourth place as most of the opposition dropped out with transmission troubles.

Mansell's injury meant that he was replaced by test driver Roberto Moreno in Holland and by Geoff Lees in France. It was hoped that with rest Mansell would be fit to run in the British GP.

Zandvoort's long straight was tailor-made for the turbos, and it was hardly surprising that Arnoux's Renault took pole and that Pironi's Ferrari won. Although testing had been promising, Moreno was plainly out of his depth, finding the rock-solid 91 a completely different experience from anything he had previously driven and he non-qualified. De Angelis was slowed by porpoising caused by lack of balance, and in the race he stopped twice to replace damaged skirts before retiring with impossible handling.

Nothing could stop Mansell from driving at Brands Hatch – he was determined to avenge his 1981 Silverstone disappointment – despite a painful left wrist cast; the injury would affect him all season. In both tyre-testing and the first untimed practice session Lotus hopes were raised, but official qualifying brought disappointment. De Angelis tried pull-rod suspension whilst a determined Mansell qualified despite his injury. In the race his car's skirts failed, which at least relieved his wrist. De Angelis ran in third for thirty-five laps but unhappily had to yield this when, on the last lap, fuel starvation, caused by a faulty metering unit arose.

Brands Hatch had made it obvious that Mansell was not fully recovered and he decided to miss the French GP, being replaced by Geoff Lees.

Lees was Lotus's highest finisher at Paul Ricard in twelfth place, having blown two engines but also mastered the understeering 91 in practice. In the race he pitted on lap 8 with a punctured right rear tyre, but he then rose to twelfth place. De Angelis retired after seventeen laps with fuel pressure failure; he had suffered from a misfire brought about by his fuel system during practice, which was still cured in time for him to show Lees the track's lines. Chapman was more concerned about Lotus's future as John Player demanded results before guaranteeing to continue their sponsorship. Winning meant having a turbo engine and Renault, for whom Arnoux had won with an EF1 engine in France, had been courted to the point where they made an engine offer to Lotus for 1983.

Whilst in Hockenheim practice Pironi suffered a huge accident that ended his F1 career, Mansell was back with a healed wrist but having trouble balancing his car, while De Angelis's misfired. Front pull-rod suspension was briefly tested but both drivers had to replace skirts during the GP itself. On Mansell's return to the race he fought with Laffite's fourth-placed Ligier whilst being lapped, and the Frenchman spun off on to the grass at the first corner; the Lotus seemed perched on the verge of disaster but Mansell caught it to finish ninth. An unwell De Angelis had earlier retired with transmission failure as Tambay won for Ferrari. Chapman again met with Renault at Hockenheim and prior to the Austrian GP, Renault-Sport boss Gerard

After a lapse of three seasons, De Angelis scored a memorable Lotus victory in Austria, when he beat Rosberg's Williams to the line by a mere 0.5 seconds! The Lotus 91 was ideally suited to fast circuits.

Larrousse finalized the deal for Lotus to use Renault engines from 1983 onwards.

De Angelis's 91 handled perfectly at the Österreichring and after practice he was seventh, with Mansell twelfth, behind the turbos. The Lotuses fought their way up the field only for Mansell's engine to fail on lap 17; nine other cars would go the same way! De Angelis led the non-turbos from the start, eventually taking the overall lead on lap 48, when Prost's (Renault) fuel injection faltered. Shortly afterwards the Lotus's fuel pressure played up, bringing back memories of Brand Hatch, and Keke Rosberg's Williams started to reel De Angelis in. With two laps to go, the gap was less than 2 seconds, but exiting the final Rindtkurve De Angelis fought the Finn to give Lotus its first win for three years – by half a second! An emotional Chapman congratulated De Angelis on his superb effort.

This was also the Ford-Cosworth DFV's 150th GP win and how appropriate it was that Lotus, which had débuted the DFV in F1, should record this milestone. Ironically in Austria Chapman finally negotiated the use of Renault's turbo engines and an official announcement was made at Dijon. De Angelis simultaneously signed his contract for 1983.

The revived Swiss GP was held at Dijon-Prenois in France, which was also Renault's main test track. They therefore expected to win, and prepared for just such an occurrence, only for Rosberg's Williams to spoil their plans. Following practice Mansell was on the last row, having crashed when, flat out on qualifiers, he had collided with Henton's Toleman at Bretelle. De Angelis was in mid-grid after the 91's 'perfect' handling

had evaporated. By mid-race Mansell had caught the battle that De Angelis was having with Patrese, Alboreto and Daly on his way to sixth. With his sprained wrist Mansell fought on to finish eighth, despite having the wrong gearing for the long straight.

At Monza the mechanics had an abnormal work load, thanks to De Angelis crashing in early practice and then the next day being rammed by Arnoux's Renault as the two braked for a chicane. Mansell too had a car-damaging trip into the barriers, so it was hardly surprising that the two Lotuses were well down the grid. On race day De Angelis retired his ill-handling 91, after a tyre stop on lap 18 failed to give any more grip and a throttle slide was sticking anyway. A solitary Mansell persevered to finish seventh.

Testing revealed that rising-rate front suspension improved the 91's handling considerably in preparation for Caesars Palace, which was to be the highly inappropriate setting for the 300th appearance of Team Lotus. Whilst Rosberg took the Championship for Williams both Lotuses were in the background, totally lacking grip. They both retired with Mansell having an accident on lap 8, when Baldi rammed him, and De Angelis surviving another twenty laps before his vain chase of Surer was rewarded with engine failure.

An era came to an end when 'ground effect' was banned in November. Flat-bottoms were now required and the minimum weight was reduced by 40kg (88lb) to 540kg (1,190lb); Chapman's response was the stop-gap Lotus 92.

TEAM LOTUS RESULTS 1982

Drivers:
Elio de Angelis: Italian; Nigel Mansell: British; Roberto Moreno: Brazilian; Geoff Lees: British
Car:
Lotus 87B and 91 Engine: Ford Cosworth DFV

CAR	CHASSIS	DRIVER	PRACTICE SESSION	GRID	RACE	LAPS	%	REASON	CHAMPIONSHIP POSITION	POINTS
S AFRICAN GP, Kyalami – 23rd January – 77 L, 196.35 miles (315.99km) (286)										
87 B	3	De Angelis	1m 10.685s 2	15th	8th	76	98.7	–	–	–
87 B	5	Mansell	1m 11.227s 2	18th	R	0	0.0	Electrics	–	–
87	2	(Spare)								
87	4	(Spare)								
BRAZILIAN GP, Jacarepagua – 21st March – 63 L, 196.945 miles (316.953km) (287)										
91	7	Mansell	1m 32.228s 1	14th	3rd	63	100.0	–	4th=	4
91	6	De Angelis	1m 31.790s 1	11th	R	21	33.3	Accident	–	–
87 B	3	(Spare)								
US GP, Long Beach – 4th April – 75 L, 160.81 miles (258.81km) (288)										
91	6	De Angelis	1m 29.694s 2	16th	5th	74	98.6	–	10th=	2
91	7	Mansell	1m 29.758s 2	17th	7th	72	96.0	–	7th=	4
87 B	3	(Spare)								
BELGIAN GP, Zolder – 9th May – 70 L, 185.38 miles (298.34km) (289)										
91	6	De Angelis	1m 17.762s 2	11th	4th	68	97.1	–	9th	5
91	7	Mansell	1m 16.944s 2	7th	R	9	12.8	Clutch	10th=	4
91	8	(Spare)								
MONACO GP, Monte Carlo – 23rd May – 76 L, 156.406 miles (251.712km) (290)										
91	7	Mansell	1m 25.642s 2	11th	4th	75	98.6	–	8th=	7
91	6	De Angelis	1m 26.456s 2	15th	5th	75	98.6	–	8th=	7
91	8	(Spare)								
91	9	(Spare)								
US GP, Detroit – 6th June – 62 L, 154.566 miles (248.749km) (291)										
91	7	Mansell	1m 50.294s 1	7th	R★	44	70.9	Engine	9th=	7
91	9	De Angelis	1m 50.443s 1	8th	R★★	17	27.4	Gearbox	9th=	7
91	6	(Spare)								
CANADIAN GP, Montreal – 13th June – 70 L, 191.82 miles (308.70km) (292)										
91	6	De Angelis	1m 29.228s 2	10th	4th	69	98.5	–	8th=	10
91	7	Mansell	1m 30.048s 2	14th	R	1	1.4	Accident	11th	7
91	9	(Spare)								
DUTCH GP, Zandvoort – 3rd July – 72 L, 190.228 miles (306.144km) (293)										
91	6	De Angelis	1m 17.620s 1	15th	R	40	50.5	Handling	8th=	10
91	7	Moreno	1m 21.149s 1	DNQ	–	–	–	–	–	–
91	8	(Spare)								
91	9	(Spare)								
BRITISH GP, Brands Hatch – 18th July – 76 L, 198.63 miles (319.67km) (294)										
91	8	De Angelis	1m 10.650s 1	7th	4th	76	100.0	–	8th	13
91	7	Mansell	1m 13.212s 2	23rd	R	30	39.4	Handling	11th=	7
91	6	(Spare)								
91	5	(Spare)	N.B. 87 B/5 conversion							
FRENCH GP, Ricard – 25th July – 54 L, 194.95 miles (313.74km) (295)										
91	6	Lees	1m 40.974s 2	24th	12th	52	96.2	–	–	–
91	8	De Angelis	1m 39.118s 2	13th	R	17	31.4	Pressure	8th=	13
91	7	(Spare)								
91	5	(Spare)								
GERMAN GP, Hockenheim – 8th August – 45 L, 190.055 miles (305.865km) (296)										
91	7	Mansell	1m 55.866s 1	17th	9th	43	95.5	–	13th=	7
91	8	De Angelis	1m 54.476s 1	12th	R	21	46.6	Gears	11th	13
91	6	(Spare)								
91	5	(Spare)								

AUSTRIAN GP, Österreichring – 15th August – 53 L, 195.699 miles (314.9472km) (297)

91	8	De Angelis	1m 31.626s	2	7th	1st W	53	100.0	–	6th	22
91	7	Mansell	1m 32.881s	2	12th	R	17	32.0	Engine	13th=	7
91	6	(Spare)									
91	5	(Spare)									

SWISS GP, Dijon – 29th August – 80 L, 188.88 miles (304.00km) (298)

91	8	De Angelis	1m 04.967s	1	15th	6th	79	98.7	–	6th	23
91	7	Mansell	1m 06.211s	2	26th	8th	79	98.7	–	13th=	7
91	6	(Spare)									
91	9	(Spare)									

ITALIAN GP, Monza – 12th September – 52 L, 187.403 miles (301.600km) (299)

91	7	Mansell	1m 34.964s	1	17th	7th	51	98.0	–	13th=	7
91	8	De Angelis	1m 33.629s	2	23rd	R	34	65.3	Throttle	8th	23
91	6	(Spare)									
91	9	(Spare)									

CAESARS PALACE GP, Las Vegas – 25th September – 75 L, 170.1 miles (273.75km) (300)

91	9	De Angelis	1m 19.302s	2	20th	R	28	37.3	Engine	9th	23
91	8	Mansell	1m 19.439s	2	21st	R	8	10.6	Accident	14th	7
91	6	(Spare)									
91	7	(Spare)									
91	10	(Spare)									

Key:
DNQ = Did Not Qualify
* = Mansell was 4th in Part 1
** = De Angelis was 12th in Part 1
W = Win
R = Retired
L = Laps

WORLD CHAMPIONSHIP RESULTS 1982

Position	Driver	Points
1	Keke Rosberg	44
2=	Didier Pironi	39
	John Watson	39
4	Alain Prost	34
5	Niki Lauda	30
6	Rene Arnoux	28
7=	Patrick Tambay	25
	Michele Alboreto	25
9	**Elio de Angelis**	**23**
10	Riccardo Patrese	21
11	Nelson Piquet	20
12	Eddie Cheever	15
13	Derek Daly	8
14	**Nigel Mansell**	**7**

CONSTRUCTORS' CUP 1982

Position	Constructor	Points
1	Ferrari	74
2	McLaren	69
3	Renault	62
4	Williams	58
5	Brabham	41
6	**Lotus-Ford**	**30**

Lotus 92

Two Cosworth-powered 92s were built for Mansell, as initially there were insufficient Renault turbos to go round. One chassis possessed Wright's 'active' suspension and, like the other 92, it comprised modified bodywork fitted to an existing 91 carbon/Kevlar tub. Riding on hydraulic jacks instead of the normal coil springs, the active suspension was designed to absorb bumps.

On an unremarkable Norfolk morning Dave Scott was the first to experience active suspension at Snetterton on 16 December 1982. The Team were intent that morning on using the 92's on-board data-gathering equipment, which provided them with a read-out in the pits. The test was tragically interrupted by Peter Warr, who arrived to inform the Team that Colin Chapman had died from a heart attack earlier that morning at the age of just fifty-four. He had returned by plane from an FISA meeting in Paris the previous evening, and whatever the cause, an era of motor racing had concluded.

CHAPTER 8

French Connection

Until shortly before his death Chapman, being a FOCA-loyalist, had avoided using a turbo engine, but eventually he accepted that if Lotus were to be competitive, he would have to swallow his pride. Turbocharged Renault engines were therefore negotiated for 1983, although initially availability was very limited. The season was characterized by mid-race refuelling and tyre-changing initiated by Brabham, who had found that approaching a race in two halves, only ever carrying half a 'normal' fuel load and using two sets of fresh tyres, gave a substantial performance advantage.

Lotus 93T

The Martin Ogilvie-designed 93T, boasting the Renault EF1 turbo engine, was launched at London Airport on the 8 February 1983, where it was revealed that the tub was constructed from folded Kevlar/carbon sheet with unusually long side-pods; there was also new pull-rod front suspension and the mandatory 1983 flat bottom. Pirelli radial ply tyres, the race version of which would cause many problems, had replaced Goodyear. Thanks partly to those tyres, so uncompetitive was the 93T to become, that by mid-season Gerard Ducarouge would be lured from Alfa Romeo to design the 94T in a mere five weeks!

In Norfolk Peter Wright had been working for two years on an active suspension system as a way of overcoming the 6cm ground clearance rule. Having ignored ride height controls he persevered with a basic 'fully active' system, which attempted to control not only ride height, but also pitching and damping.

In Brazil, Lotus handicapped itself by running two different cars and power plants – the Renault being a totally unknown quantity in a race – whilst simultaneously evaluating active suspension. Pirelli's radial tyres hardly helped, but Chapman's management was sorely missed too. The spare was extensively used in practice as De Angelis complained of Rosberg's blocking tactics, as did Mansell where Surer was concerned; improved times evaporated as a result. De Angelis's turbo failed in the warm-up, so he raced the Cosworth-powered spare, starting from the pit lane.

He was later disqualified for having practised and qualified different cars, even though he had actually practised the spare; his appeal was unsuccessful. He finished in thirteenth on the road just behind Mansell, who had been hampered by a lack of straight-line speed because his rear wing was larger than necessary. A tyre stop on lap 31 dropped him back, and neither Lotus came anywhere near rivalling the winning Brabham of Piquet.

Bumpy Long Beach was suitable for the second airing of active suspension in Mansell's hands. Still feeling the vacuum of Chapman's death, Tony Rudd – the director of engineering at Lotus – honed the longer-wheelbase 93T of De Angelis sufficiently for him to qualify fifth, whilst at the same time tending the active suspension on Mansell's ill-handling 92. The suspension's computer couldn't cope with the fiercer bumps and a battered Mansell qualified well in thirteenth with an active system that seriously 'concerned' him. In the race (won by Watson's McLaren) both Lotuses struggled as Pirelli's race tyres couldn't cope. After a bad start, De Angelis went twenty-nine laps after stopping for tyres as early as lap 16, whilst Mansell had changed on lap 4! He repeated the operation twice more on laps 29 and 51 to finish twelfth and last! After the US GP Mansell's car was converted to standard suspension to save weight. The active system, funded by Lotus Engineering, would not be seen again until 1987.

Mansell's first Renault-powered race (Brands Hatch's Race of Champions) ended with his retirement after six laps with ill-handling, officially caused by an 'assembly fault'. The driver was too 'concerned' to comment . . .

Both Lotuses retired in the French GP, where Pirelli's excellent qualifiers had yielded fifth fastest time for De Angelis, despite a broken side-pod. Mansell had tested a new Cosworth DFY, but still watched the turbos blast past on Paul Ricard's Mistral straight. Ironically his race retirement was caused by the spare, on solid metal set-up wheels, being rolled over his foot; after six laps the pain was too much and he gave up in sympathy with his tyres. Prost's Renault won, while De Angelis fought with Lauda and Laffite for twenty laps before his fuel injection's electrics failed and he parked.

Pirelli modified their race tyres in time for Imola and again De Angelis practised brilliantly but was unable to maintain this form in the race. His engine blew in the warm-up so he raced the spare, which didn't possess refuelling couplings; he was thus handicapped with double the fuel load of the opposition. He stopped twice, on laps 38 and 44, but having run in eighth, his handling and tyres deteriorated and on his second visit he disconsolately dismounted and left, without waiting to see Tambay's Ferrari win at home. Mansell's clutch had failed in practice as he persevered with a new large rear wing. From fifteenth on the grid he had two stops (on laps 29 and 46), during which the refuelling kit was successfully débuted. With four laps to go, the new rear wing broke off at the 175mph Curva Villeneuve, spinning the Lotus violently before it struck the wall backwards; a lucky Mansell somehow got away unharmed.

Mansell's luck was out again at Monaco as he retired on the opening lap after arguing with Alboreto's Tyrrell just after Tabac – having already passed Serra by taking to the Mirabeau pavement. Mansell's demise was caused by his wish to make the most of his wets but De Angelis made no such mistake, having fitted slicks, which helped him climb up to sixth on lap 12. He was then forced into three pitstops (on laps 18, 28 and 50), of which two were for tyres, and finally a drive-shaft forced his retirement when he was in eleventh place. Rosberg won for Williams.

Lotus relished their Belgian GP return to Spa, but the 93Ts refused to be obedient. A frustrated De Angelis damaged his suspension on a kerb in practice as the handling failed to match the available horsepower, whilst Mansell's Cosworth-powered 92 was too slow to keep up with the opposition, including Prost's Renault, which would win the race. The first start was aborted when both De Angelis and Laffite stalled. In the second attempt Mansell retired with gearbox oil-pump failure after thirty laps, having already stopped once (on lap 23) and De Angelis finished ninth after a single pitstop on lap 18.

After Belgium it was revealed that Gerard Ducarouge, formerly with Alfa Romeo, would be joining Lotus as chief designer to produce a car capable of handling the Renault Turbo's power. De Angelis was particularly pleased at this news.

Detroit's twisty street circuit was ideal for the Cosworth engine and as Alboreto won for Tyrrell, using a DFY, Mansell finished sixth to score the Team's first point of the season. Mansell really earned that point, having spun dramatically in practice when fourth gear had refused to engage. Using the turbo car's rear wing he was fourteenth fastest, but unable to match De Angelis's fourth, which had been achieved by turning up the boost when the track was at its quickest. De Angelis

eagerly jumped the start but only lasted for five laps before his transmission pinion broke. Mansell pushed his 92 very hard to rise through the field without a stop, demonstrating both his liking for street circuits and his grit and determination.

A week after Detroit the Canadian GP was the unloved 93T's swan-song: De Angelis retired when his throttle cable broke after two racing laps and a practice with hopeless handling, although new springs had helped slightly. Mansell's 92 was in fact made up of two cars hastily cobbled together, after the transmission failed on the original, but he still languished at the rear with a tired Cosworth engine. In the race he was in and out of the pits, eventually exhausting the Pirelli supply and retiring after forty-three laps, giving up the unequal struggle. Arnoux's Ferrari was the victor.

For Silverstone and the British GP Mansell was to get his first World Championship drive with a turbo engine bolted into the back of the new 94T.

Lotus 94T

For the 94T Ducarouge modified the 91 carbon-Kevlar tub to accept the Renault EF1 engine. The 91 was readily adaptable with the bulkheads being easily changed and a new fuel tankage arrangement was easily created for the fuel stops. Unusually, front rocker-arm suspension was utilized, and overall the 94T was a much lighter car than its predecessor with the Pirelli tyres, too, suiting the design. Ducarouge, who had slept at the factory, created the new bodywork in a mere five weeks and the 94T was to return Lotus to the front of the field, giving Mansell, in particular, the opportunity he wanted.

Over-heating and electrical troubles denied Mansell even one Silverstone practice lap in the 94 so his time was set in the 93T. The wiring loom was faulty so a new one was commissioned overnight and installed just in time for the warm-up. The Renault engines hadn't seemed powerful enough either and the manufacturer blamed the 94's very small radiators. Now fully competitive, Mansell drove from eighteenth to fourth by the time of the race's finish with the loss of a front-wheel balance weight, which affected the handling, being his only problem. The result vindicated not only Mansell, who demonstrated his determination, but also the effort to construct the 94T.

De Angelis enthused about his 94T, which was in fourth position on the grid; in the event, he retired after only two race laps when his Renault engine failed spectacularly, forcing him to park at Becketts.

Hockenheim practice saw De Angelis both spin and then have his 94T's nose come adrift on his fast lap! Mansell suffered engine troubles and switched to the

Ducarouge modified the 91's tub to create the pleasing 94T. Seen here débuting at Silverstone, the car was fourth fastest, but only lasted for two laps before the engine failed here at Becketts.

93T, in which he was seventeenth fastest, but he retired after one race lap when his engine expired. De Angelis had engine trouble, too, after eight race laps, thanks to a blown spark plug, and he became another engine-induced retirement shortly afterwards.

Mansell outshone an embarrassed De Angelis, the previous year's victor, in Österreichring practice using the large 'Imola' wing to finish third fastest in his reliable 94T, with its modified radiators. The Texaco chicane caught De Angelis out – bending his 94T's nose – only for the spare 93T literally to come apart at the seams; a weak engine denied any improvement on his twelfth-fastest time. A chaotic start saw Mansell being slow away, as De Angelis spun into the barriers, but he circulated for eighteen laps in sixth before his Pirellis failed, although in the end he seized fifth while Prost's Renault won.

In Holland, Lotus attacked pole position with Mansell initially being fastest, although then Prost pipped him, and De Angelis overtook them both! The 94Ts handled superbly on their Pirelli qualifiers although their multiple-layer rear wings slowed them on Zandvoort's long straight. Piquet's Brabham finally took pole with Lotus third and fifth fastest. On lap 1 Mansell attacked his team-mate before over-cooking things at Gerlach; in climbing back up the field he misjudged an attack on Warwick entering Tarzan on lap 27 and slid into retirement. De Angelis had already retired (after twelve laps) with fuel-metering unit failure, leaving Arnoux to win for Ferrari.

Monza required top speed and the Lotuses were lower down the grid than normal, with both drivers unhappy with their engines. Mansell could do no better than finish eleventh in the race, while De Angelis fought past Prost on lap 10 to come in fifth. He limped across the line lacking both third and fifth gears, but having at last scored two points! Mansell let his seventh place go to Giacomelli, when on the last lap he slowed at the Parabolica to avoid a track full of invading spectators. Mansell later condemned Giacomelli for risking the spectators' lives for a minor placing.

As Piquet was winning at Monza, Brazilian Ayrton Senna had a controversial F3 crash with Martin Brundle at Oulton Park. Such was Senna's talent that Lotus had already approached him for the following season, possibly putting Mansell's long-term position in jeopardy.

De Angelis practised superbly to take pole for Brands Hatch's European GP, despite having spun the spare into the Druids catch-fencing. An inspired Mansell was third fastest, and in the race itself he scored Lotus's best 1983 result, thereby ensuring that John Player wanted him retained – thoughts of a Brazilian replacement were abandoned. Competition between the Lotus drivers was high and De Angelis pushed hard, only to touch Patrese's Brabham on lap 11 during an unwise overtaking manoeuvre by the Lotus at Surtees. Having spun off, De Angelis 'buzzed' his engine in frustration whilst regaining the tarmac, which caused his retirement two laps later. Mansell was third overall at the time of his 9.62-second pitstop (lap 42), indulging in a contest with first Patrese and then Tambay before finishing third and also recording the fastest lap time.

De Angelis was second quickest in private practice at

After extensive testing, De Angelis took pole position for the European Grand Prix at Brands Hatch. Under pressure from Mansell, the Italian touched Patrese and spun off; he then damaged his engine regaining the circuit, which caused his retirement.

Kyalami, but in the official sessions he could only manage eleventh, four places behind Mansell, with intercooler troubles. The race, which was eventually won by Patrese's Brabham, saw De Angelis stop for engine repairs, but it gave out after twenty laps when he was in last place. Mansell's gear linkage failed him and he stopped three times on his way to an unclassified thirteenth place.

A thoroughly unreliable season for Lotus was thus concluded. With hindsight Mansell felt that he should have left Lotus at the end of 1983, but he agreed to stay for 1984.

TEAM LOTUS RESULTS 1983

Drivers:
Elio de Angelis: Italian; Nigel Mansell: British
Car:
Lotus 92 (standard and active) Engine: Ford Cosworth DFV
Lotus 93T   Renault EF1
Lotus 94T   Renault EF1

CAR	CHASSIS	DRIVER	PRACTICE	SESSION	GRID	RACE	LAPS	%	REASON	CHAMPIONSHIP POSITION	POINTS
BRAZILIAN GP, Jacarepagua – 13th March – 63 L, 196.945 miles (316.953km) (301)											
92 T	10A	Mansell	1m 39.154s	2	22nd	12th	61	96.8	–	–	–
92	5	De Angelis	1m 40.056s	1	SFP	DSQ	60	95.2	Swapped	–	–
93 T★	1	De Angelis	1m 36.454s	2	13th	–	–	–	–	–	–
US GP, Long Beach – 27th March – 75 L, 152.625 miles (245.625km) (302)											
92	10A	Mansell	1m 29.167s	2	13th	12th	72	96.0	–	–	–
93 T	1	De Angelis	1m 27.982s	2	5th	R	29	38.6	Tyres	–	–
92	5	(Spare)									
FRENCH GP, Ricard – 17th April – 54 L, 194.95 miles (313.74km) (303)											
93 T	1	De Angelis	1m 39.312s	2	5th	R	20	37.0	Electrics	–	–
92	10	Mansell	1m 42.650s	2	18th	R	6	11.1	Injury	–	–
92	5	(Spare)									
93 T	2	(Spare)									
SAN MARINO GP, Imola – 1st May – 60 L, 187.90 miles (302.40km) (304)											
92	10	Mansell	1m 35.703s	2	15th	12th	56	93.3	Accident	–	–
93 T	2	De Angelis	1m 34.332s	2	9th	R	44	73.3	Handling	–	–
92	5	(Spare)									
93 T	1	(Spare)									

MONACO GP, Monte Carlo – 15th May – 76 L, 156.406 miles (251.712km) (305)

93 T	1	De Angelis	1m 29.518s	1	20th	R	50	65.7	D/Shaft	–	–
92	10	Mansell	1m 28.721s	1	13th	R	0	0.0	Accident	–	–
92	5	(Spare)									
93 T	2	(Spare)									

BELGIAN GP, Spa – 22nd May – 40 L, 173.127 miles (278.622km) (306)

93 T	1	De Angelis	2m 09.310s	1	13th	9th	39	97.5	–	–	–
92	10	Mansell	2m 09.924s	1	19th	R	30	75.0	Gearbox	–	–
92	5	(Spare)									
93 T	2	(Spare)									

US GP, Detroit – 5th June – 60 L, 150 miles (241.401km) (307)

92	10	Mansell	1m 48.395s	2	14th	6th	59	98.3	–	13th=	1
93 T	1	De Angelis	1m 46.258s	2	4th	R	5	8.3	Gears	–	–
92	5	(Spare)									
93 T	2	(Spare)									

CANADIAN GP, Montreal – 12th June – 70 L, 191.82 miles (308.70km) (308)

92	10	Mansell	1m 33.588s	1	18th	R	43	61.4	Handling	13th=	1
93 T	1	De Angelis	1m 31.822s	2	11th	R	2	2.8	Throttle	–	–
92	5	(Spare)									
93 T	2	(Spare)									

BRITISH GP, Silverstone – 16th July – 67 L, 196.44 miles (316.173km) (309)

94 T	2	Mansell	(1m 15.133s)**		18th	4th	67	100.0	–	11th=	4
94 T	1	De Angelis	1m 10.771s	1	4th	R	1	1.4	Engine	–	–
93 T	1	(Spare)									
93 T	2	(Spare)	1m 15.133s	2							

GERMAN GP, Hockenheim – 17th August – 45 L, 190.055 miles (305.865km) (310)

94 T	1	De Angelis	1m 54.831s	1	11th	R	10	22.2	Temp	–	–
93 T	1	Mansell	1m 56.490s	1	17th	R	1	2.2	Engine	12th=	4
94 T	2	(Spare)									

AUSTRIAN GP, Österreichring – 14th August – 53 L, 195.699 miles (314.9472km) (311)

94 T	2	Mansell	1m 30.457s	2	3rd	5th	52	98.1	–	11th=	6
94 T	1	De Angelis	(1m 34.818s)***	1	R	0	0.0	Accident	–	–	
93 T	1	(Spare)	1m 34.818s	1							

DUTCH GP, Zandvoort – 28th August – 72 L, 190.228 miles (306.144km) (312)

94 T	2	Mansell	1m 16.711s	2	5th	R	26	36.1	Accident	11th=	6
94 T	3	De Angelis	1m 16.411s	1	3rd	R	12	16.6	Metering	–	–
4 T	1	(Spare)									

ITALIAN GP, Monza – 11th September – 52 L, 187.403 miles (301.600km) (313)

94 T	1	De Angelis	1m 31.628s	2	8th	5th	52	100.0	–	17th=	2
94 T	3	Mansell	1m 32.423s	2	11th	8th	52	100.0	–	11th=	6
94 T	2	(Spare)									

EUROPEAN GP, Brands Hatch – 25th September – 76 L, 198.63 miles (319.67km) (314)

94 T	2	Mansell	1m 12.623s	1	3rd	3rd	76	100.0	–	10th=	10
(Fastest Lap: 1m 14.342s – 126.563mph (203.683kmh) on lap 70)											
94 T	1	De Angelis	1m 12.092s	2	1st P	R	13	17.1	Engine	17th=	2
94 T	3	(Spare)									

S AFRICAN GP, Kyalami – 15th October – 77 L, 196.35 miles (315.99km) (315)

94 T	2	Mansell	1m 07.643s	2	7th	13th NC	68	88.3	—	12th=	10
94 T	3	De Angelis	1m 07.937s	1	11th	R	20	25.9	Engine	17th=	2
94 T	1	(Spare)									

Key:
SFP = Started From Pit Lane
DSQ = Disqualified
* = 93 T/1 was intended race car but turbo failure necessitated swap to 92
** = Grid time recorded in 93 T/2
*** = Grid time set in 93 T/1
NC = Not Classified
R = Retired
L = Laps
P = Pole
A = Active

WORLD CHAMPIONSHIP RESULTS 1983

Position	Driver	Points
1	Nelson Piquet	59
2	Alain Prost	57
3	Rene Arnoux	49
4	Patrick Tambay	40
5	Keke Rosberg	27
6=	John Watson	22
	Eddie Cheever	22
8	Andrea de Cesaris	15
9	Riccardo Patrese	13
10	Niki Lauda	12
11	Jacques Laffite	11
12=	**Nigel Mansell**	**10**
	Michele Alboreto	10
14	Derek Warwick	9
15	Marc Surer	4
16	Mauro Baldi	3
17=	**Elio de Angelis**	**2**

CONSTRUCTORS' CUP 1983

Position	Constructor	Points
1	Ferrari	89
2	Renault	79
3	Brabham	72
4	Williams	38
5	McLaren	34
6	Alfa Romeo	18
7=	**Lotus**	**12**
	Tyrrell	12

1984

Lotus 95T

Launched in Paris in December, the Ducarouge-penned 95T was both slimmer and lighter than its predecessor, with a new Kevlar/carbon monocoque and interchangeable aerodynamics. The Bruno Mauduit EF1 turbo engine was not as powerful as some power plants but Lotus would frequently humble the other Renault-powered runners! Pirelli's tyres were abandoned for Goodyears, but their first radials were to be less competitive than Michelin's offerings. The 95T was to be regarded as the best handling F1 chassis of 1984, such was its grip and balance, and was to be the main threat to the McLarens. The permitted fuel load was reduced to 220 litres and mid-race refuelling banned, so designers chilled their petrol, thus enabling more than 220 litres to be squeezed aboard. The consumption rate of cold fuel, though, was higher, requiring intercoolers to be fitted between the tank and engine; the pumps often iced up!

Mansell was retained, after John Watson had turned Lotus down, but he and De Angelis clashed, leading to several unwise inter-Lotus jousts. The Italian finished in the points in nine of the first ten races, thanks to intense application, and he excelled in the rain, but amazingly didn't win a race in 1984. Following a week of testing the new high temperature-resistant Garrett turbochargers, Lotus left for Rio full of confidence, unaware of McLaren's new competitiveness.

A searingly fast practice lap by Mansell, during which he had slid outside Ghinzani's Osella, set the early Brazilian pace. De Angelis subsequently annexed pole as Mansell spun to miss Prost's McLaren, which had swerved on to the racing line to miss a Ligier. The incident caused Prost – the eventual race winner – to blame Mansell for denying him pole position! After a delayed race start Mansell was initially third, before Lauda's McLaren passed him, after which he held fourth until he spun off into the fences on lap 36 after failing to fend off Tambay's Renault. After four laps, De Angelis was so unhappy with his engine response, caused by faulty electronics, that he almost retired; he decided to continue, and was rewarded by third place.

Using Garrett turbochargers and larger radiators Mansell was third fastest at Kyalami as De Angelis struggled with KKK turbos before switching to Garretts, and rising to seventh. Mansell gambled on running with a single set of Goodyears and seized second place, behind Rosberg's Williams, on the first lap run to Crowthorne. His engine suddenly stuttered and he dropped to a furious twelfth; then, after a battle with Patrese and Arnoux, he retired from sixth place on lap 50 when his turbo's inlet failed. Whilst in second place behind eventual winner Lauda, De Angelis's throttle linkage collapsed, forcing him to pit. He fought back to seventh, having dropped to eighteenth.

Having created problematic high temperatures, the 95T was given cooling bodywork for Zolder, which ironically iced up the fuel system! De Angelis went through the Belgian GP on hard tyres whilst Mansell was afflicted by a slipping clutch, which caused his retirement after only fourteen laps. De Angelis fought with the impressive Rosberg and Bellof to take a thoroughly deserved fifth place at the end.

Mansell's two-lap San Marino GP ended when his brakes failed and he spun into the Acque Minerale sand; it turned out that some experimental components hadn't been removed. His practice had been similarly frantic as Gartner had driven over his front wheels and Alliot had spun him at the Rivazza. The 95T overheated again in the warm-up, forcing him to race the spare. De Angelis quietly drove to third, despite running out of fuel and parking on the penultimate lap as Prost won the fuel-consumption race.

In France, a new rear spoiler helped De Angelis to be fastest, as the 95T handled superbly, but he was later pipped for pole by Tambay's Renault which was 'obliged' to go very fast in France! Mansell was a disappointed sixth fastest, and considering his emotional state (his mother had just died) he drove stirringly after an eleventh-hour engine change. The two Lotuses were attacked by Piquet on the first lap before Tambay took the lead. De Angelis lost second to Prost on Lap 18 as Mansell fought with Warwick, but this ended abruptly on lap 54 with the Renault embedded in the fences after a contretemps with Surer. De Angelis changed tyres, which caused oversteer, but Lotus were still able to celebrate two drivers in the top five.

The day after Dijon's high Mansell returned to England for his mother's funeral, and her coffin was poignantly draped with the third-place flowers that he had received in France.

On his favourite circuit Mansell joined the front row at Monaco, having survived a contretemps with Arnoux's Ferrari as well as having kissed the barriers. When his spare expired with a dead engine, he sprinted back for his race car and promptly posted the second-best time, after Prost. Mansell led a GP for the first time and his elation lasted from lap 11 to lap 15, when he lost the back end and swiped the barriers. In the torrential rain he had already forced past Prost, who had been delayed by a minor accident at Portier. He was criticized for throwing away an easy win, but critics overlooked the conditions that led to the race being stopped after thirty-one laps. Mansell had been caught out on the white road markings approaching the Casino, which caused his tyres to lose adhesion. He was deeply affected by both the incident and the subsequent criticism, which filled him with a new urge to prove himself. The severely understeering De Angelis had only been eleventh on the grid, and had halted to avoid a first lap Ste Devote accident, but he drove steadily to sixth place. Having been trapped behind Ghinzani for eighteen laps, he speeded up once he had overtaken.

Early in Montreal's Circuit Gilles Villeneuve practice, Mansell was fastest but he dropped back as firstly mechanical (metering unit, pinion and engine) and then on-track troubles (De Cesaris's and Prost's engine blow-ups) enabled others to pass him. De Angelis made up for Monaco, being third fastest, but both drivers complained that there was only one spare car, which curtailed their possible mileage. Mansell had another last-minute engine change and De Angelis raced the spare, only for his engine to lose power. As the fuel load lightened, the handling of Mansell's 95T improved, but he was blocked by his team-mate for nine laps, during which the two Lotuses nearly collided on

several occasions. Their unruly fight was unwise and by the time (lap 55) Mansell was in fourth, his gearbox was failing and on lap 60 he was overtaken by De Angelis, who eventually finished fourth, while Mansell salvaged sixth.

Piquet had won Canada convincingly and a week later he was in exactly the right mood to take pole position in Detroit. Mansell had again been fastest in early practice, but dropped to third after Bellof had ruined his fastest lap by spinning into the wall just in front of him. De Angelis was fifth fastest. On the riverside run to Turn 1 Mansell was the centre of an accident that involved both the slow-starting Piquet and Prost as well as Alboreto (Ferrari) and Surer (Arrows). Mansell was subsequently fined $6,000 by FISA for dangerous driving in having gone for a non-existent gap – though photographic evidence later vindicated him – and it was felt that his desperate need to win a race after the Monaco débâcle contributed to his high risk manoeuvre. The race was restarted, with Mansell's car being undamaged, and having forced past Prost on lap 9 he ran in second for seventeen laps whilst closing right in on Piquet. At this moment (lap 25) in the Atwater Tunnel, his second gear disappeared only to be followed two laps later by complete gearbox failure, denying him any chance of a win. De Angelis took second place fourteen laps from the flag only for his gearbox to fail too while he was catching the leader, although he did manage to finish third. Lotus were concerned by the gearbox failures, but it would take until Monza for a solution to be found.

Mansell's determination yielded him pole at Dallas with De Angelis second, to make an all-Lotus front row for the first time in six years. Mansell's first-ever pole was achieved on a track that was breaking up in the sun, and De Angelis thoroughly disliked the circuit. The latter also criticized Mansell for his attitude at Detroit and they expressed their feelings for each other during a hectic all-Lotus battle between Dallas's concrete walls. Mansell led the race for thirty-five laps as De Angelis's engine gave out, and he then came under pressure from Warwick until the Renault spun off. For seven laps De Angelis had tried to pass Mansell, and then on lap 19 Rosberg's lighter Williams eventually barged its way through. Mansell had a heavier fuel load than the Williams, which affected his ride height as the race progressed. Having stopped for tyres on lap 39, Mansell lost his gears after swiping a wall, and he then tried to push his car over the line in the intense heat only to collapse from exhaustion just feet from his goal. He did at least take sixth place for his efforts, with De Angelis third. At the conclusion of the race Rosberg, the winner, loudly criticized Mansell for his 'blocking' tactics.

The Texan weekend of gearbox troubles forced Lotus to create a complete replacement; at Brands Hatch newer, tougher, gears were used instead and by the time of the British GP, Lotus had undertaken no less than forty-one days of testing. Mansell was fastest in Brands Hatch tyre-testing and in official practice the Lotuses performed well despite little grip. Piquet, allegedly, had held the Italian up whilst the Englishman had a down-on-power engine only for his gearbox to promptly give out! It did the same in the GP causing Mansell's retirement after only twenty-four laps of the restarted race. De Angelis fought manfully with Senna's Toleman with the latter eventually forcing his way past at Paddock on lap 66; the Italian, however, overcame shredding Goodyears on his way to a good fourth place behind Lauda's winning McLaren.

In early Hockenheim practice De Angelis was fastest as Lotus seemed to have successfully cured the understeer so obvious in Kent. He just lost a duel for pole with eventual winner Prost's McLaren after Fabi's Brabham proved just too wide at the chicane on his quick retaliatory lap. Mansell had similar problems with De Cesaris (Ligier), having already cured all manner of gearbox troubles, and he came in an angry sixteenth as a result. De Angelis launched his 95T away from the grid to lead for the first seven laps, only for Piquet to slide past when the Lotus's turbo failed. It was widely acknowledged that nobody would have caught De Angelis had his mechanical failure not have occurred. His team-mate's turbo failure noted, Mansell decided to ease up and run a most calculating and thoughtful race as he preserved not only his left-hand Goodyears but also his engine until the end.

After Hockenheim F3 charger Johnny Dumfries successfully tested a 95T at Donington. That tired Donington engine was used at the Österreichring by De Angelis who was the best Goodyear qualifier in third place, despite having blown an engine and later spun off. Having observed the Italian's engine troubles, Mansell ran low boost on his, but still suffered a blow-up, causing another change for final qualifying; thanks to blistering tyres he was only eighth fastest. Both engines failed in the race, but this was only after an aborted start when De Angelis's car refused to move, causing start-line chaos. Once the race was under way for real, De Angelis's misfiring and blazing engine went first, and he eventually parked on lap 28, having fought off an inspired Senna. In returning to the pits the Italian had left a slick of oil on the circuit; this caught Prost unawares at the Rindtkurve and he crashed out of second place. On lap 33, Mansell's engine blew too, so that the Lotus challenge was removed. Lauda brought his McLaren in first for a home win.

In Holland, Prost and McLaren continued their winning ways, in the process breaking Lotus's 1978 record of eight wins in a single season. In the paddock Lotus revealed that Senna had been signed for the following year, much to the annoyance of Toleman, who insisted he was contracted to them; as a direct result Senna would not be provided with a Toleman to drive at Monza. Mansell found out by accident that he would not be with Lotus the following year! De Angelis, meantime, qualified an outstanding third behind Prost and Piquet, whilst Mansell could only manage twelfth after a whole series of niggling problems. For much of the Dutch GP De Angelis ran in fifth, despite the insensitivity of Winkelhock to his existence. By lap 52 he was closing on Rosberg and decided to have had a go at overtaking at Tarzan. At just this moment, Mansell dodged outside De Angelis and then, a lap later, Rosberg, in a brave move down the inside of the same corner. At the finish the two Lotuses took third and fourth positions.

Mansell, having ably demonstrated his talent, started to shop around for a replacement drive and his Zandvoort performance meant that finding a new home at Williams for 1985 didn't take him very long.

At Monza De Angelis was the only driver capable of usurping the McLarens at the top of the World Championship table. This looked achievable when he was initially quickest in Friday practice, whilst Mansell could only struggle to take seventh place in the grid. The 'heavy-duty' development gearbox on De Angelis's car played its part in the Championship outcome when it let go on lap 15. A lap before, Mansell had hit an oil slick and plunged terminally into a sand-trap, thereby once again ending Lotus's day prematurely. The World Championship would now be a McLaren battle to the finish, following Lauda's Italian win.

A double Lotus retirement occurred in the European GP at the Nurburgring. A series of turbo failures dogged De Angelis, as did a wet track, and all he could manage was twenty-third, while Mansell was a somewhat lucky eighth. A five-car accident at the first corner delayed Mansell, who dropped to twentieth but by lap 46 he was sixth, only to have his engine let go on lap 52. De Angelis had already departed on lap 26, thanks to turbo failure. Prost won again for McLaren.

At the last race of the season at Estoril, an angry De Angelis was cut up by Streiff in qualifying, but the two Lotuses were still fifth and sixth fastest. Controversially, the Team only possessed one set of large brake pads for the GP and despite protestations Mansell didn't get them, and his subsequent retirement was caused by brake failure! He had earlier fought with Rosberg, whom he would be joining at Williams the following year, and the Finn allegedly banged wheels just to make sure everyone knew who was going to be boss!

```
┌──────────────────────────────────────────────────────────────────────────────────────┐
│                           TEAM LOTUS RESULTS 1984                                      │
```

Drivers:
Elio de Angelis: Italian; Nigel Mansell: British
Car:
Lotus 95 T Engine: Renault EF4
Lotus 94 T   Renault EF4

CAR	CHASSIS	DRIVER	PRACTICE	SESSION	GRID	RACE	LAPS	%	REASON	CHAMPIONSHIP POSITION	POINTS
BRAZILIAN GP, Jacarepagua – 25th March – 61 L, 190.692 miles (306.889km) (316)											
95 T	3	De Angelis	1m 28.392s	2	1st P	3rd	61	100.0	–	3rd	4
95 T	2	Mansell	1m 29.364s	1	5th	R	35	57.3	Accident	–	–
95 T	1	(Spare)									
94 T	1	(Spare)									
S AFRICAN GP, Kyalami – 7th April – 75 L, 191.247 miles (307.783km) (317)											
95 T	3	De Angelis	1m 05.953s	2	7th	7th	71	94.6	–	4th=	4
95 T	2	Mansell	1m 05.125s	2	3rd	R	51	68.0	Turbo	–	–
95 T	1	(Spare)									
BELGIAN GP, Zolder – 29th April – 70 L, 185.38 miles (298.339km) (318)											
95 T	3	De Angelis	1m 15.979s	2	5th	5th	69	98.5	–	6th	6
95 T	2	Mansell	1m 16.720s	2	10th	R	14	20.0	Clutch	–	–
95 T	1	(Spare)									
SAN MARINO GP, Imola – 6th May – 60 L, 187.90 miles (302.400km) (319)											
95 T	3	De Angelis	1m 31.173s	2	11th	3rd	59	98.3	–	3rd=	10
95 T	1	Mansell	1m 34.477s	2	18th	R	2	3.3	Accident	–	–
95 T	2	(Spare)									
FRENCH GP, Dijon – 20th May – 79 L, 186.535 miles (300.200km) (320)											
95 T	2	Mansell	1m 03.200s	1	6th	3rd	79	100.0	–	9th	4
95 T	3	De Angelis	1m 02.336s	1	2nd	5th	79	100.0	–	5th	12
95 T	1	(Spare)									
95 T	4	(Spare)									
MONACO GP, Monte Carlo – 3rd June – 31 L, 63.797 miles (102.672km) (321)											
95 T	3	De Angelis	1m 24.426s	2	11th	6th	31	100.0	–	5th	12.5
95 T	2	Mansell	1m 22.752s	2	2nd	R	15	48.3	Accident	10th=	4
95 T	4	(Spare)									
CANADIAN GP, Montreal – 17th June – 70 L, 191.82 miles (308.70km) (322)											
95 T	4	De Angelis	1m 26.306s	2	3rd	4th	69	98.5	–	4th	15.5
95 T	2	Mansell	1m 27.246s	2	7th	6th	68	97.1	–	10th=	5
95 T	3	(Spare)									
US GP, Detroit – 24th June – 63 L, 157.500 miles (253.471km) (323)											
95 T	4	De Angelis	1m 42.434s	2	5th	3rd	63	100.0	–	3rd	19.5
95 T	2	Mansell	1m 42.172s	2	3rd	R	27	42.8	Gearbox	11th=	5
95 T	3	(Spare)									
US GP, Dallas – 8th July – 67 L, 162.408 miles (261.370km) (324)											
95 T	3	De Angelis	1m 37.635s	1	2nd	3rd	66	98.5	—	3rd	23.5
95 T	2	Mansell	1m 37.041s	1	1st P	6th NR	64	95.5	Gearbox	11th	6
BRITISH GP, Brands Hatch – 22nd July – 71 L, 185.566 miles (298.638km) (325)											
95 T	3	De Angelis	1m 11.573s	2	4th	4th	70	98.5	–	3rd	26.5
95 T	2	Mansell	1m 12.435s	2	8th	R	24	33.8	Gearbox	11th	6
95 T	4	(Spare)									
GERMAN GP, Hockenheim – 5th August – 44 L, 185.83 miles (299.068km) (326)											
95 T	2	Mansell	1m 51.715s	2	16th	4th	44	100.0	–	9th	9
95 T	3	De Angelis	1m 47.065s	2	2nd	R	8	18.1	Turbo	3rd	26.5
95 T	4	(Spare)									
AUSTRIAN GP, Österreichring – 19th August – 51 L, 188.313 miles (303.062km) (327)											
95 T	2	Mansell	1m 27.558s	2	8th	R	32	62.7	Engine	9th	9
95 T	3	De Angelis	1m 26.318s	2	3rd	R	28	54.9	Engine	3rd	26.5
95 T	4	(Spare)									

DUTCH GP, Zandvoort – 26th August – 71 L, 187.586 miles (301.892km) (328)

95 T	2	Mansell	1m 15.811s	2	12th	3rd	71	100.0	–	9th	13
95 T	3	De Angelis	1m 13.883s	2	3rd	4th	70	98.5	–	3rd	29.5
95 T	4	(Spare)									

ITALIAN GP, Monza – 9th September – 51 L, 183.801 miles (295.800km) (329)

95 T	3	De Angelis	1m 27.538s	2	3rd	R	14	27.4	Gearbox	3rd	29.5
95 T	2	Mansell	1m 28.969s	2	7th	R	13	25.4	Accident	9th	13
95 T	4	(Spare)									

EUROPEAN GP, Nurburgring – 7th October – 67 L, 189.091 miles (304.314km) (330)

95 T	2	Mansell	1m 21.170s	1	8th	R	51	76.1	Engine	9th	13
95 T	3	De Angelis	1m 26.161s	1	23rd	R	25	37.3	Turbo	3rd	32
95 T	4	(Spare)									

PORTUGUESE GP, Estoril – 21st October – 70 L, 189.207 miles (304.500km) (331)

95 T	4	De Angelis	1m 22.291s	2	5th	5th	70	100.0	–	3rd	34
95 T	2	Mansell	1m 22.319s	2	6th	R	52	74.2	Accident	9th	13
95 T	3	(Spare)									

Key:
NR = Not Running
P = Pole
R = Retired
L = Laps

Mansell's second place with twenty-five laps to go – Prost was first and Lauda third – was all that was keeping the Austrian from the World title. It didn't seem as if Lauda would catch the dominant Lotus, which had a 25-second advantage, but fate intervened with the Lotus losing its brake fluid and spinning. Lauda took his third Championship thanks to his inherited second-place finish and Mansell's last race for Lotus was concluded with honour. De Angelis came in fifth as Prost took the laurels. By winning in Portugal, Prost equalled Jim Clark's 1963 record of seven wins in a single season, although it was pointed out that Clark had had ten opportunities against Prost's sixteen!

1985

Lotus 97T

In February the 97T, which possessed a composite/ aluminium foil sandwich tub and a mandatory crash-resistant nose, commenced testing. To overcome the FISA ban of sidestep rear winglets, Ducarouge had added rear side-pod flaps and the CART tweak of vertical spoilers behind the front wheels. The simple design became the season's best-handling chassis, but it suffered from the lack of power, reliability and low fuel consumption of its Renault engine, unlike the Porsche/McLaren opposition. Renault, thanks to Mecachrome in Bourges, raced their EF15 engine and used their high-boost EF4B in qualifying, giving Senna seven poles. In fifteen of the year's thirty GP practice sessions the 97T was fastest – Senna twelve and De Angelis three times.

Mansell was replaced by Ayrton Senna who established himself as no. 1 by outperforming De Angelis, much to the Italian's annoyance. Senna's presence was a confidence boost for Team Lotus, which would have its best season since 1978.

Senna arrived at Lotus and immediately impressed both his engineer, Steve Hallam, and the entire Team with his single-mindedness. He would occupy a grid's front row ten times in 1985 but his home Brazilian GP

WORLD CHAMPIONSHIP RESULTS 1984

Position	Driver	Points
1	Niki Lauda	72
2	Alain Prost	71.5
3	**Elio de Angelis**	**34**
4	Michele Alboreto	30.5
5	Nelson Piquet	29
6	Rene Arnoux	27
7	Derek Warwick	23
8	Keke Rosberg	20.5
9=	**Nigel Mansell**	**13**
	Ayrton Senna	13

CONSTRUCTORS' CUP 1984

Position	Constructor	Points
1	McLaren	143.5
2	Ferrari	57.5
3	**Lotus-Renault**	**47**

Ayrton Senna joined De Angelis to drive the 97T in 1985. The Italian would score eleven times and win at Imola, whilst the Brazilian won in Portugal and Belgium. The car was derived from the 95T using the Renault EF15 engine for racing.

would be an exception. At Jacarepagua the Olympus-sponsored Lotuses were competitive, being fastest in the opening session with De Angelis slightly the quicker. The car's suspensions were covered when they were stationary to stop any espionage, as competition came from Alboreto's Ferrari and Rosberg's Williams, which bumped Lotus on to the second row. McLaren improved in the warm-up as De Angelis required a new engine. The Lotuses ran together in the top five for most of the race, despite two slow tyre stops, but were unable to join the Alboreto v. Prost lead battle. A mature Senna conserved his tyres climbing to third before retiring on lap 49 when his old fuel pump burned out. De Angelis was thus promoted to third for the first of seven points-scoring races.

Lotus flew from Brazil directly to Portugal, and, not having visited Norfolk, it was feared that any South American gremlins might recur. At Estoril the aerodynamics were refined by attaching rear wing modifications, and De Angelis was initially fastest as Senna had a misfire, while the spare lost its clutch. In qualifying, the offending fuel pump was replaced giving Senna fastest time – De Angelis was fourth – for his first pole. After the warm-up Senna needed a new engine and gearbox assembly so the mechanics set to work as the skies darkened. The rain became heavier as Senna seized the lead at the start, with his team-mate second, to defend himself against Prost, who eventually spun into the barriers. Only ten of the twenty-six starters finished in the torrential rain, with a calm Senna leading them home. Out of control, Senna had been right off the circuit at one point, but had rejoined to lead

from start to finish! De Angelis went off too and picked up a puncture before slowing to fourth place on a marvellous Lotus day.

In San Marino practice Senna used a second, lower rear wing and side-pod winglets to head the times on a circuit that he disliked; during his fastest laps he used race tyres. De Angelis was third after a turbo failure. Senna evaluated the new long-stroke EF14 engine and decided to race it with the EF4B being reserved for qualifying. The universal worry at Imola, though, was fuel consumption. The two Lotuses led away but after ten laps De Angelis's brakes faded, and at mid-distance Prost pressurized Senna, who resisted before trapping the Frenchman behind Tambay. Senna, who was leading, realized he was low on fuel and actually ran out on the fifty-seventh lap. Johansson, meanwhile, forced past De Angelis only to cough to a halt in his Ferrari, leaving Prost as the leader. De Angelis resigned himself to second, only to be promoted to the win (and the Championship lead) when Prost's victorious McLaren was disqualified for being below the minimum weight.

De Angelis used the 'old' steel brakes in Monaco practice taking ninth, but was forced to race the carbon-equipped spare. Monegasque observers noticed Senna's throttle dabbing in the corners that gained him pole, asking why he tortured his engine so. The Team's telemetry (a black box in the left side-pod) showed that he kept the boost pressure up, yielding extra horse-power and speed! Senna knew he had pushed his engine too far in practice, but unwisely it wasn't changed. Lauda complained that Senna had blocked him but the Brazilian pointed out that his laps on race tyres were

From pole position De Angelis led for fifteen laps in Canada before dropping back to finish fifth at the flag. Senna was delayed by a broken turbo clip.

quicker than the Austrian's with qualifiers! In the race Senna drove into the distance, but paid the price when his engine blew after thirteen laps, handing Alboreto the lead. The cautious De Angelis ran in second for

De Angelis boards his 97T and prepares for the start of the Canadian Grand Prix. The 97T had become the best handling chassis of the 1985 season, helped in no small way by the CART vertical winglets, seen here behind the front suspension.

thirty-two laps only to be bumped down to third as Prost won.

The intended Belgian race at Spa saw Lotus take second and third grid positions behind Alboreto, but the actual race was postponed when the track surface broke up badly. The circus would return in mid-September.

Canadian practice concluded with De Angelis on pole and Senna just behind, after the Ferrari challenge had wilted. Despite Senna needing a new engine after the warm-up, the two Lotuses headed the field for the first five laps as Senna conserved fuel. After six laps a broken turbo clip made him pit, where he remained for five frustrating laps; when he returned he proceeded to better the lap record. An understeering De Angelis led for the first fifteen laps but Alboreto, Johansson, Prost and Rosberg got past, leaving him to finish a disappointed fifth.

Senna disliked Detroit but he still took pole during the sole dry session, using, like Mansell, race tyres. The winglets were employed again, with Senna preferring the carbon brakes, unlike De Angelis, who was eighth. Earlier the Italian had, unobserved, struck the rear of Tambay's warming-up Renault, ripping off a front corner. Mansell's Williams led the first few yards of the US GP but at Turn 3 Senna ruthlessly cut inside to seize the lead in an amazing cold-tyre manoeuvre! Senna's soft tyres caused his lead to be reduced and he stopped on lap 9, returning in fourteenth place. He glanced the Turn 3 tyres, leaving the concrete bare only for Mansell to strike this heavily on lap 27. Ironically Senna, who had stopped again before taking fastest lap, hit that very same wall on lap 52 whilst trying to pass Alboreto. De Angelis climbed to second by lap 20, but then damaged a nose fin, causing him to pit on lap 29; he rejoined in ninth, eventually finishing fifth as Rosberg won for Williams.

De Angelis was fifth again in Paul Ricard's French GP, where Senna had had his engine explode whilst trying unsuccessfully to beat Rosberg's pole time; lacking an EF4B, De Angelis was seventh fastest. Senna led at the start but Rosberg was quickly past on the Mistral straight, where the Honda engine's superiority showed. On lap 9 Senna pitted as his third gear gave out but he quickly returned, a lap in arrears. Driving fast, his engine expired as he approached Signes flat out; spinning on its own oil, the 97T demolished several rows of catch-fencing before striking the tyre barrier. Luckily Senna had taken his feet and hands off everything and stepped out unscathed. A lap from the end De Angelis, thinking he was securely fourth, was annoyed when he was unable to alter his boost to keep Johansson behind him.

Rosberg took pole at Silverstone and Senna was eventually fourth after his engine had cut out at the vital qualifying moment. De Angelis was eighth, after turbo troubles and selecting the wrong gear ratios; in the warm-up he and Martini collided, necessitating new rear suspension on the 97T. Senna led for fifty-seven laps as Rosberg's and Prost's challenges faded. Then his engine went off-song and Prost closed in, taking the lead on lap 58. Senna ground to a halt by the pit wall with dry tanks because his engine had run too rich; it was suspected that he had increased boost to fend off Prost, but the on-car telemetry disproved this theory. De Angelis' run of points finishes ended on lap 13 when, with a dead engine, he had dismounted. During later checks the engine promptly burst into life and after half an hour he rejoined the race, finishing unclassified.

In Germany the 97Ts sported narrower front wings, and a Renault-produced fuel consumption gauge, and De Angelis also used an on-board radio for the first time. Senna was fifth and De Angelis seventh with fuel pump and engine management system troubles evident. Senna led part of the first lap, only for Rosberg to power past for fifteen laps until his tyres went off. Senna seized the lead back at the hairpin and stayed there for eleven laps before the modified rear suspension caused a rear CV joint to fail. De Angelis climbed up to third place, only for his engine to blow just when he was poised to attack Alboreto's winning Ferrari. In the post-race wash-up the telemetry scotched ideas that Senna had been using low boost to enhance his engine's reliability.

Senna's 97T wouldn't handle over the Öster-reichring's bumps and he qualified a lowly fourteenth. Contributory factors were acknowledged to be a lack of testing, unsuitable qualifying tyres and low turbo boost. In early dry practice he was seventh fastest before the rains came. He eventually raced the spare, with a new front and rear suspension configuration, after a multiple start-line shunt stopped the first Austrian GP. The second start went to plan, and De Angelis held an early fourth place, only for the meteoric Senna to take fifth by lap 23. De Angelis made his tyre stop as Senna suffered a vibration, but he continued cautiously to take second to Prost when Lauda's turbo failed. De Angelis was a secure fifth.

During Zandvoort practice Senna's sixth 'mechanical' sense spotted that his water temperature was fractionally too high; nothing untoward was found but after the race he had only ⅓ gallon (1.5 litres) left! For returning to the paddock when his car caught fire, he was rewarded with a $5,000 fine, but still he qualified fourth, with De Angelis eleventh, and for the first thirteen laps of the Dutch race he ran in second behind Rosberg. Lauda got past, but when he stopped for tyres almost simultaneously with Rosberg's Honda blowing, Senna regained second. Lauda pressurized until lap 48, when he squeezed past at Tarzan and Senna eventually finished third, two places ahead of De Angelis, having been nudged by Alboreto's Ferrari on the final lap. Renault announced their decision to quit F1 as an entrant, although it was made clear that Lotus would still receive their engines.

The 97Ts porpoised at Monza necessitating rear underbody modifications, and on his first visit to the Autodromo Senna took his fifth pole of the season, having scythed across the Lesmo grass in the process. De Angelis was sixth, with both cars making use of a 200mph (320kph) final-drive set-up for the first time in fifteen years. Just after the start of the Italian GP Rosberg forced Senna over the chicane kerbs and he was lucky to rejoin in fourth place. Both his inappropriate tyre choice and his engine slowed him up on his way to third, whilst De Angelis drove conservatively, fearing high fuel consumption – his gauges turned out to be wrong – finishing an annoyed sixth. Prost won the race. De Angelis was somewhat dismayed to be offered the no. 2 drive (after Senna) for 1986! An insulted, formerly loyal Italian immediately started looking for alternative employment.

On the return to Spa Senna was initially only eighteenth fastest after both fire and gearbox troubles but finally, with an unbalanced and understeering 97T, he ended up second fastest to Prost. De Angelis (still third in the Championship) suffered similarly and was only ninth. Race day was rainy, but Piquet helped a fast-starting Senna by spinning in front of the pack at La Source, allowing the Brazilian to sprint away. In a show of brilliance he drove to a massive 28-second win. Both Rosberg and Mansell initially gave chase

TEAM LOTUS RESULTS 1985

Drivers:
Elio de Angelis: Italian; Ayrton Senna: Brazilian
Car:
Lotus 97 T Engine: Renault EF4, EF4B, EF15

CAR	CHASSIS	DRIVER	PRACTICE	SESSION	GRID	RACE	LAPS	%	REASON	CHAMPIONSHIP POSITION	POINTS

BRAZILIAN GP, Jacarepagua – 7th April – 61 L, 190.692 miles (306.889km) (332)

CAR	CHASSIS	DRIVER	PRACTICE	SESSION	GRID	RACE	LAPS	%	REASON	POSITION	POINTS
97 T	3	De Angelis	1m 28.081s	1	3rd	3rd	60	98.3	–	3rd	4
97 T	2	Senna	1m 28.389s	2	4th	R	48	78.6	Electrics	–	–
97 T	1	(Spare)									

PORTUGUESE GP, Estoril – 21st April – 67 L, 181.098 miles (291.450km) (333)

CAR	CHASSIS	DRIVER	PRACTICE	SESSION	GRID	RACE	LAPS	%	REASON	POSITION	POINTS
97 T	2	Senna	1m 27.007s	2	1st P	1st W	67	100.0	–	2nd=	9

Fastest Lap: 1m 44.121s – 93.455mph (150.401km/h) on lap 15

CAR	CHASSIS	DRIVER	PRACTICE	SESSION	GRID	RACE	LAPS	%	REASON	POSITION	POINTS
97 T	3	De Angelis	1m 22.159s	2	4th	4th	66	98.5	–	4th	7
97 T	1	(Spare)									

SAN MARINO GP, Imola – 5th May – 60 L, 187.90 miles (302.400km) (334)

CAR	CHASSIS	DRIVER	PRACTICE	SESSION	GRID	RACE	LAPS	%	REASON	POSITION	POINTS
97 T	1	De Angelis	1m 27.852s	2	3rd	1st W	60	100.0	–	1st	16
97 T	2	Senna	1m 27.327s	2	1st P	7th NR	57	95.0	Fuel	4th=	9
97 T	3	(Spare)									

MONACO GP, Monte Carlo – 19th May – 78 L, 160.522 miles (258.336km) (335)

CAR	CHASSIS	DRIVER	PRACTICE	SESSION	GRID	RACE	LAPS	%	REASON	POSITION	POINTS
97 T	1	De Angelis	1m 21.465s	2	9th	3rd	78	100.0	–	1st	20
97 T	2	Senna	1m 20.450s	2	1st P	R	13	16.6	Engine	5th	9
97 T	3	(Spare)									
97 T	4	(Spare)									

CANADIAN GP, Montreal – 16th June – 70 L, 191.82 miles (308.70km) (336)

CAR	CHASSIS	DRIVER	PRACTICE	SESSION	GRID	RACE	LAPS	%	REASON	POSITION	POINTS
97 T	3	De Angelis	1m 24.567s	2	1st P	5th	70	100.0	–	2nd=	22
97 T	2	Senna	1m 24.816s	2	2nd	16th	65	92.8	–	5th	9

Fastest Lap and Record: 1m 27.445s – 112.812mph (181.554kmh) on lap 45

CAR	CHASSIS	DRIVER	PRACTICE	SESSION	GRID	RACE	LAPS	%	REASON	POSITION	POINTS
97 T	4	(Spare)									

US GP, Detroit – 23rd June – 63 L, 157.500 miles (253.471km) (337)

CAR	CHASSIS	DRIVER	PRACTICE	SESSION	GRID	RACE	LAPS	%	REASON	POSITION	POINTS
97 T	3	De Angelis	1m 44.769s	1	8th	5th	63	100.0	–	2nd	24
97 T	2	Senna	1m 42.051s	1	1st P	R	51	80.9	Accident	7th	9

Fastest Lap and Record: 1m 45.612s – 85.2175mph (137.144kmh) on lap 51

CAR	CHASSIS	DRIVER	PRACTICE	SESSION	GRID	RACE	LAPS	%	REASON	POSITION	POINTS
97 T	4	(Spare)									

FRENCH GP, Ricard – 7th July – 53 L, 191.337 miles (307.928km) (338)

CAR	CHASSIS	DRIVER	PRACTICE	SESSION	GRID	RACE	LAPS	%	REASON	POSITION	POINTS
97 T	3	De Angelis	1m 34.022s	1	7th	5th	53	100.0	–	2nd=	26
97 T	4	Senna	1m 32.835s	1	2nd	R	26	49.0	Accident	8th	9
97 T	2	(Spare)									

BRITISH GP, Silverstone – 21st July – 65 L, 190.580 miles (306.708km) (339)

CAR	CHASSIS	DRIVER	PRACTICE	SESSION	GRID	RACE	LAPS	%	REASON	POSITION	POINTS
97 T	4	Senna	1m 06.324s	1	4th	10th NR	60	92.3	Fuel	8th	9
97 T	3	De Angelis	1m 07.581s	1	8th	NC	37	56.9	–	3rd	26
97 T	2	(Spare)									

GERMAN GP, Nurburgring – 4th August – 67 L, 189.091 miles (304.314km) (340)

CAR	CHASSIS	DRIVER	PRACTICE	SESSION	GRID	RACE	LAPS	%	REASON	POSITION	POINTS
97 T	3	De Angelis	1m 19.120s	1	7th	R	40	59.7	Engine	3rd	26
97 T	4	Senna	1m 18.729s	1	5th	R	27	40.2	CV-joint	9th=	9
97 T	2	(Spare)									

AUSTRIAN GP, Österreichring – 18th August – 52 L, 191.993 miles (308.984km) (341)

CAR	CHASSIS	DRIVER	PRACTICE	SESSION	GRID	RACE	LAPS	%	REASON	POSITION	POINTS
97 T	4	Senna	1m 28.123s	1	14th	2nd	52	100.0	–	6th	15
97 T	2	De Angelis	1m 26.799s	1	7th	5th	52	100.0	–	3rd	28
97 T	3	(Spare)									

DUTCH GP, Zandvoort – 25th August – 70 L, 184.944 miles (297.640km) (342)

CAR	CHASSIS	DRIVER	PRACTICE	SESSION	GRID	RACE	LAPS	%	REASON	POSITION	POINTS
97 T	4	Senna	1m 11.837s	1	4th	3rd	70	100.0	–	4th=	19
97 T	3	De Angelis	1m 13.078s	1	11th	5th	69	98.5	–	3rd	30
97 T	2	(Spare)									

ITALIAN GP, Monza – 8th September – 51 L, 183.801 miles (295.800km) (343)

CAR	CHASSIS	DRIVER	PRACTICE	SESSION	GRID	RACE	LAPS	%	REASON	POSITION	POINTS
97 T	4	Senna	1m 25.084s	2	1st P	3rd	51	100.0	–	4th	23
97 T	3	De Angelis	1m 26.044s	2	6th	6th	50	98.0	–	3rd-	31
97 T	2	(Spare)									

BELGIAN GP, Spa – 15th September – 43 L, 185.669 miles (298.807km) (344)											
97 T	4	Senna	1m 55.403s	2	2nd	1st W	43	100.0	–	3rd	32
97 T	3	De Angelis	1m 57.322s	2	9th	R	19	44.1	–	4th	31
97 T	2	(Spare)									
EUROPEAN GP, Brands Hatch – 6th October – 75 L, 196.050 miles (315.511km) (345)											
97 T	4	Senna	1m 07.169s	2	1st P	2nd	75	100.0	–	3rd	38
97 T	3	De Angelis	1m 10.014s	2	9th	5th	74	98.6	–	4th	33
97 T	2	(Spare)									
S AFRICAN GP, Kyalami – 19th October – 75 L, 191.247 miles (307.783km) (346)											
97 T	3	De Angelis	1m 04.129s	2	6th	R	52	69.3	Engine	4th	33
97 T	4	Senna	1m 02.825s	2	4th	R	8	10.6	Engine	3rd	38
97 T	2	(Spare)									
AUSTRALIAN GP, Adelaide – 3rd November – 82 L, 192.498 miles (309.796km) (347)											
97 T	4	Senna	1m 19.843s	2	1st P	R	62	75.6	Engine	4th	38
97 T	3	De Angelis	1m 23.077s	2	10th	DSQ	(17)	(20.7)	–	5th	33
97 T	2	(Spare)									

Key:
DSQ = Disqualified
NR = Not Running
NC = Not Classified
R = Retired
L = Laps
P = Pole
W = Win

with the Briton emerging just ahead of Senna after his tyre change, but he was easily disposed of on the downhill run to Eau Rouge. De Angelis's engine failed, making Senna nervous about his Renault, but luckily it held.

Derek Warwick spent a day testing for Lotus at Brands Hatch to set the 97Ts up successfully for the forthcoming European GP. In official practice Senna established Brands as a 140mph (225kph) circuit and he described his car as 'fantastic' after crushing Piquet's challenge. De Angelis tried a four-piece biplane rear wing but crashed heavily at Westfield, straining his neck. Senna fought off Mansell at the first corner of the race and led for eight laps before Rosberg and Piquet attacked him at Surtees. The Finn suffered a puncture and pitted, only to emerge a lap later in front of Senna effectively to block him. This permitted Rosberg's Williams team-mate, Mansell, to pass (allegedly under a yellow flag) and to score his first win, as second-placed Senna admitted to being powerless to challenge him. De Angelis was fifth behind Prost, whose fourth position was enough to secure him the World Championship.

At Kyalami the Lotus-Renaults played second fiddle to the Williams-Hondas. Lack of boost at altitude meant that Senna was 10mph (16kph) slower than Piquet on the straight, but he was still fourth. De Angelis was sixth in a car that proved very difficult to balance. In the South African GP Surer's Brabham briefly seized third, but at Sunset Senna forced past him, only for De

Angelis to take third from his team-mate as they crossed the line. Both 97T's engines failed, Senna's on lap 9 and De Angelis's on lap 53. Earlier De Angelis had been forced well off line at Crowthorne by Prost.

Adelaide hosted the inaugural World Championship Australian GP, where Senna gained pole while De Angelis could only manage tenth before being disqualified in the race. Having had troubles on the parade lap he drove through the field to take up his original starting position before the green light. This contravened the rules and after only seventeen laps he was called in by the officials. Using carbon brakes Senna had an untypically erratic race. He pushed Mansell across a kerb to take second place behind Rosberg on the first lap and then bounced off kerbs himself until lap 42, when he damaged his aerofoil on the back of the Williams. Without downforce it eventually took a dramatic grassy slide to convince him that he should stop for repairs. He reappeared and took the lead again on lap 58, only for his engine to blow. Following a pitstop, and a further slow lap, his wild day ended.

Following this result, Lotus finished the season in equal third place in the World Championship, but dropped to fourth behind Williams because they had won fewer races. Senna had led more laps than any other driver, in a season during which Lotus seemed unable to run two drivers competitively and simultaneously.

WORLD CHAMPIONSHIP RESULTS 1985

Position	Driver	Points
1	Alain Prost	73
2	Michele Alboreto	53
3	Keke Rosberg	40
4	**Ayrton Senna**	**38**
5	**Elio de Angelis**	**33**

CONSTRUCTORS' CUP 1985

Position	Constructor	Points
1	McLaren	90
2	Ferrari	82
3	Williams	71
4	**Lotus-Renault**	**71**

1986

For the new season, former works Renault driver Derek Warwick was widely expected to become Senna's partner, possessing as he did great experience of the French engines. Senna, though, saw things differently and promptly exercised his contractual veto, unconvinced that Lotus could run two no. 1 drivers simultaneously. He threatened to go to Brabham if Warwick was hired, but the fact that Senna's view prevailed upset many British enthusiasts. Mauricio Gugelmin had been another suggestion but Johnny Dumfries was eventually hired, although he was to be treated hostilely by the press, being perceived as a Warwick-replacement. To his great credit, he coped with the difficult situation in a very diplomatic way.

Lotus 98T

For 1986 Ducarouge emulated Ferrari, McLaren and Williams by producing a moulded Kevlar carbon-composite tub, filled with aluminium foil, for the first time. Held together with solid aluminium bulkheads, the tub was much lower than its predecessor, thanks to the reduction in size of the fuel load (42 gallons/195 litres) and cell, but the 98T was to suffer from fuel consumption problems. The record eight pole positions were to be achieved through Ducarouge's qualifying modifications, which produced high download whilst also adjusting the attitude of the car to hug the track more closely than normal. The car boasted very similar front suspension to the 97T, although the rear suspension was completely altered, now boasting a top triangular wishbone. Renault had closed down their own F1 team but now supplied their 1986 EF15bis engines to Lotus directly from their Viry-Chatillon headquarters. Bernard Dudot had created a DP (Distribution Pneumatique) version, which allowed the lightweight engine to rev to 12,500rpm.

The Lotus 98T possessed a carbon-composite tub and was much lower than the 97T. Fuel consumption was a recurrent problem throughout 1986 and its suspension, which FISA checked out here at Imola, proved controversial but effective.

Previous sponsorship by Olympus was replaced by new backing from DeLonghi, Micromax and Reporter.

Senna had a dashboard-mounted fuel-level read-out for the first time in Jacarepagua qualifying. He celebrated his twenty-sixth birthday jousting with Piquet's Williams, which was fastest until he spun out. With only one minute of the final session remaining, Senna put in a stunning lap, even dropping a wheel on to the grass at top speed, to snatch pole, whilst observing that his fuel consumption was worryingly high. Dumfries had a flash fire and then sat idly – not being allowed to touch Senna's spare car – only to suffer turbo failure before qualifying eleventh.

At the start Senna shot ahead, but Mansell's Williams tried to out-brake him at the end of the back straight only to lift off and crash out. Piquet then attacked Senna, who thought he had a puncture, on lap 3 and succeeded where his team-mate had misjudged. On lap 19 Prost overtook Senna too for second and the Brazilian then stopped for tyres before recovering second place on lap 29, which is where he stayed although at the finish his fuel tanks were dry. Piquet still had some fuel in hand, making Lotus realize the handicap that was revealing itself. Although Dumfries was ninth he did record the fourth fastest race lap being very unlucky indeed not to score points on his Lotus début. At mid-race a misunderstanding in the pit saw a misfiring Dumfries arrive and be mistakenly fitted with Senna's tyres; he was waved out again whilst the Brazilian pitted before being allowed to return to have his Renault engine rectified!

Pre-GP testing at Jerez saw Dumfries bounce across the kerbs and damage the underneath of his car. Senna was to dominate at the new Spanish circuit although the final margin would be unbelievably small. He took Lotus's 100th pole position, to the disbelief of the Williams and McLaren teams, thanks to the 98T's perfect handling – some suggested too perfect – around the new bumpy track in a spray of titanium sparks.

He carefully led the first thirty-nine laps of the race from firstly Piquet's and then Mansell's Williams, only for the latter to nip through as Brundle was being lapped. Mansell looked set to win but suddenly slowed with a puncture and pitted, so that on lap 62 Senna regained the lead. Mansell returned to chase after Senna relentlessly, though with eight laps to go he had the impossible disadvantage of being 19 seconds behind with Prost in between. On the final run to the flag a physically shattered Senna, who had agonized over his fuel consumption, won by a mere 0.014 seconds, which was the closest margin since Monza back in 1971! Dumfries, who thought he had overcome practice gearbox troubles, retired from a good fifth place with a recurrence of the same. He had run the six-speed version – Senna preferred the more reliable five-speed – and would fall foul of its fragility on a number of occasions as the year progressed.

After the Spanish GP Peter Warr discussed with Honda the possibility of using their engines, as Senna set off for Willi Dungl's Austrian clinic, so battered was he after the strains of the Jerez track.

Lotus only completed nineteen laps of racing in the

In one of the closest finishes ever in Grand Prix racing, Senna just reached the Jerez finish line first. Here, early in the race, he leads Piquet's Williams but it was to be Mansell who would push Senna to the limit.

On the podium the Briton, who had missed out by a mere 0.014 of a second, still cannot believe that Senna got there before him. On the warm-down lap Mansell was sure that he had won and Williams had to break it to him gently that he hadn't.

San Marino GP but Senna controversially took pole. The hydraulic suspension qualifying set-up created more downforce than that available to the opposition, with the car so close to the track that it produced a huge spray of sparks; it was subsequently inspected by FISA and pronounced completely legal. Dumfries was way down the grid because of an engine change that thoroughly messed up his qualifying. In the race itself a pair of incorrectly machined wheel bearings failed, eliminating both drivers, which was particularly galling for Senna who was fourth at the time. Prost took an untroubled win.

Dumfries failed to qualify at Monaco thanks to an early accident at Massenet; after that, six-speed gearbox troubles stopped him from whittling his times down. Senna, on the other hand, was frustrated at not capturing pole, but was third. Making use of a double rear-wing set-up, he finished third in a processional race, during which he passed Prost to lead for seven laps only to be retaken by both the Frenchman and Rosberg before the end.

During testing at Paul Ricard on 14 May, Elio de Angelis fatally crashed his Brabham BT55; the whole racing world was stunned and saddened.

Senna was fourth fastest at Spa as a rear suspension change altered the 98T's balance and his gears kept jumping out. Dumfries qualified thirteenth. At the start a first-corner accident was triggered by Senna's attempt to overtake Berger. As mayhem ensued, Senna chased Piquet away and Dumfries swept between the spinning cars to be fifth at the end of the first lap! Sadly, after seven laps he spun at Stavelot holing a radiator and thus causing his own retirement. Piquet's electrics failed on lap 16, leaving Mansell and Senna once again jousting. Tyre stops were to be the deciding factor with Mansell's taking just 7.9 seconds; Lotus were unable to reply. As Senna accelerated out of the pits Mansell passed him to win by turning up the boost of his fuel-efficient Honda whenever Senna's guzzler threatened. An emotional Mansell dedicated his victory to Elio de Angelis.

In Montreal in heavy rain, Senna set the bench-mark (1 minute 24.188 seconds) for the others, particularly Mansell, to tilt at once the track dried. Mansell just snatched pole and an unusually untidy Senna failed, even with the qualifying suspension, to overtake the Briton. A lack of parts for the better rear suspension arrangement meant that Dumfries was only sixteenth. As Mansell stretched away into an unassailable lead of the Canadian GP, Senna held up the pack from his insecure second place. Prost forced his way past on lap 4 in the fast curves after the pits and rudely chopped the Brazilian out; Senna went sideways on to the grass in a hurried avoidance as he dropped to sixth to fight with Arnoux. In a classic misunderstanding, Dumfries emerged from the pits to be struck from behind by Johansson's Ferrari, putting both cars out; Alboreto very nearly piled into the wreckage too. Stopping for tyres on lap 34, Senna managed to take fifth at the flag, but was unhappy with his race set-up.

Given Senna's open dislike of the Detroit street circuit, the final result of the US GP was quite a surprise. This year he avoided the walls and safely took pole, having beaten off Mansell and, exuding confidence, he preferred watching Brazil play football on the television to attending the press conference! Dumfries hit the walls, however, only managing fourteenth. Senna led at the start but came under pressure from Mansell, who in turn was fending off Arnoux. At the end of lap 2, Senna missed a gear and Mansell sliced through, only for his brakes to start going off, allowing Senna to get back past again on lap 8. Four laps later Senna's car started to slide because of a puncture, and his pitstop dropped him down to eighth; but he fought back. His first stop had been for 11.67 seconds but his next was only 8.28 seconds, so that on returning to the track on lap 40 he was in the lead, which was where he would finish. Dumfries boosted his confidence with a seventh-place finish.

Meanwhile the discussions with Honda continued,

Despite his intense dislike for the circuit, Senna took his 98T to his second 1986 victory at Detroit. Having started from pole he fought with Mansell and stopped to replace a puncture before fighting back from eighth place.

and after Detroit Warr flew to Japan to confirm and sign the contract for their engine supply for 1987.

Senna crashed out of the French GP despite the new Renault 15C engine, which boasted improved consumption thanks in part to a new cylinder head. On the shortened track Senna again took pole, but he lost out at the start to Mansell and, after only three laps, he spun

off, losing a front wheel against the barriers. From twelfth on the grid, a confident Dumfries made an excellent start -- he was sixth at the end of the first lap -- but was struck from the rear by Rothengatter on lap 35 and his engine failed twenty laps later.

Poor handling and a misfire at Brands Hatch stopped Senna from gaining the front row as Dumfries scraped

Senna was firmly on pole at Paul Ricard but he was beaten away at the start by Mansell's second-fastest Williams. After a mere three laps he spun off into the barriers and lost a wheel.

into the top ten on a circuit he knew well. The two Williams cars topped the charts and dominated the restarted race, with Mansell eventually winning. Senna had chased them both, limited by his fuel consumption, and briefly held third, only to retire shortly afterwards when fourth gear deserted him. For thirty-nine laps Dumfries fought with Streiff eventually to take seventh.

Senna endured another bad practice at Hockenheim as engine changes and Berg's Ostkurve accident delayed him. He eventually took third place on his one flying lap just after the chequered flag had come out! Dumfries was twelfth on his first visit to the circuit. Senna led the first lap until his turbo boost failed, allowing Rosberg's McLaren and Piquet's Williams through. Senna played the fuel-consumption game well, and a patient second place to Piquet was his reward. Dumfries had stopped for new tyres on lap 17 when in seventh place, but the mechanics spotted a holed radiator, thus ending his race on the spot.

At Hockenheim both the existing Honda-Williams Team and the hopeful McLaren learned officially from Yoshitoshi Sakuri, Honda's director of research and development, that Lotus were to have the Japanese engines for two years starting in 1987.

Formula One visited Hungary for the first time in 1986 and Senna made history by taking the inaugural pole at the Hungaroring, although he spun more than once; Dumfries excelled himself to take eighth. The huge crowd of 200,000 saw Senna lead the first eleven laps before Piquet nipped past as the Renault EF15B couldn't match the power of the Honda. Even so, on lap 36 Senna regained the lead as Piquet pitted for tyres. His 8-second advantage over Piquet was, though, soon closed and on lap 55 Senna forced his fellow Brazilian into a slide at the first corner, when he wouldn't give way. Two laps later Piquet did eventually get past, establishing what would be the finishing order, with Dumfries a superb fifth.

From Hungary the Team travelled to Austria for a weekend they would rather forget. Williams alleged that the 98T's undertrays were flexing too much, and rather than face a FISA investigation, these were modified along with the car's skid plates. Senna and Dumfries shared the same car when the Brazilian's engine failed; Dumfries was pleasantly surprised to be only half a second slower in identical equipment, but he sideswiped the Rindtkurve barriers later as well as going grass-cutting. Senna was only eighth on the grid, and in the Austrian GP itself, Dumfries damaged his car's nose on the first lap on the back of a Ferrari; after stopping for a replacement, he trailed at the rear only to suffer a misfire and a jammed plug, which caused his retirement. Senna too retired with a misfire problem on lap

At Hockenheim, Senna led initially only for his turbo to let him down; eventually he took second place behind Piquet (6), having driven a tactical race, looking very closely at his fuel consumption gauge.

12, having pitted several times as Prost took another McLaren victory.

The Team commenced extensive testing to find the root cause of the mysterious misfire and eventually incompatible electrical components were blamed.

At Monza the transmissions again became troublesome. Fastest in first qualifying, Senna was fifth at the end of practice, when he couldn't recover after a spectacular engine blow-up. Dumfries bounced across a sand-trap to a lowly seventeenth, although he lasted nineteen laps of the race before his gearbox failed. Senna's clutch expired as Piquet went on to win for Williams.

In Estoril practice, a rejuvenated Senna with new turbochargers trounced the opposition, taking pole by 0.8 seconds! Dumfries again had gear problems and took to the gravel avoiding a Ferrari, to take fifteenth place. For all but two laps an oversteering Senna ran in second place in the race, whilst calculatingly using backmarkers to fend off Piquet and to tail eventual winner Mansell. On lap 31 he stopped for tyres without losing ground, and with one lap to go, his fuel

TEAM LOTUS RESULTS 1986

Drivers:
Ayrton Senna: Brazilian; Johnny Dumfries: British
Car:
Lotus 98 T Engine: Renault EF15B, EF15C

CAR	CHASSIS	DRIVER	PRACTICE	SESSION	GRID	RACE	LAPS	%	REASON	CHAMPIONSHIP POSITION	POINTS

BRAZILIAN GP, Jacarepagua – 23rd March – 61 L, 190.692 miles (306.889km) (348)

CAR	CHASSIS	DRIVER	PRACTICE	SESSION	GRID	RACE	LAPS	%	REASON	POSITION	POINTS
98 T	3	Senna	1m 25.501s	2	1st P	2nd	61	100.0	–	2nd	6
98 T	2	Dumfries	1m 25.503s	2	11th	9th	58	95.08	–	–	–
98 T	1	(Spare)									

SPANISH GP, Jerez – 13th April – 72 L, 188.708 miles (303.696km) (349)

CAR	CHASSIS	DRIVER	PRACTICE	SESSION	GRID	RACE	LAPS	%	REASON	POSITION	POINTS
98 T	3	Senna	1m 21.605s	1	1st P	1st W	72	100.0	–	1st	15
98 T	2	Dumfries	1m 25.107s	2	10th	R	52	72.2	Gearbox	–	–
98 T	1	(Spare)									

SAN MARINO GP, Imola – 27th April – 60 L, 187.90 miles (302.40km) (350)

CAR	CHASSIS	DRIVER	PRACTICE	SESSION	GRID	RACE	LAPS	%	REASON	POSITION	POINTS
98 T	3	Senna	1m 25.050s	1	1st P	R	11	18.3	Wheel	2nd	19
98 T	2	Dumfries	1m 29.244s	1	17th	R	8	13.3	Wheel	–	–
98 T	1	Spare									

MONACO GP, Monte Carlo – 11th May – 78 L, 161.298 miles (259.584km) (351)

CAR	CHASSIS	DRIVER	PRACTICE	SESSION	GRID	RACE	LAPS	%	REASON	POSITION	POINTS
98 T	3	Senna	1m 23.175s	2	3rd	3rd	78	100.0	–	1st=	15
98 T	2	Dumfries	1m 27.826s	2	DNQ	–	–	–	–	–	–
98 T	1	Senna									

BELGIAN GP, Spa – 25th May – 43 L, 185.429 miles (298.420km) (352)

CAR	CHASSIS	DRIVER	PRACTICE	SESSION	GRID	RACE	LAPS	%	REASON	POSITION	POINTS
98 T	3	Senna	1m 54.576s	2	4th	2nd	43	100.0	–	1st	25
98 T	2	Dumfries	1m 57.462s	2	13th	R	7	16.2	Accident	–	–
98 T	1	(Spare)									

CANADIAN GP, Montreal – 15th June – 69 L, 189.07 miles (304.29km) (353)

CAR	CHASSIS	DRIVER	PRACTICE	SESSION	GRID	RACE	LAPS	%	REASON	POSITION	POINTS
98 T	3	Senna	1m 24.188s	2	2nd	5th	68	98.5	–	2nd=	27
98 T	1	Dumfries	1m 28.521s	2	16th	R	28	40.5	Accident	–	–
98 T	2	(Spare)									

US GP, Detroit – 22nd June – 63 L, 157.500 miles (253.471km) (354)

CAR	CHASSIS	DRIVER	PRACTICE	SESSION	GRID	RACE	LAPS	%	REASON	POSITION	POINTS
98 T	3	Senna	1m 38.301s	2	1st P	1st W	63	100.0	–	1st	36
98 T	2	Dumfries	1m 42.511s	2	14th	7th	61	96.8	–	–	–
98 T	1	(Spare)									

FRENCH GP, Ricard – 6th July – 80 L, 189.543 miles (305.04km) (355)

CAR	CHASSIS	DRIVER	PRACTICE	SESSION	GRID	RACE	LAPS	%	REASON	POSITION	POINTS
98 T	2	Dumfries	1m 08.544s	2	12th	R	56	70.0	Engine	–	–
98 T	3	Senna	1m 06.526s	1	1st P	R	3	3.7	Accident	3rd	36
98 T	1	(Spare)									

BRITISH GP, Brands Hatch – 13th July – 75 L, 196.050 miles (315.511km) (356)

CAR	CHASSIS	DRIVER	PRACTICE	SESSION	GRID	RACE	LAPS	%	REASON	POSITION	POINTS
98 T	2	Dumfries	1m 10.304s	1	10th	7th	72	96.0	–	–	–
98 T	1	Senna	1m 07.524s	2	3rd	R	27	36.0	Gearbox	3rd	36
98 T	3	(Spare)									

GERMAN GP, Hockenheim – 27th July – 44 L, 185.83 miles (299.068km) (357)

CAR	CHASSIS	DRIVER	PRACTICE	SESSION	GRID	RACE	LAPS	%	REASON	POSITION	POINTS
98 T	4	Senna	1m 42.329s	2	3rd	2nd	44	100.0	–	3rd	42
98 T	2	Dumfries	1m 44.768s	2	12th	R	17	38.6	Radiator	–	–
98 T	1	(Spare)									

HUNGARIAN GP, Hungaroring – 10th August – 76 L, 189.557 miles (305.064km) (358)

CAR	CHASSIS	DRIVER	PRACTICE	SESSION	GRID	RACE	LAPS	%	REASON	POSITION	POINTS
98 T	4	Senna	1m 29.450s	2	1st P	2nd	76	100.0	–	2nd	48
98 T	2	Dumfries	1m 31.886s	2	8th	5th	74	97.3	–	12th=	2
98 T	1	(Spare)									

AUSTRIAN GP, Österreichring – 17th August – 52 L, 191.933 miles (308.984km) (359)

CAR	CHASSIS	DRIVER	PRACTICE	SESSION	GRID	RACE	LAPS	%	REASON	POSITION	POINTS
98 T	4	Senna	1m 25.249s	2	8th	R	13	25.0	Engine	3rd	48
98 T	2	Dumfries	1m 27.212s	1	15th	R	9	17.3	Engine	13th=	2
98 T	1	(Spare)									

ITALIAN GP, Monza – 7th September – 51 L, 183.801 miles (295.800km) (360)

CAR	CHASSIS	DRIVER	PRACTICE	SESSION	GRID	RACE	LAPS	%	REASON	POSITION	POINTS
98 T	2	Dumfries	1m 28.024s	2	17th	R	19	37.2	Gearbox	13th=	2
98 T	4	Senna	1m 24.916s	2	5th	R	0	0.0	Gearbox	4th	48
98 T	1	(Spare)									

PORTUGUESE GP, Estoril – 21st October – 70 L, 189.207 miles (304.50km) (361)

98 T	4	Senna	1m 16.673s	2	1st P	4th	69	98.5	–	4th	51
98 T	2	Dumfries	1m 21.594s	2	15th	9th	68	97.1	–	13th=	2
98 T	1	(Spare)									

MEXICAN GP, Mexico – 12th October – 68 L, 186.801 miles (300.628km) (362)

98 T	4	Senna	1m 16.990s	2	1st P	3rd	68	100.0	–	4th	55
98 T	2	Dumfries	1m 20.479s	1	17th	R	53	77.9	Electrics	13th=	2
98 T	1	(Spare)									

AUSTRALIAN GP, Adelaide – 26th October – 82 L, 192.498 miles (309.796km) (363)

98 T	2	Dumfries	1m 22.664s	2	14th	6th	60	97.5	–	13th=	3
98 T	4	Senna	1m 18.906s	2	3rd	R	43	52.4	Engine	4th	55
98 T	1	(Spare)									

Key:
DNQ = Did Not Qualify
R = Retired
L = Laps
P = Pole
W = Win

monitor suggested that second place was guaranteed. At that moment he ground to a halt with a dry tank, being two litres short! He was extremely disappointed, having undoubtedly driven his best race to date. Dumfries came in an untroubled ninth.

Following a break of sixteen years, the Mexican GP returned to the calendar with Senna annexing pole; on his last lap he hit a bump in the final corner. For forty-five race laps Senna held a top two position with Piquet, but Prost eventually forced past, dropping the Lotus driver to an eventual third. Senna's demise had been brought about by a second stop to replace blistered tyres; luckily Johansson's threatening Ferrari blew up. Dumfries climbed as high as ninth, but retired with electrical failure on lap 53. During the race Senna set the fastest-ever Lotus record, with an official speed of 215.228mph (346.3kph)!

A blown tyre denied Mansell his Championship aspirations in Adelaide whilst Senna remonstrated with himself for hitting a wall in practice. Yellow flags curtailed his best lap and he was third to Dumfries's fourteenth. Quickest in the warm-up, he fought with Piquet and Rosberg as if the race were a ten-lap sprint, only for his engine to fail at half-distance. Dumfries scored another personal best with a single point on the eve of his Honda-necessitated departure from the Team. The forthcoming Honda engines were to be accompanied by Satoru Nakajima for 1987: Dumfries had earned great respect but he was not Japanese.

Finally, the old Renault-powered 98T would be fondly remembered as the last Lotus to carry the distinctive John Player Special livery.

WORLD CHAMPIONSHIP RESULTS 1986

Position	Driver	Points
1	Alain Prost	72
2	Nigel Mansell	70
3	Nelson Piquet	69
4	**Ayrton Senna**	**55**
5	Stefan Johansson	23
6	Keke Rosberg	22
7	Gerhard Berger	17
8=	Jacques Laffite	14
	Rene Arnoux	14
	Michele Alboreto	14
11	Martin Brundle	8
12	Alan Jones	4
13=	**Johnny Dumfries**	**3**

CONSTRUCTORS' CUP 1986

Position	Constructor	Points
1	Williams	141
2	McLaren	96
3	**Lotus-Renault**	**58**

CHAPTER 9

Japanese Technology –
Japanese Driver

Camel's yellow colour scheme, Honda engines and a new driver in Satoru Nakajima joined Lotus for the 1987 season. Nakajima's inclusion was Honda's justification for their support of a second GP team but there was widespread concern about his overall lack of experience. Senna in turn made an ultimatum that if he didn't win the Championship in 1987 he would leave Lotus.

Lotus 99T

The 99T possessed a single carbon composite sheet tub, containing a protected aluminium-foil honeycomb, with both suspension and engine attached to solid aluminium bulkheads. The 80-degree Honda engines were not nearly as smooth as their 90-degree Renault predecessors and took some learning, although previous Honda-user Nakajima knew the characteristics of the narrower V design, which produced about 900bhp. The vibrations meant that many of the rear ancillaries had to be strengthened before they were shaken apart! A special six-speed Lotus gearbox harnessed the wide rev range, but the 99T's basic aerodynamics needed much more power and fuel to push it along the straights than the rival Williams FW11B.

One 99T was sent to Japan for F3000 driver Kazuyoshi Hoshino to test for Honda whilst engineers Steve Hallam and Tim Densham oversaw the race cars of Senna and Nakajima respectively.

Despite its extra weight and slight power penalty, hydraulically actuated 'active' suspension featured on the 99T. The system fed off an exhaust camshaft-powered hydraulic pump, which fed fluid to electronically (computer/gyro) controlled pressure-regulating valves in each suspension. It responded to chassis movement and motion as well as the steering, using both air-speed and suspension sensors. The ride-height and suspension movement were controlled by the system developed by Peter Wright and Dave Williams along with Cranfield and the special Active Technology Engineering Group of Lotus Research and Development. So competent was Senna, though, that it was sometimes difficult to decide whether performance improvements were down to him or the suspension!

In Rio's pre-season testing Senna was alarmed by his

Camel Team Lotus now boasted Honda engines in the 99T, and as a result, Nakajima (following Senna) joined the driver line-up for 1987. Vibrations were an initial problem but here at Monaco, Senna took the first-ever race win for an 'active'-suspension F1 car.

Honda engine's vibration but Nakajima reassured him! Senna enthused about the active suspension so more time was devoted to it, with all three cars being so equipped. Acclimatizing to the suspension required time and Senna suffered a monumental qualifying spin in Brazil as a result. Thanks to programming difficulties, the 99T handled badly over bumps and in Jacarepagua's long radius corners. Senna overtook Piquet's Williams on lap 7 of the race and led for five laps before his car's handling required a pitstop. He was second again by lap 22 only to retire thirty-seven laps later when an oil tank vibrated so much that air entered the lubricant, causing the engine to threaten seizure. Prost's McLaren was then left unchallenged. Nakajima showed promise by finishing seventh despite a failed water-filled helmet-lining that should have helped his personal cooling.

Following Piquet's massive Imola practice accident, Senna took a 'cautious' pole as suspicion centred on a tyre failure. In the race itself Senna couldn't catch Mansell and trailed home 27.5 seconds behind. Prost, Alboreto and Patrese all got past Senna but he regained some distance and held on to second place on lap 50 by carefully judging his fuel consumption. Nakajima again went well to finish sixth after his active suspension collapsed in the warm-up because of battery failure; he raced Senna's spare, having started from the pits.

At Spa, over-masked brake cooling ducts prevented Senna from attacking the Williams cars in final qualifying, while another battery failure dropped Nakajima to fifteenth. Senna was second when the Belgian GP was stopped after Boutsen and Berger tangled, but he led the restarted first lap until Les Fagnes, where the closely following Mansell thought he had missed a gear. Senna denied this but they touched and spun off the track in unison. Senna was stranded – his car was stuck in the sand trap – but a furious Mansell rejoined only to retire and make his way to the Lotus pit. There an altercation took place, during which neither driver apologized! It was left to the Lotus mechanics to cool things down. Nakajima, thanks to a failing gearbox during the last ten laps, just failed to wrest fourth place as Prost won.

In Lotus's most important test of the season at Donington, revised underbodies and air boxes were conceived for the two slow circuits coming up.

Memories of their Spa feud worried everyone at Monaco when Mansell took pole and Senna – having modified his suspension's computer program – shared the front row. At the start Mansell got the jump on Senna and avoided the possible Ste Devote contretemps only to retire after thirty dominant laps, leaving Senna, who had stopped for tyres on lap 42, to take an 'active' car's first win. The system had worked perfectly, giving Senna a much smoother ride than the previous year. Nakajima had recovered from an airborne moment at the first corner and after a precautionary stop he climbed up to a tenth-place finish.

Detroit suited the active suspension too and the Donington aerodynamics and high downforce wings were deployed as well. Mansell took pole with Senna again in second place, rekindling the first corner worries. In a repeat of Monaco, Mansell started best but

Detroit in 1987 was at the time of writing the last Lotus GP win. Senna took his 99T, complete with special aerodynamics, past Mansell to make the most of his active suspension advantage for Lotus's 79th Grand Prix victory.

lost the lead on lap 33 when a wheel nut jammed during a tyre change. Senna went by to win, although he had brake pedal troubles, deciding not to stop for tyres and putting in arguably the best individual drive of the entire season. As graphically broadcast by his on-board TV camera Nakajima assaulted two cars and the wall on the first lap before retiring!

Silverstone testing yielded some much-needed extra speed in time for the ultra-fast Paul Ricard race. There, in practice, Senna suffered from diabolical handling, thanks to incorrect tyre pressures. He had also jumped a kerb and suffered an unusual engine failure, so he was lucky indeed to be third; Nakajima was sixteenth. In the race an aggravated Senna ran for all but four laps in fourth place, thoroughly disliking his car's balance and finding he could not keep up with the Williams car. Mansell, Piquet and Prost led him home after the three-wheeled Nakajima had pitted with a puncture and stopped several more times before finishing an un-classified eleventh.

Senna damaged the front of his car on some debris in Silverstone practice and was lucky to be third fastest, with Nakajima twelfth. A new Williams-style rear wing was delivered late on Saturday evening. The crowd only had eyes for Mansell as he scored an epic British GP victory; Senna, meanwhile, worried about fuel consumption and drove economically to third, de-liberately letting the Williams twins lap him as he knew his fuel duration was marginal. Nakajima scored his best result of the season with a fine fourth.

Lotus tested at Hockenheim before the German GP, only for Senna to suffer a 200mph (320kph) puncture, which ripped his rear suspension off. Luckily this oc-curred on a straight. So worried were Lotus that they contacted Goodyear but no tyre design fault was found. Only a downpour in final Hockenheim qualify-ing kept Senna from capturing Mansell's pole; he had already crashed, though, when a gear jumped out, while later he unusually spun. Nakajima was four-teenth fastest. In the race the active suspension was unreliable and failed, giving the car hydraulic failure, but Senna's eventual placing was unaffected. Nakajima retired when an electrical sensor broke, affecting his car's attitude. Senna led the first lap in the spare – his race car had engine maladies – but two stops for tyres, one to replace a damaged front wing and another to investigate why the car had mysteriously gone light, meant that he was very lucky to finish third!

In Germany Senna had decided that both Williams and McLaren were better bets for the World Cham-pionship and he informed Lotus that he would exercise his release clause and leave. Shortly afterwards, in a counter move, Nelson Piquet was signed by Warr for 1988. Lotus had not only protected its position by retaining a top driver but had surprised Senna, who was left out in the cold until he subsequently signed for McLaren for 1988.

Before Hungary the 99T received new bodywork and a much-narrowed cockpit surround. Senna qualified a lowly sixth, complaining of lack of grip, whilst Nakajima was similarly afflicted in seventeenth. The Japanese driver's race was no consolation, as a drive-shaft broke on the first lap and he retired in the pits. Senna fought off Boutsen to take third place on lap 43, following the demise of the Ferraris. Mansell lost a wheel nut only six laps from the flag, handing Senna second place, where he finished even though his gear-box was jumping out and he was being badly bruised by a chassis fault. Piquet was Williams's lucky winner.

Lotus assumed that Silverstone's suspension settings would work at the Österreichring but they were caught out as Senna's car refused to handle. Rain, too, meant that Senna was back in seventh place and Naka-jima, who was unsettled by the high speeds, thirteenth. Both Lotuses avoided the multiple accident at the start and were able to take the restart, although Senna stalled and had to be pushed. He fought back all afternoon and by lap 25 he was third and locked into a battle with Alboreto, which terminated when he bent his nose wings. Now ninth, Senna benefited from the late re-tirements and finished fifth, eight places ahead of Nakajima. Mansell's Williams was the victor.

Imola testing produced a new rear underbody for Monza, where Honda announced that McLaren and Lotus would be their two 1988 teams, much to the consternation of Williams supporters. Senna decided to join McLaren, which some people uncharitably at-tributed to necessity rather than choice after Lotus had blocked any other moves by retaining Honda engines.

Having overcome brake troubles, Senna was fourth fastest as the Williams drivers headed the sheets. Naka-jima was down in fourteenth and in the race he spun off on lap 4 before climbing back to eleventh at the flag. Piquet's active Williams FW11B led for the first twenty-three laps, by which time Senna had caught up to second. Piquet then made a tyre stop, letting Senna into the lead. Against advice over the radio from Goodyear and Warr, Senna single-mindedly decided to go for the finish without a stop. All went to plan until, with six laps to go, he lost the lead whilst lapping Ghinzani at the Parabolica, spinning through the sand-trap; the active suspension saved him as he smoothly regained the track. He had lost valuable time, but still took fastest lap on the penultimate tour to finish a fighting second.

The Portuguese GP didn't go so well for Lotus as Prost scored his record twenty-eighth GP win. Senna had a new intercooler bypass, but could only manage fifth, having spun off twice and swiped a barrier before both his and Nakajima's fifteenth-placed 99T caught fire! In the race, having run third for the first ten laps, Senna was passed by Piquet and shortly afterwards he pitted for three laps as a malfunctioning throttle sensor was replaced. By then, there was only one car behind him as; he managed to climb back to seventh, taking third-fastest lap on lap 62. Nakajima finished one place behind.

At Jerez for the Spanish GP, Senna was fifth fastest behind the Williams and Ferraris. Senna's 99T had been a practice handful, whilst Nakajima was down in eighteenth on a track that was new to him. Senna took third at the start as the two Ferraris of Berger and Alboreto made a tactical error in not elbowing him out. Seemingly oblivious to outsiders, Senna fended a pack of cars off for sixty-two laps, stubbornly ignoring the need for a tyre stop. Berger, Alboreto, Prost, Boutsen and Piquet all failed to get past until lap 63, when Senna's tyres cried enough and he slid wide; his final position of fifth place was assured, however. Nakajima finished ninth.

FISA president Jean-Marie Balestre threatened to ban active suspension in Mexico but subsequently denied that he'd done so after a discussion with Ducarouge. During practice, Senna was right on the edge, but it was a mystery as to whether it was the Team, the car or the circuit that was causing him concern? In vainly trying to gain pole he had a number of spins, even though the active suspension seemed to cope well with the bumps. It was then that he took a 120mph (193kph) trip into the wall at the banked Peralta cor-

ner. Luckily he emerged unscathed but was considerably shaken up, only to later have a tussle with de Cesaris. Nakajima was all at sea, qualifying sixteenth; on lap two of the race he drove into the back of Warwick's Arrows in full view of his on-board TV audience, who saw his front-right wheel wrenched off! If that wasn't enough for Lotus, when Senna seemed assured of third place with nine laps to go, he got his braking wrong while coping with a dud clutch and spun off into retirement. This effectively ended his Championship aspirations, leaving Piquet and Mansell in with a chance.

Japan was unlucky for the Williams drivers as Mansell had a heavy practice accident and Piquet, who was now assured of the title, embarrassingly retired with a blown Honda engine. Nakajima put in an excellent performance on the Suzuka circuit he knew well, by qualifying eleventh and finishing sixth, to the glee of his 100,000 fellow countrymen. Senna was only seventh on the grid, having had his fire extinguisher go off, but he drove well in the race to second place behind Berger's Ferrari, and forcefully fought off Piquet in the process.

Intense heat was anticipated in Adelaide, so the 99Ts sported extra cooling piping for their front brakes. Senna qualified fourth, whilst the spinning Nakajima was ten places behind. From lap 42 Senna ran in second place to Berger's Ferrari, having overcome Alboreto, Prost and Piquet *en route*, although Prost complained of wheel banging. Senna finished second whilst Nakajima retired after only twenty-two laps, when his suspension collapsed as the hydraulic fluid drained out. Benetton

---

TEAM LOTUS RESULTS 1987

Drivers:
Ayrton Senna: Brazilian; Satoru Nakajima: Japanese
Car:
Lotus 99 T Engine: Honda RA166-E, RA167-G

CAR	CHASSIS	DRIVER	PRACTICE	SESSION	GRID	RACE	LAPS	%	REASON	CHAMPIONSHIP POSITION	POINTS
BRAZILIAN GP, Jacarepagua – 12th April – 61 L, 190.692 miles (306.891km) (364)											
99 T	1	Nakajima	1m 32.276s	2	12th	7th	59	96.7	–	–	–
99 T	4	Senna	1m 28.408s	2	3rd	R	50	81.9	Engine	–	–
99 T	3	(Spare)									
SAN MARINO GP, Imola – 3rd May – 59 L, 185.30 miles (297.36km) (365)											
99 T	4	Senna	1m 25.826s	2	1st P	2nd	59	100.0	–	4th=	6
99 T	3	Nakajima	1m 29.579s	1	12th SFP	6th	57	96.9	–	10th	1
99 T	1	Spare									
BELGIAN GP, Spa – 17th May – 43 L, 185.429 miles (298.420km) (366)											
99 T	1	Nakajima	1m 58.649s	2	15th	5th	42	97.6	–	8th=	3
99 T	4	Senna	1m 53.426s	2	3rd	R	0	0.0	Accident	4th=	6
99 T	3	(Spare)									

MONACO GP, Monte Carlo – 31st May – 78 L, 161.298 miles (259.584km) (367)

99 T	4	Senna	1m 23.711s	2	2nd	1st W	78	100.0	–	2nd	15
Fastest Lap: 1m 27.685s – 84.901mph (136.635kmh) on lap 72											
99 T	1	Nakajima	1m 28.890s	2	17th	10th	75	96.1	–	9th=	3
99 T	3	(Spare)									

US GP, Detroit – 21st June – 63 L, 157.500 miles (253.471km) (368)

99 T	4	Senna	1m 40.607s	2	2nd	1st W	63	100.0	–	1st	24
Fastest Lap and Record: 1m 40.464s – 89.584mph (144.171kmh) on lap 39											
99 T	1	Nakajima	1m 48.801s	2	24th	R	0	0.0	Accident	10th	3
99 T	5	(Spare)									

FRENCH GP, Ricard – 5th July – 80 L, 189.543 miles (305.04km) (369)

99 T	4	Senna	1m 07.024s	2	3rd	4th	79	98.7	–	1st	27
99 T	1	Nakajima	1m 10.652s	2	16th	NC	71	88.7	–	10th	3
99 T	5	(Spare)									

BRITISH GP, Silverstone – 12th July – 65 L, 192.985 miles (310.579km) (370)

99 T	4	Senna	1m 08.181s	2	3rd	3rd	64	98.4	–	1st	31
99 T	5	Nakajima	1m 10.619s	1	12th	4th	63	96.9	–	8th	6
99 T	3	(Spare)									

GERMAN GP, Hockenheim – 26th July – 44 L, 185.83 miles (299.068km) (371)

99 T	4	Senna	1m 42.873s	1	2nd	3rd	43	97.7	–	2nd	35
99 T	3	Nakajima	1m 46.760s	1	14th	R	9	20.4	Turbo	8th	6
99 T	5	(Spare)									

HUNGARIAN GP, Hungaroring – 9th August – 76 L, 189.557 miles (305.064km) (372)

99 T	4	Senna	1m 30.387s	2	6th	2nd	76	100.0	–	2nd	41
99 T	3	Nakajima	1m 34.297s	1	17th	R	1	1.3	D/shaft	8th	6
99 T	6	(Spare)									

AUSTRIAN GP, Österreichring – 16th August – 52 L, 191.933 miles (308.984km) (373)

99 T	6	Senna	1m 25.429s	1	7th	5th	50	96.1	–	2nd	43
99 T	3	Nakajima	1m 28.786s	1	13th	13th	49	94.2	–	10th	6
99 T	4	(Spare)									

ITALIAN GP, Monza – 6th September – 50 L, 180.197 miles (290.000km) (374)

99 T	4	Senna	1m 24.907s	2	4th	2nd	50	100.0	–	2nd	49
Fastest Lap and Record: 1m 26.796s – 149.479mph (240.564kmh) on lap 49											
99 T	3	Nakajima	1m 28.160s	2	14th	11th	47	94.0	–	10th	6
99 T	6	(Spare)									

PORTUGUESE GP, Estoril – 21st September – 70 L, 189.207 miles (304.50km) (375)

99 T	4	Senna	1m 18.354s	2	5th	7th	68	97.1	–	2nd	49
99 T	3	Nakajima	1m 26.946s	2	15th	8th	68	97.1	–	10th	6
99 T	6	(Spare)									

SPANISH GP, Jerez – 27th September – 72 L, 188.708 miles (303.696km) (376)

99 T	4	Senna	1m 24.320s	2	5th	5th	72	100.0	–	3rd	51
99 T	3	Nakajima	1m 28.367s	2	18th	9th	70	97.2	–	10th	6
99 T	6	(Spare)									

MEXICAN GP, Mexico – 18th October – 63 L, 173.065 miles (278.523km) (377)

99 T	6	Senna	1m 19.089s	2	7th	R	54	85.7	Accident	3rd	51
99 T	3	Nakajima	1m 22.214s	2	16th	R	1	1.5	Accident	11th=	6
99 T	4	(Spare)									

JAPANESE GP, Suzuka – 1st November – 51 L, 185.670 miles (298.809km) (378)

99 T	6	Senna	1m 42.723s	2	7th	2nd	51	100.0	–	3rd	57
99 T	3	Nakajima	1m 43.685s	2	11th	6th	51	100.0	–	11th	7
99 T	4	(Spare)									

AUSTRALIAN GP, Adelaide – 15th October – 82 L, 192.454 miles (309.796km) (379)

99 T	3	Nakajima	1m 20.891s	2	14th	R	22	26.8	Hydraulics	11th=	7
99 T	4	Senna	1m 18.488s	2	4th	(2nd) DSQ	(82)	(100.0)	Brakes	3rd	57
99 T	6	(Spare)									

Key:
SFP = Started from Pits
NC = Not Classified
P = Pole
W = Win
R = Retired
L = Laps

then successfully protested about the extra brake-cooling pipes on Senna's car and he was disqualified.

This was an unfortunate way in which to bid farewell to Senna who, in his three years with Lotus, had been widely respected and had performed miracles in 1987 with a car that was accepted as uncompetitive. Active suspension was put into retirement as Lotus Engineering, its originators, concentrated on road-car work. There was optimism for 1988, though, as not only had the reigning World Champion been signed, but Camel funding combined with the all-important Honda engines, gave the impression that nothing could stop progress being made.

WORLD CHAMPIONSHIP RESULTS 1987

Position	Driver	Points
1	Nelson Piquet	73
2	Nigel Mansell	61
3	**Ayrton Senna**	**57**
4	Alain Prost	46
5	Gerhard Berger	36
6	Stefan Johansson	30
7	Michele Alboreto	17
8	Thierry Boutsen	16
9	Teo Fabi	12
10	Eddie Cheever	8
11=	**Satoru Nakajima**	**7**
	Jonathan Palmer	7

CONSTRUCTORS' CUP 1987

Position	Constructor	Points
1	Williams	137
2	McLaren	76
3	**Lotus-Honda**	**64**

1988

Lotus 100T

Announced at Paul Ricard in February, the small and conventionally suspended 100T never provided the anticipated results and was to be the last Ducarouge-designed Lotus. The car was never competitive – rumours suggested that the design had been based upon incorrect wind tunnel information – and 1988 was to be a year best forgotten. During 1987 Lotus had developed an excellent working relationship with Honda, and the openness of Ketteringham Hall and its staff was perceived to be one of the reasons that the engine deal was retained for the last year in which turbos would be permitted. McLaren was the other team to possess the

powerful Honda engines and all season Lotus would be compared, unfavourably, with the Woking-based equipe. The deficiencies in performance could not be laid at the feet of Honda, who supplied identical units to both teams, but seemed rooted firmly in the problematic Lotus chassis.

Reigning world champion Nelson Piquet joined the driver strength at Lotus, but the 100T was never to do him justice, whilst he failed to generate the loyalty that his predecessor had engendered. His lack of motivation behind the wheel, in a year when he was not threatened in any way by his team-mate, reflected in his results.

Nakajima, meanwhile, found that the 100T was unable to allow him to build on his previous year's experience, although this was not evident in the first race of the year in Brazil.

Understeer that abruptly changed to oversteer was Piquet's overriding concern in qualifying for the Brazilian GP; he took fifth place. He was the centre of much press attention in his home country and put under great pressure to compete with fellow-countryman Senna in what was also perceived as a battle of the cigarette companies – Marlboro McLaren v. Camel Lotus! The GP itself was led from flag to flag by Prost's McLaren, and whilst Piquet was initially fourth, he was soon to come under pressure from Boutsen's Benetton. Piquet pitted on lap 20 for fresh tyres – his hope of going without a stop being denied him – letting Nakajima past to lead him briefly on laps 21 and 22. Piquet climbed back to third place but later his ill-handling chassis caused such a deterioration in his tyres that he had to pit again for his third set! Back in third by lap 46, this is where he stayed until the end of the race. On the face of it this may have appeared to have been a good result, but in reality the Lotus was not able to stay with the McLarens even though it possessed an identical Honda engine. Nakajima finished in the points in sixth place.

Back in Europe at Imola, Piquet's eventual third place result in the San Marino GP again concealed Lotus's problems. In qualifying, Piquet was 3 seconds slower than Senna's pole position time even though he was in third place on the grid! He had to overcome gear and grip troubles whilst Nakajima had a huge spin on his way to twelfth. The 100Ts boasted changed front suspension in an attempt to cure the Brazilian problems. Senna took a flag to flag win in the race being shadowed home by McLaren team-mate Prost, and these two were the only finishers to go the full distance. Piquet was third, a lap behind, his Lotus being unable to emulate the McLaren-Honda fuel consumption. Piquet had been second for the first seven laps but soon had to drive according to the fuel consumption read-out. His practice form was repeated, as he had to drive at about 3 seconds a lap slower than the McLarens, whilst fending off attacks from the likes of both Nannini's and then Boutsen's Benettons. Eventually Piquet was lapped by the McLarens, but he did at least manage to hold on until the flag for another four points, whilst Nakajima was eighth.

A year previously Monaco had been a great race for Lotus as Senna had taken an actively suspended win, but this year was different. Having qualified seventeenth on his first visit to Monte Carlo, this year Nakajima failed to qualify and never realistically looked like getting anywhere near the field; Piquet was way down in eleventh, being unable to put his power on to the track. The sole Lotus to start the 1988 Monaco GP in fact went only as far as the hurly-burly of the first corner before it touched the rear right wheel of Warwick's Arrows. A visit to the pits revealed that the fixing points were so damaged that a new nose could not be fitted, so less than one lap of Lotus racing was all that could be recorded that May weekend. Prost took the flag first.

The Honda engines should have been a distinct benefit to Lotus in the altitude of Mexico but this was not to be the case. Both engines failed in the race and the blame was placed on fuel trouble, which holed pistons. All initially went well when Piquet qualified fourth and

Nelson Piquet joined Nakajima to run the unloved Lotus 100T in 1988. The car disappointed and Piquet found himself unable to respond. The Honda race engines both expired in Mexico after a promising practice and should have performed better at altitude.

Nakajima only two places behind, with both drivers liking the fast circuit. Suspension alterations were obviously proving effective, but it had to be borne in mind that the Honda runners had nearly 200bhp advantage over their rivals at 7,000 feet (2,100 metres) above sea level. Having initially been third, Piquet ran from laps 9 to 58 in fourth place whilst fending off Alboreto's Ferrari. He had kept some fuel in reserve but this was all to no avail as his engine promptly gave out on him on lap 59. Nakajima's Honda had already let him down to add still further to the Lotus gloom as the McLaren-Hondas rolled on to another crushing one-two, with Prost again heading the field.

Lotus went testing at Croix-en-Ternois to try to sort the aerodynamics as well as the suspension out in preparation for the trip to North America. As a result, in Detroit Piquet was to run a short-wheelbase, widertrack version of the 100T, along with a much modified rear suspension.

At least in Canada both of the Team's cars would finish the GP. To achieve this, Piquet worked tirelessly to capture sixth place on the grid and circuit rookie Nakajima was thirteenth, having surmounted engine troubles. This weekend it was Senna's turn to lead the McLarens home, whilst Piquet fended off Streiff's AGS for nineteen laps before the Frenchman dumped his car across a kerb. The Brazilian eventually came home a lapped fourth, whilst Nakajima struggled back from twenty-second on lap 15, to eleventh at the end.

Nakajima failed to qualify for the second time that season at Detroit, as he thoroughly disliked the proximity of the concrete walls. His Lotus had also been rudely assaulted from behind by Alliot's Lola, doing neither car any good. Piquet, too, had hit a wall early in practice, but despite this and boiling brake fluid, ended up eighth fastest. This weekend the McLaren result was Senna first and Prost second, whilst Piquet circulated in midfield, stopped for tyres on lap 24, and then promptly crashed out as a victim of terminal wheelspin.

McLaren staged yet another Prost-led walkover in France whilst Piquet mysteriously could not repeat his encouraging unofficial time in qualifying, although Nakajima did manage eighth place on the grid now that he was on a far roomier circuit. In the race Piquet spent sixty-six laps in fifth place, and apart from a couple of brief bursts into fourth, this was where he remained until the end, a lap behind the McLarens. He was also hampered by the lack of second gear. Nakajima did well to finish only two places behind Piquet in seventh, but had unwittingly contributed to Warwick's heavy avoidance accident when he missed a gear.

From Sunny Paul Ricard it was off to rainy Silverstone, where it would be Senna's turn to win for

McLaren. For two races Lotus had been trying out computer-controlled Bilstein shock absorbers, but they were not to be used in the British GP itself. Piquet tried them in early practice but soon reverted to the standard set-up; he was happier with his car in the corners, but plainly unable to keep up with even the ill-handling McLarens on Hangar straight. In the very inclement race Nakajima had fifth gear go this time as he came home tenth, while Piquet slithered to fifth.

In Germany for his 150th GP, Piquet was not happy with his engine, but he was still fifth fastest with Nakajima in eighth. In the drizzle that led up to the GP start, Piquet threw caution to the wind and changed to slicks, only to regret this bitterly after the warm-up lap. On the second lap he was to spin into the tyres as his car pirouetted at the Ostkurve chicane, and his landmark race was well and truly over. Nakajima was left as the sole Lotus representative and, apart from holding Prost up at one stage (lap 32), he had an uneventful cruise to ninth place.

On to Hungary, where Piquet improved from his initial twenty-second place to thirteenth – 2.77 seconds behind the similarly engined pole-sitting McLaren of Senna – whilst Nakajima was nineteenth. In the Senna-dominated race Piquet collided with Martini's Minardi on lap 9, which cost him a lot of time and nine places as he had to fit a new nose; he then climbed back through the field to be in eighth place at the flag. Nakajima beat the reigning World Champion by coming in seventh after winning a fight with Tarquini's Coloni.

In the Monza tests after the Hungarian GP, Johnny Herbert went particularly well during a one-off Lotus drive, only to suffer grievous leg injuries the next weekend at Brands Hatch in a European F3000 race.

By the time of Spa and the Belgian GP, Nakajima seemed to be getting much more into the swing of things, as he enjoyed the faster circuits. Indeed at one point, in the Ardennes rain, he was second fastest overall, but he had to settle for eighth on the grid in the end. Piquet was very unhappy with his 100T, and when his clutch went the best he could achieve was ninth. Senna won the Belgian race whilst Nakajima's enthusiasm was thwarted by an engine failure at a time when he was holding a strong sixth place. He had been fifth, but his Brazilian team-mate had got past him on lap 16. Piquet in turn came under attack from Nannini's Benetton, which was particularly threatening in the corners; he forced past Piquet at La Source on lap 37, to be followed shortly afterwards by Capelli's March, leaving the Lotus sixth at the flag.

Prior to Monza, Derek Warwick was offered a drive at Lotus for the following season, but he declined as he was not willing to be subservient to Piquet who, it was insisted, would be no. 1 driver.

Exactly a decade after his death at Monza, Senna beat Ronnie Peterson's previous record with his tenth pole position of the year. Lotus, meanwhile, were plagued by oversteer and Piquet also suffered at the hands of his experimental suspension system. In the GP, neither Lotus lasted beyond fourteen laps, as firstly Piquet spun terminally into the sand on lap 12 when his clutch gave out and then Nakajima's engine blew as a result of a seized piston on his fifteenth lap. The crowd were ecstatic, though, at the Ferrari one-two that was the eventual result, with Berger being the winner.

Piquet was to retire in Portugal too, thanks to his clutch, and it would be Nakajima's turn to spin off out of the race. This followed great optimism in practice when Piquet seemed to be finally taming the 100T, and even though he was only eighth on the grid he was most enthusiastic. An unwell Nakajima could only manage sixteenth, thanks again to the clutch, which was becoming a common problem. At the first corner of the GP a mêlée of midfield runners occurred, amongst whom was Nakajima, and the race was red-flagged. His car, which had suffered a puncture as well as the loss of its rear wing, was repaired on the grid, only for its driver to crash out on lap 16 of the restarted event. Piquet, drove well, but again fell foul of his clutch after thirty-four laps, so neither Lotus was to make it to the end as Prost took the McLaren laurels yet again.

In Spain the Lotus twins were in all sorts of handling trouble in practice, and even though at one point Piquet was third fastest, he subsequently dropped to ninth; Nakajima was fifteenth. As Prost tore off into an unassailable lead Nakajima fell off the circuit into a sand-trap after only fourteen laps, having crossed swords with Dalmas and Caffi. As the marshals made a real pig's ear of recovering 100T/1, Piquet and Warwick had a lengthy ten-lap fight, which eventually saw the Arrows damage itself on a kerb. The Brazilian felt that Warwick had unfairly held him up but at least he was able to continue to the end and eighth place, unlike the Arrows driver, who was forced to retire.

Piquet went to Japan and was rewarded for his long journey by being sick. Nakajima, who made himself ill in the process, was initially faster of the two on his home track, but honour was restored when the Brazilian recorded an identical time – 1 minute 43.693 seconds – and as a result they shared the third row of the grid together. Nakajima was a firm favourite of the home crowd but managed to select the wrong gear at the start and was swamped by the opposition. He dropped to twentieth place at the end of the first lap but was soon to fight back through the field, fired up as he was.

TEAM LOTUS RESULTS 1988

Drivers:
Nelson Piquet: Brazilian; Satoru Nakajima: Japanese
Car:
Lotus 100 T Engine: Honda RA16 8-E

CAR	CHASSIS	DRIVER	PRACTICE	SESSION	GRID	RACE	LAPS	%	REASON	CHAMPIONSHIP POSITION	POINTS
BRAZILIAN GP, Jacarepagua – 3rd April – 60 L, 187.566 miles (301.860km) (380)											
100 T	2	Piquet	1m 30.087s	2	5th	3rd	60	100.0	–	3rd	4
100 T	1	Nakajima	1m 31.280s	2	10th	6th	59	98.3	–	6th	1
100 T	3	(Spare)									
SAN MARINO GP, Imola – 1st May – 60 L, 187.902 miles (302.400km) (381)											
100 T	2	Piquet	1m 30.500s	2	3rd	3rd	59	98.3	–	3rd=	8
100 T	1	Nakajima	1m 31.647s	2	12th	8th	59	98.3	–	8th=	1
100 T	3	Spare									
MONACO GP, Monte Carlo – 15th May – 78 L, 161.298 miles (259.584km) (382)											
100 T	2	Piquet	1m 28.403s	2	11th	R	1	1.2	Nose	4th	8
100 T	1	Nakajima	1m 30.611s	1	DNQ	–	–	–	–	9th=	1
100 T	3	(Spare)									
MEXICAN GP, Mexico – 29th May – 67 L, 184.054 miles (296.207km) (383)											
100 T	2	Piquet	1m 18.946s	2	4th	R	58	86.5	Engine	5th=	8
100 T	4	Nakajima	1m 20.275s	2	6th	R	27	40.2	Engine	9th=	1
100 T	3	(Spare)									
CANADIAN GP, Montreal – 12th June – 69 L, 188.21 miles (302.91km) (384)											
100 T	2	Piquet	1m 23.995s	2	6th	4th	68	98.5	–	4th	1
100 T	4	Nakajima	1m 25.373s	1	13th	11th	66	95.6	–	10th=	1
100 T	3	(Spare)									
US GP, Detroit – 19th June – 63 L, 157.500 miles (253.471km) (385)											
100 T	2	Piquet	1m 43.314s	2	8th	R	26	41.2	Accident	4th=	11
100 T	4	Nakajima	1m 47.243s	1	DNQ	–	–	–	–	11th=	1
100 T	3	(Spare)									
FRENCH GP, Ricard – 3rd July – 80 L, 189.543 miles (305.04km) (386)											
100 T	3	Piquet	1m 09.734s	1	7th	5th	79	98.7	–	4th=	13
100 T	1	Nakajima	1m 10.250s	2	8th	7th	79	98.7	–	12th=	1
100 T	2	(Spare)									
BRITISH GP, Silverstone – 10th July – 65 L, 192.985 miles (310.579km) (387)											
100 T	3	Piquet	1m 12.040s	2	7th	5th	65	100.0	–	4th	15
100 T	1	Nakajima	1m 12.862s	2	10th	10th	64	98.4	–	14th=	1
100 T	2	(Spare)									
GERMAN GP, Hockenheim – 24th July – 44 L, 185.83 miles (299.068km) (388)											
100 T	1	Nakajima	1m 48.781s	2	5th	9th	43	97.7	–	14th=	1
100 T	2	Piquet	1m 47.681s	2	8th	R	1	2.2	Accident	5th	15
100 T	3	(Spare)									
HUNGARIAN GP, Hungaroring – 7th August – 76 L, 189.557 miles (305.064km) (389)											
100 T	2	Nakajima	1m 31.646s	2	19th	7th	73	96.0	–	15th=	1
100 T	1	Piquet	1m 30.405s	2	13th	8th	73	96.0	–	6th	15
100 T	3	(Spare)									
BELGIAN GP, Spa – 28th August – 43 L, 185.429 miles (298.420km) (390)											
100 T	2	Piquet	1m 57.821s	1	9th	6th	43	100.0	–	5th=	16
100 T	1	Nakajima	1m 57.616s	1	8th	R	21	48.8	Engine	15th=	1
100 T	3	(Spare)									
ITALIAN GP, Monza – 11th September – 51 L, 183.801 miles (295.800km) (391)											
100 T	1	Nakajima	1m 29.541s	1	12th	R	14	27.4	Engine	16th=	1
100 T	2	Piquet	1m 28.044s	2	7th	R	11	21.5	Accident	6th	16
100 T	3	(Spare)									
PORTUGUESE GP, Estoril – 25th September – 70 L, 189.207 miles (304.50km) (392)											
100 T	2	Piquet	1m 19.551s	1	8th	R	34	48.5	Clutch	6th	16
100 T	1	Nakajima	1m 20.783s	2	16th	R	16	22.8	Accident	16th=	1
100 T	3	(Spare)									

SPANISH GP, Jerez – 2nd October – 72 L, 188.708 miles (303.696km) (393)

100 T	2	Piquet	1m 25.648s	2	9th	8th	72	100.0	–	6th	16
100 T	1	Nakajima	1m 27.171s	2	15th	R	14	19.4	Accident	16th=	1
100 T	3	(Spare)									

JAPANESE GP, Suzuka – 30th October – 51 L, 185.670 miles (298.809km) (394)

100 T	1	Nakajima	1m 43.693s	2	6th	7th	50	98.0	–	16th=	1
100 T	2	Piquet	1m 43.693s	2	5th	R	34	66.6	Illness	6th	16
100 T	3	(Spare)									

AUSTRALIAN GP, Adelaide – 13th November – 82 L, 192.498 miles (309.796km) (395)

100 T	2	Piquet	1m 19.535s	2	5th	3rd	82	100.0	–	6th	20
100 T	1	Nakajima	1m 20.852s	2	13th	R	45	54.8	Accident	16th=	1
100 T	3	(Spare)									

Key:
DNQ = Did Not Qualify
R   = Retired
L   = Laps

Having dodged the lagging Senna at the start, Piquet felt increasingly unwell as the race progressed. Having already spun, he retired on lap 34 as nausea overtook him. Nakajima meanwhile came in seventh as Senna celebrated not only his Japanese win but also the 1988 World Championship, which he had now secured.

Having overcome problems with a pop-off valve and made use of a larger turbo than those on the McLarens, Piquet took eighth on the grid in Australia, with Nakajima thirteenth, having overcome an engine failure. The Brazilian had a scintillating first lap ending it in fourth place, and he built on this position to take third, after the demise of Berger's Ferrari, on lap 25. Second-placed Senna was already in trouble with his second gear, which is used heavily in Adelaide, and he changed the richness of his fuel mixture several times a lap to compensate for this with the intention of keeping Piquet at bay, in which he was successful. On lap 46 Nakajima had collided heavily with the rear of Gugelmin's March as the latter was avoiding the spinning Benetton of Martini. The Lotus was unfortunately retired there and then, as Piquet stayed on course for his third place, which would leave him sixth overall in the World Championship.

Gerard Ducarouge left Lotus towards the end of 1988 to be replaced by former Williams aerodynamicist Frank Dernie. As the 1,500cc turbo era had come to a conclusion, the Team were to say goodbye to their Honda power plants.

WORLD CHAMPIONSHIP RESULTS 1988

Position	Driver	Points
1	Ayrton Senna	90 (94)
2	Alain Prost	87 (105)
3	Gerhard Berger	41
4	Thierry Boutsen	31
5	Michele Alboreto	24
6	**Nelson Piquet**	**20**
7=	Ivan Capelli	15
	Alessandro Nannini	15
	Derek Warwick	15
10	Nigel Mansell	12
11	Riccardo Patrese	8
12=	Eddie Cheever	5
	Mauricio Gugelmin	5
	Jonathan Palmer	5
15	Andrea de Cesaris	3
16=	**Satoru Nakajima**	**1**
	Pierluigi Martini	1

CONSTRUCTORS' CUP 1988

Position	Constructor	Points
1	McLaren	199
2	Ferrari	65
3	Benetton	46
4	**Lotus-Honda**	**21**

1989

Lotus 101

1989 was to be the most disappointing season since the Team had first involved itself in F1 back in 1958. Everything sank to a new low and, just as a climb out of the doldrums started, Spa heralded an even bigger setback. It was then recognized that enough was enough. Radical changes had to occur; the price of failure would be the Lotus name disappearing from GP racing.

An important factor in 1989 was that, unbeknown to many, Peter Warr was planning to leave; he

The Judd-powered Lotus 101 was a rushed design for the 1989 season. Boasting the same suspension as the 100T, performance gradually improved in Piquet's hands, but the complete disaster of Spa caused a major managerial restructuring. Nakajima (pictured) was often off the pace.

continued in post until just after the British GP. Other moves included Rupert Mainwaring becoming team manager and Bob Dance moving from being chief mechanic – a position now taken by Richard Taylor – to engine shop manager. Steve Hallam was race operations engineer.

Following Ducarouge's departure Williams aerodynamicist Frank Dernie had arrived in November 1988 as technical director in time to rush through the design of the Judd-powered 101. This was the first time that Dernie had constructed a whole car and it was chief designer Mike Coughlan who in fact actually penned the alterations to the 100T to create the longer, compact, carbon-fibre/nomex honeycomb 101, which possessed the same suspension and fuel system as the 100T. Dernie had to book the Imperial College wind tunnel in London but despite this inconvenience the 101 was to be the second fastest of the Judd contenders, possessing a number of neat design features such as the tucking away of the cockpit-adjustable suspension dampers along the bottom of the monocoque.

The Judd V8 engines produced roughly 125bhp less than the much-lamented Hondas in qualifying, and when a piston ring problem was added into the equation, Lotus uncompetitiveness was predicted. Judd's main interest lay with March, which ran the EV engine variant; Warr, therefore, reached an arrangement with Tickford to research a troublesome new five-valve-per-cylinder head. This was not raced, as it was never proven that the increased valve area actually enabled better breathing at high revs. It was also argued that if the existing two drivers couldn't achieve results with Honda engines there was little likelihood of them doing much with the Judds. Tyres too were an addi-

tional problem, as what was on offer had been designed for McLaren and Ferrari, both of whom had tested and tuned them unlike Lotus.

In a year of Prost and McLaren domination Piquet had another miserable time, as the machinery did not give him the advantage that his mentality required. Lotus didn't really know how to handle his personality whilst Nakajima never proved that he warranted promotion to the drivers' first division. Impressive Martin Donnelly was signed as test driver in January, and his attitude led to a full-time job in 1990. He went to Brazil as doubts hung over the injured Piquet's participation.

The 101 was launched at the six-day test prior to the Brazilian GP, after both Piquet and Donnelly had shaken the machine down for twenty-five laps of Snetterton. Mansell was a surprise winner on his Ferrari début in Rio as Piquet suffered from the consequences of a fall on his yacht; he did take ninth starting position, however. The drivers bemoaned the lack of power, which Nakajima demonstrated with a twenty-first place on the grid and two over-revved Judds. Piquet only lasted for ten laps of the race before his fuel pump failed – never having got higher than eleventh – whilst Nakajima finished eighth as others dropped by the wayside.

Mid-April Imola testing saw Piquet seventh fastest (1 minute 29.10 seconds), having overcome Rio-style fuel pump trouble, although the Judd engines were still underpowered. In the San Marino race proper hopes were raised as Piquet managed to last for twenty-nine laps and to run in a strong fourth before his engine let go. On a day that will be remembered more for Berger's miraculous escape from his burning Ferrari,

Piquet had started eighth on the original grid and had looked much more confident. By contrast, Nakajima had qualified well down in twenty-fourth, and was unclassified twelve laps behind the winner, Senna.

Prior to Monaco, Piquet successfully tested 'standard' Goodyear tyres, but was dismayed when a new version introduced for Monaco proved unsuitable for the 101. Some time later it would be realized that the car's bad handling and acute low-speed understeer were caused by the construction of those new Goodyear tyres.

At Monaco the Team was all at sea and their confidence took a severe knock. Nakajima – plagued by severe understeer – didn't qualify, and Piquet just scraped into nineteenth place, having overcome both gearbox and tyre troubles. As Senna won again, Piquet contributed to a silly accident on lap 32. On the slowest corner – Loews hairpin – as he was being lapped by the fourth placed De Cesaris, the two cars locked wheels, only for the beached drivers to hurl abuse at each other. Eventually the two cars were separated by the marshals but Piquet's was sufficiently damaged to retire. For some time Piquet had plodded around in a Coloni's wake, raising questions about whether he was actually sufficiently motivated even to try to pass . . .

After Monaco, Lotus moved to nearby Paul Ricard to test. Piquet could only manage seventeenth fastest (1 minute 10.73 seconds) and Nakajima nineteenth (1 minute 11.07 seconds). Donnelly, meanwhile, set the fastest non-aspirated lap of Snetterton at 51.2 seconds (134.81mph/216.9kph) despite coping with a little understeer!

By the time of the Mexican fourth round Lotus were thoroughly frustrated, and Piquet had to cope with a leaking cooling system as well as engines unsuited to the high altitude. A new underbody was hardly used; in fifteenth place, Nakajima out-qualified Piquet, who was last! The Japanese had persisted to 'tame' the 101, unlike the team leader. The GP itself was another Senna/McLaren benefit whilst Nakajima climbed from nineteenth to thirteenth only for his gears to jump out on lap 35 causing him to spin off. Piquet was an unimpressive eleventh at the flag.

Phoenix was the new venue for the United States GP, and whilst the McLaren steamroller continued – Prost was victor this time – there was still no joy for Camel Team Lotus. A lacklustre Piquet was only just ahead of Nakajima in twenty-second on the grid for the Team's 400th GP! In the race Piquet had to have a paper bag removed from his radiator intake, but then benefited from the large number of retirements to get as high as seventh before hitting a wall and deranging his suspension on lap 52. Nakajima had retired from thirteenth when his throttle cable broke. In taking pole

at Phoenix, Senna had broken Jim Clark's twenty-one-year-old record of thirty-three pole positions from seventy-two starts.

Sadly a day after the United States GP former Lotus designer Maurice Phillipe was found dead at his home in Surrey.

The Canadian GP saw Team Lotus at last finishing in the points, which had seemed unlikely at the outset, as Piquet had been only nineteenth fastest and Nakajima had not qualified; both cars had proven difficult to balance. As Boutsen won for Williams in the rainy conditions, Piquet forged on throughout the event, rising from sixteenth at the end of lap 1 to fourth at the flag.

During Silverstone testing the Tickford-headed Judd engine appeared publicly for the first time in back-to-back tests against the normal V8. After 450 miles (724km) it became the Team's firm intention to race the engine in the French GP. All three Lotus drivers were present, but Donnelly really made his mark with eighth-fastest time on qualifiers (1 minute 11.80 seconds). This was well ahead of Piquet (1 minute 13.08 seconds), who was fifteenth, and seventeenth-placed Nakajima (1 minute 13.27 seconds). Dernie greatly appreciated Donnelly's feedback and the 101 was improved as a result.

In France Nakajima out-qualified Piquet who had tried the Tickford-modified engine in practice and decided against using it for qualifying or the race. Gugelmin's somersaulting March meant the GP itself had to be restarted; Piquet then rose from twentieth to eighth at the finish despite being slow on the Mistral straight. Nakajima had his bodywork come apart only for a fuel problem to cause him to pull off and retire on his fiftieth lap. Prost won again.

By this time Camel were becoming frustrated with Lotus's lack of results and Piquet was allegedly given an ultimatum to improve or else . . .

Strangely Piquet seemed rejuvenated at Silverstone and his tenth place on the grid was well earned after all the testing at the Northamptonshire track. Nakajima was sixteenth. In the race a confident Piquet bowled along for thirty-two laps in third place until Nannini's Benetton got past with just nine laps remaining. Nakajima came home eighth as Prost won yet again for McLaren. Piquet regenerated morale within the team and from this time onwards seemed more and more likely to score points.

Following Silverstone the Chapman family – the shareholders in Team Lotus International – decided that enough was enough. After a formal meeting they announced that Peter Warr would leave, as, surprisingly, would chairman Fred Bushell. He was about to face allegations concerning the DeLorean affair; just before the British GP, he had been arrested in London before appearing before Belfast Crown Court. He was charged with conspiring with others (John DeLorean and Colin Chapman) to defraud the DeLorean Motor Company of £3.5 million. His departure allowed Tony Rudd to come over from Group Lotus – where he was group technical director and chairman of Lotus Engineering – to become executive chairman of Team Lotus. Rudd had been BRM's chief engineer in their 1962 World Championship season and was a true racer, taking over the newly formed senior management team of Frank Dernie, Rupert Mainwaring, Noel Stanbury and Manning Buckle. The last two were respectively in charge of marketing/commercial matters, and company secretary. Additionally, Rudd set about re-establishing the Team's research and development base, which had not operated fully since Chapman's death. Investment in facilities was needed, and a business plan dependent upon income was quickly put in hand to facilitate this fully.

A new era dawned at Lotus as it was quite evident that for the Team to continue as it had been would have meant oblivion.

At Hockenheim an optimistic atmosphere pervaded the Lotus pit with the management change being welcomed. The Tickford head engines were finally abandoned and once understeer was ironed out the Team were happier with the improving 101. Racing the spare as his intended car had a misfire, Piquet found it handled brilliantly and he was motivated enough to finish in fifth place on what was a power circuit. He could not, however, catch winner Senna. Nakajima closed in on Warwick's sixth-placed Arrows but in trying to overtake at the chicane on lap 37, the resulting closing of the door saw the Lotus rudely bundled off the track and into retirement. Nakajima would suffer at Warwick's hands again in Hungary.

Rumours that Lotus was up for sale were strenuously denied by Tony Rudd. Meanwhile, in Hungaroring qualifying Piquet was initially eleventh fastest until his less powerful engine dropped him to seventeenth. Nakajima suffered a succession of missed gear changes. On a day when Mansell was to win for Ferrari, Piquet climbed through the field to an eventual sixth whilst Nakajima again collided with Warwick, who had just exited the pits on lap 34. With its right rear wheel pointing high in the air Nakajima's Lotus spun across the gravel and into a premature retirement. The leading Williams of Patrese was later to suffer from the after-effects of this accident, as his FW12C hit a piece of wreckage – probably a half-shaft – causing his engine to over-heat and his retirement!

On the way to Spa, three days of testing were undertaken at Monza; Piquet was a disappointing fifteenth

fastest (1 minute 29.48 seconds) and Nakajima was twenty-ninth (1 minute 13.12 seconds).

Camel Team Lotus's trip to Spa can only be described as a complete logistical disaster! A series of misfortunes struck in practice as Piquet spun several times, denying himself any time to improve; in fact he had been sixth fastest through the speed trap. Nakajima had been eighth fastest through the same trap but suffered from appalling balance that stopped him from getting into the groove at all as others improved. At the end of the day, for the first time since Lotus had entered F1 back in 1958, there wasn't a works Lotus on a GP grid at the very track on which Clark had won four times in succession! Rupert Mainwaring admitted that the last day of practice at Spa was 'the worst day of my life'. For both of a team's cars to fail to qualify is not new for some outfits (it had even happened to McLaren at Monaco in 1983), but it was still the worst result for Lotus in all of their 406 GP meetings. The Team was visibly knocked.

Following such disappointments, it came as no surprise when it was revealed at Monza that for 1990 both existing Lotus drivers would be leaving, to be replaced by Derek Warwick and Martin Donnelly. The Judd engines were to go too, in favour of Lamborghini V12s. Interestingly, Camel (R.J. Reynolds) decided to continue their sponsorship with Lotus, which had seemed unlikely. A flu-ridden Piquet qualified eleventh in Italy and Nakajima was nineteenth, having looked like not qualifying again. Piquet only completed twenty-three laps before coming across Gachot's crashing Onyx and spinning in sympathy into retirement from tenth place. Nakajima was then the sole Lotus representative, coming in tenth as Prost won, virtually assuring himself of the Championship.

During the Portuguese GP Mansell and Senna eliminated each other, allowing Berger to win for Ferrari. Nakajima had taken the penultimate position on the grid and Piquet was in twentieth place, but the Brazilian crashed out at mid-race after a contretemps with Caffi, and the Japanese finished just outside the points.

Nakajima had an opening lap accident at Jerez during the Spanish GP having clipped Capelli's March. His car's rear wing had been found to be too high (by one millimetre!) during Friday practice and his day's times were therefore erased from the record, but he started from eighteenth place. Piquet's 101 seemed to suit Jerez ideally and he qualified seventh, despite having been caught up in traffic, to his annoyance. In the race he dropped as low as eighteenth following a Nannini-enforced trip across a corner, which damaged his undertray, and then having a rear tyre punctured by Warwick's Arrows. Race winner Senna was not amused at being held up by Piquet either.

TEAM LOTUS RESULTS 1989

Drivers:
Nelson Piquet: Brazilian; Satoru Nakajima: Japanese
Car:
Lotus 101 Engine: Judd CV★

CAR	CHASSIS	DRIVER	PRACTICE	SESSION	GRID	RACE	LAPS	%	REASON	CHAMPIONSHIP POSITION	POINTS

BRAZILIAN GP, Jacarepagua – 26th March – 61 L, 190.692 miles (306.981km) (396)

CAR	CHASSIS	DRIVER	PRACTICE	SESSION	GRID	RACE	LAPS	%	REASON	POSITION	POINTS
101	1	Nakajima	1m 30.375s	2	21st	8th	60	98.3	–	–	–
101	2	Piquet	1m 27.437s	2	9th	R	10	16.3	Pump	–	–

SAN MARINO GP, Imola – 23rd April – 58 L, 181.638 miles (292.32km) (397)

101	1	Nakajima	1m 30.697s	2	24th	NC	–	–		–	–
101	3	Piquet	1m 29.057s	2	8th	R	29	50.0	Engine	–	–
101	2	Spare									

MONACO GP, Monte Carlo – 7th May – 77 L, 159.229 miles (256.256km) (398)

101	2	Piquet	1m 27.046s	2	19th	R	32	41.5	Accident	–	–
101	3	Nakajima	1m 28.419s	2	DNQ	–	–	–	–	–	–
101	1	(Spare)									

MEXICAN GP, Mexico – 28th May – 69 L, 189.548 miles (305.049km) (399)

101	2	Piquet	1m 21.831s	2	26th	11th	68	98.5	–	–	–
101	3	Nakajima	1m 20.943s	2	15th	R	35	50.7	Gearbox	–	–
101	1	(Spare)									

US GP, Phoenix – 4th June – 75 L, 177.00 miles (284.858km) (400)

101	2	Piquet	1m 33.745s	1	22nd	R	52	69.3	Accident	–	–
101	3	Nakajima	1m 33.782s	2	23rd	R	24	32.0	Throttle	–	–
101	1	(Spare)									

CANADIAN GP, Montreal – 18th June – 69 L, 188.21 miles (302.91km) (401)

101	2	Piquet	1m 24.029s	1	19th	4th	69	100.0	–	15th=	3
101	3	Nakajima	1m 25.051s	1	DNQ	–	–	–	–	–	–
101	1	(Spare)									

FRENCH GP, Ricard – 9th July – 80 L, 189.543 miles (305.04km) (402)

101	4	Piquet	1m 10.135s	2	20th	8th	78	97.5	–	15th=	3
101	2	Nakajima	1m 10.119s	2	19th	R	49	61.2	Engine	–	–
101	–	(Spare)									

BRITISH GP, Silverstone – 16th July – 64 L, 190.080 miles (305.904km) (403)

101	4	Piquet	1m 10.925s	2	10th	4th	64	100.0	–	7th=	6
101	2	Nakajima	1m 11.960s	2	16th	8th	63	98.4	–	–	–
101	3	(Spare)									
101	1	(Spare)									

GERMAN GP, Hockenheim – 30th July – 45 L, 190.055 miles (305.865km) (404)

101	4	Piquet	1m 45.474s	2	8th	5th	44	97.7	–	7th	8
101	3	Nakajima	1m 47.663s	2	18th	R	36	80.0	Accident	–	–
101	2	(Spare)									

HUNGARIAN GP, Hungaroring – 13th August – 77 L, 189.850 miles (305.536km) (405)

101	4	Piquet	1m 22.406s	2	17th	6th	77	100.0	–	7th	9
101	3	Nakajima	1m 22.630s	2	20th	R	33	42.8	Accident	–	–
101	2	(Spare)									

BELGIAN GP, Spa – 27th August – 44 L, 189.741 miles (305.360km) (406)

101	4	Piquet	1m 57.771s	2	DNQ	–	–	–	–	7th	9
101	3	Nakajima	1m 57.251s	2	DNQ	–	–	–	–	–	–
101	2	(Spare)									

ITALIAN GP, Monza – 10th September – 53 L, 191.009 miles (307.400km) (407)

101	3	Nakajima	1m 28.441s	2	19th	10th	51	96.2	–	–	–
101	4	Piquet	1m 27.508s	2	11th	R	23	43.3	Accident	7th	9
101	2	(Spare)									

PORTUGUESE GP, Estoril – 24th September – 71 L, 191.910 miles (308.850km) (408)

101	3	Nakajima	1m 19.165s	2	25th	7th	70	98.5	–	–	–
101	4	Piquet	1m 18.482s	1	20th	R	33	46.4	Accident	8th	9
101	2	(Spare)									

SPANISH GP, Jerez – 1st October – 73L, 191.328 miles (307.914km) (409)

101	4	Piquet	1m 21.922s	2	7th	8th	71	97.2	–	8th	9
101	3	Nakajima	1m 23.309s	2	18th	R	0	0.0		–	–
101	2	(Spare)							Accident		

JAPANESE GP, Suzuka – 22nd October – 53 L, 192.952 miles (310.527km) (410)

101	4	Piquet	1m 41.802s	2	11th	4th	53	100.0	–	8th	12
101	3	Nakajima	1m 41.988s	2	12th	R	41	77.3		–	–
101	2	(Spare)							Engine		

AUSTRALIAN GP, Adelaide – 5th November – 70 L, 164.290 miles (264.460km) (411)

| 101 | 3 | Nakajima | 1m 20.066s | 1 | 23rd | 4th | 70 | 100.0 | – | 21st | 3 |

Fastest Lap: 1m 38.480s – 85.860mph (138.180kmh) on lap 64)

| 101 | 4 | Piquet | 1m 19.392s | 1 | 18th | R | 19 | 27.1 | Accident | 8th | 12 |
| 101 | 2 | (Spare) | | | | | | | | | |

Key:
NC = Not Classified
DNQ = Did Not Qualify
R = Retired
L = Laps

Piquet took a deserved fourth in Japan after the two Lotus cars had sorted out practice tyre troubles and qualified on the sixth row of the grid together. Piquet yet again blocked Senna for a whole race lap only to benefit later from an altercation between Senna and Prost to take fourth place; as he crossed the line his engine blew up! Nakajima had forcefully helped Sala off the road on the opening lap only for his engine to fail after forty-one laps. A surprised Nannini won for Benetton.

The Australian GP was controversially run in torrential rain. Having collided with Mansell in qualifying, Piquet hit a wall hard, deranging his suspension. As Boutsen won for Williams, Piquet was lucky to emerge unscathed when, blinded by spray, he drove into the back of Ghinzani's Osella; that car's rear tyre cracked his helmet. Subsequently, he was critical of the stewards for allowing the race to be run in such conditions. Meanwhile Nakajima put in the race of his F1 career as he confidently mastered the wet to climb from twenty-second place on the first lap to fourth, taking fastest lap too.

Despite the Team's overall improvement in the second half of the season morale remained low, and Piquet in particular was glad to leave behind what he now regarded as a completely uncompetitive car.

In early December Warwick was fourteenth fastest (1 minute 20.16 seconds) in Estoril testing, with an engine test-bed 101B for the Lamborghini V12 engine. Donnelly was eighteenth (1 minute 20.65 seconds) with Judd power.

WORLD CHAMPIONSHIP RESULTS 1989

Position	Driver	Points
1	Alain Prost	78
2	Ayrton Senna	60
3	Riccardo Patrese	40
4	Nigel Mansell	38
5	Thierry Boutsen	37
6	Alessandro Nannini	32
7	Gerhard Berger	21
8	**Nelson Piquet**	**12**
9	Jean Alesi	8
10	Derek Warwick	7
11=	Stefan Johansson	6
	Michele Alboreto	6
	Eddie Cheever	6
14=	Johnny Herbert	5
	Pierluigi Martini	5
16=	Andrea de Cesaris	4
	Mauricio Gugelmin	4
	Stefano Modena	4
	Alex Caffi	4
	Martin Brundle	4
21=	**Satoru Nakajima**	**3**
	Christian Danner	3

CONSTRUCTORS' CUP 1989

Position	Constructor	Points
1	McLaren	141
2	Williams	77
3	Ferrari	59
4	Benetton	39
5	Tyrrell	16
6	**Lotus-Judd**	**15**

1990

Lotus suffered badly during 1990 because of a lack of money, although Derek Warwick's arrival gave a new purposeful air; his positive attitude lifted morale and bounced nicely off up-and-coming Ulsterman Martin Donnelly, who had impressed greatly with his testing prowess, and was now the full-time no 2.

Johnny Herbert was signed as test driver, a task which dovetailed neatly in with his Japanese F3000 commitments. He had already completed forty laps of Silverstone acclimatizing himself to the 101-Judd. Amidst driver optimism the 102, with its heavy and thirsty engine, desperately needed more testing time than was available.

Lotus 102

The 102 was announced in February, and with its Lamborghini Tipo 3512 V12 engine it promised much. Rudd's personal friendship with Mauro Forghieri had brought about the Italian engine's use and the first example had been delivered back in mid-September. Dernie and Coughlan kept the 102's overall length within 2in (50mm) of the 101 and the tub was tailored for the taller drivers. A new transverse six-speed gearbox was jointly produced by Lotus and Lamborghini. The suspension was unchanged in concept although it was tidied up at the front with horizontal longitudinal dampers and a semi-integrated roll bar. BP developed several special fuels during a season in which Lotus's Lamborghini engines proved far more unreliable than those at Larrousse. It was uncharitably suggested that the latter team had at least followed the basic installation instructions!

After initial Snetterton testing the 102 was taken to Estoril where engines started to blow. It took the personal intervention of Lamborghini's Forghieri to establish that the cause of the problem was the insufficient capacity of the oil tank. A hurried modification took place amidst further concern about the gearbox casing. Warwick eventually was the faster with a 1 minute 18.12 second time, against Donnelly's 1 minute 22.44 seconds. Immediately before Phoenix, Chrysler's USA test track at Witton was used for some eleventh-hour running-in.

At Phoenix a plague of breakages were caused by attempts to save weight to compensate for the heavier engine; already 5 per cent had been pruned from the original specification. Annoyingly Larrousse's Lamborghini-powered cars out-performed Lotus after Warwick's rear suspension failed. Donnelly bravely took nineteenth as the Team kept their fingers crossed that his suspension wouldn't fail — he had already collided with Alboreto and been into the wall. He failed to start after his starter motor refused to work and was pushed ignominiously off the dummy grid, whilst Warwick compounded Lotus's disastrous day with another rear suspension failure after only six laps.

Hopes were raised in Interlagos when Donnelly was quickest in the first wet unofficial practice session; however, race day was much drier. Controversially, Warwick's car was towed back to the pits for an engine change whilst cars were still circulating, and he just made the race in twenty-fifth with Donnelly fourteenth. The Brazilian GP was dismal as Warwick retired with electrical failure again and Donnelly spun off when his seating position induced cramp; his right foot jammed on to the throttle and he abruptly left the track!

The popular Derek Warwick at long last joined the Team in 1990 to drive the Lotus 102. The car's Lamborghini engine proved unreliable compared with those at Larrousse, and ill-handling in high-speed corners led to big accidents for both Donnelly and Warwick.

In Imola testing Warwick was tenth fastest, just behind Mansell, with a 1 minute 27.07 second time and Donnelly was fourteenth (1 minute 27.763 seconds). In further Imola tests everyone reduced their times considerably, with Donnelly being thirteenth fastest (1 minute 26.386 seconds) and Warwick fifteenth (1 minute 26.721 seconds).

San Marino GP qualifying improved morale when the Lotuses were tenth and eleventh on the grid despite oversteer, gearbox and electrical failures. In the race itself, a confident Donnelly spun to the rear of the field on the first lap before catching Warwick again on lap 30; the two then ran in a Camel train until they finished in respectable seventh and eighth places.

For Monaco the gearbox casings were strengthened and Warwick was initially fastest, while Piquet's Benetton held up Donnelly's best qualifying lap. The race was stopped shortly after the start when Berger and Prost collided at the Mirabeau. Warwick and Donnelly became involved when Modena's Tyrrell ignored all the slowing cars and launched over the back of Donnelly in a damaging knock-on accident. Donnelly quickly transferred to the spare for the restart only to retire after five laps with transmission failure. By lap 43 Warwick was up to fifth place; then he let Mansell briefly get past him, only to regain fifth again on lap sixty-four. Two laps later he spun and stalled at the swimming-pool; the car was narrowly missed by eventual winner Senna as it was craned away. At Monaco rumours circulated that Camel would move their sponsorship in 1991, with both Eddie Jordan's fledgling F1 team and Peugeot's Group C programme being suggested as alternatives. Testing at Paul Ricard, though, was certainly encouraging, with Donnelly coming seventh overall (1 minute 05.84 seconds) having been fastest on the first day, and Warwick coming thirteenth (1 minute 06.57 seconds).

Warwick was troubled in Montreal practice by both clutch and engine failures whilst Donnelly concentrated on learning the island track. On a treacherously damp circuit off-line, the Lotuses ran sixth and seventh from lap 44 to lap 57 of the GP before Donnelly's engine suddenly failed, denying him seventh place but leaving Warwick, his car boasting an arched diffuser for the first time, to finish sixth.

The Lotuses again had strengthened gearbox casings in Mexico, where Warwick was just faster, even though a series of engine problems had left him stranded at one point. Donnelly cautiously learned the circuit and ended up twelfth fastest; he then passed Warwick on the fourth race lap before spending the balance of the event conserving his tyres to finish eighth. Warwick had an underpowered engine in Mexico's altitude and neither driver was able to evalu-

ate his new diffuser. Two days later in Silverstone testing, Donnelly and Warwick found the 102 hopeless to balance in the long corners; still, Donnelly was tenth fastest (1 minute 10.31 seconds) and Warwick thirteenth (1 minute 11.01 seconds). The following Sunday Herbert demonstrated a 102 at Brands Hatch and recorded a 39.07-second Indy circuit lap.

The 102's handling in Paul Ricard practice was 'nervous' and the drivers couldn't repeat their promising testing times. Adding insult to injury, Lotus lost its record number of pole positions to Ferrari when Mansell took the Italian marque's 108th. Alain Prost scored Ferrari's 100th GP victory too, whilst all Lotus could manage was eleventh and twelfth place.

At Silverstone Donnelly qualified ahead of Warwick; the 102s were still unstable and also suffering from gearbox problems. In the Foster's British GP, the Lamborghini engines blew almost simultaneously: Warwick's went first, on lap 46, and then Donnelly's two laps later. Ironically both Lamborghini-Larrousses finished in the points.

Hockenheim's high-speed corners were the next testing venue and Warwick surprisingly managed seventh fastest (1 minute 45.22 seconds) amidst rumours that Team Lotus was for sale! High-speed stability was again questionable in official qualifying, when the 102s lacked grip. Both cars were well down the grid with their tyres unable to last a complete lap, and in the race Warwick suffered vibration-induced vision troubles while Donnelly's clutch failed after a single lap. Worst fears were confirmed when Camel (R.J. Reynolds Tobacco International) announced their move to Benetton and Williams for 1991. More positive news was that Peter Collins and Peter Wright were to become Lotus's marketing consultants.

Warwick confidently qualified eleventh in Hungaroring practice on a track that suited the 102. Donnelly recorded 1 minute 19.911 seconds in practice but was blocked in qualifying and ended up eighteenth fastest. Brakes were Warwick's only problem on his way to fifth place and Donnelly was a commendable seventh although the Team's mood was one of depression.

In Monza's FOCA tests Herbert was a revelation, being tenth fastest (1 minute 27.54 seconds) on qualifiers, rekindling memories of his similar testing performance in 1988. When one considers that on race tyres Warwick was back in twentieth place (1 minute 28.46 seconds) and Donnelly was twenty-fifth (1 minute 29.14 seconds), this puts his fine performance into perspective!

Gerhard Berger sympathized with the Lotus drivers during Belgian GP practice for having to control the ill-handling Lotuses around Spa's switchbacks. In spinning to miss his stricken McLaren, Donnelly nearly eliminated Senna when a right rear wheel nut sheared and the errant wheel just missed the Brazilian's helmet! Meanwhile, Warwick was frustrated with the lack of grip. The race was quickly stopped after Mansell had been nudged into the barriers and in the aftermath Warwick collided with his team-mate. Warwick took the spare for the second start as Donnelly commentated on TV, only for the race to be stopped yet again. By this time the second Lotus was repaired and Donnelly started Belgian GP no. 3 from the pit lane to finish twelfth with a fractured exhaust, just behind his team-mate's misfiring steed. In winning, Senna equalled Clark and Lauda's previous best of twenty-five World Championship victories.

Donnelly was twelfth fastest in Monza testing (1 minute 27.32 seconds) and in official practice he improved to 1 minute 25.629 seconds. At this time, Lamborghini announced that they were withdrawing from Lotus in 1991 as the Team concentrated on testing a new Bilstein front suspension. The first lap of the race saw Warwick tigering along behind Gugelmin's Leyton House, and as the gaggle of cars pulled through the Parabolica a yellow blur was already on the grass and heading for the barriers at an acute angle – Warwick had got too close to Gugelmin and had lost grip terminally. Amidst the ensuing explosion of debris the Lotus rebounded, now upside-down, to skid along the track trailing a shower of sparks from the roll bar. Mercifully all the pack missed the inverted 102 and Warwick coolly climbed out and walked to the trackside before jogging back to the pits! There, having been cleared by a doctor, he climbed aboard the spare before taking the restart seemingly unruffled. In an amazing display of single-mindedness he raced for fifteen laps before his clutch failed, whilst Donnelly's clutch only lasted for thirteen laps. Both Warwick's courage and the strength of Dernie's Lotus 102 design would be tested to the limit again in the Spanish GP.

With the 102's front suspension once again altered for Estoril, the two drivers couldn't balance their cars and came a miserable fifteenth and twenty-first. The race was even worse as Donnelly retired when his alternator broke on lap 14 and Warwick's throttle linkage gave out after five laps.

Just as Jerez's first day's qualifying concluded, the session was abruptly halted after an aeroplane-type accident. Horrified onlookers identified the car as a Lotus from the shattered yellow debris scattered across the track. Further back was the rear of a 102B with nothing left in front of the naked fuel bags except the gear lever and its linkage where the driver should have been sitting. It transpired that the front suspension had broken, pitching Donnelly headlong into the barriers. His lonely, hunched form lay motionless on the track and, as Martini parked his Minardi to protect him, the emergency vehicles raced round and a relieved Horst Roeger found a pulse. Professional help having arrived, Prof. Syd Watkins moved the Lotus driver to the medical centre and then, once stabilized, on to hospital in Seville.

The accident had occurred at 140–160mph (225–258kph) whilst the car was in sixth gear. It has now been calculated that Donnelly survived an impact of 100g, but his peak physical fitness helped him to start to pull through after a six-week fight. By this time he had been air-lifted back from the Virgen de Rocio Hospital in Seville to the London Hospital in Whitechapel where Prof. Watkins was head of neurosurgery. Donnelly had suffered a fractured cheek-bone, collar-bone, left lower leg and thigh and a broken right leg. Whilst the 102 was devastated in the accident, it was recognized that by shattering it had dissipated an enormous amount of energy and that even though Donnelly was ejected his life had been saved by good design.

A rocker arm failure was suspected so the others were reinforced overnight. A gritty Warwick then continued practice taking an amazing tenth place around the very corners that the 102 hated. The sooner the race 'was over the better, but Warwick rose as high as sixth before retiring with gearbox failure whilst seventh. His brave efforts had helped considerably to restore Lotus's morale.

The 102s went to Japan with beefed-up front suspension but Herbert was in electrical trouble from the start before taking fifteenth place. Warwick's gearbox played up but he managed twelfth as he maintained optimism. In the race, Lotus was plagued by unreliability as Herbert retired on lap 31 when his engine blew and Warwick joined him seven laps later thanks to a failed gearbox. The unloved 102s understeered in practice at Adelaide, and a miserable season was rounded off in the Australian sun as firstly Warwick's gears and clutch dropped him back into eventual retirement and then Herbert's clutch went after a tyre stop.

Throughout 1990 the 102 had proved a let down – some would say a liability – there being insufficient resources to develop, test or replace it; fragility had led to disastrous structural failures. Financially and technically Lotus had survived on Camel sponsorship and Lamborghini engines and with both gone the future looked bleak. A disappointed Warwick left, and Donnelly would take many months to recover. With few sponsors and no drivers the end looked nigh. The Team had had the stuffing knocked out of it and the staff started leaving: Tyrrell snapped up team manager

TEAM LOTUS RESULTS 1990

Drivers:
Derek Warwick: British; Martin Donnelly: British; Johnny Herbert: British
Car:
Lotus 101 B Engine: Lamborghini 3512 V12
Lotus 102

CAR	CHASSIS	DRIVER	PRACTICE	SESSION	GRID	RACE	LAPS	%	REASON	CHAMPIONSHIP POSITION	POINTS
US GP, Phoenix – 11th March – 72 L, 169.920 miles (273.460km) (412)											
102	1	Warwick	1m 32.400s	1	22nd	R	6	8.3	Suspension	–	–
102	2	Donnelly	1m 31.650s	1	19th	DNS	0	0.0	Gearbox	–	–
101 B	1	(Spare)									
BRAZILIAN GP, Interlagos – 25th March – 71 L, 190.807 miles (307.075km) (413)											
102	2	Donnelly	1m 20.032s	1	14th	R	43	60.5	Accident	–	–
102	1	Warwick	1nr 20.998s	2	24th	R	25	35.2	Electrics	–	–
101 B	1	(Spare)									
SAN MARINO GP, Imola – 13th May – 61 L, 191.033 miles (307.440km) (414)											
102	4	Warwick	1m 26.682s	2	10th	7th	60	98.3	–	–	–
102	3	Donnelly	1m 26.714s	2	11th	8th	60	98.3	–	–	–
102	2	Spare							–	–	–
MONACO GP, Monte Carlo – 27th May – 78 L, 161.297 miles (259.584km) (415)											
102	4	Warwick	1m 23.656s	2	13th	R	66	84.6	Accident	–	–
102	3	Donnelly	1m 23.600s	2	11th	R	6	7.6	Gearbox	–	–
CANADIAN GP, Montreal – 10th June – 70 L, 190.947 miles (307.300km) (416)											
102	4	Warwick	1m 22.673s	1	11th	6th	68	97.1	–	12th=	1
102	3	Donnelly	1m 22.703s	1	12th	R	57	81.4	Engine	–	–
102	2	(Spare)									
MEXICAN GP, Mexico – 24th June – 69 L, 189.548 miles (305.049km) (417)											
102	3	Donnelly	1m 18.994s	2	12th	8th	69	100.0	–	–	–
102	4	Warwick	1m 18.951s	2	11th	10th	68	98.5	–	12th=	1
102	1	(Spare)									
FRENCH GP, Ricard – 8th July – 80 L, 189.543 miles (305.04km) (418)											
102	4	Warwick	1m 06.624s	1	16th	11th	79	98.7	–	13th=	1
102	3	Donnelly	1m 06.647s	1	17th	12th	79	98.7	–	–	–
102	5	(Spare)							–	–	–
BRITISH GP, Silverstone – 15th July – 64 L, 190.080 miles (305.904km) (419)											
102	3	Donnelly	1m 09.751s	2	14th	R	48	75.0	Engine	–	–
102	4	Warwick	1m 10.092s	2	19th	R	46	71.8	Engine	14th=	1
102	5	(Spare)									
GERMAN GP, Hockenheim – 29th July – 45 L, 190.195 miles (306.090km) (420)											
102	4	Warwick	1m 45.244s	2	16th	8th	44	97.7	–	14th=	1
102	3	Donnelly	1m 45.790s	2	20th	R	1	2.2	Clutch	–	–
102	1	(Spare)									
HUNGARIAN GP, Hungaroring – 12th August – 77 L, 189.850 miles (305.536km) (421)											
102	4	Warwick	1m 19.839s	2	11th	5th	77	100.0	–	12th	3
102	3	Donnelly	1m 20.602s	2	18th	7th	76	98.7	–	–	–
102	1	(Spare)									
BELGIAN GP, Spa – 25th August – 44 L, 189.741 miles (305.360km) (422)											
102	1	Warwick	1m 55.068s	2	18th	11th	43	97.7	–	12th	3
102	3	Donnelly	1m 55.304s	2	22nd	12th	43	97.7	–	–	–
102	5	(Spare)		SFP							
ITALIAN GP, Monza – 9th September – 53 L, 191.009 miles (307.400km) (423)											
102	1	Warwick	1m 25.677s	2	12th	R	15	28.3	Clutch	12th	3
102	3	Donnelly	1m 25.629s	2	11th	R	13	24.5	Engine	–	–
102	4	(Spare)									

PORTUGUESE GP, Estoril – 23rd September – 61 L, 164.880 miles (265.350km) (424)

102	3	Donnelly	1m 16.762s	2	15th	R	14	22.9	Electrics	–	–
102	4	Warwick	1m 17.259s	2	21st	R	5	8.1	Throttle	12th	3
102	1	(Spare)									

SPANISH GP, Jerez – 30th September – 73 L, 191.328 miles (307.914km) (425)

102	4	Warwick	1m 20.610s	2	10th	R	63	86.3	Gearbox	12th	3
102	2	Donnelly	1m 22.659s	1	–	DNS	–	–	Accident		
102	1	(Spare)									

JAPANESE GP, Suzuka – 21st October – 53 L, 192.952 miles (310.527km) (426)

102	4	Warwick	1m 41.024s	2	12th	R	38	71.6	Gearbox	14th=	3
102	2	Herbert	1m 41.448s	2	15th	R	31	58.4	Engine	–	–
102	1	(Spare)									

AUSTRALIAN GP, Adelaide – 4th November – 81 L, 190.107 miles (306.018km) (427)

102	1	Herbert	1m 19.091s	1	18th	R	57	70.3	Clutch	–	–
102	4	Warwick	1m 18.351s	2	11th	R	43	53.0	Gearbox	14th=	3
102	2	(Spare)									

Key:
SFP = Started From Pits
R = Retired
L = Laps

WORLD CHAMPIONSHIP RESULTS 1990

Position	Driver	Points
1	Ayrton Senna	78
2	Alain Prost	71
3=	Nelson Piquet	43
	Gerhard Berger	43
5	Nigel Mansell	37
6	Thierry Boutsen	34
7	Riccardo Patrese	23
8	Alessandro Nannini	21
9	Jean Alesi	13
10=	Ivan Capelli	6
	Roberto Moreno	6
	Aguri Suzuki	6
13	Eric Bernard	5
14=	**Derek Warwick**	**3**

CONSTRUCTORS' CUP 1990

Position	Constructor	Points
1	McLaren	121
2	Ferrari	110
3	Benetton	71
4	Williams	57
5	Tyrrell	16
6	Leyton House	7★
7	**Lotus-Lamborghini**	**3**

★ The Larrousse team was initially sixth but its position and points were subsequently removed by FISA

Rupert Mainwaring whilst Dernie departed to Ligier and Mike Coughlan and Steve Hallam went to Benetton and McLaren respectively.

As Christmas approached it seemed unlikely that Team Lotus would appear on a GP grid again. Indeed *Autosport*'s columnist Nigel Roebuck was moved to write: 'Is this the end of Lotus? I hope not, but fear so . . . A lot of Formula One teams you wouldn't notice by their absence. But not this one.'

CHAPTER 10

Born Again

A dank, dismal and depressing Norfolk December was forgotten when it became apparent that Lotus might just survive. Against many predictions a lifeline had been thrown just when Team Lotus appeared to be going under for the final time. The hearts of everyone with a passion for motor racing were gladdened when it was announced that the much-respected Australian Peter Collins was to head up a rescue bid along with Peter Wright and German Horst Schubel. Enrique Scalabroni would handle the technical side of Frank Coppuck's 1991 Lotus 102B. This alliance of Lotus enthusiasts earnestly desired to keep Team Lotus afloat by re-establishing its credibility, even if this had to be undertaken on a financial shoestring.

Lotus 102B

In March Julian Bailey replaced Donnelly, who was at Willi Dungl's Austrian clinic after a brief visit home for Christmas, beating both Johnny Herbert and Bernd Schneider (Schubel's suggestion) for the drive. The reigning British F3 Champion, Finn Mika Hakkinen, also joined, confident that he would benefit from being with the restructuring Team.

With only two months to prepare for racing, the 102 was modified to B specification as Judd engines were bought from Brabham and David Brabham himself set the car up. Hakkinen's familiarization took forty laps in a 101 on the redesigned Silverstone track, setting the bench-mark F1 time of 1 minute 30.70 seconds.

Hakkinen liked street circuits and was happy to début at Phoenix, where the two 102Bs displayed their new green and white colours on the tunnel-like walled track. Bailey overcame a minor hydraulic fire only for his Judd to refuse to run cleanly over 9,100rpm throughout the rest of practice; despite resorting to Hakkinen's car, he didn't qualify. Hakkinen was well in control, being thirteenth fastest on his first experience of soft qualifying tyres. His subsequent race was a high spot of the meeting as he survived a perilous moment when, characteristically hunched over the steering wheel, it came loose at 150mph! To regain his composure, and to make sure the replacement was firmly attached, Hakkinen stopped before proceeding to fight back. He impressed many until an oil union ruptured, causing a second fire. Having already avoided Blundell's spinning Brabham, the Finn made a name for himself on his GP début as a new, purposeful air permeated Team Lotus.

During Interlagos practice Hakkinen's Judd misfired and cut out so much that he looked in danger of non-qualifying, but when a broken injector trumpet was

Mika Hakkinen was the regular Lotus 102B driver in 1991 in the hastily prepared Judd-engined machine. The 'new' Lotus organization was finding its feet, but at Imola the Finnish driver – a protege of Keke Rosberg – did well to finish fifth.

replaced, he managed to rise to twenty-second fastest. Both electrical problems and a fire dogged Bailey's efforts after he had been the quicker of the two in the wet first practice. He subsequently failed to qualify again in the tense eight minutes left to him of the second session, after yet another fire and suspension troubles. Hakkinen raced to ninth place – taking ninth fastest lap too – shadowing the McLaren of winner Senna towards the end. The Finn had taken things easily in a car that handled much better than he had expected, but the physical endurance required had surprised him.

Martin Donnelly, following a visit from Niki Lauda at Dungl's Austrian clinic, married Diane McWhirter in Norfolk and kept his promise to walk unaided down the church's aisle.

In the break before the San Marino GP Lotus tested at Imola and, whilst both drivers were present, only Bailey actually drove for 113 laps. He achieved the twenty-second fastest time (1 minute 30.438 seconds) despite electrical and fuel-pressure difficulties.

The Imola meeting was tragically marred by an accident when Lotus mechanic David Jacques fell through a skylight at the Team's hotel. He later died in a Bologna hospital but his parents encouraged Lotus to compete rather than withdraw; both drivers wore black armbands for the rest of the weekend. The Team recovered from this setback, and on the track the San Marino race was to be a much-needed tonic after early qualifying concern. The 102B's balance set-up had to be radically altered to cure front suspension-induced understeer, and this set-up gamble squeezed the Lotuses on to the back of the grid. In the wet Saturday practice Bailey was consistently second fastest and Hakkinen was third fastest in free practice, so optimism predominated as Lotus prayed for race day rain. The deluge just before the start delighted the drivers, but Bailey had sticking gears and he accidentally selected first, causing him to spin at the Acque Minerale. He stopped twice, once because of his brakes and secondly because of over-heating, and actually overtook Hakkinen four times, only for the Finn to repass when it mattered. The Finn had had no clutch from lap 14 on but he still fought over sixth place with Bailey until the final lap, when Van de Poele retired, handing Lotus fifth and sixth place and the first points of the season.

Monaco was not so good, as Bailey missed qualifying by two seconds, having struck the perilous barriers, in both cars, and spun spectacularly at Ste Devote too. The cars were extremely difficult to set up and Hakkinen scraped into the race last, having tried a variety of wings, and cured gearbox and throttle maladies. In the race he circulated impressively behind Gachot and Bernard during their ninth-placed fight. Hakkinen was

quicker than the other two – setting the tenth fastest lap of the race (1 minute 26.627 seconds) – before he was sidelined by a loose oil pipe that sprayed lubricant on to his exhaust, causing a fire; he then retired on lap 64. Even though Senna won, Hakkinen's talent had not gone unnoticed.

Before Canada Bailey was replaced by Johnny Herbert, whose Japanese F3000 exploits seemed likely to lure a Japanese sponsor to Lotus. Herbert was initially seventeenth fastest in Montreal, but was then afflicted by gear selection problems on his own car and an ill-handling spare and he unexpectedly non-qualified. Against the rules, his qualifying tyres were retrieved and a $5,000 fine was thus incurred! Hakkinen was twenty-fourth fastest, coping with both oversteer and understeer on a new track with a faster team-mate! Sadly his rise through the field to sixteenth place in the race ended on lap 21 when he leaped across a sand-trap in a vain passing manoeuvre, damaging his rear suspension and retiring. Mansell's dominant Williams also ground to a halt within sight of the flag.

The Team left Montreal to visit General Motors' Michigan Black Lake testing facility to undertake attitude measurement tests. Hakkinen was very encouraged by the results as rumours persisted that an Isuzu (a GM subsidiary) inspired engine was on the cards for 1992.

In Mexico both Lotuses just qualified with the drivers beset by balance problems and Hakkinen suffering a dodgy clutch; a hindrance that continued in the race. It gave out on him after thirty laps during a fight with Boutsen's Ligier, and the tired and aching Finn eventually finished ninth. Herbert was immediately behind, having twice been pushed off the circuit by other thoughtless drivers; as a consequence his 'dirty' tyres stopped him from attacking his team-mate.

After Mexico Herbert won the Le Mans 24-hour race in a Mazda 787B shared with Bertrand Gachot and Volker Weidler. Without respite he spent the following day testing at Silverstone and notched up a time of 1 minute 26.96 seconds, which was faster than Senna's 1 minute 27.43 seconds. Donnelly was there egging everyone on, appearing in a F1 pit lane for the first time since his accident.

President Mitterand's new French circuit of Magny-Cours then hosted its first GP; in the over-crowded pit road Lotus mechanic Peter Vale broke his ankle on the Friday after being struck by Morbidelli's Minardi. On the circuit Herbert liked his 102B's brakes but the Team ran out of time setting his downforce and therefore knew that he could have done better than his eventual twentieth-fastest time. Clutch trouble stopped Hakkinen from qualifying. Just as the Finn was using his second set of qualifiers, Olivier Grouillard spread oil all over the track's racing line and Hakkinen's chances evaporated as arch-rival J.J. Lehto snapped up the final grid placing. Lack of gears let Herbert down at the start and he got away last. The Le Mans winner then proved his mettle by disposing of drivers such as Alboreto, Blundell and Brundle with apparent ease. His plan was to keep going on his Goodyear C tyres without a pitstop; this strategy, combined with his driving talent, earned him a meritorious tenth place at the flag.

For his first British GP Herbert was just quicker than Hakkinen at the end of the Mansell-dominated Silverstone practice sessions, but a spate of problems kept the two Lotuses at the back of the grid. Oil surge claimed one of Hakkinen's Judds and both drivers found the circuit very slippery. Herbert's Judd holed a piston as the two drivers bemoaned the lack of power. The huge crowd of Mansell disciples (Nigosi!) cheered as their hero raced off into the distance in his Williams FW14 while Herbert, the second of only four British drivers, benefited from the surge of patriotism too. Hakkinen spun at Club on lap 29, but finished twelfth, sitting on several painful gravel stones! Herbert drove strongly and should have finished ninth – the position he took on lap 48 following a long battle with Martini's Minardi. He actually finished fourteenth as oil starvation forced him to slow up and switch off.

Engines were the centre of press attention after Peter Collins revealed that for 1992 either a V10 or a V12 would be used from one of two European sources or from Japan. The contenders were rumoured to be Judd, Lamborghini and Isuzu.

Young German driver Michael Bartels ran in the German, Hungarian, Italian and Spanish events whilst Herbert was away racing F3000 in Japan. It was hoped that his experience of Hockenheim would be particularly useful, and he was the centre of enormous pre-event hype when, in the circuit's mid-July testing, he was nineteenth fastest. At this time Lotus also purchased Williams's one-quarter scale wind-tunnel in which to develop the forthcoming 107 design. Benetton's former chief mechanic Nigel Stepney rejoined Lotus – having last worked with Lotus alongside Collins and De Angelis – as former chief mechanic, Richard Taylor, left.

Bartels surprisingly did not qualify at Hockenheim as a result of an untimely puncture, amongst other problems. Engine failures were frequent for Hakkinen, who also managed to crash heavily at the first corner on his first flying lap, severely damaging the spare. In the race he went wide at the Ostkurve chicane, a marker cone having to be removed in a pitstop, and he retired just before half distance when his Judd gave out.

Lotus 102C

In the break before Hungary, Scalabroni left the Team as part of 'the continued restructuring of Lotus'. His last task before leaving had been to adapt a 102 chassis to C specification as a test-bed for an Isuzu V12 F1 engine; Hakkinen ran the car at Hethel and also for two days at Silverstone, where the power plant proved most reliable. Informed sources still insisted that Judd engines would continue to be utilized in 1992.

Hungary was very similar to Hockenheim in that Bartels again non-qualified; this time his car suffered from low fuel pressure and bad balance. Hakkinen scraped into last place on the grid; in the GP itself his performance improved as his car lightened and he finished fourteenth, having at one stage recorded lap times faster than the leading McLaren and Williams after a tyre stop on lap 38.

Lack of engines meant that the Team was unable to attend the FOCA test session at Monza and the next appearance was therefore to be the Belgian GP. Herbert returned to his favourite power circuit of Spa and managed to get as high as nineteenth – one place behind his team mate – before slipping to twenty-first. In the race he came home a steady seventh, having been unable to communicate an intended pitstop for fresh tyres when his radio failed. Hakkinen meanwhile had huge engine blow-ups both in practice and in the race. Both drivers needed more top-end speed and less understeer at Spa.

Monza again required top-end speed and from the start of practice Lotus's cars languished at the back of the grid despite all their drivers' skill. Spa's high-speed set-up couldn't be replicated at Monza and neither Bartels nor Hakkinen could qualify in the first session. All rested on second practice, when the young German was unlucky enough to be held up by a Lola on his fast lap and was thus knocked out. By contrast, Hakkinen, on his first-ever visit to the Italian track, took the spare to twenty-fifth on the grid and in the race, whilst coping with a misfire, drove steadily if disappointedly through to an eventual fourteenth place at the flag.

Portuguese practice seemed destined to be a disaster for Hakkinen until literally the last moment. Initially he was only twenty-eighth fastest in his gripless 102B but he then just squeezed into last place as Herbert used the spare to qualify twenty-second. The latter completed just one race lap before his Judd blew spectacularly as he passed the pits. Hakkinen plugged on for the second successive race to a fourteenth-place finish, three laps behind the leaders, having suffered from the G-forces on Estoril's constant-radius corners and regretting that he had refused a helmet-brace.

At the new Spanish Circuit de Catalunya, Bartels

TEAM LOTUS RESULTS 1991

Drivers:
Mika Hakkinen: Finnish; Julian Bailey: British; Johnny Herbert: British; Michael Bartels: German
Car:
Lotus 102 B Engine: Judd V8

CAR	CHASSIS	DRIVER	PRACTICE	SESSION	GRID	RACE	LAPS	%	REASON	CHAMPIONSHIP POSITION	POINTS
US GP, Phoenix – 10th March – 81 L, 184.68 miles (297.10km) (428)											
102 B	1	Hakkinen	1m 25.488s	2	13th	R	59	72.8	Fire	–	–
102 B	2	Bailey	1m 28.570s	2	DNQ	–	–	–	–	–	–
BRAZILIAN GP, Interlagos – 24th March – 71 L, 190.777 miles (307.00km) (429)											
102 B	2	Hakkinen	1m 20.611s	2	22nd	9th	68	95.7	–	–	–
102 B	1	Bailey	1m 23.590s	2	DNQ	–	–	–	–	–	–
SAN MARINO GP, Imola – 28th April – 61 L, 191.052 miles (307.46km) (430)											
102 B	3	Hakkinen	1m 27.432s	1	25th	5th	58	95.0	–	9th=	2
102 B	2	Bailey	1m 27.976s	1	26th	6th	58	95.0	–	11th=	
102 B	1	(Spare)									
MONACO GP, Monte Carlo – 12th May – 78 L, 161.297 miles (259.57km) (431)											
102 B	3	Hakkinen	1m 24.829s	2	26th	R	64	82.0	Oil fire	12th=	2
102 B	2	Bailey	1m 26.995s	2	DNQ	–	–	–	–	14th=	1
102 B	1	(Spare)									
CANADIAN GP, Montreal – 2nd June – 69 L, 189.957 miles (305.69km) (432)											
102 B	3	Hakkinen	1m 29.932s	2	24th	R	21	30.4	Spun off	13th=	2
102 B	2	Herbert	1m 24.732s	2	DNQ	–	–	–	–	–	–
102 B	1	(Spare)									
MEXICAN GP, Mexico – 16th June – 67 L, 184.049 miles (296.19km) (433)											
102 B	3	Hakkinen	1m 20.823s	1	24th	9th	65	97.0	–	13th=	2
102 B	2	Herbert	1m 20.830s	1	25th	10th	65	97.0	–	–	–
102 B	1	(Spare)									
FRENCH GP, Magny-Cours – 7th July – 72 L, 191.078 miles (307.50km) (434)											
102 B	2	Herbert	1m 18.185s	2	20th	10th	70	97.2	–	–	–
102 B	3	Hakkinen	1m 19.491s	2	DNQ	–	–	–	–	13th=	2
102 B	1	(Spare)									
BRITISH GP, Silverstone – 14th July – 59 L, 191.573 miles (308.31km) (435)											
102 B	3	Hakkinen	1m 25.872s	2	25th	12th	57	96.6	–	14th=	2
102 B	2	Herbert	1m 25.689s	2	24th	14th	55	93.2	–	–	–
102 B	1	(Spare)									
GERMAN GP, Hockenheim – 28th July – 45 L, 190.180 miles (306.06km) (436)											
102 B	3	Hakkinen	1m 42.726s	2	23rd	R	19	42.2	Engine	14th=	2
102 B	2	Bartels	1m 43.624s	2	DNQ	–	–	–	–	–	–
102 B	1	(Spare)									
HUNGARIAN GP, Hungaroring – 11th August – 77 L, 189.805 miles (305.46km) (437)											
102 B	3	Hakkinen	1m 22.355s	2	26th	14th	74	96.1	–	14th=	2
102 B	2	Bartels	1m 23.248s	2	DNQ	–	–	–	–	–	–
102 B	1	(Spare)									
BELGIAN GP, Spa – 25th August – 44 L, 189.742 miles (305.36km) (438)											
102 B	2	Herbert	1m 53.361s	2	21st	7th	44	100.0	–	–	–
102 B	3	Hakkinen	1m 53.799s	2	24th	R	25	56.8	Engine	14th=	2
102 B	1	(Spare)									
ITALIAN GP, Monza – 8th September – 53 L, 191.009 miles (307.400km) (439)											
102 B	3	Hakkinen	1m 25.941s	2	25th	14th	49	92.4	–	14th=	2
102 B	2	Bartels	1m 26.828s	2	DNQ	–	–	–	–	–	–
102 B	1	(Spare)									
PORTUGUESE GP, Estoril – 22nd September – 71 L, 191.913 miles (308.84km) (440)											
102 B	3	Hakkinen	1m 17.714s	2	26th	14th	68	95.7	–	14th	2
102 B	2	Herbert	1m 17.015s	2	22nd	R	1	1.4	Engine	–	–
102 B	1	(Spare)									

SPANISH GP, Barcelona – 29th September – 65 L, 191.750 miles (308.56km) (441)											
102 B	3	Hakkinen	1m 22.646s	1	21st	R	5	7.7	Accident	15th=	2
102 B	2	Bartels	1m 25.392s	2	DNQ	–	–	–	–	–	–
102 B	1	(Spare)									
JAPANESE GP, Suzuka – 20th October – 53 L, 193.117 miles (310.78km) (442)											
102 B	2	Herbert	1m 40.170s	2	23rd	R	32	60.3	Electrical	–	–
102 B	3	Hakkinen	1m 40.024s	2	21st	R	5	9.4	Accident	15th=	2
102 B	1	(Spare)									
AUSTRALIAN GP, Adelaide – 3rd November – 14 L, 32.882 miles (54.53km) (443)											
102 B	2	Herbert	1m 18.091s	2	21st	11th	14	100.0	–	–	–
102 B	3	Hakkinen	1m 18.271s	2	25th	19th	13	92.8	–	15th=	2

Key:
DNQ = Did Not Qualify
R   = Retired
L   = Laps

missed the first exploratory day because of a lack of engines and then crashed heavily on the Friday, failing to qualify. Hakkinen, by contrast, was initially ninth fastest before striking a wall hard. He ended up twenty-first on the grid and was a superb tenth in the eventful race when he incurred a rear wheel puncture after Alboreto punted him into a wall on lap 5; he had once again shown his class. Against all odds Mansell won the race, with Senna only fifth.

Leyton House's Chris Murphy joined Lotus as chief designer and took on the responsibility for the forthcoming 107 design. He was soon to be joined by two other former Leyton House employees, Jean-Claude Martens (wind-tunnel modelling) and Tim Robathan.

The long trek to Japan, where F1 fever was on the ascendancy, was rewarded by a number of additional home-country sponsors in the form of Yellow Hat, Phenix and Nichibutsu. Racing on a circuit he knew particularly well from his Japanese F3000 exploits, Herbert started his weekend off in excellent form with an eleventh-fastest time and then a fifteenth; he was full of praise for the alterations that had been made to the rear suspension geometry. He was to fall to twenty-third as a low wing experiment failed and when the others learned the circuit, but the omens were good. Hakkinen went off into the sand at one point in practice but ended up a confident twenty-first. Sadly, on the day Mansell finally lost the Championship to Senna, Hakkinen was to last only five laps before he spun off again, suffering a momentary fire. Herbert went well after a superb start to rise as high as eleventh before a loose lead cut his engine out after thirty-two laps.

In Adelaide's final race of the year Herbert was initially fifteenth fastest in the Australian sunshine only to fall back with grip problems, finishing up twenty-first whilst Hakkinen was twenty-fifth. The Finn had side-

WORLD CHAMPIONSHIP RESULTS 1991

Position	Driver	Points
1	Ayrton Senna	96
2	Nigel Mansell	72
3	Riccardo Patrese	53
4	Gerhard Berger	43
5	Alain Prost	34
6	Nelson Piquet	26.5
7	Jean Alesi	21
8	Stefano Modena	10
9	Andrea De Cesaris	9
10	Roberto Moreno	8
11	Pierluigi Martini	6
12=	JJ Lehto	4
	Bertrand Gachot	4
	Michael Schumacher	4
15=	**Mika Hakkinen**	**2**
	Martin Brundel	2
	Satoru Nakajima	2
18	**Julian Bailey**	**1**
	Aguri Suzuki	1
	Emanuele Pirro	1
	Eric Bernard	1
	Ivan Capelli	1
	Mark Blundell	1

CONSTRUCTORS' CUP 1991

Position	Constructor	Points
1	McLaren-Honda	139
2	Williams-Renault	125
3	Ferrari	55.5
4	Benetton-Ford	38.5
5	Jordan-Ford	13
6	Tyrrell-Honda	12
7	Minardi-Ferrari	6
8	BMS Dallara-Judd	5
9	**Lotus-Judd**	**3**
	Brabham-Yamaha	3

swiped a wall and aviated over one of the chicane kerbs as he learned the circuit. In the inclement race, which was stopped early because of the downpour that flooded the track and the fact that Mansell's Williams was stuck in a wall, Herbert finished an impressive, although soaked, eleventh. Hakkinen was back in nineteenth on a day when nobody would have blamed the drivers if they had decided not to race at all.

1992

Lotus 102D

For 1992 it was announced that Ford would be supplying the Team's engines again, and from the start of practice on the 'new' Kyalami circuit, Herbert was extremely pleased with the performance of his Ford HB V8 in what was essentially a two-year-old chassis. He found himself a fine eleventh fastest, whilst Hakkinen was plagued with a difficult gearbox and an engine he pushed too hard; he was an unhappy twenty-first. He was to race the spare when his 102D developed an oil leak. For sixty laps of the South African GP Herbert kept the Ligiers of Comas and Boutsen – and after the latter retired for eleven laps just Comas – at bay in a fantastic drive. Towards the end he pulled away from Senna, who was on his way to third. Herbert's sixth place was widely acclaimed and the British driver became a desirable property immediately. Hakkinen took ninth in a car with gear troubles, but all in all Lotus had started the season well.

Polluted Mexico City boasted the rougher than normal Circuit Hermanos Rodriguez, which caught Senna out in practice, hurling his McLaren into a wall. The Peraltdata corner, altered since Senna's practice accident in 1991, proved very difficult for Herbert, who took twelfth on the grid; Hakkinen was back in eighteenth after blowing a Ford engine. The race start was chaotic, with Herbert spinning at the first corner before driving from a lowly twenty-first place back to seventh sixty-nine laps later, once again earning praise for his determination. Hakkinen made a superb start but was soon stuck behind Alesi's smoking Ferrari, which made it hard for him to see. When the former dropped by the wayside on lap 31, the Finn climbed up to sixth place, taking that final championship point. Lotus had now been in the points for two successive 1992 races.

After Mexico, sponsorship guru Guy Edwards joined Lotus to head up the marketing department, with a target of £50m for the next three seasons!

From the high altitude of the first two races it was down to sea level at Sao Paulo's Interlagos circuit. Down to earth it was literally, as Herbert had to use a

kamikaze lap to just qualify last on the grid! Both he and Hakkinen, who was two places ahead, had suffered from a severe lack of grip. Herbert made a storming start and climbed from last to eighteenth on the first lap alone! He continued upwards to seventh until he became the innocent victim of a coming together between the Ligiers of Boutsen and Comas at the end of the pit straight. As the two French cars bounced each other off the pit's wall, Herbert was pushed on to the gravel-trap on the outside of the first corner, from where he was unable to get going again; this was a poor reward for another dogged drive. Hakkinen, too, had got as high as eighth only for his gearbox to give out, and he had to settle for tenth at the flag.

The 107 was launched in Spain but the 102Ds continued as the Team's spearhead, with Imola being the new car's intended début venue. Lack of grip again blighted Lotus in Barcelona; Hakkinen was being thirtieth after the first session as his clutch played up, but he improved to twenty-first. Herbert made a mistake in the first qualifying session, in which he spun at the Wurth corner. In the spare he just scraped on to the back of the grid. Hakkinen made a superb start in the damp race picking up seven places on the first lap, and he was running in twelfth when he tangled with Alesi's overtaking Ferrari on lap 40. Afterwards he returned to twelfth place only to spin and retire seventeen laps later. Herbert only lasted for fourteen laps before spinning into retirement, thanks to a stalled engine.

Lotus 107

The drivers went straight to Imola to test the 107 after Olivier Beretta had shaken it down at Hethel. The 107 was the product of the combined work of Peter Wright (technical director), Chris Murphy (chief designer), John Davis (head of research), Jean-Paul Gousset, Jean-Claude Martens, Tim Robotham and Peter Weston. It featured a new, simple 'semi-active' suspension system, which used Cranfield Group electronics to control conventional springs and dampers. The cars were intended to go 'fully active' by season's end, with both traction control and an automatic gearbox under development. A standard gear change was used initially with Weston's lightweight box. The car had significantly better rigidity and aerodynamics than the 102 and the Ford HB engine was particularly neatly packaged.

In Imola testing, Herbert was happy to record 1 minute 26.686 seconds in the 107 despite some minor oil leaks, against Hakkinen's 1 minute 27.595 seconds in the 102D. At Misano, Hakkinen then ran the 107 for twenty-five laps before buzzing an engine, and unfortunately gearbox trouble didn't reveal itself until

As more sponsors gradually appeared, the Lotus 107 was run in 1992, boasting a 'simple' active-suspension system. Here Herbert leads Hakkinen with the former's best result being sixth in Canada and the latter's being sixth in Japan.

official Imola practice. As Mansell's Williams dominated the San Marino meeting, the 107's fuel pressure and transmission played up. The 102Ds circulated, as engineering attention was lavished on the 107, but Herbert qualified last and Hakkinen didn't qualify at all. The 107 was tenth fastest in the warm-up so the Team decided to race the new car, but Wendlinger broke its steering in a first-lap collision. After a lengthy stop, Herbert only completed eight laps before the transmission failed again.

Before Monaco, Lotus tested the 107 at Paul Ricard whilst the second chassis was run in by Beretta at Hethel. In Monte Carlo Herbert's 107 understeered after problems with the active suspension's computer. Third gear played up, and then first gear, but he still took ninth! He copied Hakkinen's settings for the race but crashed heavily on lap 18, leaving Lotus temporarily with a singleton 107. Hakkinen's 107 arrived during practice after he had found that the 102D coped well with the bumps. Having locked a wheel and hit the Rascasse barriers he then crashed at the Casino, and was ordered to go easy for the rest of practice as 107 spares were dwindling! He finished up fourteenth in an imperfect car. During the race he felt very uncomfortable as he pressurized Alboreto's Footwork, only for his clutch to fail, causing the gearbox to give out in sympathy on lap 30 at Ste Devote.

Montreal boosted morale with the 107s sixth and tenth on the grid, which were Lotus's highest grid positions since 1988. Herbert liked the third chassis in practice and kept ahead of the Ferraris until a gearbox problem intervened; meanwhile, a lead dropping off spoiled Hakkinen's time. At the start Brundle and Herbert jousted before Hakkinen caught up to shadow the

leading bunch of eight cars. When Mansell fell off on lap 15, Herbert and Hakkinen were promoted to sixth and seventh, but the former's gearbox was already weakening and his clutch failed on lap 35. A lap later Hakkinen's gearbox let him down, too, but it was felt that a podium finish was getting closer.

During Silverstone tyre-testing, Herbert was fourteenth fastest (1 minute 25.96 seconds) and Hakkinen nineteenth (1 minute 27.09 seconds) amidst rumours that Guy Edwards would soon announce a major sponsor, such as Castrol or Budweiser.

Active-suspension hydraulic troubles meant that Hakkinen's 107 was shared for much of Magny-Cours practice. Herbert couldn't adjust, having a big spin, whilst an inspired Hakkinen was eleventh fastest with the passive set-up. In the warm-up, the two Lotuses were fourth and fifth, but the French GP became another Mansell demonstration before the race was stopped after eighteen laps when the heavens opened. Hakkinen and Herbert, running at the time in fifth and eighth, restarted in these positions. Hakkinen subsequently finished fourth on the road but was just pipped on combined times by Comas's Ligier. Hakkinen's Ford engine had pulled him right up behind the Ligier in the final few laps. The understeering Herbert was sixth before the rain returned at race's end. Sadly, mechanic Andy Fulford had had his foot broken in the pits and John Miles collapsed through exhaustion, although both quickly recovered. The French lorry drivers' blockade was outwitted as Lotus's transporter returned via Dunkirk for Silverstone the following weekend.

Before the British GP, Castrol was announced as Lotus's new sponsor and they financed full development of the 107. Four cars were fielded at Silverstone with Dirt Devil, the car vacuum-cleaner manufacturer, providing sponsorship too. Seventh (Herbert) and ninth (Hakkinen) fastest, the former bent his right front top wishbone during a Luffield spin. Hakkinen was booked for dangerous driving on his way to the track on race day and missed the warm-up; Herbert had to prepare his car. An annoyed Hakkinen tackled Alesi's Ferrari for sixteen laps and forced past on lap 20. He had climbed to fifth by lap 34, but Schumacher (Benetton) and Berger (McLaren) got past on lap 48 as he stopped for tyres. Herbert had run strongly in sixth, wisely conserving his tyres, but retired on lap 31 when his gearbox's clutch release bearing failed.

Lotus next visited Brands Hatch's FF1600 Silver Jubilee meeting and Herbert broke the late Paul Warwick's Indy circuit lap record with a time of 36.67 seconds in the 102D.

At Hockenheim, Herbert's 107 was uncontrollable on the straights, and he reverted to the understeering spare after a huge spin exiting the third chicane. With a modified front wing he was eleventh fastest whilst Hakkinen (thirteenth) believed his straight line problem was caused by mismatched Goodyears. The German GP saw Mansell win for the eighth time, whilst both Lotuses retired simultaneously when their series V Ford HBs expired with low fuel pressure. The two Lotus drivers had briefly fought with each other before Herbert's engine lost power and Hakkinen was then left to chase Boutsen's Ligier. Herbert stopped for tyres on lap 13 and then harried Alboreto's ninth-placed Footwork, only to have his engine fail as he exited the Ostkurve. Hakkinen changed tyres on lap 15 but his engine cut out too six laps later.

In Hungary practice Herbert just avoided Suzuki's spinning Footwork; Mansell then arrived at full chat only to swipe the barriers in avoidance. On the race's first lap Herbert couldn't avoid Comas's spinning Ligier, which had just struck the second Ligier! Hakkinen set an early fastest lap before fighting with the Benettons. He passed Brundle but spun when his engine died on the final lap still, though, retaining a fine fourth place, putting him on several teams' shopping lists. Senna won the race but Mansell finished second, guaranteeing him the World Championship.

In Spa practice Hakkinen attacked Blanchimont in sixth gear in the wet! He was sixth at the end of the race's first lap and got up to fourth before he changed to wets as the weather deteriorated. He held fifth, but stopped again for slicks on lap 32, when he was only overtaken by Senna's McLaren with two laps to go. Herbert suffered an engine fire in the race day warm-up but he was soon up to sixth in the race, only to drop back to eleventh after a tyre stop on lap 7. He fought back up again to sixth but lost his engine with three laps to go after another tyre stop. Whilst Benetton driver Schumacher won his first GP, the two Lotuses set fourth and fifth fastest race laps on lap 42!

Both Lotuses retired early in the Italian GP at Monza. Hakkinen, whose steering wheel loosened during practice, retired from seventh place after only five laps. Herbert was next, after eighteen laps, when his power plant failed as he was sixth on the road. He had endured engine problems all weekend. At Monza Hakkinen apparently signed a contract for another year with Lotus.

Herbert retired early again at Estoril when his steering was terminally damaged during some wheel-banging on the opening lap. Hakkinen performed superbly to finish sixth. The Finn had qualified a fine seventh, and having dodged Schumacher's stranded Benetton on the grid, he had fought off Brundle. The new World Champion won for Williams and Patrese emulated him, winning in Japan.

The 107 was more competitive but less reliable than the Benettons at Suzuka; excellent in the fast corners, its straight-line speed was problematical. In the race Schumacher held up the fourth- and fifth-placed Lotuses, but shortly after the German's gearbox failed Herbert went the same way. Hakkinen continued, to charge through to a fighting fourth on lap 44 only for his engine to let him down, forcing him to pull off.

Adelaide's finale saw thirty-three-year-old 1987 500cc motorcycle World Champion Wayne Gardner undertake some 107 demonstration laps, thoroughly enjoying himself. In qualifying, Herbert spun three times on the slippery track hitting the wall mightily at one point. Hakkinen trapped his feet in the pedals and only just avoided another hefty collision after flying over a kerb! The Lotus twins were tenth and twelfth fastest. Berger won the race for McLaren as Hakkinen spun from ninth place down to twentieth in a confusion with Suzuki (Footwork), Andrea de Cesaris (Tyrrell) and Schumacher (Benetton). Hakkinen pushed on to seventh place at the flag after Herbert was the innocent victim of a first-lap contretemps with Grouillard's Tyrrell. He could only salvage thirteenth place at the end as three laps in the pits dropped him back.

Herbert's promising season had been affected too many times by the crashing Ligiers of Comas and Boutsen as well as by mechanical unreliability. The Team still hadn't possessed a sufficiently large budget to permit regular testing and had suffered as the car had to be developed at race meetings.

Lotus 107B

The 107B was really a derivative of Chris Murphy's previous chassis, possessing as it did the only 'real active

TEAM LOTUS RESULTS 1992

Drivers:
Mika Hakkinen: Finnish; Johnny Herbert: British
Car:
Lotus 102 D and Lotus 107 Engine: Ford HB v8

CAR	CHASSIS	DRIVER	PRACTICE	SESSION	GRID	RACE	LAPS	%	REASON	CHAMPIONSHIP POSITION	POINTS
S AFRICAN GP, Kyalami – 1st March – 72 L, 191.727 miles (308.55km) (444)											
102 D	2	Herbert	1m 18.626s	2	11th	6th	71	98.6	–	6th	1
102 D	3	Hakkinen	1m 19.672s	1	21st	9th	70	97.2	–	–	–
102 D	1	(Spare)									
MEXICAN GP, Mexico City – 22nd March – 69 L, 189.543 miles (305.03km) (445)											
102 D	3	Hakkinen	1m 20.145s	1	18th	6th	68	98.5	–	7th=	1
102 D	1	Herbert	1m 19.509s	2	12th	7th	68	98.5	–	7th=	1
102 D	2	(Spare)									
BRAZILIAN GP, Interlagos – 5th April – 71 L, 190.807 miles (307.06km) (446)											
102 D	3	Hakkinen	1m 20.577s	1	24th	10th	67	94.4	–	9th=	1
102 D	1	Herbert	1m 20.650s	2	26th	R	36	50.7	Accident	9th=	1
102 D	2	(Spare)									
SPANISH GP, Barcelona – 3rd May – 65 L, 191.681 miles (308.47km) (447)											
102 D	3	Hakkinen	1m 25.202s	1	21st	R	56	86.1	Accident	10th=	1
102 D	1	Herbert	1m 25.786s	1	26th	R	13	20	Accident	10th=	1
102 D	2	(Spare)									
SAN MARINO GP, Imola – 17th May – 60 L, 187.920 miles (302.42km) (448)											
107	1	Herbert	1m 27.270s★	1	26th	R	8	13.3	Accident	12th=	1
102 D	3	Hakkinen	1m 27.437s	1	DNQ	–	–	–	–	12th=	1
102 D	2	Spare									
102 D	1	(Spare)									
MONACO GP, Monte Carlo – 31st May – 78 L, 161.298 miles (259.584km) (449)											
107	2	Hakkinen	1m 22.886s★★	2	14th	R	30	38.5	Gearbox	12th=	1
107	1	Herbert	1m 22.579s	2	9th	R	17	21.8	Accident	12th=	1
102 D	2	(Spare)									
102 D	1	(Spare)									
CANADIAN GP, Montreal – 14th June – 69 L, 189.934 miles (305.670km) (450)											
107	1	Herbert	1m 21.645s	1	6th	R	35	50.7	Clutch	13th=	1
107	2	Hakkinen	1m 22.360s	1	10th	R	36	52.2	Gears	13th=	1
102 D	2	(Spare)									
FRENCH GP, Magny-Cours – 5th July – 69 L, 183.126 miles (294.70km) (451)											
107	1	Hakkinen	1m 17.257s	2	12th	4th	68	98.5	–	9th=	4
107	2	Herbert	1m 16.999s	2	11th	6th	68	98.5	–	13th=	2
102 D	2	(Spare)									
BRITISH GP, Silverstone – 12th July – 59 L, 191.589 miles (308.334km) (452)											
107	2	Hakkinen	1m 23.813s	1	9th	6th	59	100.0	–	8th=	5
107	1	Herbert	1m 23.605s	1	7th	R	31	52.5	Gearbox	13th=	2
102 D	3	(Spare)									
GERMAN GP, Hockenheim – 26th July – 45 L, 190.181 miles (306.067km) (453)											
107	1	Herbert	1m 42.645s	2	11th	R	23	51.1	Engine	13th=	2
107	2	Hakkinen	1m 42.749s	2	13th	R	21	46.6	Engine	8th=	5
107	3	(Spare)									
HUNGARIAN GP, Hungaroring – 16th August – 77 L, 189.850 miles (305.536km) (454)											
107	2	Hakkinen	1m 19.587s	1	16th	4th	77	100.0	–	8th	8
107	1	Herbert	1m 19.143s	2	13th	R	0	0.0	Accident	14th=	2
107	3	(Spare)									
BELGIAN GP, Spa – 30th August – 44 L, 189.741 miles (305.360km) (455)											
107	2	Hakkinen	1m 54.812s	1	8th	6th	44	100.0	–	8th	9
107	1	Herbert	1m 55.027s	1	10th	13th NR	42	95.4	Engine	14th	2
107	3	(Spare)									

ITALIAN GP, Monza – 13th September – 53 L, 191.009 miles (307.400km) (456)

Model	No.	Driver									
107	1	Herbert	1m 25.140s	2	13th	R	18	33.9	Engine	14th=	2
107	2	Hakkinen	1m 24.807s	2	11th	R	5	9.4s	Engine	8th	9
107	3	(Spare)									

PORTUGUESE GP, Estoril – 27th September – 71 L, 191.91 miles (308.85km) (457)

Model	No.	Driver									
107	4	Hakkinen	1m 16.173s	1	7th	5th	70	98.6	–	8th	11
107	3	Herbert	1m 16.628s	2	9th	R	2	2.8	Accident	14th	2
107	2	(Spare)									

JAPANESE GP, Suzuka – 25th October – 53 L, 193.117 miles (310.792km) (458)

Model	No.	Driver									
107	4	Hakkinen	1m 41.415s	1	6th	R	44	83.0	Engine	8th	11
107	3	Herbert	1m 41.030s	1	7th	R	15	28.3s	Diff	14th=	2
107	2	(Spare)									

AUSTRALIAN GP, Adelaide – 8th November – 81 L, 290.269 miles (306.180km) (459)

Model	No.	Driver									
107	4	Hakkinen	1m 16.863s	1	10th	7th	80	98.7	–	8th	11
107	3	Herbert	1m 16.944s	1	12th	13th	77	95.1	–	14th=	2
107	2	(Spare)									

Key:
★   = time set in 102 D
★★ = time set in 102 D/2
NR = not running
DNQ = Did Not Qualify
R   = Retired
L   = Laps

suspension in F1'; it had neither conventional springs nor dampers. This proved particularly innovative during pitstops when the car lowered itself on to a special tray and raised its own wheels off the ground! Wright referred to the car as the model that the Team had wanted to build ever since the new management had taken over. An early season problem, though, would be that the new wings were ineffectual.

In the third season for the rejuvenated Team another element of the jigsaw slotted into place when Peter Hall became a director of Team Lotus. He had competed in the British Touring Car Championship and was also chairman of the ICS Group. 1993 witnessed not only a new sponsor in the form of Loctite but also increased budgets from both Hitachi and Castrol. Air UK were to fly Team personnel to races too.

In December Herbert had won the Bologna Motor Show F1 knockout pursuit with his 107, before visiting Paul Ricard, where he was fourth fastest (1 minute 04.35 seconds) in the 107B. He suffered two component-damaging accidents but still managed three and a half GP distances!

WORLD CHAMPIONSHIP RESULTS 1992

Position	Driver	Points
1	Nigel Mansell	108
2	Ricardo Patrese	56
3	Michael Schumacher	53
4	Ayrton Senna	50
5	Gerhard Berger	49
6	Martin Brundle	38
7	Jean Alesi	18
8	**Mika Hakkinen**	**11**
9	Andrea De Cesaris	8
10	Michele Alboreto	6
11	Erik Comas	4
12=	Karl Wendlinger	3
	Ivan Capelli	3
14=	**Johnny Herbert**	**2**
	Pierluigi Martini	2
	Thierry Boutsen	2

CONSTRUCTORS' CUP 1992

Position	Constructor	Points
1	Williams-Renault	164
2	McLaren-Honda	99
3	Benetton-Ford	91
4	Ferrari	21
5	**Lotus-Ford**	**13**

1993

At the turn of the year Herbert tested firstly at Snetterton and then at Estoril, coming away fifth fastest (1 minute 15.47 seconds) in Portugal as he concentrated on collecting data for the 107B's active suspension computerized control system. In February it was officially revealed that Hakkinen was to leave Lotus for McLaren, as the F1 Contract Recognition Board had confirmed that this was contractually possible. He had

Initial testing of the Lotus 107B indicated that podium finishes were now a distinct possibility. These findings flattered to deceive and Herbert – seen here driving superbly at Donington – did well to maintain his enthusiasm amidst much frustration.

supposedly been talking to both Ligier and Williams as well; anyway, shortly afterwards Italian Alessandro Zanardi was announced as his replacement.

Zanardi tested the 107B at Snetterton shortly before the 1993 campaign was launched at Claridges in London at the end of February. The season saw a number of new regulations: tyres had to be 3in narrower than previously at 15in, and there would only be seven sets per car available for each race meeting. Lotus tested briefly at Silverstone before going to South Africa, and the Team set off for Kyalami with very high hopes.

The optimism evaporated in South Africa as Zanardi could only manage sixteenth fastest in practice as he acclimatized himself to the 107B albeit with a misfiring engine caused by incorrect mapping. At one point Herbert was sixth fastest, but the 107B just would not turn in as it had done in testing; whilst trying to sort this out he collided with Badoer's Lola. It was in fact to be the 107B of Zanardi that was the faster of the two Lotuses in the race day warm-up as he took eleventh (1 minute 22.233 seconds) to Herbert's sixteenth (1 minute 22.370 seconds). Zanardi started well by gaining three places on the first lap, whilst, on his début for Williams, fourth-placed Damon Hill had spun down the field causing many a heart to miss a beat. Lotus's Italian driver got caught up in the mêlée with not only an angry Hill but also with Alliot (Larrousse) and Berger (Ferrari). The Italian tried vainly to overtake Hill on lap 17 and misjudged everything, locked up his brakes and took both himself and the Williams into the sand-trap, enforcing retirement. By contrast, Herbert paced himself well before his pitstop on lap 23 whilst he was in twelfth place, but fuel pressure troubles caused his retirement on lap 39 when he was in seventh. Prost took a début win for Williams, having

fought off Senna's McLaren, which used its Ford HB engine to tremendous effect.

Before Brazil it was announced that Trevor Foster, formerly team manager at Jordan, would join Castrol Team Lotus as director of racing. Suzanne Radbone would become the logistical co-ordinator later in the season.

The oversteering 107Bs felt much better in Brazil and Lotus achieved first points of the season at Interlagos. Herbert was just getting well into his stride when oil sprayed out of the back of his car, causing him to spin and a small fire to start. He extinguished this himself – the marshal on the scene being unable to operate the extinguisher he had carried across the track – but the delay caused him to drop back from sixth to twelfth on the grid. Zanardi had already managed to get on to the grass early in practice, and following hydraulic problems he was fifteenth. The accident-marred race – thanks mainly to a deluge of mid-race rain – brought out the newly prepared pace car for the first time when Herbert was in ninth. He cleverly nipped into the pits – making use of the curious toboggan arrangement that allowed the 107B to raise its own wheels to facilitate a change – and as the rain subsided came out on slicks in fifth; then, despite a quick spin, he was soon up to third, which he held for twenty-six laps. He was subsequently only just pipped by Schumacher's charging Benetton with three laps remaining, thus missing a podium place by finishing fourth. Whilst Herbert had been regaining his confidence Zanardi had consistently motored on – stopping twice – only to be hit on the neck by a stone with twenty laps to go; he drove particularly well to finish a one-handed sixth as he fought to support his head. Senna won for McLaren.

Before the GP of Europe at Donington, Guy

Edwards was awarded the freedom of the City of London. Donington would be the second successive race where Team strategy would pay big dividends. Herbert had hit the McLeans wall backwards early in practice – Zanardi struck that at the Old Hairpin – but started the race from eleventh place in the drizzle, climbing to eighth before his stop for slicks on lap 10. He then decided tactically, unlike most others, to stay out in the wet conditions and his reward was fourth place, as Senna mastered the conditions, while Prost stopped eight times! Zanardi was eighth after four stops.

Following more testing at Snetterton, Herbert was to start from twelfth place in the San Marino GP after an oil leak, but he selected too much wing for Imola's straights and was therefore handicapped throughout the race. After taking on new tyres on lap 10, he climbed as high as fifth (for eight laps) before his engine blew on lap 58. Engine problems ruined Zanardi's practice but he was faster in the race, having made a better choice of aerodynamics than his team-mate, only to spin out of fifth place into the chicane wall on lap 53. He had been trying to pass Lehto's Sauber and he now tried to rejoin, but the spectacular flames from his damaged car eventually forced him to pull off at Tamburello, where he knew there would be some experienced fire marshals.

Team manager Paul Bussey left Lotus before Spain, where Herbert was plagued by lack of active suspension reliability, which eventually stranded his vibrating car humiliatingly on the grid, thanks to a loose wire! Having qualified well in tenth, he managed only two ignominious laps before retiring. Zanardi, by contrast, had no such troubles and spent his oversteering race climbing up the field to sixth place, before his engine blew on lap 61, sending Schumacher across the gravel in avoidance. Prost won again for Williams.

Before Monaco the Team tested twice at Silverstone and once at Snetterton in an attempt to eradicate the obvious handling troubles further. Zanardi then crashed heavily in the Tunnel during Monaco practice when his car suddenly gripped. He was disappointed to end up twentieth fastest on the grid but he climbed through the field to seventh place at the end of the GP, having fought through the traffic and benefited from the retirements. Herbert had been fourteenth fastest, also complaining about lack of grip. His gearbox played him up during the race whilst he was dicing with both Fittipaldi and Barrichello; it then failed completely on lap 62, causing him to crash out. By winning his sixth Monaco GP Senna finally beat Graham Hill's previous record of five wins in the Principality.

Herbert, still afflicted by grip and active-suspension problems, started from twentieth on the grid in Montreal and finished tenth in what was Prost's race.

Zanardi crashed spectacularly in Saturday qualifying, and also lacked grip in the race; he spun off at one point, before rejoining to take on new tyres and to finish eleventh.

Prior to Magny-Cours, 500cc motorcycle Champion Wayne Gardner had a run in a 107B at Snetterton; the Team then moved to Silverstone testing, in which Herbert was seventh fastest (1 minute 23.37 seconds) and Zanardi ninth (1 minute 24.17 seconds).

In France, Herbert was extremely depressed that the Team wasn't making progress. In practice he over-revved whilst on his slowing-down lap, and Zanardi similarly bent an engine. The latter had active-suspension reliability troubles throughout, with a faulty actuator causing him to spin at least once in practice, although he was seventeenth fastest to Herbert's nineteenth. In the Williams-dominated race, Zanardi lasted a hairy three laps before that suspension actuator nearly put him off the track just before Lycee. Herbert only lasted until lap 17, when he was caught in a monumental fight with Berger (Ferrari) and Warwick (Footwork): he lost downforce and spun off to complete a disappointing weekend.

Before Silverstone the Team launched a 'racing for charities' scheme, whereby £5,000 per point would be donated to certain charities. John Miles also tested the 107B at Hethel, following which the active software was modified, and the car improved greatly.

The performance advantage was very evident at Silverstone after the Snetterton test, but Zanardi crashed heavily at Copse in qualifying, ending up fourteenth using his team-mate's car. Herbert himself was fifth fastest at one point, but dropped to an eventual seventh place; then, after a good start and just after the safety car had pulled off, he passed Patrese for sixth on lap 42 of the GP. Whilst lapping Alliot, the Italian repassed, but Herbert was still destined to finish fourth (Senna and Brundle had dropped out) only 0.925 seconds behind him. A notably relaxed Herbert was now very pleased with a result achieved for once through performance gain. Zanardi had spun off on lap 42 following a long midfield battle with, amongst others, Alesi (Ferrari).

Unusually Zanardi tested on a Saturday evening at Snetterton in advance of the German GP, but at Hockenheim he drove with a broken foot after falling from his bicycle in a road accident in Italy. Having qualified fifteenth, he spun off on lap 20 of the race. Herbert started from thirteenth place and decided to go without a tyre stop, finishing tenth after an actuator played up towards the end. Hill had again failed to win almost within sight of the flag, letting Prost through. In the paddock rumours abounded that Lotus would use Mugen (Honda) engines in 1994.

TEAM LOTUS RESULTS 1993

Drivers:
Johnny Herbert: British; Alessandro Zanardi: Italian; Pedro Lamy: Portuguese
Car:
Lotus 107 B Engine: Ford HBV8

CAR	CHASSIS	DRIVER	PRACTICE	SESSION	GRID	RACE	LAPS	%	REASON	CHAMPIONSHIP POSITION	POINTS

S AFRICAN GP, Kyalami – 14th March – 72 L, 190.631 miles (396.78km) (460)

CAR	CHASSIS	DRIVER	PRACTICE	SESSION	GRID	RACE	LAPS	%	REASON	POSITION	POINTS
107 B	3	Herbert	1m 19.498s	2	17th	R	38	52.7	Pressure	–	–
107 B	2	Zanardi	1m 19.936s	2	16th	R	16	22.2	Accident	–	–
107 B	1	(Spare)									

BRAZILIAN GP, Interlagos – 28th March – 71 L, 190.807 miles (307.06km) (461)

CAR	CHASSIS	DRIVER	PRACTICE	SESSION	GRID	RACE	LAPS	%	REASON	POSITION	POINTS
107 B	3	Herbert	1m 19.435s	2	12th	4th	71	100.0	–	6th=	3
107 B	2	Zanardi	1m 19.804s	2	15th	6th	70	98.6	–	9th=	1
107 B	1	(Spare)									

EUROPEAN GP, Donington – 11th April – 76 L, 189.982 miles (305.73km) (462)

CAR	CHASSIS	DRIVER	PRACTICE	SESSION	GRID	RACE	LAPS	%	REASON	POSITION	POINTS
107 B	3	Herbert	1m 13.328s	2	11th	4th	75	98.7	–	4th=	6
107 B	2	Zanardi	1m 13.560s	2	13th	8th	72	94.7	–	10th=	1
107 B	1	(Spare)									

SAN MARINO GP, Imola – 25th April – 61 L, 191.034 miles (307.43km) (463)

CAR	CHASSIS	DRIVER	PRACTICE	SESSION	GRID	RACE	LAPS	%	REASON	POSITION	POINTS
107 B	3	Herbert	1m 25.115s	2	12th	8th NR	57	93.4	Engine	6th	6
107 B	2	Zanardi	1m 26.465s	1	20th	R	53	86.8	Accident	13th=	1
107 B	1	Spare									

SPANISH GP, Barcelona – 9th May – 65 L, 191.727 miles (308.54km) (464)

CAR	CHASSIS	DRIVER	PRACTICE	SESSION	GRID	RACE	LAPS	%	REASON	POSITION	POINTS
107 B	2	Zanardi	1m 23.026s	2	15th	R	60	92.3	Engine	15th	1
107 B	3	Herbert	1m 22.470s	2	10th	R	2	3.1	Suspension	5th=	6
107 B	1	(Spare)									

MONACO GP, Monte Carlo – 23rd May – 78 L, 161.298 miles (259.56km) (465)

CAR	CHASSIS	DRIVER	PRACTICE	SESSION	GRID	RACE	LAPS	%	REASON	POSITION	POINTS
107 B	2	Zanardi	1m 24.888s	2	20th	7th	76	97.4	–	16th	1
107 B	3	Herbert	1m 23.812s	2	14th	R	61	78.2	Accident	5th=	6
107 B	1	(Spare)									

CANADIAN GP, Montreal – 13th June – 69 L, 189.934 miles (305.66km) (466)

CAR	CHASSIS	DRIVER	PRACTICE	SESSION	GRID	RACE	LAPS	%	REASON	POSITION	POINTS
107 B	3	Herbert	1m 23.223s	2	20th	10th	67	97.1	–	6th=	6
107 B	1	Zanardi	1m 23.240s	1	21st	11th	67	97.1	–	16th=	1
107 B	2	(Spare)									

FRENCH GP, Magny-Cours – 4th July – 72 L, 190.139 miles (305.99km) (467)

CAR	CHASSIS	DRIVER	PRACTICE	SESSION	GRID	RACE	LAPS	%	REASON	POSITION	POINTS
107 B	3	Herbert	1m 17.706s	2	19th	R	16	22.2	Spun off	6th=	6
107 B	2	Zanardi	1m 17.862s	1	17th	R	3	4.2	Suspension	16th=	1
107 B	1	(Spare)									

BRITISH GP, Silverstone – 11th July – 59 L, 191.589 miles (308.32km) (468)

CAR	CHASSIS	DRIVER	PRACTICE	SESSION	GRID	RACE	LAPS	%	REASON	POSITION	POINTS
107 B	3	Herbert	1m 22.487s	2	7th	4th	59	100.0	–	5th=	9
107 B	2	Zanardi	1m 23.533s	2	14th	R	41	69.5	Spun off	16th=	1
107 B	1	(Spare)									

GERMAN GP, Hockenheim – 25th July – 45 L, 190.559 miles (306.66km) (469)

CAR	CHASSIS	DRIVER	PRACTICE	SESSION	GRID	RACE	LAPS	%	REASON	POSITION	POINTS
107 B	3	Herbert	1m 41.564s	1	13th	10th	44	97.7	–	7th=	9
107 B	2	Zanardi	1m 41.858s	1	15th	R	19	42.2	Spun off	16th=	1
107 B	1	(Spare)									

HUNGARIAN GP, Budapest – 15th August – 77 L, 189.851 miles (305.52km) (470)

CAR	CHASSIS	DRIVER	PRACTICE	SESSION	GRID	RACE	LAPS	%	REASON	POSITION	POINTS
107 B	2	Zanardi	1m 19.485s	2	21st	R	45	58.4	Gearbox	18th	1
107 B	3	Herbert	1m 19.444s	2	20th	R	38	49.3	Spun off	19th	9
107 B	1	(Spare)									

BELGIAN GP, Spa – 29th August – 44 L, 190.671 miles (306.85km) (471)

CAR	CHASSIS	DRIVER	PRACTICE	SESSION	GRID	RACE	LAPS	%	REASON	POSITION	POINTS
107 B	3	Herbert	1m 51.139s	2	10th	5th	43	97.7	–	6th=	11
107 B	2	Zanardi	–	–	–	–	–	–	–	18th	1
107 B	1	(Spare)							Accident		

ITALIAN GP, Monza – 12th September – 53 L, 191.009 miles (306.34km) (472)

107 B	1	Lamy	1m 26.324s	2	26th	11th	NR	49	92.4	Engine	–	–
107 B	6	Herbert	1m 23.769s	2	7th	R		14	26.4	Accident	6th=	11
107 B	3	(Spare)										

PORTUGUESE GP, Estoril – 26th September – 71 L, 191.910 miles (307.78km) (473)

107 B	1	Lamy	1m 15.920s	2	18th	R		61	85.9	Accident	–	–
107 B	6	Herbert	1m 15.183s	2	14th	R		60	84.5	Accident	8th	11
107 B	3	(Spare)										

JAPANESE GP, Suzuka – 24th October – 53 L, 193.117 miles (310.01km) (474)

107 B		Herbert	1m 41.488s	1	19th	11th		51	96.2s	–	8th	11
107 B		Lamy	1m 41.600s	2	20th	R		49	92.4s	Accident	–	–
107 B		(Spare)										

AUSTRALIAN GP, Adelaide – 7th November – 79 L, 185.553 miles (297.58km) (475)

107 B	6	Herbert	1m 17.450s	2	20th	R		9	11.39	Hydraulics	9th	11
107 B	1	Lamy	1m 19.369s	2	23rd	R		0	0.0	Accident	–	–
107 B	3	(Spare)										

Key:
NR = Not Running

After Germany, Lotus tested the traction control system. At the Hungaroring a sticking throttle stopped Herbert from beating twentieth place, but he started well in the GP only to be forced back on the opening lap. He stopped for tyres on lap 22 and took seventh place until a data box came loose, causing him to spin off and stall on lap 39. Using traction control for the first time, Zanardi spun to a qualifying position of twenty-first. In the race he was delayed while avoiding the spinning Alliot on lap 14 and gravel got into his radiator intakes. He stopped to have them cleared only to repeat the process nine laps later and to retire on lap 46 when his gearbox gave out.

Early in free practice at Spa, Zanardi had a horrifying accident climbing out of the 150mph Eau Rouge. Amazingly he escaped major injury as, having lost control, his car cannoned from barrier to barrier, spinning like a top, before coming to rest in the sand-trap with a dazed, but outwardly unhurt, driver slumped at the wheel. He was whisked off to hospital and wasn't allowed to take any further part in proceedings. Herbert started tenth and finished a fine fifth in probably his best performance of the season, having stopped for tyres on lap 16. He had only just missed the slow-starting Benetton of Schumacher, nearly involving Brundle in a hairy moment just after the start, but the 107B handled perfectly through Eau Rouge to allow him to pass Warwick, Lehto and finally Suzuki. Hill won again, which statistically was the seventieth for Williams and the fiftieth for Renault, taking Williams past Lotus into third place behind McLaren and Ferrari in the table for the highest number of points scored since the World Championship had begun.

The much-rumoured official announcement that V10 Mugen Honda engines would be used for 1994 was made at Monza as Portuguese F3000 driver Pedro Lamy stood in for the still injured Zanardi. Wright acknowledged that more power was needed for Lotus to be up at the front, and it was anticipated that Mugen would oblige.

Herbert went surprisingly well on the Milanese power circuit, ending up a creditable seventh on the grid after spinning off early in practice. For the first four laps of the race he was fifth, before being demoted by the fast recovering, and eventual race winner, Hill. Whilst in sixth place on lap 15, Herbert missed the apex as he tried too hard to get round Berger at the Parabolica; he slid heavily into the barriers and retirement. Lamy had handling troubles, which dropped him to last place on the grid, from an early fifteenth, and he drove sensibly in the GP looking assured of ninth place with four laps to go, when his engine let go, dropping him to eleventh.

Being the centre of huge home media interest, Lamy was extremely pressurized at Estoril and this undoubtedly caused him to complete one too many practice laps in the first session. After several spins in his restricted second session he was eighteenth fastest – 0.7 seconds behind Herbert – and rose as high as tenth in the race before his pitstop; he then crashed out at Turn 3 on lap 62. A dispirited Herbert had similarly hit the Parabolica tyre wall a lap earlier, having struggled with his car's handling, which had been troublesome all weekend. The perceived improvements made at Spa and then Monza seemed to have evaporated. With second place, Prost clinched the Championship for Williams and promptly announced his retirement at the end of the season.

Before Japan it was announced that Lamy would replace Zanardi for the two remaining races and become full-time with Herbert in 1994. Zanardi had proven unfit during a brief Silverstone test.

Sadly, at the age of sixty-three, former Lotus driver Innes Ireland lost his fight against cancer on the eve of the Japanese race. Lamy had to learn Suzuka and in the process he spun at the Degner Curve on his way to twentieth fastest, one place behind an upset Herbert, who suffered actuator and gearbox failure. In the damp race Herbert stopped several times for tyres, having flat-spotted one set, to finish eleventh. Lamy had climbed up to eleventh place, but on lap 50 he plunged off the circuit (without injury) when his active suspension played up. Winner Senna would slug it out with GP débutant Eddie Irvine both on and off the track!

The Australian finale to the 1993 season was unfortunate for Team Lotus as both drivers spent much of practice spinning. The 107Bs proved very nervous on the tortuous street circuit, and in the race Lamy was punted out on the first lap at the first corner by the Tyrrell of Ukyo Katayama, who was trying to make up for having had to start from the back of the grid. Herbert did at least complete nine laps, having risen from twenty-third starting place to fourteenth on the first lap! His hydraulic pump then broke and the lack of active suspension caused the frustrated Briton to retire.

Ford's two-year association with Lotus concluded in Australia with Mugen/Hondas then being the power plants to be used in the quest for more power in 1994. A test version of the 107B, named the 107C, would be used to evaluate the Mugen/Honda engine.

WORLD CHAMPIONSHIP RESULTS 1993

Position	Driver	Points
1	Alain Prost	99
2	Ayrton Senna	73
3	Damon Hill	69
4	Michael Schumacher	52
5	Riccardo Patrese	20
6	Jean Alesi	16
7	Martin Brundle	13
8	Gerhard Berger	12
9	**Johnny Herbert**	**11**

CONSTRUCTORS' CUP 1993

Position	Constructor	Points
1	Williams-Renault	168
2	McLaren-Ford	84
3	Benetton-Ford	72
4	Ferrari	28
5	Ligier-Renault	23
6=	**Lotus-Ford**	**12**
	Sauber	12

Epilogue

Senna's win in Adelaide promoted McLaren past Ferrari to become the most successful Grand Prix team, with its 104th victory. McLaren's performance indicators are obviously good, but we must also examine Team Lotus's outstanding record.

Since 1958 Team Lotus has entered 475 races and won seventy-nine of them (16.6 per cent) and on 107 (22.5 per cent) of those occasions it has captured pole position; seventy-one (14.9 per cent) fastest laps have been chalked up and the Team has also led 5,496 (17.4 per cent) laps of racing. On the reliability front the Team has amassed 954 race starts, managing to be counted as a finisher 497 (52.09 per cent) times.

The Team's most successful design was the Lotus 72, which notched up twenty wins between 1970 and 1973, although the Lotus 25 led 1,071 race laps between 1962 and 1965. The most successful individual chassis constructed and raced by Team Lotus was undoubtedly 25/R4, which took a record seven wins in 1963 whilst also leading no less than 506 (71.5 per cent) race laps.

It is hardly surprising when one acknowledges the domination of the Lotus 25 that the Team's most successful driver was Jim Clark, who led 1,932 laps of Grand Prix racing in a Lotus as well as winning no less than twenty-five times. Interestingly, the driver who started the most races behind the wheel of a Lotus Grand Prix car was Elio de Angelis, who did so ninety times, finishing on fifty-one (56.6 per cent) occasions.

It is significant that most of these achievements occurred whilst Colin Chapman was still alive, and his personal influence as a factor in Lotus's success cannot be ignored. As the 1994 regulations exclude most of the accepted 1993 electronic driver aids, one cannot help but feel that had Chapman still been around, he would very early on have turned his mind to the problem and sketched his innovative response on the corner of a tablecloth . . .

Appendix

LOTUS FORMULA 1 CAR SPECIFICATIONS 1958–92★

1958: Lotus 12

Battery	: –
Bearings	: –
Brakes	: Girling
Brake Pads	: –
Capacity	: 1,960cc or 2,207cc
Carburettors	: –
Clutch	: –
Dampers	: –
Engine	: Coventry Climax FPF
Fuel	: –
Fuel capacity	: –
Fuel system	: –
Fuel tanks	: –
Gearbox	: Lotus five-speed
Gearbox weight	: 49lb (22.2kg)
Half-shafts	: –
Height overall	: –
Ignition	: –
Instruments	: –
Length overall	: 131in (3,327mm)
Maximum power	: (1.9-litre) 176bhp; (2.2-litre) 194bhp
Oil	: –
Pistons	: –
Plugs	: –
Radiator	: –
Rim width front	: –
Rim width rear	: –
Rings	: –
Rpm	: (1.9-litre) 6,500; (2.2-litre) 6,250
Steering	: –
Suspension front	: Double wishbones, transverse link, coil/spring dampers
Suspension rear	: Hub casting, radius rod, coil/spring dampers, De Dion
Track front	: 48in (1,209mm)
Track rear	: 48in (1,209mm)
Turbocharger/s	: –
Tyres	: –
Weight (engine)	: 280lb (127kg)
Weight (tub)	: –
Weight (dry)	: 660lb (299.4kg)
Weight (start)	: 700lb (317.5kg)
Formula weight	: –
Wheelbase	: 88in (2,235mm)
Wheel diameter-f	: –
Wheel diameter-r	: –

1958–59: Lotus 16

Battery	: –
Bearings	: –
Brakes	: Girling
Brake Pads	: Ferodo PF3
Capacity	: 2,2210cc
Carburettors	: Weber
Clutch	: Lotus/Borg & Beck
Dampers	: Armstrong
Engine	: Coventry Climax FPF
Fuel	: Avgas
Fuel capacity	: 22 gallons (100 litres)
Fuel system	: AC
Fuel tanks	: –
Gearbox	: Lotus 5-speed
Gearbox weight	: –
Half-shafts	: –
Height overall	: 35in (889mm)
Ignition	: Lucas
Instruments	: –
Length overall	: 140in (3,556mm)
Maximum power	: 194bhp
Oil	: –
Pistons	: –
Plugs	: Champion NA12
Radiator	: –
Rim width front	: –
Rim width rear	: –
Rings	: –
Rpm	: 6,250
Steering	: Lotus rack and pinion
Suspension front	: Double wishbones, transverse link, coil/spring dampers
Suspension rear	: Strut, hub casting, forward radius arms, coil/spring dampers
Track front	: 47in (1,194mm)
Track rear	: 47in (1,194mm)
Turbocharger/s	: –
Tyres	: Dunlop
Weight (engine)	: –
Weight (tub)	: –
Weight (dry)	: 1,080lb (489.9kg)
Weight (start)	: –
Formula weight	: –
Wheelbase	: 88in (2,235mm)
Wheel diameter-f	: 15in
Wheel diameter-r	: 15in

★ Some early specification data is unavailable.

1960: Lotus 18

Battery	: –
Bearings	: –
Brakes	: Girling
Brake Pads	: –
Capacity	: 2,495cc
Carburettors	: –
Clutch	: Borg & Beck
Dampers	: –
Engine	: Coventry Climax FPF
Fuel	: –
Fuel capacity	: 31.5 gallons (143 litres)
Fuel system	: –
Fuel tanks	: –
Gearbox	: Lotus 5-speed
Gearbox weight	: –
Half-shafts	: –
Height overall	: –
Ignition	: –
Instruments	: –
Length overall	: 135in (3,429mm)
Maximum power	: 237bhp
Oil	: –
Pistons	: –
Plugs	: –
Radiator	: –
Rim width front	: 5in (127mm)
Rim width rear	: 6.5in (165mm)
Rings	: –
Rpm	: –
Steering	: –
Suspension front	: Unequal double wishbones, coil/ spring dampers
Suspension rear	: Lower wishbones reversed, twin radius rods, coil/spring dampers
Track front	: 52in (1,321mm)
Track rear	: 53.25in (1,353mm)
Turbocharger/s	: –
Tyres	: Dunlop R5
Weight (engine)	: –
Weight (tub)	: –
Weight (dry)	: 770lb (349.3kg)
Weight (start)	: 950lb (430.9kg)
Formula weight	: 980lb (444.5kg)
Wheelbase	: 90in (2,286mm)
Wheel diameter-f:	15in
Wheel diameter-r:	15in

1961: Lotus 21

Battery	: Varley
Bearings	: Vandervell Thinwall
Brakes	: Girling
Brake Pads	: Ferodo
Capacity	: 1,497.8cc
Carburettors	: Wever 45 DCOE/9
Clutch	: Borg & Beck
Dampers	: Armstrong
Engine	: Coventry Climax FPF Mk 2
Fuel	: Esso
Fuel capacity	: –
Fuel system	: –
Fuel tanks	: –
Gearbox	: Lotus ZF SD510 5-speed
Gearbox weight	: –
Half-shafts	: Hardy Spicer
Height overall	: –
Ignition	: –
Instruments	: Smiths
Length overall	: 141in (3,581mm)
Maximum power	: 151bhp
Oil	: Esso
Pistons	: Brico
Plugs	: Champion
Radiator	: Lotus/Serck
Rim width front	: –
Rim width rear	: –
Rings	: Brico
Rpm	: 7,500
Steering	: Lotus/Triumph rack and pinion
Suspension front	: Outboard coil/spring dampers, upper rocking arms, unequal double lower wishbones
Suspension rear	: Reversed lower wishbones, twin transverse radius rods, upper links, outboard coil/spring dampers
Track front	: –
Track rear	: 53.25in (1,352mm)
Turbocharger/s	: –
Tyres	: Dunlop
Weight (engine)	: –
Weight (tub)	: –
Weight (dry)	: 1,003.1lb (455kg)
Weight (start)	: –
Formula weight	: 995lb (451.3kg)
Wheelbase	: 90in (2,286mm)
Wheel diameter-f:	15in
Wheel diameter-r:	15in

1962: Lotus 24

Battery	: –
Bearings	: –
Brakes	: –
Brake Pads	: –
Capacity	: 1,498cc
Carburettors	: –
Clutch	: –
Dampers	: –
Engine	: Coventry Climax FWMV V8
Fuel	: –
Fuel capacity	: –
Fuel system	: –
Fuel tanks	: –
Gearbox	: ZF 5-speed
Gearbox weight	: –
Half-shafts	: –
Height overall	: –
Ignition	: –
Instruments	: –
Length overall	: 142in (3,607mm)
Maximum power	: 182bhp
Oil	: –
Pistons	: –
Plugs	: –
Radiator	: –
Rim width front	: –
Rim width rear	: –
Rings	: –
Rpm	: –
Steering	: –
Suspension front	: Lower wishbones, inboard coil/spring dampers, upper cantilever rocking arms
Suspension rear	: Reversed lower wishbones, twin radius rods, upper links, outboard coil/spring dampers
Track front	: –
Track rear	: 53.25in (1,352mm)
Turbocharger/s	: –
Tyres	: –
Weight (engine)	: –
Weight (tub)	: –
Weight (dry)	: 996lb (451.8kg)
Weight (start)	: –
Formula weight	: 1,000lb (453.6kg)
Wheelbase	: 90in (2,286mm)
Wheel diameter-f:	–
Wheel diameter-r:	–

1962–65: Lotus 25

Battery	: Varley
Bearings	: Vandervell
Brakes	: Girling
Brake Pads	: Ferodo
Capacity	: 1,495cc
Carburettors	: Weber 38 DCN
Clutch	: AP/Borg & Beck
Dampers	: Armstrong
Engine	: Coventry Climax FWMV V8
Fuel	: Esso
Fuel capacity	: 26 gallons (118 litres)
Fuel system	: –
Fuel tanks	: –
Gearbox	: ZF 5-speed
Gearbox weight	: –
Half-shafts	: Lotus/Metalastic
Height overall	: –
Ignition	: Lucas
Instruments	: Smiths
Length overall	: 142in (3,607mm)
Maximum power	: 200bhp
Oil	: Esso
Pistons	: Brico
Plugs	: Lodge RL50
Radiator	: Serck
Rim width front	: –
Rim width rear	: –
Rings	: AE/Brico
Rpm	: 8,600
Steering	: Lotus rack and pinion
Suspension front	: Upper rocker arms, double lower wishbones, inboard coil/spring dampers
Suspension rear	: Outboard rear coil/spring dampers, reversed lower wishbones, twin radius rods, upper links
Track front	: 53in (1,346mm)
Track rear	: 54in (1,372mm)
Turbocharger/s	: –
Tyres	: Dunlop
Weight (engine)	: 269lb (122kg)
Weight (tub)	: –
Weight (dry)	: 996lb (452kg)
Weight (start)	: –
Formula weight	: 995lb (451kg)
Wheelbase	: 94in (2,388mm)
Wheel diameter-f:	15in
Wheel diameter-r:	15in

1964–65: Lotus 33

Battery	: Varley
Bearings	: Vandervell
Brakes	: Girling
Brake Pads	: Ferodo
Capacity	: 1,496cc
Carburettors	: –
Clutch	: Borg & Beck
Dampers	: Armstrong
Engine	: Coventry Climax FWMV 32-valve V8
Fuel	: Esso
Fuel capacity	: –
Fuel system	: Lucas port injection
Fuel tanks	: –
Gearbox	: ZF 5DS10 5-speed
Gearbox weight	: –
Half-shafts	: Lotus Metalastic/Hardy Spicer
Height overall	: –
Ignition	: Lucas transistor
Instruments	: Smiths
Length overall	: 142in (3,607mm)
Maximum power	: 205bhp +
Oil	: Esso
Pistons	: Brico/Mahle
Plugs	: Champion
Radiator	: Serck
Rim width front	: –
Rim width rear	: –
Rings	: Brico
Rpm	: 9,800/10,000rpm
Steering	: Lotus rack and pinion
Suspension front	: Inboard spring/damper, unequal double wishbone
Suspension rear	: Outboard spring/damper, transverse link/radius arms, reversed lower wishbones
Track front	: 55in (1,397mm)
Track rear	: 56in (1,422mm)
Turbocharger/s	: –
Tyres	: Dunlop R6/R7
Weight (engine)	: –
Weight (tub)	: –
Weight (dry)	: –
Weight (start)	: –
Formula weight	: 995lb (451kg)
Wheelbase	: 92in (2,337mm)
Wheel diameter-f	: 13in
Wheel diameter-r	: 13in

1966–67: Lotus 43

Battery	: Varley
Bearings	: Vandervell
Brakes	: Girling
Brake Pads	: Ferodo
Capacity	: 2,998cc
Carburettors	: –
Clutch	: Borg & Beck 7.25in
Dampers	: Armstrong AT9
Engine	: BRM H16 Type 75
Fuel	: Esso
Fuel capacity	: 50 gallons
Fuel system	: Lucas injection
Fuel tanks	: FPT
Gearbox	: BRM 6-speed
Gearbox weight	: –
Half-shafts	: Lotus/BRD/Mercedes
Height overall	: –
Ignition	: Lucas transistor
Instruments	: Smiths
Length overall	: 160in (4,064mm)
Maximum power	: 420bhp
Oil	: Esso
Pistons	: Hepolite
Plugs	: Marchal
Radiator	: Serck
Rim width front	: 8/10in
Rim width rear	: 10/12in
Rings	: Hepolite
Rpm	: 10,500
Steering	: Lotus rack and pinion
Suspension front	: Lower wishbones, upper rocking arms, inboard coil/spring dampers
Suspension rear	: Lateral upper links, reversed lower wishbones, twin radius rods, coil/spring dampers
Track front	: 60in (1,524mm)
Track rear	: 60in (1,524mm)
Turbocharger/s	: –
Tyres	: Firestone
Weight (engine)	: –
Weight (tub)	: –
Weight (dry)	: –
Weight (start)	: –
Formula weight	: 1,250lb (567kg)
Wheelbase	: 96in (2,438mm)
Wheel diameter-f	: 15in
Wheel diameter-r	: 15in

1967: Lotus 49

		1968: Lotus 49B
Battery	: Varley	Varley
Bearings	: Vandervell	Vandervell
Brakes	: Girling	Girling
Brake Pads	: Ferodo DS11	Ferodo
Capacity	: 2,995cc	2,995cc
Carburettors	: —	
Clutch	: Borg & Beck 7.25in	Borg & Beck
Dampers	: Armstrong	Armstrong
Engine	: Ford Cosworth DFV	Ford Cosworth DFV
Fuel	: Esso	Shell
Fuel capacity	: —	—
Fuel system	: Lucas injection	Lucas injection
Fuel tanks	: FPT	FPT
Gearbox	: ZF 5DS 12	Hewland FG400/DG300
Gearbox weight	: 98lb (44.5kg)	105/122lb (47.5/55.3kg)
Half-shafts	: BRD	BRD/Hardy Spicer/Hooke
Height overall	: 29in (737mm)	32in (+ wing 61in) (812 + 1,549mm)
Ignition	: Lucas	—
Instruments	: Smiths	Smiths
Length overall	: 158in (4,013mm)	158in (4,013mm)
Maximum power	: 410bhp	415bhp
Oil	: Esso	Shell
Pistons	: Hepolite	Hepworth
Plugs	: Autolite	Autolite
Radiator	: Serck	Serck/Coventry
Rim width front	: 9in	—
Rim width rear	: 13in	—
Rings	: —	Grandage
Rpm	: 9,000	9,500
Steering	: Alford & Alder rack and pinion	Cam Gears rack and pinion
Suspension front	: Unequal wishbones, coil/spring, anti-roll bar	Plus new geometry/uprights
Suspension rear	: Unequal wishbones, coil/spring, anti-roll bar	Plus new geometry/uprights
Track front	: 60in (1,524mm)	62.6in (1,590mm)
Track rear	: 61in (1,549mm)	61in (1,549mm)
Turbocharger/s	: —	—
Tyres	: Firestone	Firestone
Weight (engine)	: 356lb (161.5kg)	370lb (168kg)
Weight (tub)	: 91lb (41kg)	—
Weight (dry)	: 1,102lb (500kg)	1,180lb (535kg)
Weight (start)	: 1,562lb/1,105lb (708.5/501kg)	1,640lb (744kg)
Formula weight	: 1,102lb (500kg)	1,130lb (512.5kg)
Wheelbase	: 95in (2,413mm)	98in (2,489mm)
Wheel diameter-f	: 8/10in	12in
Wheel diameter-r	: 13in	15in

1969: Lotus 49C

Battery	: –	
Bearings	: –	
Brakes	: Girling	
Brake Pads	: –	
Capacity	: 2,995cc	
Carburettors	: –	
Clutch	: Borg & Beck	
Dampers	: Armstrong	
Engine	: Ford Cosworth DFV	
Fuel	: –	
Fuel capacity	: –	
Fuel system	: Lucas injection	
Fuel tanks	: –	
Gearbox	: Hewland DG300	
Gearbox weight	: –	
Half-shafts	: Hardy Spicer CV	
Height overall	: 32in (+ wing 38in) (812mm + 965mm)	
Ignition	: –	
Instruments	: Lucas transistor	
Length overall	: 158in (4,013mm)	
Maximum power	: 430bhp	
Oil	: –	
Pistons	: –	
Plugs	: Autolite	
Radiator	: Serck/Coventry	
Rim width front	: 13in	
Rim width rear	: –	
Rings	: –	
Rpm	: 10,000	
Steering	: Cam Gears rack and pinion	
Suspension front	: Unequal wishbones, coil/spring, anti-roll bar	
Suspension rear	: Unequal wishbones, coil/spring, anti-roll bar	
Track front	: 62.6in (1,590mm)	
Track rear	: 61in (1,549mm)	
Turbocharger/s	: –	
Tyres	: Firestone	
Weight (engine)	: –	
Weight (tub)	: –	
Weight (dry)	: 1,190lb (540kg)	
Weight (start)	: 1,640lb (744kg)	
Formula weight	: –	
Wheelbase	: 98in (2,489mm)	
Wheel diameter-f	: 12in	
Wheel diameter-r	: 15in	

1970: Lotus 49D

–
–
Girling
–
2,995cc
–
Borg & Beck
Armstrong
Ford Cosworth DFV
–
–
Lucas injection
–
Hewland DG300
–
BRD/Hardy Spicer/Hooke
32in (812mm)

–
Lucas transistor
158in (4,013mm)
430bhp
–
–
Autolite
Serck/Coventry
–
–
10,000
Cam Gears rack and pinion
(As 49B)

(As 49B)

62.6in (1,590mm)
61in (1,549mm)
–
Firestone
–
–
1,190lb (540kg)
1,640lb (744kg)
–
98in (2,489mm)
13in
15in

1968: Lotus 56(B)

Battery	: —
Bearings	: —
Brakes	: Girling
Brake Pads	: —
Capacity	: 14,999sq. in
Carburettors	: —
Clutch	: —
Dampers	: —
Engine	: Pratt & Whitney STN6/76 turbine
Fuel	: Shell kerosene
Fuel capacity	: 62 US gallons
Fuel system	: —
Fuel tanks	: Firestone Racesafe
Gearbox	: —
Gearbox weight	: —
Half-shafts	: ZF spiral bevel Hardy Spicer
Height overall	: 32in (812mm)
Ignition	: —
Instruments	: —
Length overall	: 170in (4,318mm)
Maximum power	: 500+ bhp
Oil	: —
Pistons	: —
Plugs	: —
Radiator	: —
Rim width front	: —
Rim width rear	: —
Rings	: —
Rpm	: —
Steering	: Cam Gears rack and pinion
Suspension front	: Double wishbones/link top rocking arms
Suspension rear	: Double wishbone/link top rocking arms
Track front	: —
Track rear	: 62.5in (1,587mm)
Turbocharger/s	: —
Tyres	: Firestone
Weight (engine)	: —
Weight (tub)	: —
Weight (dry)	: —
Weight (start)	: —
Formula weight	: 1,350lb (612kg)
Wheelbase	: 102in (2,591mm)
Wheel diameter-f	: 15in
Wheel diameter-r	: 15in

1969: Lotus 63

Battery	: —
Bearings	: —
Brakes	: Girling
Brake Pads	: Ferodo
Capacity	: 2,995cc
Carburettors	: —
Clutch	: —
Dampers	: Armstrong Patents Ltd
Engine	: Ford Cosworth DFV V8
Fuel	: Shell
Fuel capacity	: 40 imperial gallons (181.8 litres)
Fuel system	: —
Fuel tanks	: FPT
Gearbox	: Lotus/Hewland 5-speed
Gearbox weight	: —
Half-shafts	: ZF spiral level crownwheel and pinion
Height overall	: 34in
Ignition	: —
Instruments	: —
Length overall	: 152in (3,861mm)
Maximum power	: 430bhp
Oil	: —
Pistons	: —
Plugs	: Autolite
Radiator	: Serck
Rim width front	: 12in
Rim width rear	: 14in
Rings	: —
Rpm	: —
Steering	: Cam Gears rack and pinion
Suspension front	: —
Suspension rear	: —
Track front	: 59in (1,499mm)
Track rear	: 59in (1,499mm)
Turbocharger/s	: —
Tyres	: Firestone
Weight (engine)	: —
Weight (tub)	: —
Weight (dry)	: —
Weight (start)	: —
Formula weight	: 1,170lb (530kg)
Wheelbase	: 98in (2,589mm)
Wheel diameter-f	: 13in
Wheel diameter-r	: 13in

1970: Lotus 72

Battery	: Varley	
Bearings	: Vandervell	
Brakes	: Girling	
Brake Pads	: Ferodo	
Capacity	: 2,995cc	
Carburettors	: –	
Clutch	: Borg & Beck	
Dampers	: Armstrong	
Engine	: Ford Cosworth DFV	
Fuel	: Shell	
Fuel capacity	: 45 gallons (204 litres)	
Fuel system	: Lucas injection	
Fuel tanks	: FPT fuel cells	
Gearbox	: Hewland FG400	
Gearbox weight	: 95lb (43kg)	
Half-shafts	: Lotus/Hardy Spicer/Lobro	
Height overall	: –	
Ignition	: Lucas transistor	
Instruments	: Smiths	
Length overall	: 165in (4,191mm)	
Maximum power	: 440bhp	
Oil	: Shell	
Pistons	: Hepworth	
Plugs	: Autolite	
Radiator	: Serck	
Rim width front	: 10in	
Rim width rear	: 15in	
Rings	: Grandage	
Rpm	: 10,000	
Steering	: Cam Gears rack and pinion	
Suspension front	: Torsion bars and double wishbones	
Suspension rear	: Torsion bars and double wishbones	
Track front	: 57in (1,448mm)	
Track rear	: 57in (1,448mm)	
Turbocharger/s	: –	
Tyres	: Firestone	
Weight (engine)	: 380lb (172kg)	
Weight (tub)	: 65lb (29.5kg)	
Weight (dry)	: –	
Weight (start)	: –	
Formula weight	: 1,170lb (530kg)	
Wheelbase	: 100in (2,540mm)	
Wheel diameter-f	: 13in	
Wheel diameter-r	: 15in	

1971: Lotus 72C/D

Varley
Cosworth/Vandervell
Girling
Ferodo
2,993cc
–
Borg & Beck
Koni
Ford Cosworth DFV
Shell
45 gallons (204 litres)
Lucas injection
FPT
Hewland FG400
98lb (44.5kg)
Lotus/Hardy Spicer/Lobro
–
Lucas transistor
Smiths
–
440bhp
Shell
Cosworth
Motorcraft
Serck
–
–
Hepolite
10,000
Cam Gears rack and pinion
Torsion bars and double wishbones
Torsion bars, twin radius rods, single top, parallel lower links
57in (1,448mm)
57in (1,448mm)
–
Firestone
365lb (165.5kg)
65lb (29.5kg)
–
–
1,165lb (528kg)
100in (2,540mm)
13in
13/15in

1972: Lotus 72D

Battery	:	Varley
Bearings	:	Vandervell
Brakes	:	Girling
Brake Pads	:	Ferodo DS11
Capacity	:	2,993cc
Carburettors	:	–
Clutch	:	Borg & Beck 7.25in
Dampers	:	Koni
Engine	:	Ford Cosworth DFV
Fuel	:	Texaco
Fuel capacity	:	42 gallons (190 litres)
Fuel system	:	Lucas injection
Fuel tanks	:	FPT fuel cells
Gearbox	:	Hewland FG400
Gearbox weight	:	98lb (44.5kg)
Half-shafts	:	Lotus/GKN
Height overall	:	–
Ignition	:	Lucas OPUS
Instruments	:	Smiths
Length overall	:	165in (4,191mm)
Maximum power	:	480bhp
Oil	:	Havoline
Pistons	:	Cosworth
Plugs	:	Autolite
Radiator	:	Serck
Rim width front	:	10/11in
Rim width rear	:	15/17in
Rings	:	Hepolite
Rpm	:	10,800
Steering	:	Cam Gears rack and pinion
Suspension front	:	Torsion bars and double wishbones
Suspension rear	:	Torsion bars/lower parallel links/ top single link/rad. rods
Track front	:	58in (1,473mm)
Track rear	:	61in (1,549mm)
Turbocharger/s	:	–
Tyres	:	Firestone
Weight (engine)	:	365lb (165.5kg)
Weight (tub)	:	68lb (31kg)
Weight (dry)	:	–
Weight (start)	:	–
Formula weight	:	1,213lb (550kg)
Wheelbase	:	99in (2,514mm)

Wheel diameter-f: 13in
Wheel diameter-r: 13/15in
★ 1974 differences shown in ( ) brackets.
★★1975 differences shown in [ ] brackets.

1973 (1974)★ [1975]★★: Lotus 72D/E

Varley
Vandervell
Girling [Lockheed]
Ferodo
2,993cc

–
Borg & Beck
Koni
Ford Cosworth DFV
Texaco
40 gallons (181 litres)
Lucas injection
FPT (Marston)
Hewland FG400
100lb (102lb) (45kg)
Lotus
–
Lucas OPUS
Smiths
–
460bhp [465bhp]
Texaco (Duckhams)
Cosworth
Champion
Serck
10in (10/11in) [10in]
17in (+18/19in) [+20in]
Hepolite [Cosworth]
10,250 [10,500]
Cam Gears (Lotus) rack and pinion
Torsion bars and double wishbones
Torsion bars/lower parallel links/ top single link/rad. rods
58in (1,473/1,575mm) [58/62in (1,473mm)]
62in (1,626mm) [64in (1,575mm)]
–
Goodyear
365lb (165.5kg)
70lb (31.75kg)
–
–
1,270lb (576kg)
100in (2,540mm) [100/105in (2,540/2,667mm)]
13in
13in

1974: Lotus 76 (JPS Mk1)

Battery	: Varley
Bearings	: Vandervell
Brakes	: Girling
Brake Pads	: Ferodo
Capacity	: 2,993cc
Carburettors	: –
Clutch	: Borg & Beck/AP
Dampers	: Koni
Engine	: Ford Cosworth DFV
Fuel	: –
Fuel capacity	: 40 gallons (181 litres)
Fuel system	: Lucas
Fuel tanks	: Marston Excelsior
Gearbox	: Hewland FGA400
Gearbox weight	: 102lb (46.25kg)
Half-shafts	: BRD
Height overall	: –
Ignition	: Lucas Opus
Instruments	: Smiths
Length overall	: –
Maximum power	: 460bhp
Oil	: Duckhams
Pistons	: Cosworth-Hepolite
Plugs	: Champion
Radiator	: Serck
Rim width front	: 10/11in
Rim width rear	: 17/18/19in
Rings	: Cosworth-Hepolite
Rpm	: 10,250
Steering	: Lotus rack and pinion
Suspension front	: Torsion bars, double wishbones
Suspension rear	: Lower links, parallel top links, torsion bars, twin radius rods
Track front	: 58in (1,473mm)
Track rear	: 62in (1,574mm)
Turbocharger/s	: –
Tyres	: Goodyear
Weight (engine)	: 365lb (165.5kg)
Weight (tub)	: –
Weight (dry)	: –
Weight (start)	: –
Formula weight	: 1,268lb (575kg)
Wheelbase	: 101in (2,565mm)
Wheel diameter-f	: 13in
Wheel diameter-r	: 13in

1976: Lotus 77 (JPS Mk 2)

Battery	: Varley
Bearings	: Vandervell
Brakes	: Lockheed/Lotus
Brake Pads	: Ferodo
Capacity	: 2,993cc
Carburettors	: –
Clutch	: Borg & Beck
Dampers	: Koni
Engine	: Ford Cosworth DFV
Fuel	: Shell
Fuel capacity	: 39 gallons (177 litres)
Fuel system	: Lucas
Fuel tanks	: Marston
Gearbox	: Hewland FG400 5-speed
Gearbox weight	: 102lb (46kg)
Half-shafts	: Lotus
Height overall	: –
Ignition	: Lucas RITA
Instruments	: Smiths
Length overall	: –
Maximum power	: 465bhp
Oil	: Texaco
Pistons	: Cosworth
Plugs	: Champion
Radiator	: Serck
Rim width front	: 10/11in
Rim width rear	: 18/20in
Rings	: Hepworth & Grandage
Rpm	: 10,500
Steering	: Lotus rack and pinion
Suspension front	: Outboard springs, double wishbones
Suspension rear	: Outboard springs, radius rods, single lower and top parallel links
Track front	: 50in (1,475mm)
Track rear	: 61in (1,550mm)
Turbocharger/s	: –
Tyres	: Goodyear
Weight (engine)	: –
Weight (tub)	: 1,267lb (575kg)
Weight (dry)	: –
Weight (start)	: –
Formula weight	: 1,300lb (589kg)
Wheelbase	: 110in (2,795mm)
Wheel diameter-f	: 13in
Wheel diameter-r	: 13in

1977–78: Lotus 78 (JPS Mk3)

Battery	: Yuasa
Bearings	: Vandervell
Brakes	: Lotus/Lockheed
Brake Pads	: Ferodo
Capacity	: 2,993cc
Carburettors	: –
Clutch	: Borg & Beck
Dampers	: Koni
Engine	: Ford Cosworth DFV
Fuel	: –
Fuel capacity	: 39 gallons (177 litres)
Fuel system	: Lucas
Fuel tanks	: Marston
Gearbox	: Hewland FG400 5-speed
Gearbox weight	: 102lb (46kg)
Half-shafts	: Lobro
Height overall	: –
Ignition	: Lucas
Instruments	: Smiths
Length overall	: –
Maximum power	: 465bhp
Oil	: Valvoline
Pistons	: Cosworth
Plugs	: NGK
Radiator	: Serck/Marston
Rim width front	: 10in
Rim width rear	: 18.5in
Rings	: Hepworth & Grandage
Rpm	: 10,500
Steering	: Knight rack and pinion
Suspension front	: Inboard springs, double wishbones
Suspension rear	: Outboard springs, bottom wishbones, parallel top, links, twin radius rods
Track front	: 67in (1,700mm)
Track rear	: 63in (1,600mm)
Turbocharger/s	: –
Tyres	: Goodyear
Weight (engine)	: 365lb (166kg)
Weight (tub)	: 90lb (41kg)
Weight (dry)	: –
Weight (start)	: –
Formula weight	: 1,310lb (594kg)
Wheelbase	: 107in (2,720mm)
Wheel diameter-f	: 13in
Wheel diameter-r	: 13in

1978–79: Lotus 79 (JPS Mk 4)

Battery	: Yuasa
Bearings	: Vandervell
Brakes	: Lotus/Lockheed
Brake Pads	: Ferodo
Capacity	: 2,993cc
Carburettors	: –
Clutch	: Borg & Beck
Dampers	: Koni
Engine	: Ford Cosworth DFV
Fuel	: –
Fuel capacity	: 38 gallons (168 litres)
Fuel system	: Lucas
Fuel tanks	: Marston
Gearbox	: Hewland FG400/5-speed
Gearbox weight	: 121lb (55kg)
Half-shafts	: Lobro
Height overall	: –
Ignition	: Lucas
Instruments	: Smiths
Length overall	: –
Maximum power	: 475bhp
Oil	: Valvoline
Pistons	: Cosworth
Plugs	: NGK
Radiator	: Serck
Rim width front	: 10in
Rim width rear	: 18.5in
Rings	: Hepworth & Grandage
Rpm	: 10,750
Steering	: Rack and pinion (Knight)
Suspension front	: Lower wishbones, upper rocking arms, inboard coil/spring dampers
Suspension rear	: Lower wishbones, upper rocking arms, inboard coil/spring dampers
Track front	: 68in (1,730mm)
Track rear	: 64in (1,630mm)
Turbocharger/s	: –
Tyres	: Goodyear
Weight (engine)	: 365lb (166kg)
Weight (tub)	: 86lb (39kg)
Weight (dry)	: –
Weight (start)	: –
Formula weight	: 1,268lb (575kg)
Wheelbase	: 108in (2,718mm)
Wheel diameter-f	: 13in
Wheel diameter-r	: 13in

1979: Lotus 80

Battery	: Yuasa
Bearings	: Vandervell
Brakes	: Lockheed
Brake Pads	: Ferodo/Mintex
Capacity	: 2,993cc
Carburettors	: –
Clutch	: Borg & Beck
Dampers	: Koni
Engine	: Ford Cosworth DFV
Fuel	: –
Fuel capacity	: 40 gallons (182 litres)
Fuel system	: Lucas
Fuel tanks	: Aerotech
Gearbox	: Lotus/Hewland FGA 5-speed
Gearbox weight	: 125lb (57kg)
Half-shafts	: –
Height overall	: –
Ignition	: Lucas
Instruments	: Smiths
Length overall	: –
Maximum power	: 470bhp (min)
Oil	: Valvoline
Pistons	: Cosworth
Plugs	: NGK
Radiator	: Marston
Rim width front	: 11in
Rim width rear	: 18.5
Rings	: Cosworth
Rpm	: 10,800
Steering	: Rack and pinion (Knight)
Suspension front	: Lower wishbones, upper rocking arms, inboard coil/spring dampers
Suspension rear	: Lower wishbones, upper rocking arms, inboard coil/spring dampers
Track front	: 70in (1,778mm)
Track rear	: 64in (1,626mm)
Turbocharger/s	: –
Tyres	: Goodyear
Weight (engine)	: 360lb (163kg)
Weight (tub)	: 85lb (38.5kg)
Weight (dry)	: –
Weight (start)	: –
Formula weight	: 1,378lb (625kg)
Wheelbase	: 108in (2,743mm)
Wheel diameter-f	: 13in
Wheel diameter-r	: 13in

1980* [1981]: Lotus 81 & 81B

Battery	: Yuasa
Bearings	: Vandervell
Brakes	: Lockheed
Brake Pads	: Ferodo
Capacity	: 2,993cc
Carburettors	: –
Clutch	: Borg & Beck
Dampers	: Koni
Engine	: Ford Cosworth DFV
Fuel	: Valvoline
Fuel capacity	: 38.5 gallons (175 litres) [35.5 gallons/161.4 litres]
Fuel system	: Lucas
Fuel tanks	: Aerotech
Gearbox	: Lotus/Hewland FGA 5-speed
Gearbox weight	: –
Half-shafts	: Lobro
Height overall	: –
Ignition	: Lucas
Instruments	: Smiths/Veglia
Length overall	: –
Maximum power	: 470bhp (min)
Oil	: Valvoline
Pistons	: Cosworth
Plugs	: NGK
Radiator	: Serck/Marston [Serck]
Rim width front	: 11in
Rim width rear	: 18.5in [16in]
Rings	: Cosworth
Rpm	: 10,800 [11,100]
Steering	: Rack and pinion (Knight)
Suspension front	: Lower wishbones, upper rocking arms, inboard coil/spring dampers
Suspension rear	: Lower wishbones, upper rocking arms, inboard coil/spring dampers
Track front	: 70in (1,778mm) [66in (1,676mm)]
Track rear	: 64in (1,626mm)
Turbocharger/s	: –
Tyres	: Goodyear [Michelin/Goodyear]
Weight (engine)	: 360lb (163kg)
Weight (tub)	: 75lb (34kg) [85lb (39kg)]
Weight (dry)	: –
Weight (start)	: –
Formula weight	: 1,268lb (575kg) [1,290lb (585kg)]
Wheelbase	: 108in (2,743mm) [111in (2,819)]
Wheel diameter-f	: 13in or 15in
Wheel diameter-r	: 13in

* 1981 differences shown in [ ] brackets

1980: Lotus 86

Battery	: –
Bearings	: –
Brakes	: –
Brake Pads	: –
Capacity	: –
Carburettors	: –
Clutch	: –
Dampers	: –
Engine	: Ford Cosworth DFV
Fuel	: –
Fuel capacity	: –
Fuel system	: –
Fuel tanks	: –
Gearbox	: Lotus/Hewland FGA
Gearbox weight	: –
Half-shafts	: –
Height overall	: –
Ignition	: –
Instruments	: –
Length overall	: –
Maximum power	: –
Oil	: –
Pistons	: –
Plugs	: –
Radiator	: –
Rim width front	: –
Rim width rear	: –
Rings	: –
Rpm	: –
Steering	: –
Suspension front	: Lower wishbones, upper rocking arms, inboard coil/spring dampers
Suspension rear	: Lower wishbones, upper rocking arms, inboard coil/spring dampers
Track front	: 66in (1,676mm)
Track rear	: 64in (1,626mm)
Turbocharger/s	: –
Tyres	: –
Weight (engine)	: –
Weight (tub)	: –
Weight (dry)	: –
Weight (start)	: –
Formula weight	: 1,286lb (583kg)
Wheelbase	: 111in (2,819mm)
Wheel diameter-f:	–
Wheel diameter-r:	–

1981: Lotus 87

Battery	: Yuasa
Bearings	: Vandervell
Brakes	: Lockheed
Brake Pads	: Ferodo
Capacity	: 2,993cc
Carburettors	: –
Clutch	: Borg & Beck
Dampers	: Koni
Engine	: Ford Cosworth DFV
Fuel	: –
Fuel capacity	: 42 gallons (191 litres)
Fuel system	: Lucas
Fuel tanks	: Aerotech
Gearbox	: Lotus/Hewland FGA
Gearbox weight	: –
Half-shafts	: Lobro
Height overall	: –
Ignition	: Lucas
Instruments	: Smiths/Veglia
Length overall	: –
Maximum power	: 470bhp (min)
Oil	: –
Pistons	: Cosworth
Plugs	: NGK
Radiator	: Serck
Rim width front	: 11in
Rim width rear	: 16in
Rings	: Cosworth
Rpm	: 11,100
Steering	: Knight
Suspension front	: Lower wishbones, top rocker arms, inboard coil/spring dampers
Suspension rear	: Lower wishbones, top rocker arms, inboard coil/spring dampers
Track front	: 70in (1,778mm)
Track rear	: 63in (1,600mm)
Turbocharger/s	: –
Tyres	: Michelin/Goodyear
Weight (engine)	: 360lb (163kg)
Weight (tub)	: 1,290lb (585kg)
Weight (dry)	: –
Weight (start)	: –
Formula weight	: 1,286 (583kg)
Wheelbase	: 107in (2,718mm)
Wheel diameter-f:	13/15in
Wheel diameter-r:	13in

1982: Lotus 87B

Battery	: Yuasa
Bearings	: —
Brakes	: Lockheed
Brake Pads	: Ferodo
Capacity	: —
Carburettors	: —
Clutch	: Borg & Beck
Dampers	: Koni
Engine	: Ford Cosworth DFV
Fuel	: —
Fuel capacity	: 42 gallons (191 litres)
Fuel system	: —
Fuel tanks	: Aerotech
Gearbox	: Lotus/Hewland FGA
Gearbox weight	: 98lb (44.5kg)
Half-shafts	: Lobro
Height overall	: —
Ignition	: —
Instruments	: Smiths/Veglia
Length overall	: —
Maximum power	: —
Oil	: Valvoline
Pistons	: —
Plugs	: NGK
Radiator	: Serck
Rim width front	: 11in
Rim width rear	: 16in
Rings	: —
Rpm	: —
Steering	: Knight
Suspension front	: —
Suspension rear	: —
Track front	: 68.89in (1,750mm)
Track rear	: 63.78in (1,620mm)
Turbocharger/s	: —
Tyres	: —
Weight (engine)	: —
Weight (tub)	: 75lb (34kg)
Weight (dry)	: —
Weight (start)	: —
Formula weight	: 1,279lb (580kg)
Wheelbase	: 110in (2,794mm)
Wheel diameter-f:	15in
Wheel diameter-r:	13/15in

1981: Lotus 88/88B

Battery	: Yuasa
Bearings	: Vandervell
Brakes	: Lockheed
Brake Pads	: Ferodo
Capacity	: 2,993cc
Carburettors	: —
Clutch	: Borg & Beck
Dampers	: Koni
Engine	: Ford Cosworth DFV
Fuel	: —
Fuel capacity	: 42 gallons (191 litres)
Fuel system	: Lucas
Fuel tanks	: Aerotech
Gearbox	: Lotus/Hewland FGA 5-speed
Gearbox weight	: —
Half-shafts	: Lobro
Height overall	: —
Ignition	: Lucas
Instruments	: Smiths/Veglia
Length overall	: —
Maximum power	: 470bhp (min)
Oil	: —
Pistons	: Cosworth
Plugs	: NGK
Radiator	: Serck
Rim width front	: 11in
Rim width rear	: 16in
Rings	: Cosworth
Rpm	: 11,100
Steering	: Knight
Suspension front	: Lower wishbones, upper rocking arms inboard coil/spring dampers
Suspension rear	: Lower wishbones, upper rocking arms, inboard coil/spring dampers
Track front	: 70in (1,778mm)
Track rear	: 63in (1,600mm)
Turbocharger/s	: —
Tyres	: Michelin/Goodyear
Weight (engine)	: 360lb (163kg)
Weight (tub)	: 75lb (34kg)
Weight (dry)	: —
Weight (start)	: —
Formula weight	: 1,290lb (585kg)
Wheelbase	: 107in (2,718mm)
Wheel diameter-f:	13in/15in
Wheel diameter-r:	13in

1982: Lotus 91

Battery	: Yuasa
Bearings	: Vandervell
Brakes	: Girling/Lockheed (rear)
Brake Pads	: Ferodo
Capacity	: 2,993cc
Carburettors	: –
Clutch	: Borg & Beck
Dampers	: Koni
Engine	: Ford Cosworth DFV
Fuel	: –
Fuel capacity	: 42 gallons (191 litres)
Fuel system	: Lucas
Fuel tanks	: Aerotech
Gearbox	: Lotus/Hewland FGA (5)
Gearbox weight	: 98lb (44.5kg)
Half-shafts	: Lobro
Height overall	: –
Ignition	: Lucas/Contactless
Instruments	: Smiths/Contactless
Length overall	: –
Maximum power	: 480bhp
Oil	: Valvoline
Pistons	: Cosworth
Plugs	: NGK
Radiator	: Serck/IPRA
Rim width front	: 11in
Rim width rear	: 16in
Rings	: Cosworth
Rpm	: 11,100
Steering	: Lotus/Knight
Suspension front	: Lower wishbones, upper rocker arms, inboard coil/spring dampers
Suspension rear	: Lower wishbones, upper rocker arms, inboard coil/spring dampers
Track front	: 68.89in (1,750mm)
Track rear	: 63.78in (1,620mm)
Turbocharger/s	: –
Tyres	: Goodyear
Weight (engine)	: 360lb (163kg)
Weight (tub)	: 75lb (34kg)
Weight (dry)	: –
Weight (start)	: –
Formula weight	: 1,279lb (580kg)
Wheelbase	: 110in (2,794mm)
Wheel diameter-f	: 15in
Wheel diameter-r	: 13/15in

1983: Lotus 92

Battery	: Yuasa
Bearings	: Vandervell
Brakes	: Girling/Lockheed
Brake Pads	: Ferodo
Capacity	: 2,993cc [2,994cc]
Carburettors	: –
Clutch	: Borg & Beck
Dampers	: Koni
Engine	: Cosworth DFV (Stage 1) and [Short Stroke]
Fuel	: Elf
Fuel capacity	: 42 gallons (191 litres)
Fuel system	: Lucas
Fuel tanks	: ATL
Gearbox	: Lotus/Hewland FGA (5)
Gearbox weight	: 98lb (44.5kg)
Half-shafts	: Lobro
Height overall	: –
Ignition	: Lucas Contactless
Instruments	: Contactless
Length overall	: –
Maximum power	: 495bhp [510bhp]
Oil	: Elf
Pistons	: Cosworth
Plugs	: Champion
Radiator	: IPRA
Rim width front	: 11in
Rim width rear	: 16.5/17in
Rings	: Goetze
Rpm	: 11,000
Steering	: Lotus/Knight
Suspension front	: Pull-rods, double wishbones, inboard coil/spring dampers
Suspension rear	: Lower wishbones, upper rocking arms, inboard coil/spring dampers
Track front	: 68.89in (1,750mm)
Track rear	: 62.36in (1,584mm)
Turbocharger/s	: –
Tyres	: Pirelli
Weight (engine)	: 330lb (150kg) [320lb (145kg)]
Weight (tub)	: 75lb (34kg)
Weight (dry)	: –
Weight (start)	: –
Formula weight	: 1,191lb (540kg)
Wheelbase	: 110in (2,794mm)
Wheel diameter-f	: 15in
Wheel diameter-r	: 13/15in

1983: Lotus 93T

Battery	: Yuasa
Bearings	: Glyco
Brakes	: AP/Lockheed
Brake Pads	: Ferodo
Capacity	: 1,492cc
Carburettors	: –
Clutch	: AP/Borg & Beck
Dampers	: Koni
Engine	: Renault EF1 V6
Fuel	: Elf
Fuel capacity	: 55 gallons (250 litres)
Fuel system	: Kugelfischer electronic
Fuel tanks	: ATL
Gearbox	: Lotus/Hewland FGB (5)
Gearbox weight	: 98lb (44.5kg)
Half-shafts	: Lobro
Height overall	: –
Ignition	: Renault 'Renix'/Marelli
Instruments	: Contactless/Poinsot
Length overall	: –
Maximum power	: 650bhp
Oil	: Elf
Pistons	: Mahle
Plugs	: Champion
Radiator	: Secan
Rim width front	: 11in
Rim width rear	: 16.5in
Rings	: Goetze
Rpm	: 12,000
Steering	: Lotus/Knight
Suspension front	: Pull-rods, double wishbones, inboard coil/spring dampers
Suspension rear	: Lower wishbones, upper rocking arms, inboard, coil/spring dampers
Track front	: 70.9in (1,800mm)
Track rear	: 63in (1,600mm)
Turbocharger/s	: KKK
Tyres	: Pirelli
Weight (engine)	: 375lb (170kg)
Weight (tub)	: 75lb (34kg)
Weight (dry)	: –
Weight (start)	: –
Formula weight	: 1,191lb (540kg)
Wheelbase	: 106in (2,692mm)
Wheel diameter-f	: 15in
Wheel diameter-r	: 13/15in

1983: Lotus 94T

Battery	: Yuasa
Bearings	: Glyco
Brakes	: Girling/Lockheed
Brake Pads	: Ferodo
Capacity	: 1,492cc
Carburettors	: –
Clutch	: AP/Borg & Beck
Dampers	: Koni
Engine	: Renault EF1 V6
Fuel	: Elf
Fuel capacity	: 40 gallons (182 litres)
Fuel system	: Kugelfischer electronic
Fuel tanks	: ATL
Gearbox	: Lotus/Hewland FGB (5)
Gearbox weight	: 95lb (43kg)
Half-shafts	: Lotus/Lobro
Height overall	: –
Ignition	: Marelli
Instruments	: Contactless/Poinsot
Length overall	: –
Maximum power	: 650bhp
Oil	: Elf
Pistons	: Mahle
Plugs	: Champion
Radiator	: Secan
Rim width front	: 11in
Rim width rear	: 16.5in
Rings	: Goetze
Rpm	: 12,000
Steering	: Lotus/Knight
Suspension front	: Lower wishbones, upper rocking arms, inboard coil spring dampers
Suspension rear	: Double wishbones, pull-rods, inboard coil spring dampers
Track front	: 71in (1,800mm)
Track rear	: 68in (1,730mm)
Turbocharger/s	: KKK
Tyres	: Pirelli
Weight (engine)	: 375lb (170kg)
Weight (tub)	: 75lb (34kg)
Weight (dry)	: –
Weight (start)	: –
Formula weight	: 1,191lb (540kg)
Wheelbase	: 106in (2,692mm)
Wheel diameter-f	: 15in
Wheel diameter-r	: 13in

1984: Lotus 95T

Battery	: Yuasa
Bearings	: Glyco
Brakes	: Brembo/Lotus/SEP
Brake Pads	: Ferodo/SEP
Capacity	: 1,492cc
Carburettors	: –
Clutch	: AP
Dampers	: Koni
Engine	: Renault EF1 V6
Fuel	: Elf
Fuel capacity	: 48.4 gallons (220 litres)
Fuel system	: Electronic Renix
Fuel tanks	: ATL
Gearbox	: Lotus/Hewland FGB 5-speed
Gearbox weight	: 95lb (43kg)
Half-shafts	: Lobro
Height overall	: –
Ignition	: Marelli
Instruments	: Contactless/Poinsot
Length overall	: –
Maximum power	: 750bhp
Oil	: Elf
Pistons	: Mahle
Plugs	: Champion
Radiator	: IPRA/Secan
Rim width front	: 11in
Rim width rear	: 16.5in
Rings	: Goetze
Rpm	: 11,500
Steering	: Lotus/Knight
Suspension front	: Double wishbones, pull-rods, inboard coil spring dampers
Suspension rear	: Double wishbones, pull-rods, inboard coil/spring dampers
Track front	: 70.9in (1,800mm)
Track rear	: 63in (1,600mm)
Turbocharger/s	: Garret
Tyres	: Goodyear radials
Weight (engine)	: –
Weight (tub)	: 81.57lb (37kg)
Weight (dry)	: –
Weight (start)	: –
Formula weight	: 1,191lb (540kg)
Wheelbase	: 107in (2,720mm)
Wheel diameter-f	: 13in
Wheel diameter-r	: 13in

1985: Lotus 97T

Battery	: Yuasa
Bearings	: Glyco
Brakes	: SEP/Brembo
Brake Pads	: SEP/Ferodo
Capacity	: 1,492cc/1,494cc
Carburettors	: –
Clutch	: AP
Dampers	: Koni
Engine	: Renault EF4B/15
Fuel	: Elf
Fuel capacity	: 48.4 gallons (220 litres)
Fuel system	: Electronic Renix/Weber injectors
Fuel tanks	: ATL
Gearbox	: Lotus/Hewland DGB 5-speed
Gearbox weight	: 99lb (45kg)
Half-shafts	: Lotus/Lobro
Height overall	: –
Ignition	: Marelli
Instruments	: Brion Leroux/Mors
Length overall	: –
Maximum power	: 760bhp/810bhp
Oil	: Elf
Pistons	: Mahle/Goetze
Plugs	: Champion
Radiator	: IPRA/Secan
Rim width front	: 11.5in
Rim width rear	: 16.25in
Rings	: Mahle/Goetze
Rpm	: 11,500
Steering	: Knight/Lotus
Suspension front	: Double wishbones, pull-rods, inboard coil/spring dampers
Suspension rear	: Double wishbones, pull-rods, inboard coil/spring dampers
Track front	: 70.9in (1,800mm)
Track rear	: 63.7in (1,620mm)
Turbocharger/s	: 2 × Garrett AiResearch
Tyres	: Goodyear
Weight (engine)	: –
Weight (tub)	: 81.57lb (37kg)
Weight (dry)	: –
Weight (start)	: –
Formula weight	: 1,191lb (540kg)
Wheelbase	: 107in (2,720mm)
Wheel diameter-f	: 13in
Wheel diameter-r	: 13in

1986: Lotus 98T

Battery	: Yuasa
Bearings	: Glyco
Brakes	: Brembo/SEP
Brake Pads	: SEP
Capacity	: 1,494cc
Carburettors	: –
Clutch	: AP
Dampers	: Koni
Engine	: Renault EF15B/C V6
Fuel	: Elf
Fuel capacity	: 42.9 gallons (195 litres)
Fuel system	: Bendix/Renault
Fuel tanks	: ATL
Gearbox	: Lotus/Hewland DGB (5/6-speed)
Gearbox weight	: 99lb (45kg)
Half-shafts	: Lotus/Lobro
Height overall	: –
Ignition	: Renault
Instruments	: Brion Leroux/Mors
Length overall	: –
Maximum power	: –
Oil	: Elf
Pistons	: Mahle/Goetze
Plugs	: Champion
Radiator	: Secan/IPRA
Rim width front	: 11.5in
Rim width rear	: 16.25in
Rings	: Mahle/Goetze
Rpm	: 12,000
Steering	: Knight/Lotus
Suspension front	: Double wishbones, pull-rods, coil/spring dampers
Suspension rear	: Double wishbones, pull-rods, coil/spring dampers
Track front	: 70.9in (1,800mm)
Track rear	: 63.7in (1,620mm)
Turbocharger/s	: Garrett × 2
Tyres	: Goodyear
Weight (engine)	: 308lb (140kg) (less intercooler)
Weight (tub)	: 81.61lb (37kg)
Weight (dry)	: –
Weight (start)	: –
Formula weight	: 1,190lb (540kg)
Wheelbase	: 107in (2,720mm)
Wheel diameter-f	: 13in
Wheel diameter-r	: 13in

1987: Lotus 99T

Battery	: Yuasa
Bearings	: –
Brakes	: Brembo/SEP
Brake Pads	: SEP carbon
Capacity	: 1,500cc
Carburettors	: –
Clutch	: AP/Tilton carbon-fibre
Dampers	: Lotus active
Engine	: Honda RA166-E/167-G V6
Fuel	: Elf
Fuel capacity	: 42.9 gallons (195 litres)
Fuel system	: Honda/PCM-F1
Fuel tanks	: ATL
Gearbox	: Lotus/Hewland 6-speed
Gearbox weight	: –
Half-shafts	: Lotus
Height overall	: –
Ignition	: Honda
Instruments	: Honda electronic
Length overall	: –
Maximum power	: 1,050bhp (qualifying), 870bhp (race)
Oil	: Elf
Pistons	: Honda
Plugs	: NGK
Radiator	: Secan
Rim width front	: 11.5in
Rim width rear	: 16in
Rings	: Honda
Rpm	: 12,000/13,000
Steering	: Lotus rack and pinion
Suspension front	: 'Active' pull rods, double wishbones
Suspension rear	: 'Active' pull rods, double wishbones
Track front	: 70.5in (1,790mm)
Track rear	: 64.6in (1,640mm)
Turbocharger/s	: IHI × 2
Tyres	: Goodyear
Weight (engine)	: –
Weight (tub)	: –
Weight (dry)	: 1,187lb (538kg)
Weight (start)	: –
Formula weight	: 1,190.5lb (540kg)
Wheelbase	: 107.5in (2,730mm)
Wheel diameter-f	: 13in
Wheel diameter-r	: 13in

1988: Lotus 100T

Battery	: Yuasa
Bearings	: Vandervell
Brakes	: Brembo/SEP
Brake Pads	: SEP carbon
Capacity	: 1,494cc
Carburettors	: –
Clutch	: AP
Dampers	: Bilstein
Engine	: Honda RA 168-E
Fuel	: Elf
Fuel capacity	: –
Fuel system	: Honda PGM F1
Fuel tanks	: ATL
Gearbox	: Lotus/Hewland 6-speed
Gearbox weight	: –
Half-shafts	: Lotus/Glaenzer
Height overall	: –
Ignition	: Honda PGM 1G
Instruments	: Honda
Length overall	: –
Maximum power	: –
Oil	: Elf
Pistons	: Honda
Plugs	: NGK
Radiator	: Secan
Rim width front	: 11.5in
Rim width rear	: 16.3in
Rings	: Honda
Rpm	: 12,500
Steering	: Lotus rack and pinion
Suspension front	: Push-rod, double wishbones, coil spring/dampers
Suspension rear	: Push-rod, double wishbones, coil spring/dampers
Track front	: 70.8in (1,798mm)
Track rear	: 53in (1,651mm)
Turbocharger/s	: Twin IHI
Tyres	: Goodyear
Weight (engine)	: 330.7lb (150kg)
Weight (tub)	: –
Weight (dry)	: 1,186lb (538kg)
Weight (start)	: –
Formula weight	: 1,190.5lb (540kg)
Wheelbase	: 109.3in (2,776mm)
Wheel diameter-f	: 13in
Wheel diameter-r	: 13in

1989: Lotus 101

Battery	: Panasonic
Bearings	: Vandervell
Brakes	: Brembo/SEP
Brake Pads	: SEP
Capacity	: 3,496cc
Carburettors	: –
Clutch	: AP/Borg & Beck
Dampers	: Bilstein
Engine	: Judd CV V8
Fuel	: Elf
Fuel capacity	: 41.7 gallons (190 litres)
Fuel system	: Zytek
Fuel tanks	: ATL
Gearbox	: Lotus/Hewland 6-speed
Gearbox weight	: –
Half-shafts	: Lotus
Height overall	: –
Ignition	: Lucas
Instruments	: Stack
Length overall	: –
Maximum power	: 610bhp
Oil	: Elf
Pistons	: Omega
Plugs	: NGK
Radiator	: Behr/Secan
Rim width front	: 11.5in
Rim width rear	: 17in
Rings	: Omega
Rpm	: 11,000
Steering	: Lotus
Suspension front	: Pull-rod, double wishbone, coil spring/damper
Suspension rear	: Push-rod, double wishbone, coil spring/damper
Track front	: 71in (1,803mm)
Track rear	: 66in (1,676mm)
Turbocharger/s	: –
Tyres	: Goodyear
Weight (engine)	: 284.4lb (129kg)
Weight (tub)	: –
Weight (dry)	: 1,099lb (498.5kg)
Weight (start)	: –
Formula weight	: 1,102.3lb (500kg)
Wheelbase	: 114in (2,895mm)
Wheel diameter-f	: 13in
Wheel diameter-r	: 13in

1990: Lotus 102

Battery	: –
Bearings	: Clevite/Vandervell
Brakes	: Brembo
Brake Pads	: Carbone Industrie
Capacity	: 3,493cc
Carburettors	: –
Clutch	: AP
Dampers	: Bilstein
Engine	: Lamborghini 3512 V12
Fuel	: BP
Fuel capacity	: 48.4 gallons (220 litres)
Fuel system	: Bosch
Fuel tanks	: ATL
Gearbox	: Lotus/Lamborghini 6-speed
Gearbox weight	: –
Half-shafts	: Lotus
Height overall	: –
Ignition	: Bosch
Instruments	: Bosch
Length overall	: –
Maximum power	: 640bhp
Oil	: BP
Pistons	: Mahle/Goetze
Plugs	: Champion
Radiator	: Behr/Secan
Rim width front	: 11.5in
Rim width rear	: 16.3in
Rings	: Mahle/Goetze
Rpm	: 13,000
Steering	: Lotus
Suspension front	: Pull-rod, double wishbone
Suspension rear	: Push-rod, double wishbone
Track front	: 70.9in (1,800mm)
Track rear	: 65in (1,650mm)
Turbocharger/s	: –
Tyres	: Goodyear
Weight (engine)	: 321.8lb (146kg)
Weight (tub)	: –
Weight (dry)	: –
Weight (start)	: –
Formula weight	: 1,102lb (500kg)
Wheelbase	: 116.1in (2,590mm)
Wheel diameter-f	: 13in
Wheel diameter-r	: 13in

1991: Lotus 102B

Battery	: Yuasa
Bearings	: –
Brakes	: Brembo/AP/Hitco
Brake Pads	: AP/Hitco
Capacity	: 3,500cc
Carburettors	: –
Clutch	: AP
Dampers	: Lotus/OMZ
Engine	: Judd EV
Fuel	: BP
Fuel capacity	: 46.2 gallons (210 litres)
Fuel system	: —
Fuel tanks	: ATL
Gearbox	: Lotus/Lamborghini (6)
Gearbox weight	: –
Half-shafts	: –
Height overall	: –
Ignition	: –
Instruments	: Cranfield
Length overall	: –
Maximum power	: 640bhp
Oil	: BP
Pistons	: –
Plugs	: Champion
Radiator	: Behr
Rim width front	: 11.5in
Rim width rear	: 16.3in
Rings	: –
Rpm	: 12,500
Steering	: Lotus/Jack Knight
Suspension front	: Pull-rod, inboard spring/damper unit
Suspension rear	: Push-rod, inboard spring/damper unit
Track front	: 70.9in (1,800mm)
Track rear	: 64.6in (1,640mm)
Turbocharger/s	: –
Tyres	: Goodyear
Weight (engine)	: –
Weight (tub)	: –
Weight (dry)	: –
Weight (start)	: –
Formula weight	: 1,102.3lb (500kg)
Wheelbase	: 116.1in (2,950mm)
Wheel diameter-f	: 13in
Wheel diameter-r	: 13in

1992: Lotus 107

Battery	: Panasonic
Bearings	: –
Brakes	: AP
Brake Pads	: AP/Hitco
Capacity	: 3,494cc
Carburettors	: –
Clutch	: AP
Dampers	: Penske
Engine	: Ford HB V8
Fuel	: Castrol
Fuel capacity	: 43.9 gallons (200 litres)
Fuel system	: Cosworth
Fuel tanks	: ATL
Gearbox	: Lotus transverse 6-speed
Gearbox weight	: –
Half-shafts	: Lotus
Height overall	: –
Ignition	: Cosworth
Instruments	: Cranfield
Length overall	: –
Maximum power	: 730bhp
Oil	: Castrol
Pistons	: –
Plugs	: NGK
Radiator	: Lotus/Secan
Rim width front	: 11.5in
Rim width rear	: 16.3in
Rings	: –
Rpm	: 13,800
Steering	: Lotus
Suspension front	: Double wishbones, push-rod, 'fast-ride' single spring/damper
Suspension rear	: Double wishbones, push-rod, 'fast-ride' double spring/dampers
Track front	: –
Track rear	: –
Turbocharger/s	: –
Tyres	: Goodyear
Weight (engine)	: –
Weight (tub)	: –
Weight (dry)	: –
Weight (start)	: –
Formula weight	: 111.3lb (505kg)
Wheelbase	: –
Wheel diameter-f	: 13in
Wheel diameter-r	: 13in

1993: Lotus 107B

Battery	: Panasonic
Bearings	: –
Brakes	: AP/Carbone Industrie/Hitco
Brake Pads	: Carbone Industrie/Hitco
Capacity	: –
Carburettors	: –
Clutch	: AP
Dampers	: –
Engine	: Ford HB V8
Fuel	: Burmah
Fuel capacity	: 43.9 gallons (200 litres)
Fuel system	: –
Fuel tanks	: ATL
Gearbox	: Lotus/Xtrac 6-speed
Gearbox weight	: 110.23lb (50kg)
Half-shafts	: SDC/Lotus
Height overall	: 39in (1,000mm)
Ignition	: Cranfield/Cosworth
Instruments	: Stack/Lotus
Length overall	: 167in (4,260mm)
Maximum power	: –
Oil	: Castrol
Pistons	: –
Plugs	: NGK
Radiator	: Behr/Secan/Lotus
Rim width front	: 11in
Rim width rear	: 13.7in
Rings	: –
Rpm	: –
Steering	: Jack Knight/Lotus
Suspension front	: Double wishbone, twin active struts, push-rod
Suspension rear	: Double wishbone, twin active struts, push-rod
Track front	: 64.96in (1,650mm)
Track rear	: 61.02in (1,550mm)
Turbocharger/s	: –
Tyres	: Goodyear
Weight (engine)	: –
Weight (tub)	: 88.18lb (40kg)
Weight (dry)	: –
Weight (start)	: –
Formula weight	: 1,113.33lb (505kg)
Wheelbase	: 114.17in (2,900mm)
Wheel diameter-f	: 13in
Wheel diameter-r	: 13in

Index